PRIORITIES AND PATHWAYS IN SERVICES REFORM

Part I – Quantitative Studies

World Scientific Studies in International Economics

(ISSN: 1793-3641)

---

*Published**

Vol. 18 Quantitative Analysis of Newly Evolving Patterns of International Trade: Fragmentation, Offshoring of Activities, and Vertical Intra-Industry Trade
edited by Robert M Stern (University of Michigan and University of California-Berkeley, USA)

Vol. 19 The World Economy after the Global Crisis: A New Economic Order for the 21st Century
edited by Barry Eichengreen (University of California-Berkeley, USA) & Bokyeong Park (Korea Institute for International Economic Policy, Korea)

Vol. 20 Trade, Development and Agriculture: Essays in Economic Policy Analysis
edited by Kym Anderson (University of Adelaide, & Australian National University, Australia)

Vol. 21 Regulation of Foreign Investment: Challenges to International Harmonization
edited by Zdenek Drabek (Charles University, Czech Republic) & Petros Mavroidis (Columbia University, USA)

Vol. 22 International Trade Policy Formation: Theory and Politics
by Wolfgang Mayer (University of Cincinnati, USA)

Vol. 23 Priorities and Pathways in Services Reform: Part I — Quantitative Studies
edited by Philippa Dee (Australian National University, Australia)

Forthcoming

Globalizing Information: The Economics of International Technology Trade
by Keith E Maskus (University of Colorado at Boulder, USA)

Globalizing Trade and Investment: India Arrives
edited by Rajesh Chadha (National Council of Applied Economic Research (NCAER), India)

*The complete list of the published volumes in the series can be found at http://www.worldscientific.com/series/wssie.

23 World Scientific Studies in International Economics

PRIORITIES AND PATHWAYS IN SERVICES REFORM

Part I — Quantitative Studies

Editor

Philippa Dee

Australian National University, Australia

World Scientific

NEW JERSEY · LONDON · SINGAPORE · BEIJING · SHANGHAI · HONG KONG · TAIPEI · CHENNAI

Published by

World Scientific Publishing Co. Pte. Ltd.
5 Toh Tuck Link, Singapore 596224
USA office: 27 Warren Street, Suite 401-402, Hackensack, NJ 07601
UK office: 57 Shelton Street, Covent Garden, London WC2H 9HE

British Library Cataloguing-in-Publication Data
A catalogue record for this book is available from the British Library.

World Scientific Studies in International Economics — Vol. 23
PRIORITIES AND PATHWAYS IN SERVICES REFORM
Part I — Quantitative Studies

ISBN 978-981-4447-72-0

In-house Editor: Lee Xin Ying

Printed in Singapore.

Preface

Methodological frameworks for prioritizing services reforms have often lagged policy commitments. An important impetus for catch-up was the establishment of a global negotiating framework for services trade and investment under the World Trade Organization. Researchers responded with a first generation of empirical studies designed to quantify impediments to services trade and investment. While those studies made considerable progress, they suffered from sins of omission and commission. Further, they revealed that services trade reforms could only be properly designed and carried out in the broader context of domestic regulatory reform.

This book is designed to address the shortcomings and close the gap. It presents methodologies to address the sins of omission and commission. It also provides a quantitative assessment of structural reforms in the finance, transport, energy, telecommunications and higher education sectors in APEC member economies, where necessary combining services trade reforms (narrowly defined) with the pro-competitive domestic regulatory reforms required to ensure that the trade reforms deliver on their promise. A companion volume examines what it takes to overcome political resistance in these areas, by reporting on actual reform experiences in some of these sectors and countries.

In 2006 the Australian Research Council (ARC) funded a joint project involving the Australian National University, the University of Adelaide and the Australian Productivity Commission to address the identified shortcomings. I would like to thank Professor Jenny Corbett from the Australian National University for leading the project, Professor Christopher Findlay from the University of Adelaide for organizing some of the research, and Paul Gretton from the Productivity Commission for coordinating the support and input from that institution.

There were strong synergies between the ARC project and emerging concerns within APEC member countries. In 2004, APEC Leaders had signed on to a Leaders' Agenda to Implement Structural Reform (LAISR), where they recognized the value of well-executed structural reform, underpinned by institutional capacity building, for achieving sustainable economic growth and supporting APEC's goal of trade and investment liberalization. The newly-created APEC Policy Support Unit saw the benefits of studies that could demonstrate the potential benefits from structural reforms in key infrastructure industries. I would like to thank Philip Gaetjens, then Director of the Policy Support Unit, and Nathan Zhivov, Policy Advisor, for their enthusiasm in organizing such a project, which contributed some of the chapters in this book. I would also like to thank Professor Christopher Findlay, again, for leading that project.

The methodological frameworks and applications reported in this book have been previewed in a number of conferences and workshops, allowing comment and criticism by academics, industry representatives and/or government officials. I am grateful to all participants at those events for their comments and insights. The research in this book falls squarely in the realm where theory meets both policy and practice, so input from all these sources has been critical to closing the gap.

Philippa Dee

Contents

Contributors

Pedro Cantos is Associate Professor in Economics at the Department of Economic Analysis and ERI-CES, Universitat de Valencia.

Philippa Dee is Adjunct Associate Professor at the Crawford School of Public Policy, the Australian National University.

Huong Dinh is Research Fellow at the Faculty of Business, Government and Law, University of Canberra.

Claire Hollweg is PhD Candidate at the School of Economics, University of Adelaide.

José M. Pastor is Associate Professor in Economics at the Department of Economic Analysis, Universitat de Valencia and Ivie.

Lorenzo Serrano is Associate Professor in Economics at the Department of Economic Analysis, Universitat de Valencia and Ivie.

Patricia Sourdin is Adjunct Professor of International Economics at the Johns Hopkins University School of Advanced International Studies Bologna, Italy.

Marn-Heong Wong is Assistant Professor at the Lee Kuan Yew School of Public Policy, National University of Singapore.

List of Tables

List of Figures

Abbreviations

ADSL	Asymmetric digital subscriber line
AFAS	ASEAN Framework Agreement on Services
ANU	Australian National University
APEC	Asia Pacific Economic Cooperation
ASEAN	Association of South East Asian Nations
ASEAN+6	A group of countries comprising the ten members ASEAN plus Australia, China, India, Japan, the Republic of Korea and New Zealand
ATM	Automatic teller machine
BOD	Board of Directors
CEPII	Centre D'études Prospectives Et D'informations Internationales
CIA	Central Intelligence Agency
CPC	Central Product Classification
CPI	Consumer price index
cif	cost, insurance and freight
DEA	Data envelop analysis
DSO	Distribution System Operator
EDI	Electronic Data Interchange
EIA	Energy Information Administration
ERIA	Economic Research Institute for ASEAN and East Asia
ETO	Express Transportation Organization of Thailand
EU	European Union
FDI	Foreign direct investment
fob	free on board
FTAP	GTAP with foreign direct investment
GATS	General Agreement on Trade in Services
GDP	Gross domestic product
GNP	Gross national product
GTAP	Global Trade Analysis Project
GWh	Gigawatt hours
HS	Harmonized System

IBCA	International Bank Credit Analysis
IFS	International Financial Statistics
ILO	International Labour Organization
IMF	International Monetary Fund
ITU	International Telecommunications Union
Kcal	Kilocalories
kWh	Kilowatt hours
LNG	Liquified natural gas
LPI	Logistics Performance Index
LPS	Logistics services provider
LSCI	Liner Shipping Connectivity Index
MAT	Marine, aviation and transport
MFN	Most-favoured-nation
MWe	Megawatt electrical
NGO	Non-government organization
OECD	Organization for Economic Co-operation and Development
OLS	Ordinary least squares
PDR	People's Democratic Republic
PPP	Purchasing power parity
REPSF	Regional Economic Policy Support Facility
SCRGSP	Steering Committee for the Review of Government Service Provision
TEU	Twenty-foot equivalent
THB	Thai baht
TPA	Third party access
TRI	Trade restrictiveness index
TSO	Transmission System Operator
UK	United Kingdom
UN	United Nations
UNCTAD	United Nations Conference on Trade and Development
UPS	United Parcel Service
US	United States
USD	United States dollar
USTR	United States Trade Representative
WTO	World Trade Organization

Chapter 1

Measuring and Modelling Regulatory Restrictions in Services

Philippa Dee

1.1 Introduction

Prioritizing services reform requires an understanding of the relative costs and benefits of various reform initiatives, both against each other and against reforms in other sectors. Identifying pathways to services reform requires an understanding of how political resistance to reform, arising from the costs to various segments of society, can be overcome by a combination of leadership and reform strategy (such as bundling, sequencing and compensation). This volume is directed at measuring costs and benefits. It outlines appropriate methodologies and gives empirical estimates of the direct effects of policies in a range of services markets in different countries. Finally, it gives an overall assessment of reform priorities by presenting estimates of the relative economy-wide costs and benefits of structural reforms in the finance, transport, energy, telecommunications and higher education sectors in APEC member economies. A companion volume examines what it takes to overcome political resistance in these areas, by reporting on actual reform experiences in some of these sectors and countries.

Services reform is a behind-the-border agenda. The particular focus of some of the chapters in this volume is on services trade, in part because serious thinking about how to measure and evaluate regulatory barriers in services began in a trade context. Nevertheless, as is argued in this chapter and elsewhere (Dee 2007, Dee and Findlay 2008a), services trade reform can only be properly designed and carried out in the broader context of domestic regulatory reform. Done properly, services trade reform *is* structural reform.

In services, the development of negotiating frameworks for liberalizing trade barriers preceded proper academic understanding of how to measure or evaluate the barriers. The General Agreement on Trade in Services (GATS) under the World Trade Organization (WTO) was completed as part of the Uruguay Round in 1994. Its negotiating framework drew heavily on Sampson and Snape (1985), who pioneered the thinking about how to incorporate services into the WTO. The first attempt by Hoekman (1995) at quantifying the impact of the commitments made under the GATS was published in working paper form a year after the GATS was concluded. The simplicity of his approach reflected the lack of analytical frameworks to measure services trade barriers. He derived frequency counts of the services trade commitments that had been signed by the WTO Members — a technique that has survived with various degrees of sophistication since — but then simply imputed a 'guesstimate' of the 'tariff equivalent' of barriers that were deemed to be prohibitive, and allocated lower values to less prohibitive barriers on a *pro rata* basis.

It took a while for academics to make sense of the GATS text (and the insights from Sampson and Snape (1985) embodied in it) and to decide how this was relevant for the measurement and evaluation of services trade barriers. The GATS text combined negative-list and positive-list commitments. The commitment to most-favoured-nation (MFN) treatment was negative list, meaning that all WTO signatories were bound by it, unless they took out specific MFN exemptions. The MFN commitment was itself familiar from WTO disciplines on goods trade — WTO members could not discriminate against one trading partner in favour of another. By contrast, the commitments to national treatment and market access were positive list, meaning that they applied only to the particular sectors and modes of supply that WTO Members chose to include in their schedules of specific commitments. A version of the national treatment commitment was also familiar from the disciplines on goods trade — WTO members could not discriminate against trading partners in favour of domestic suppliers.

Warren and Findlay (2000) provided key insights into the interpretation of the GATS disciplines on national treatment and market access that were relevant for measuring services trade barriers. The first was that the GATS provision on national treatment did not draw a distinction between frontier and internal constraints, but embraced all policies that might discriminate between domestic and foreign suppliers. By contrast, the national treatment commitment in goods trade extended only to matters of internal taxation and regulation. In effect, they observed, the GATS discipline of national treatment covered both national treatment and market access as previously defined.

More importantly, the GATS discipline on market access extended beyond traditional concerns of access for foreign services or service suppliers, but covered policies that restricted any access to a market. This was a major extension of services trade disciplines into domestic regulation, in particular competition policy. Thus the GATS had incorporated a key insight from Snape (1998) that some of the key barriers to trade in services were those that protected incumbents from any competition, be it from foreign providers or from domestic new entrants.

That services trade barriers extended behind the border, and also affected domestic providers, were strong clues that the concept of a 'tariff equivalent' was not the appropriate way to think about services trade barriers. They also hinted that services trade reform should only be assessed properly in a broader context of domestic structural reform (see Dee and Findlay 2008a).

The GATS defined barriers to market access more specifically as limitations on either (i) the number of services suppliers, through quotas, monopolies, granting of exclusive rights or economic needs tests, (ii) the total value of services transactions, through quotas or economic needs tests, (iii) the total number of services operations or total quantity of service output, through quotas or economic needs tests, (iv) the total number of people employed, through quotas or economic needs tests, (v) the legal form through which a service supplier could establish, or (vi) foreign equity participation.

Thus if there is a meaningful distinction in principle between services trade reform and structural reform, it lies in measures that might restrict market access but fall outside of one of these areas. One example is measures restricting competition in upstream or downstream markets (Dee and Findlay 2008b), such as the absence of a third party access regime in markets characterized by natural monopoly (although for telecommunications there is a WTO Reference Paper prescribing basic conditions for third party access in that sector). Yet access regimes are critical if services trade reforms in upstream or downstream markets are to deliver on their promise. Another example is the restrictive provisions written into international air services agreements, which are explicitly excluded from the GATS. However, as will be seen below, some commentators have maintained a broader distinction between services trade reform and structural reform in practice, by assuming that services trade reform is only or primarily about measures that discriminate against foreign services or service suppliers.

Findlay and Warren (2000) was a seminal volume that incorporated the above general insights into the measurement and evaluation of barriers to trade in services. From the outset, their sectoral studies included any policy that might restrict access to a market, not just policies that discriminated (*de facto* or *de jure*) against foreign services or service providers. They also proposed a three step process to empirical evaluation:

- use qualitative information about services trade barriers to derive a frequency-type index;
- estimate the effect of this index on cross-national differences in domestic prices or quantities, while controlling for other relevant factors;
- incorporate the resulting counterfactual values of prices or quantities into a partial or general equilibrium model to assess economy-wide effects.

The volume contained a number of examples of the first two steps. For example, McGuire and Schuele (2000) derived an index of barriers to trade in banking services, and Kalirajan *et al.* (2000) estimated its impact on net interest margins. Warren (2000) derived an index of barriers to trade in telecommunications services, and estimated its impact on quantities. Table 1.1 gives examples of this type of analysis, from Findlay and Warren (2000) and elsewhere, that were available by 2005 — the somewhat arbitrary cut-off used here to define first-generation studies. More recently, the World Bank has produced indices of barriers to trade in services that are in practice primarily discriminatory (that is, they only affect foreign services or service providers) in a wide set of countries and sectors (Borchert, Gootiiz and Mattoo 2012a). The OECD is also developing a services trade restrictiveness index.[1] More recent studies are also surveyed in the individual chapters in this volume.

Findlay and Warren (2000) did not include an example of general equilibrium modelling, although Dee, Hardin and Holmes (2000) canvassed some of the key issues. One of the first general equilibrium assessments, which drew on two of the chapters from Findlay and Warren (2000), was Dee and Hanslow (2001). This exercise was rather stylized, because it contained only a single services sector, and applied a simple average of the estimates of the barriers to trade in banking and telecommunications (Kalirajan *et al.* 2000, Warren 2000) to this entire sector.

While the studies in Table 1.1 are examples of first-generation attempts to quantify barriers to trade in services, the purpose of this volume is to present second-generation studies of regulatory restrictions in services. Some of these address limitations of the first-generation studies. Others push the assessment of regulatory regimes into new sectors, such as health and education, and to a wider coverage of policies, including third party access regimes. The final study gives an example of state-of-the-art general equilibrium modelling of services reform, showing how far it has come from its stylized beginnings.

The following section outlines in more detail some of the key insights from first-generation empirical studies of services trade barriers. The next sections describe the methodology in more detail, and outline the sins of omission and commission in first-generation studies. The final section then assesses the extent to which the sectoral contributions in this

---

[1] www.oecd.org/trade/servicestrade/towardsaservicestraderestrictivenessindexstri.htm (accessed 23 September 2012).

Table 1.1. Some First-Generation Studies of the Effects of Services Trade (and Other Regulatory) Barriers

Sector	*Study*	*Sectoral performance measure*	*Cross country or panel*
Air passenger transport	Gonenc and Nicoletti (2000)	Airfares Load factors Airline efficiency	Cross-country
	Doove *et al.* (2001)	Airfares	Cross-country
Banking	Kalirajan *et al.* (2000)	Net interest margin	Cross-country
	Claessens, Demirgüç-Kunt and Huizinga (2001)	Net interest margin Non-interest income Overhead expenses	Panel
	Barth, Caprio and Levine (2004)	Bank development[a] Net interest margin Overhead cost Non-performing loans Prob. of bank crisis	Cross-country
	Dee (2004)	Net interest margin	Cross-country
Business/finance	Francois and Hoekman (1999)	Exports	?
Construction	Francois and Hoekman (1999)	Exports	?
Distribution	Kalirajan (2000)	Cost	Cross-country
Energy generation	Steiner (2000)	Price Utilization rates Reserve plant margins	Panel
	Doove *et al.* (2001)	Price	Panel
Maritime	Kang (2000)	Price	Cross-country
	Fink, Mattoo and Neagu (2002)	Price	Cross-country
	Clark, Dollar and Micco (2004)	Costs	Panel
Engineering	Nguyen-Hong (2000)	Price Cost	Cross-country
Telecom-munications	Warren (2000)	Quantity Price	Cross-country
	Trewin (2000)	Cost	Panel
	Boylaud and Nicoletti (2000)	Price Labour productivity Quantity	Panel
	Doove *et al.* (2001)	Price	Panel
	Dee (2004)	Quantity Price	Cross-country
	Fink, Mattoo and Rathindran (2002)	Quantity Productivity	Panel

Note: [a] Bank credit to the private sector as a share of GDP.
Source: See table for references.

volume address those limitations. It also summarizes the insights gained from putting all the sectoral estimates together into a computable general equilibrium assessment of priorities for structural reform.

1.2 The Nature of Services Trade Barriers[2]

Services are highly differentiated. Not only do they differ from one firm to the next, they also differ from one customer to the next. As Ethier and Horn (1991) noted, what makes services special is that they are customized to meet the needs of individual purchasers.

This means that the measurement of services trade barriers cannot assume services are homogeneous. Nor is it appropriate to use the price comparisons methodology often used to measure non-tariff barriers in goods trade, since this assumes homogeneity across borders. Strictly speaking, it is not even appropriate to talk about a 'tariff equivalent', since this concept (a) assumes that services are primarily traded cross-border, and (b) often also assumes that the domestic and foreign service are perfect substitutes.

Services are often delivered face to face. This means that trade in services often takes place via the movement of primary factors of production — people or capital. Therefore, the transaction typically occurs behind the border. Even when cross-border trade takes place via e-commerce, it is not easily observed by customs officials. Accordingly, services transactions are not amenable to border protection. Instead, services trade barriers are typically behind-the-border, non-price regulatory measures. As noted above, they may specifically discriminate against foreign suppliers, or they may protect incumbent service providers by discriminating against all new suppliers, be they domestic or foreign.

While services are typically not protected by tariffs, services trade barriers may or may not be tariff-like, in the following sense. Some regulatory trade restrictions, particularly quantitative restrictions, create artificial scarcity. The prices of services are inflated, not because the real resource cost of producing them has gone up, but because incumbent

[2] This and the subsequent two sections are based on Dee (2005).

firms are able to earn economic rents — akin to a tax, but with the revenue flowing to the incumbent rather than to government. Liberalization of these barriers would yield 'triangle gains' in producer and consumer surplus associated with improvements in allocative efficiency, but also have redistributive effects associated with the elimination of rents to incumbents. As Dee and Hanslow (2001) demonstrate, the former effects would not be trivial, but the latter effects could also be significant. Such rent-creating restrictions are tariff-like, with the redistribution of rent having effects similar to the redistribution of tariff revenue.

Alternatively, services trade restrictions could increase the real resource cost of doing business. An example would be a requirement for foreign professionals to retrain in a new economy, rather than have their existing qualifications recognized or undergo a proficiency test. Liberalization would be equivalent to a productivity improvement (saving in real resources), and yield 'roughly rectangle' gains associated with a downward shift in supply curves. This could increase returns for the incumbent service providers, as well as lowering costs for users elsewhere in the economy.

The distinction is critical, for two reasons. First, in a unilateral or multilateral setting, rectangle gains are likely to exceed triangle gains by a significant margin, especially given the importance of the services sectors in most economies. Secondly, in the context of preferential trade agreements, the danger of net welfare losses from net trade diversion arises only if the relevant barriers are rent-creating (see also Adams *et al.* 2003).

To understand the economic effects of services trade barriers, and to work out policy priorities, it is therefore critical to know three things:

- the 'height' of the trade barrier — the equivalent of the tariff rate in goods trade (though it applies behind rather than at the border);
- the 'incidence' of the barrier — whether it applies only to foreign suppliers, or whether it also applies to domestic operators; and
- the 'impact' of the barrier — whether the barrier has created rents or raised real resource costs.

Some generalizations from the findings of first-generation empirical studies are as follows (Dee and Findlay 2008a). In sectors such as banking and telecommunications, services trade barriers are much higher in developing than in developed economies. In sectors such as the professions, distribution (wholesale and retail trade) and electricity generation, the barriers in the developed world are non-trivial, but still generally lower than in developing countries. In a few sectors such as maritime, the barriers in the developed world can exceed those in developing countries. Across all sectors, where there are significant barriers to foreign supply, there are typically also non-trivial barriers to domestic supply. Whether barriers create rents or add to resource costs is severely under-researched, although theory can sometime provide guidance.

1.3 Measurement Methodology

Because services trade barriers operate behind the border, the research has quantified the effects of barriers on some behind-the-border measure of economic performance. In generic terms, econometric methods have been used to estimate the effects of a measure of services trade barriers (*TB*) on some measure of economic performance (*Y*) in a particular services market, controlling for all the other factors (*Z*) that affect economic performance in that market. The estimated model is then used to construct the value *Y'* that would obtain in that market if there were no services trade barriers (normally, if *TB* took a zero value). The actual models have varied from one sector to the other, but typically have been drawn from the literature on structure, conduct and performance for the sector in question. As shown in Table 1.1, the measures of economic performance have included price, cost, price-cost margin, quantity or productivity. The appropriate control variables have varied from one sector to the next.

Because services trade barriers vary across but typically not within countries, econometric studies of the effects of services trade restrictions have been cross-country or panel studies. Essentially, the studies exploit cross-country (or panel) variation in the extent of barriers to trade in a particular services sector, and cross-country variation in the subsequent economic performance of that sector, or of the economy as a whole, to quantify a 'cross-country average' relationship between barriers and performance. This can then be used to project the effects on an individual country, given its current level of barriers to services trade in that sector.

The methodology requires a quantitative measure of services trade barriers (*TB*). In the first-generation studies in Findlay and Warren (2000), qualitative information about regulatory restrictions was converted into a quantitative index (or indexes) using *a priori* judgements about the relative restrictiveness of different barriers. This was generally less contentious within a given category of barrier than between. For example, it might make sense to score a regime that restricts foreign ownership to 25 per cent or less as being twice as restrictive as one that restricts foreign ownership to 50 per cent or less. What is less obvious is how to weight the scores on foreign ownership restrictions together with those on licensing requirements, or those on restrictions on lines of business. This aspect of the methodology has been subject to criticisms that are outlined below.

Nevertheless, if the analysis proceeds to the second step of assessing the impact on performance, then in principle it is possible to use this econometric stage to test the weighs that were assigned *a priori* to different categories of restrictions in the first stage, essentially by re-estimating them. This can be done by entering the index scores for the different categories of restrictions separately into the estimating equation. The first-generation studies that achieved the most in this regard were Steiner (2000) for electricity generation, Nguyen-Hong (2000) for the engineering profession and Dee (2004) for telecommunications.

Often this approach is precluded by one of two econometric problems endemic in this work — multicollinearity, or lack of in-sample variation in one or more of the restrictiveness index components. However, the regulatory work by the OECD (Gonenc and Nicoletti 2000, Boylaud and Nicoletti 2000, Steiner 2000) showed how factor analysis (of which principal components is an application) can be used to overcome these problems in a technical sense. Prior to any econometric estimation, they used factor analysis to identify a set of orthogonal 'factors' that explained most of the variation in their original data on regulatory restrictions. But as Doove *et al.* (2001) point out, high cross-country variation in restrictions may have little or no relationship with the relative economic importance of particular restriction categories:

> … the use of factor analysis could lead to paradoxical results — in the sense that the more important restrictions, if they were applied widely and consistently across countries, could also have low cross-country variation and thus low factor analysis weights. (p. 17)

If, instead, principal components were used as the method of econometric estimation, then problems of multicollinearity would be overcome and orthogonal linear combinations of individual restrictions could be identified that explained most of the variation in economic outcomes — a truer measure of economic significance. To date, however, no study of the impact of services policy has used this methodology.

Once the econometric estimation is completed, the 'on-average, per unit' effects of services trade restrictions are given by the estimated coefficients. Total, country-specific measures of economic impact can be estimated by multiplying these coefficient(s) by their associated restrictiveness index measures for that country. *If* these estimated impacts can be interpreted as vertical shifts in supply curves (see more on this below), they can be turned into 'tax equivalents', if the trade barriers have raised price-cost margins, or 'productivity equivalents', if the trade barriers have raised real resource costs. These give the direct impact of services trade barriers in the particular sector and country in question.

One advantage of this methodology is that it can be generalized fairly easily to include additional countries or additional time periods. Once a coefficient estimate has been obtained from a particular sample, all that is required for additional countries or time periods is to produce an index score to characterize the services trade restrictions at that point in time, and the new 'tax equivalents' or 'productivity equivalents' can be calculated from the existing coefficient and the new index score without redoing the econometrics. Obviously, the original sample needs to be fairly representative for such 'out-of-sample forecasting' to be appropriate. Many of the studies in Table 1.1 included, at minimum, the APEC economies, the members of the European Union, and often key economies from the rest of the world (eg Switzerland, Turkey, India, South Africa).

A second advantage of the methodology is that it produces estimates of the effects of trade barriers that are explicitly linked to characterizations of the restrictions themselves, rather than being generated as an 'unexplained residual' (as in Francois and Hoekman 1999).

While it would be desirable to use information about every conceivable barrier affecting trade in a particular service in these exercises, this is not always possible. Where the index measures of services trade barriers are to be used in an econometric model, issues of comparability also arise. It would be inappropriate to use a dataset that showed a particular country to be very liberal (or very illiberal), simply because information on some barriers to services trade were unavailable for that country. Hence, the trade restrictiveness indexes used in econometric exercises may not be fully comprehensive, but they generally measure a broad range of barriers for which comparable data are available for all the countries in the sample.

Services trade barriers and domestic regulation

Services trade reform cannot take place in a vacuum. This is because governments often want to regulate services markets to correct for market failures and/or to meet equity objectives.[3] Unless regulation is appropriately designed, services trade liberalization may not be feasible, or if feasible, may not generate its intended benefits. The GATS recognized the right of individual governments to regulate, but required that domestic regulatory regimes be the 'least burdensome' necessary to achieve their objectives. The links between services trade barriers and

[3] For example, natural monopoly is a feature of many network infrastructure industries, financial markets are prone to systemic instability, and the problem of asymmetric information characterizes many professional and social services (eg health), requiring regulation to ensure quality.

domestic regulation are explored in more detail in Sidorenko and Findlay (2003) and Stephenson, Findlay and Yi (2002).

The analytical difficulty posed by domestic regulation in the measurement of services trade barriers is how to distinguish between restrictions that are protective and those that are designed to meet legitimate economic or social policy objectives. The literature has taken one of three possible approaches, all of which are applicable to regulatory restrictions more generally.

The first approach is to decide *a priori* which policy measures are designed to meet legitimate economic or social policy objectives, and to exclude them from the analysis at the outset. Thus, for example, estimates of the effects of services trade barriers have excluded those policy measures in air passenger transport designed to ensure the safety of passengers, and those technical regulations in electricity generation and transmission designed to ensure the integrity of the transmission network. Similarly, licensing *per se* is not necessarily treated as a restriction, but only when the licensing is not automatic or the qualification criteria are judged to be unduly restrictive. The early work on the effects of regulatory measures in banking services excluded prudential regulation (as did the GATS itself), since it was designed to ensure systemic stability. But in some sectors such as health, such a clean separation is not possible (see Chapter 9).

The second approach is to treat regulation on a continuum, and to ask the question whether the current level of regulation is 'too little' or 'too much'. Empirically, this is accomplished by allowing for a non-linear relationship between regulation and performance, and then identifying at what point the degree of regulation has the least adverse incidental effect on economic performance. For example, port services such as pilotage and towage can help to reduce costs, but eventually, having too many mandatory port services can start to add to costs. The study of Clark, Dollar and Micco (2004) identified what level of mandatory servicing minimized costs. The approach to identifying the optimal regulatory regime in electricity generation was similar (Doove *et al.* 2000), although there the regulatory choices were binary rather than continuous.

The final approach is to avoid prejudging the issue, to include all regulatory measures in the analysis, and to identify whether they have an adverse effect on some measures of economic efficiency. It is useful to policy makers to know this effect, even when the measures have a legitimate social or other objective. But if the cost to economic efficiency is found to be high, the appropriate policy conclusion need not be that the regulatory measure be removed. It could instead be that some other, less burdensome method be found to achieve that objective. For example, cross-subsidization was often used in the telecommunications industry as a way of ensuring universal service on reasonable terms, but cross-subsidization can also be a major impediment to achieving competition and lower prices generally. The regulatory solution has been to phase out cross-subsidization so as to allow the development of competition, but to find other mechanism (such as having all services providers, not just the incumbent, make financial contributions) so as to fund universal service.

All these approaches are of necessity incomplete. Ideally, the quantification process should identify the effects of services sector regulations, not just on economic outcomes such as prices or costs, but also on the social, environmental or safety outcomes that the regulations may be also designed to address. With this more complete information, the tradeoff between economic efficiency and other objectives could be evaluated directly. The difficulty is in coming up with a modelling framework that can evaluate both economic and other social, environmental or safety outcomes. The current frameworks, which focus on economic outcomes, can help in the policy evaluation process. But they do not replace the need for judgement.

1.4 Critiques of First-Generation Studies

Many of the first-generation studies relied solely or primarily on cross-country variation in policy settings, and the resulting cross-sectional variation in sectoral performance. This meant that, when quantifying the price or cost impact for a particular country, the assumption was being made that the country conformed to the sample average responsiveness of performance to policy settings. In reality, there could be country-specific factors (captured in the error term of the regression) that were likely to play an important role. One important contribution of second-generation studies would therefore be to develop panel datasets with a time dimension, so that country-specific characteristics could be more readily controlled for.

Ideally, the econometric models of sectoral performance used to quantify direct effects should be both developed and estimated at the structural level — that is, supply and demand side influences should be separately identified and estimated. In addition, the estimated supply side effects should control for the quantity of the service produced. When a quantity control is used, the effect of trade barriers on price or cost can be interpreted unambiguously as a vertical shift in the supply curve.

In practice, some models were developed structurally but then estimated in reduced form (eg Kalirajan *et al.* 2000). Other models were both developed and estimated in reduced form (eg Steiner 2000, Warren 2000). This meant that it is not always possible to identify supply and demand side influences separately, nor was it always clear that the price or cost wedge being estimated in fact corresponded to a vertical shift in the supply. On this score, at least, the direct effects may have been underestimated (Nguyen-Hong 2000).

The restrictiveness indices are in many ways crude measures of services policy, which is typically multidimensional. Even where there is enough in-sample variation to enter sub-indexes into the econometrics separately, the sub-indexes will lump together measures which may not be comparable in their economic impact.

Finally, there may be multiple dimensions to economic performance that are not always captured. An example is in electricity generation, where there are both static and dynamic considerations. Prices or costs may be measures of static performance at a point in time. But in the longer term, lower prices may reduce the incentives for investment in infrastructure. So not only are there multiple measures of performance, there can be tradeoffs between them.

There were two notable critiques of the first-generation services trade barrier measurement methodology, by Whalley (2004) and Deardorff and Stern (2005). Whalley paid insufficient attention to the importance of non-discriminatory trade restrictions, to the importance of high levels of differentiation in services such as the professions, health and education, and too easily slipped into making direct but inappropriate comparisons with the literature on tariffs and goods trade.[4] But he did state that:

> Market structure, conduct and performance are all key and all need to be evaluated when discussing quantitative impacts of global liberalization of services trade on poorer developing countries. (p. 1232)

The measurement of barriers to services trade has been firmly in the structure-conduct-performance framework, as originally identified by Findlay and Warren (2000).

Whalley made the following specific criticisms of services trade barrier measurement. First, he noted that with multiple restraints on trade, it is not clear which restrictions are binding and which are not. Ideally, this argues for continuing efforts to separate out the different dimensions of trade barriers and to enter them separately into the econometric models of sectoral performance. Borchert, Gootiiz and Mattoo (2012a, 2012b) argue instead that some judgment should be made as to when a particular measure is both binding and prohibitive, and a high overall restrictiveness score should be assigned accordingly. However, they focus primarily on producing indexes (step 1 of the above methodology), and so do not rely on econometric evidence to resolve the issue.[5]

Second, Whalley noted that the marginal effects of different restrictions on trade will typically differ. This also argues for continuing to separate out the different restrictions in econometric work.

Third, he noted that there may be country discrimination in the application of barriers, even though both *de jure* and *de facto* discrimination are breaches of national treatment under the GATS. The literature has so far dealt with this by explicitly identifying both discriminatory and non-discriminatory measures, using policy

---

[4] 'Price based measures of barriers to services trade ... ideally ... should reflect differences between domestic and foreign prices for key service categories across supplying and using countries'. (Whalley 2004, p. 1238).

[5] In practice, when a single prohibitive measure is scored within an indexing methodology that adds up the effects of a number of different restriction categories, the index result is often similar to that proposed by Borchert, Gootiiz and Mattoo (2012a). For example, see the treatment of the Myanmar's policy regimes in Dee (2010b, 2011b).

information sources that go well beyond GATS schedules. Recent assessments have confirmed the importance of looking at actual policies rather than formal trade commitments (Dee and NcNaugton 2011). Nevertheless, recent work has also documented the content of services trade commitments in regional trading arrangements, so as to identify formal deviations from most-favoured-nation treatment (eg Ochiai, Dee and Findlay 2010).

Whalley stated that quantity-based measures are 'typically based on model-generated residuals given by observations relative to econometric model predictions' (p. 1239). In reality, Francois and Hoekman (1999) was the only study in Table 1.1 to use this approach.

Finally, Whalley presumed that international price comparisons were the appropriate way to generate price-based measures of barriers to services trade, but noted that 'price differences across countries for services need not be related to barriers, even if they could be measured' (p. 1239). As stated earlier, the highly differentiated nature of services makes direct international price comparisons an inappropriate tool. So the literature has not used this approach, but has instead undertaken behind-the-border studies of market structure, conduct and performance to generate its price or cost impacts, controlling for a range of other factors that affect prices or costs.

Deardorff and Stern (2005) also paid insufficient attention to the critical importance of non-discriminatory trade barriers in services trade. This seems to be the fundamental reason why they asserted that the appropriate way to model services trade barriers was as a tariff equivalent — all the examples they gave to demonstrate that a tariff equivalent was an appropriate concept were examples of discriminatory trade barriers.

Deardorff and Stern, like Whalley, noted that if the econometric models are not structural enough to have controlled for the effects of services quantities, then estimates of the elasticities of supply and demand would be required to covert the price impacts from econometrics into vertical shifts in supply or demand curves. A solution to this issue, discussed in more detail below, is to begin to control for quantities in the econometric work.

Deardorff and Stern discussed the issue of assigning weights in a restrictiveness index by judgement or by factor analysis. They stated that:

> [Judgement] may well be the best approach if the investigator really is knowledgeable, as in the case when an index is being constructed for a specific narrowly defined industry.
>
> An alternative … is to apply factor analysis to the data …This is a purely statistical technique that is not, in our view, necessarily an improvement on the use of judgement weights. (p. 569)

Deardorff and Stern provided guiding principles for measuring barriers to services trade. They noted first that no single methodology is sufficient for documenting and measuring barriers to trade in services. Instead, investigators need to draw upon all available information, including both direct observation of particular barriers and indirect inference of barriers using data on prices and quantities. These approaches are both used in steps 1 and 2 above.

Deardorff and Stern also noted that because of the special role of incumbent firms in many services industries, regulations do not need to be explicitly discriminatory against foreign firms in order to have discriminatory effects.

This observation is true, but it misses the economic significance of non-discriminatory barriers against potential domestic new entrants. In most developing countries, indigenous firms have significant supply capability, and can compete against foreign new entrants by differentiating their services and targeting particular market niches. In banking, for example, foreign banks may specialize in servicing the local affiliates of foreign multinationals in manufacturing, while local banks specialize in rural or retail finance. Indigenous law firms have a natural advantage in practising home country law. Any analysis of services trade barriers that misses the barriers against potential domestic new entrants will miss the gains to those entrants when barriers are lifted, and will give a distorted view of who gains and who loses from services trade reform. Some of these themes were explored in Dee and Sidorenko (2005).

The first-generation work on measuring barriers to services trade suffered from sins of omission and sins of commission.

Sins of omission

The critique of Deardorff and Stern (2005) confirmed that a sector-by-sector approach to measuring barriers to services trade is the best way to proceed. Whalley (2004) confirmed that the sectoral evaluations should occur in a way that takes account of structure, conduct and performance. Experience suggests that for any given sector, there will be a combination of one-off and ongoing information sources that can be found to provide information about current policy settings on an indicative, if not always comprehensive basis. As will be explained below, a slight change of focus is required when finding measures of performance.

The sectoral coverage of the first-generation estimates in Table 1.1 was inadequate. In particular, the key service sectors of insurance, education, health, construction and tourism were missing. For education, some information about policy regimes in a number of countries had already been collected (Nguyen-Hong and Wells 2003), but the impact of these regimes on performance had yet to be analysed. Since education is one of the few services traded via all four modes of delivery, the analysis could potentially yield some interesting insights into how trade barriers could drive inter-modal substitution.[6]

Further work was also required to track how services trade barriers were changing over time. Initial experience suggested that the regimes in telecommunications and financial services were changing rapidly, while those governing distribution and the professions were far more static. The regimes affecting air passenger transport also changed fairly rapidly, although it remains difficult to obtain up-to-date information about the content of international air service agreements.

---

[6] The four modes are cross-border supply (mode 1), supply via the temporary movement of the consumer (mode 2), supply via permanent commercial presence of the provider (mode 3), and supply via the temporary movement of the provider (mode 4). All are recognized in the GATS.

A research priority was therefore to update information about policy regimes comprehensively across a range of countries. This would be required to track progress on services trade liberalization. Even more valuable, however, would be to update both the measures of policy and the measures of performance. This would allow the estimation of the costs of trade barriers to be done in a panel context. With panel data, it would be possible to control for unobserved heterogeneity across countries, and thus achieve more robust and reliable estimates.

Sins of commission

The first-generation general equilibrium studies showed that the single biggest determinant of the projected gains from services trade liberalization was whether the trade barriers were modelled as affecting markups or affecting real resource costs.[7] This 'treatment' effect often dominated the estimated 'height' of the trade barrier, and accounted for some of the variation in modelling outcomes observed by Whalley (2004).

This treatment effect also meant that the economic significance of barriers to services trade could not be gauged simply by comparing the 'heights' of the impacts on costs or price-cost margins. As noted earlier, the cost impacts have much greater implications for economic welfare than the impacts on price-cost margins. Economic modelling is therefore critical to trace through the implications of the barriers for economy-wide resource allocation and for economic welfare.

As noted above, whether barriers created rents or added to resource costs was severely under-researched in first-generation studies. In some cases, the empirical evidence was suggestive, but not conclusive because only one performance measure was used. In other cases, a price impact was estimated, and then it was simply asserted whether the effect operated through price-cost margins or costs.

To establish this properly requires using more than one measure of economic performance. Specifically, it requires estimating both a profit

---

[7] For example, Dee and Diop (2010) compared several first-generation studies of the effects of services trade liberalization in Tunisia on this basis.

function and a cost function, and determining the effects of trade barriers on both measures of performance. Only then can it be teased out whether the effects of trade barriers are operating through price-cost margins or through marginal costs. Berger, Cummins and Weiss (1997) showed how this approach could be applied to performance in the insurance industry. Berden *et al.* (2009) do a similar thing on a more informal basis for non-tariff measures in a range of manufacturing and services sectors.

A second advantage to estimating profit and cost functions is that both are structural, and correct for output quantities. This would help to overcome the critique outlined earlier about the reduced form nature of most first-generation studies.

Doing such analysis requires using datasets that provide data on prices and quantities separately. Only then can profit and cost functions be estimated. The datasets used for many first-generation studies were accounting datasets. These provide values, not prices and quantities. However, the Worldscope and Bankscope databases provide considerable additional information for the banking and insurance sectors, in addition to the usual accounting data, and are an adequate source for proper estimation of cost and profit functions for these sectors. For other sectors, alternative databases would need to be found to support the estimation of cost and profit functions, or some other structural approach to measuring supply characteristics.

1.5 Second-Generation Studies

How well have the second-generation studies in this volume overcome the sins of omission and commission?

Clearly the coverage of sectors has expanded. This volume includes a full analysis (step 1 and 2) for insurance, higher education and rail transport, and a partial analysis (step 1 only) for health services. The analysis of the education sector (Chapter 8) has indeed revealed evidence of intermodal substitution — international student mobility is being driven at least in part by restrictions on commercial presence in higher education. The analysis of the health sector has shown how full liberalization will be difficult in situations where there is an insufficient number of policy instruments to meet multiple policy objectives. Analysis of construction and tourism is still missing, although in major tourist destinations such as Thailand, the main barriers to entry in tourism services are of two types — restrictions in air transport, which are already covered, along with restrictions on resort development, which are issues of land planning, coordination and development.

The coverage of measures has also expanded. While the existence of a third party access regime was already included in the first-generation study of electricity by Steiner (2000), this regulatory feature is also covered here for rail (Chapter 6) and gas (Chapter 7). The content of air services agreements is taken into account in the analysis of air transport (Chapter 5), as it was in the original study by Gonenc and Nicoletti (2000). For banking, for example, the coverage of services trade measures has been expanded (Chapter 3). For air and maritime transport, it has been updated (Chapter 5).

In some sectors, progress has also been made in tracking the evolution of regulatory barriers over time. Panel datasets of regulatory restrictions in insurance, banking, electricity and gas have been compiled and used in econometric analysis. The recent trends over time in regulatory barriers in banking services have shed some new light on the distinction between prudential and non-prudential regulation in the wake of the global financial crisis (Chapter 3). The analysis of the electricity sector in Chapter 7 shows that in order to quantify the impact of regulatory barriers, it is important to choose countries and time periods over which sufficient policy variation has actually occurred. The discussion in Chapter 6 indicates that the same issue applies in rail.

In finance services, some significant progress has been made in determining whether regulatory barriers affect costs or price-cost margins. The evidence is that barriers in insurance create rents (Chapter 2) while those in banking have both types of effects, but primarily affect costs (Chapter 3). As intimated above, the progress has been possible because of adequate data sets. In other sectors, the necessary data has not been obtained. For example, in electricity and gas, the International Energy Agency publishes separate data on output prices and costs, but its data on inputs is incomplete and therefore inadequate to support the full estimation of cost and profit functions. In higher education services, the issue has been resolved on theoretical grounds, by observing that higher education is dominated by non-profit institutions (see the discussion in Chapter 8). In both higher education and rail, databases have nevertheless been found to support a productivity-based structural approach to estimating supply characteristics, even though only one performance measure has been used. For other sectors, data limitations still preclude a full structural approach (see Chapters 5 and 7).

The sectoral studies in this volume demonstrate that the econometric problems of multicollinearity or lack of in-sample variation continue to limit the ability to determine the separate influence (or otherwise) of every individual restriction on economic performance. However, individual restrictions can be examined separately when they are few in number (eg Chapter 7, Cantos, Pastor and Serrano 2010). Otherwise, a strategic approach can be taken to dividing a single overall restrictiveness index into several sub-components to focus attention on a particular policy issue of interest. Using this approach, the analysis of banking performance in Chapter 3 sheds new light on several 'grey area' measures whose function — whether protective or prudential — has been subject to debate. As noted above, the time series evidence on how governments have actually changed these measures over time provides circumstantial evidence to support the econometric findings. Another approach to multicollinearity is shown in Chapter 5, where a battery of potential performance measures is used, but they are entered one at a time to determine (albeit imperfectly) which one(s) affect performance. The analysis of higher education combines these two approaches (Chapter 8).

1.6 Priorities for Services Reform

To assess priorities for services reform, it is not sufficient to estimate and compare the 'heights' of the regulatory barriers, as they have been estimated in the sectoral chapters of this volume. The overall economic effects of regulatory barriers also depend on their incidence — whether they apply only to foreign suppliers or also apply to domestic operators. A distinguishing feature of the sectoral studies both here and in Findlay and Warren (2000) is that they have been careful to identify the incidence as well as the nature of the trade barriers from the raw qualitative information. The overall economic effects also depend on the impact of the barriers — whether they affect costs or price-cost margins. As noted, this has been identified, where possible, in the econometric analysis of step 2.

To assess priorities for reform, it is therefore necessary to use a multi-sectoral model to capture the overall economy-wide effects of regulatory barriers, once their height, incidence and impact is taken into account. This is done in Chapter 10, for the finance, transport, energy, telecommunications and higher education sectors of APEC member economies. This final chapter begins by summarizing the empirical findings from the relevant sectoral chapters and elsewhere, so those summaries are not repeated here.

Included in the analysis are services trade reforms (narrowly defined), along with pro-competitive domestic regulatory reforms necessary to ensure that the trade reforms deliver on their promise. This includes measures such as the removal of price controls, the establishment of third party access regimes, and the introduction of an independent regulator. However, in finance, the analysis does not explicitly include the better design or enforcement of prudential regulation, while in higher education, it does not explicitly include the design of better quality assurance and accreditation frameworks. In some APEC economies, however, these measures would need to accompany the reforms considered here.

The modelling results suggest that APEC wide, the projected gains from these structural reforms are more than three times as big as the gains from further liberalization of merchandise trade. Yet the services sectors where the reforms occur are about a third the size of those engaged in merchandise trade. When structural reforms lower real production costs, even by half as much as is modelled, they generate a 'bang for the buck' that is much greater than from merchandise trade reforms. The findings of this analysis therefore vindicate the decision of APEC Leaders to move beyond a 'border' agenda to one that focuses on behind-the-border reforms.

In all APEC economies, an overwhelming proportion of the gains would come from reforms at home, rather than reforms in other economies. In services, this result applies even more strongly than it does for goods trade. The reasons why there are so few economic gains from reciprocity in services are canvassed in Dee and Findlay (2008a). The modelling results suggest, however, that while the gains from joint reforms are considerable, there is no compelling reason for each APEC economy to wait for others to reciprocate.

Which particular services sectors should be the focus of reform depends much more on country-specific factors — not only on where the highest regulatory barriers are, but also on the underlying structure of each economy, and its ultimate sources of comparative advantage. For example, the economic fortunes of the ASEAN members of APEC are closely tied to the manufacturing production networks that operate across the region. Accordingly, the ASEAN members are projected to benefit particularly from services reforms in air and maritime transport — key sectors within the logistics chains that link the production networks together. The reader is referred to the final chapter for more of this sectoral detail. Chapter 4 does a more comprehensive job of cataloguing and indexing regulatory restrictions in logistics services, including customs restrictions, but this work has yet to be used for performance measurement or economy-wide modelling.

Structural reforms cannot generate significant gains without also generating significant structural adjustments. Some of these adjustment mechanisms are familiar from the analysis of merchandise trade liberalization, but some are new.

If a regulatory barrier in services affects costs rather than price-cost margins, then the employment effects of liberalizing it can be more severe than the employment effects of liberalizing a tariff of comparable height. The essence of a productivity improvement is that an industry can produce more with less. As a result, input usage can fall, even if output rises.

The projected results in the last chapter suggest that this concern is real. However, two of the three cases where the worst *relative* outcomes for unskilled employment are projected to occur are in sectors where substantial reform in the home economy has already taken place. In addition, relative losses need not translate into absolute losses if there is sufficiently strong underlying economic growth. To some extent, services reforms provide their own reward, in terms of stimulating activity and increasing the resilience of the economy, but prudent macroeconomic management is also crucial.

Where services reform involves removing a significant margin of discrimination against the commercial presence of foreign services providers, another fear is that reform will crowd out domestically-owned businesses in favour of foreign-invested firms. This fear can carry considerable political weight.

According to the model projections, however, crowding out is not of particularly great practical concern. Multinational services providers often focus on different market niches than local firms. Investors themselves prefer to retain a diversified portfolio of local and foreign assets. And services trade reform, when carried out on a wide enough basis, can do more than just remove discrimination against foreign providers — it can also benefit domestic new entrants. At a political level, this benefit to domestic players is a counterweight to the fear of crowding out. It also means that ignoring the non-discriminatory dimensions of services trade barriers not only distorts the economic analysis, it also gives a misleading and unhelpful view of the political economy.

The remainder of this volume is devoted to elaborating the empirical methodologies outlined in this chapter. A companion volume gives more detail on the political economy of services reforms in APEC member economies, and provides ten key lessons from the reforms to date.

One of those lessons is particularly relevant here — know the costs of the current regime. The studies in this volume contribute directly to that agenda. Another lesson is that competition is more important that ownership. The modelling results in Chapter 10 confirm significant gains in rail, electricity or gas without privatization. A third lesson is to promote engagement from within. In general terms, this means engaging with the political debate at home, rather than promoting an adversarial relationship with trading partners. And potential domestic new entrants are important stakeholders in the domestic debate.

Do these political economy forces work in practice? Chapter 4 of this volume provides direct empirical evidence, as a foretaste to the case studies in the companion volume. It shows that there is a positive empirical relationship between actual restrictions and perceived performance in the logistics sector. Furthermore, poor perceived performance has indeed created pressure from domestic traders and logistics operators and led to recent logistics reforms in Indonesia and Thailand. Many further such examples are given in the companion volume.

Chapter 2

Impact of Regulatory Barriers to Trade in Insurance Services

Philippa Dee and Huong Dinh

2.1 Introduction

As with other financial markets, insurance services markets are susceptible to problems of systemic instability. They can also be adversely affected by information asymmetry between service providers and their customers. Identifying and analysing barriers to trade in insurance services therefore requires them to be distinguished from legitimate government and private sector responses to the potential problems of market failure in the industry.

The next section describes the market failure problems that can affect insurance markets, and the government and private sector approaches to solving those problems. The following section then describes the types of regulatory restrictions that impede trade in insurance services without meeting one of these legitimate regulatory objectives. It documents the extent of such barriers in 35 countries over the period 1997 to 2004. This dataset provides valuable information about the evolution of regulatory barriers over time, providing clues as to the drivers of reform in this sector.

The dataset is then used to examine how regulatory barriers affect economic performance in the insurance industry. The barriers are found to raise the profits of insurers, but not to raise their costs. The impacts of trade barriers on firm profitability are found to vary by line of business, but not by business size. Trade barriers tend to affect developing more than developed countries.

2.2 The Rationale for Regulating Insurance Services

Insurance provides backup for individuals and organizations against shocks in their life, allowing them to limit the downside losses from possible contingencies in exchange for a fee — the insurance premium. Insurance markets also provide a broader social service. In an uncertain world, the efficient allocation of resources requires complete markets, including markets for risk-bearing and risk diversification. Without insurance markets, an important prerequisite for the efficient allocation of resources is missing.

Insurance companies thus provide a range of services that are of value to individuals and industries, and also contribute to overall market outcomes. The services include at least the following (eg Berger, Cummins and Weiss 1997).

- *Risk pooling and risk bearing services.* Insurance companies allow customers to reduce their individual risk exposure by pooling risks across customers, relying on diversification to reduce the aggregate risk of the combined portfolio. Insurers also add value by holding equity capital to bear the residual risk of the pool.
- *Real services related to insured losses.* Insurers provide a range of real services for policyholders, including risk surveys, coverage design, loss-prevention services, and loss-settlement services.
- *Intermediation.* Insurers collect premiums in advance of loss payments and hold the funds in reserve until claims are paid. This is similar to the way that banks hold deposits. Insurers invest the funds in marketable securities, and use the interest earnings to provide policyholders with a discount on their premiums, to compensate for the opportunity cost of the funds. Alternatively, they may make explicit interest payments back to policyholders, in cases where the insurance policies have an explicit savings component.

Because of the sizable funds that policyholders have invested in insurance companies, those companies can be susceptible to the same loss of confidence as banks. Poor management of, or a rash of claims against, one company may make policyholders of other companies lose confidence, leading to a rush of policy cancellations and withdrawals of savings. This can threaten the stability of the entire system.

There are additional problems that can threaten the viability of insurance markets, and thus threaten the efficient allocation of resources. A key problem is information asymmetry between insurers and their policy holders.

Problems of *moral hazard* arise when policyholders have private information about the efforts they take to avoid risky behaviour, but insurance companies do not share that information. Once policyholders are insured, they have less incentive to actively avoid risky behaviours. If insurance companies cannot monitor such behaviour, they may fail to adjust their actuarial estimates of various risks, thus putting their operations in jeopardy. This problem is more acute in insurance markets where risk avoidance behaviour is possible, for example in home contents insurance markets. It can be mitigated by insurance companies offering inducements to policyholders to undertake appropriate risk-avoidance behaviour.

Problems of *adverse selection* arise when policyholders have private information about their risk profiles, but insurance companies do not share that information. Thus insurance companies are forced to charge the same premiums to high-risk and low-risk customers. The lowest-risk customers may then feel they are being overcharged and withdraw from the market (ie self-insure), leaving the insurance companies with a pool of higher-risk customers. This may force the companies to raise premiums, leading to another wave of withdrawals. At the extreme, the particular insurance market may disappear altogether. As noted, this problem is acute in markets where policyholders have private information about their risk profile, for example in health insurance markets. This problem can be mitigated by insurance companies offering loyalty programs or no-claim discounts or requiring preliminary waiting periods before claims can be made (the insurance equivalent of a 'warranty' on the part of a policyholder).

Thus there are various market-based approaches that can be used by insurance companies to reduce the problems of moral hazard and adverse selection. Sometimes governments too may intervene to limit problems of adverse selection, particularly in private health insurance markets when those problems flow on to affect to the government funding of health services themselves, and when the standard market-based ways of dealing with adverse selection are deemed unacceptable on equity grounds. But typically there is no wholesale government intervention to deal with these problems of information asymmetry.

However, insurance companies in virtually all countries are subject to prudential regulations designed to ensure that they can meet claims when they arise, thus avoiding the possibility of a single insurance company collapsing, something that may then threaten the stability of the entire system.

Prudential regulation of insurance companies typically includes:

- minimum capital requirements;
- capital adequacy ratios;
- liquidity reserve ratios;
- possible coverage by an insolvency guarantee scheme; and
- a required frequency of publication of financial statements.

Prudential requirements may also dictate methods of valuing companies' liabilities, its reinsurance arrangements and its financial risk management strategies.

Such prudential regulations have been excluded from the scope of this study. The key reason is that the General Agreement on Trade in Services (GATS) under the World Trade Organization (WTO) recognizes the legitimate role of prudential regulation in ensuring systemic stability, and excludes such regulation from the scope of GATS disciplines.

This is not to say the levels of prudential regulation applied are always appropriate. Sometimes prudential regulation may be applied in a manner that is more burdensome than necessary to achieve the desired effect, and so become a *de facto* barrier to trade in insurance services. Indeed, some countries reduced their minimum capital requirements over the period 1997–2004 in the process of regulatory reform, suggesting that they had been deemed to be more burdensome than necessary. The key difficulty is in establishing what the minimum 'minimum capital requirements' should be for any country, within the limited scope of this study. Without a satisfactory way of resolving this issue, the above-listed regulations that are typically used for prudential reasons have been excluded altogether.

2.3 Regulatory Barriers to Trade in Insurance Services

In general terms, non-prudential regulatory restrictions may act as a barrier to trade by limiting competition in one of the following ways:

- by protecting incumbent insurance companies from new entrants, be they domestic or foreign, or by restricting the ongoing operations of those entrants;
- by protecting domestic insurance companies from foreign competition, or by restricting the ongoing operations of foreign players.

The latter type of restriction is explicitly discriminatory, while the former is not. Each type potentially may be applied to any of the ways in which services are traded:

- cross-border trade, where neither the provider nor customer moves (mode 1);
- purchases by consumers in the country of the provider (mode 2);
- commercial presence, where the provider establishes permanently in the country of the customer (mode 3); and
- sales by agents of the producer (for example, insurance brokers) who are temporarily in the country of the consumer (mode 4).

Finally, such barriers may apply to some or all of the following sub-categories of insurance:

- life;
- medical;
- property;
- marine, aviation and transport (MAT);

- automobile;
- freight;
- reinsurance; and
- auxiliary services.

Thus there is potentially a 2x4x8 matrix of possible barriers to trade in insurance services. However, for tractability and to focus on the most important barriers, this matrix has been compacted somewhat. The key distinction between barriers that affect domestic and/or foreign players has been retained. But only the prevalent barriers to each mode of service delivery have been selected. And within each category of barrier, its incidence across the various sub-categories of insurance products has sometimes been measured by a 'frequency count' across the different products.

The template for scoring the regulatory restrictions affecting trade in insurance services is shown in Table 2.1. Many of the restrictions, especially on commercial presence, are of the type that can be used in other industries — restrictions on foreign equity participation,[1] juridicial form, licensing or scope of operations, screening and approval requirements, monopoly provision, price controls, restrictions on expansion of outlets, restrictions on the short- or long-term movement of intra-corporate transferees and restrictions on the composition of the Board of Directors. Some restrictions are specific to insurance — restrictions on local companies' ability to reinsure, specific restrictions on broking activity, regulated 'ceding percentages' (the minimum percentage of premiums that a company is required to reinsure with domestically appointed reinsurers), and restrictions on companies' ability to place assets abroad.

The template is more detailed than that used by the OECD (Dihel and Shepherd 2007). In particular, the current template keeps track of whether the restrictions affecting commercial presence also apply to domestic players, thus revealing the true margin of discrimination against

---

[1] In principle, it is also possible to record equity restrictions that affect both domestic and foreign providers, in the form of minimum levels of government ownership. In practice, it was difficult to obtain comprehensive information on this from the information sources used.

Table 2.1. Template for Scoring Restrictions on Trade in Insurance Services

Restriction name	*Weight*	*Score*	*Restriction category*
M1F	0.06		***Restrictions on cross border (mode 1) — foreign***
		1.00	Non-resident insurance companies are not permitted to provide residents with any type of cross-border insurance services
		Table 2.2	Non-resident insurance companies are permitted to provide residents with certain types of cross-border insurance services
		Table 2.2	Non-resident insurance companies are permitted to provide residents with any type of cross-border insurance services, but with limitations (eg purchases subject to limits, foreign insurers prevented from soliciting business through advertising)
		0.00	Non-resident insurance companies are permitted to provide residents with any type of cross-border insurance services
M2F	0.07		***Restrictions consumption abroad (mode 2) — foreign***
		1.00	Residents are not authorized to purchase insurance services abroad
		Table 2.2	Residents are authorized to purchase some insurance services abroad, with or without restrictions
		0.00	No restrictions
			Restrictions on commercial presence (mode 3)
M3_DIF	0.07		**Foreign direct investment — foreign** The score will be the difference between 1 and the maximum foreign equity participation permitted in a domestic insurance company, with or without approval. For example, ownership to a maximum of 49 per cent of insurance companies would receive a score of 0.51.
M3_JFF	0.06		**Juridical form — foreign**
		1.00	No commercial presence permitted
		0.66	Only representative offices permitted
		0.33	Some legal forms of establishment allowed (subsidiaries and/or branches) in addition to representative offices
		0.00	All legal forms of establishment allowed

Table 2.1. Continued.

M3_JVF	0.07		**Joint venture arrangements — foreign**
		1.00	Foreign insurer entry is only through joint ventures with domestic subsidiary insurance companies in any type of insurance services
		0.66	Foreign insurer entry is only through joint ventures with domestic subsidiary insurance companies in some types of insurance services
		0.33	Joint ventures with domestic insurance companies in all or some types of insurance is prohibited
		0.00	No requirement is made for a foreign insurer to enter through a joint venture with a domestic subsidiary insurance company
M3_LICB	0.07		**Licensing — foreign/domestic**
		1.00	No new licences to insurance companies are issued
		0.75	Up to 4 new licences with only prudential restrictions are issued
		0.50	Up to 8 new licences with only prudential restrictions are issued
		0.25	Up to 12 new licences with only prudential restrictions are issued
		0.00	New licences are issued with only prudential restrictions
M3_SCREENB	0.04		**Screening and approval — foreign/domestic**
		1.00	Investors must show economic benefits
		0.66	Approval is required unless contrary to national interest
		0.33	Notification (pre or post) is required
		0.00	No screening or approval is required
M3_SCSB	0.05		**Scope of services — foreign/domestic**
		1.00	An insurance company can provide only one type of insurance
		Table 2.2	An insurance company can provide composite insurance service (2 or more)
		0.00	There are no restrictions on the number of insurance types provided by an insurance company
M3_REINB	0.04		**Restrictions on reinsurance by resident insurance companies — foreign/domestic**
		1.00	Reinsurance is prohibited
		0.50	Reinsurance is restricted (with foreigners only or limited in some geographic areas)
		0.00	No restriction is applied on reinsurance

Table 2.1. Continued.

M3_INTB	0.04		**Broking or agency restrictions — foreign/domestic**
		1.00	Broking or agency activities are prohibited
		0.50	Broking or agency activities are restricted
M3_MONOB	0.06		**Monopoly provision of insurance services — foreign/domestic**
		1.00	Two or more products are subject to national monopoly
		0.75	Two or more products are subject to regional monopoly
		0.50	One product is subject to national monopoly
		0.25	One product is subject to regional monopoly
		0.00	No monopoly provision is applied
M3_CEDB	0.05		**Ceding percentage — foreign/domestic**
			The score will be the ceding percentage (the percentage of premiums that an insurer is required to cede or reinsure with domestically appointed insurers) For example, if the ceding percentage is 20%, then the score is 0.2
M3_PRICEB	0.05		**Price control — foreign/domestic**
		1.00	Premium rates for any insurance product are fully set by the government
		0.75	Premium rates for some insurance products are fully set by the government
		0.50	Premium rates for all products need to be approved by the government
		0.25	Premium rates for some products need to be approved by the government
		0.00	Insurance companies are free to set premium rates
M3_ASSETB	0.05		**Placement of assets — foreign/domestic**
		1.00	Insurers are required to hold all assets locally
		0.50	Insurers are restricted in the amount they can invest abroad
		0.00	There are no restrictions on investing abroad
M3_EXPB	0.08		**Expanding operations (street branches, offices) — foreign/domestic**
		1.00	Only one insurance outlet is permitted
		0.75	Insurance outlets are limited in number and location
		0.25	Expansion of insurance outlets is subject to non-prudential regulatory approval
		0.00	No restriction is applied on insurance outlet expansion

Table 2.1. Continued.

			Restrictions on natural persons (mode 4)
M4_SHORTF	0.07		**Movement of people — Temporary — foreign**
		1.00	No temporary entry of executives, senior managers or specialists is allowed
		0.75	Temporary entry of executives, senior managers or specialists up to 30 days
		0.50	Temporary entry of executives, senior managers or specialists up to 60 days
		0.25	Temporary entry of executives, senior managers or specialists up to 90 days
		0.00	Temporary entry of executives, senior managers or specialists over 120 days
M4_LONGF	0.03		**Movement of People — Permanent — foreign**
		1.00	No entry of executives, senior managers or specialists is allowed
		0.80	Executives, specialists or senior managers can stay a period of up to 1 year
		0.60	Executives, specialists or senior managers can stay a period of up to 2 years
		0.40	Executives, specialists or senior managers can stay a period of up to 3 years
		0.20	Executives, specialists or senior managers can stay a period of up to 4 years
		0.00	Executives, specialists or senior managers can stay a period of more than 5 years
M4_BODF	0.05		**Movement of people — Board of Directors — foreign**
		1.00	The Board of Directors cannot comprise foreigners
		0.66	Majority of the BOD must be nationals
		0.33	At least one member of the BOD must be a national, resident, or locally licensed
		0.00	No restriction is applied on the composition of the board of directors

Source: Authors.

foreigners. The template is not quite as detailed as the questionnaire developed by the World Bank (World Bank, undated), which would only be completed effectively by government officials with detailed knowledge of the legislation affecting the insurance sector in each country. In particular, the current template lacks the detailed information about prudential regulations covered by the World Bank questionnaire. These have been excluded for reasons given above.

In the current template, restrictions that affect only foreign players have a name ending in 'F', while those affecting both domestic and foreign players have a name ending in 'B'. The restriction name prefixes 'M1_' to 'M4_' indicate which mode of service delivery is affected. There are 18 restriction categories in total. Eight of these affect only foreign insurers — those on mode 1 and mode 2 trade, along with three affecting mode 3 (restrictions on the legal form of establishment, foreign equity limits and the requirement to establish in a joint venture), and three affecting mode 4 (restrictions on the short- or long-term movement of intra-corporate transferees and nationality requirements on the Board of Directors). The remaining ten categories of restrictions can potentially affect both domestically-owned and locally-incorporated foreign insurance companies. These restrictions include limitations on establishment (licensing, screening and approval) and ongoing operations (for example, restrictions on reinsurance or the placement of assets). Whether these restrictions do in fact operate in a non-discriminatory way is captured in the scoring of the policy regimes for each country.

The template has been completed for 35 countries over the period 1997 to 2004 using information available from secondary sources. These include GATS commitments, WTO Trade Policy Reviews, Asia Pacific Economic Cooperation (APEC) Individual Action Plans and National Trade Estimate Reports on Foreign Trade Barriers by the Office of the United States Trade Representative, all of which are available from the websites of the respective organizations. This information has been supplemented occasionally by country insurance legislation and other selected publications.

In the current template, each restriction category is generally given a score between zero and one, where one is the most restrictive and zero is the least restrictive. Table 2.2 gives an indicative but not exhaustive list of the possible scoring values for the restrictions affecting modes 1 and 2, which are based on frequency counts across the various product categories.

Table 2.2. Detailed Scoring of Restrictions on Scope of Insurance Services

Type of insurance	*Score for each prohibited activity*	*Score for each restricted activity*	*No. of activities allowed*	*Without other limits*	*With other limits*
Life	0.125	0.0625	One	0.88	0.94
Medical	0.125	0.0625	Two	0.75	0.88
Property	0.125	0.0625	Three	0.63	0.81
Marine, aviation & transport	0.125	0.0625	Four	0.50	0.75
Automobile	0.125	0.0625	Five	0.38	0.69
Freight	0.125	0.0625	Six	0.25	0.63
Reinsurance	0.125	0.0625	Seven	0.13	0.56
Auxiliary	0.125	0.0625	All	0.00	0.50
Total	1.000	0.500			

Source: Authors.

In order to present the data in summary form, a weighted average across all restriction categories is computed for each country and time period, using the weights shown in the second column of Table 2.1. The weights were derived from principal component analysis.[2] It is desirable that the weights are the same for each time period, so that the time-series variation in the resulting summary indexes reflects only changes in the underlying policy regimes. Accordingly, the weights were computed from the raw scores for all countries, but averaged over all time periods. The weights are used to compute an index of all restrictions affecting foreign suppliers across all modes (TRI_F). This index ranges between 0 (fully unrestricted) and 1 (fully restricted). An appropriate subset of the weights is used to compute an index of all restrictions affecting domestic suppliers (TRI_D). This index ranges between 0 (fully unrestricted) and 0.53 (fully restricted), reflecting the subset of weights used. A further subset of the weights is used to compute an index of restrictions affecting locally-incorporated foreign firms via barriers to mode 3 and mode 4 trade (TRI_FA). This index ranges between 0 (fully unrestricted) and 0.87 (fully restricted). This last index is used in the subsequent

[2] This technique gives weights which, when applied to the raw scoring of restrictions, yield a weighted average which reproduces most of the original variation in the raw scores. A detailed explanation of the use of principal component analysis in the current context is given in Jolliffe (2002).

econometric analysis of impacts on insurers. Values for these three indexes are shown in Tables 2.A.1 to 2.A.3 at the end of this chapter.

Prevalence of restrictions

One way to look at the relative prevalence of different types of restrictions is to examine how many of the countries in the sample have a significant restriction in each category. Figure 2.1 shows the proportion of countries (among the overall sample of 35 countries) that have a significant restriction affecting foreign services suppliers in 1997, the first year of the sample (and generally the most restrictive year). Figure 2.2 shows the proportion of countries that have a significant restriction affecting domestic suppliers.

The most prevalent restrictions on foreign operators are those affecting supply by modes 1, 2 and 4. However, this may simply reflect the lack of variability in the ways in which these modes are restricted — if they are restricted at all, they are restricted in similar ways. It is expected that restrictions on modes 1 and 2 would be the least

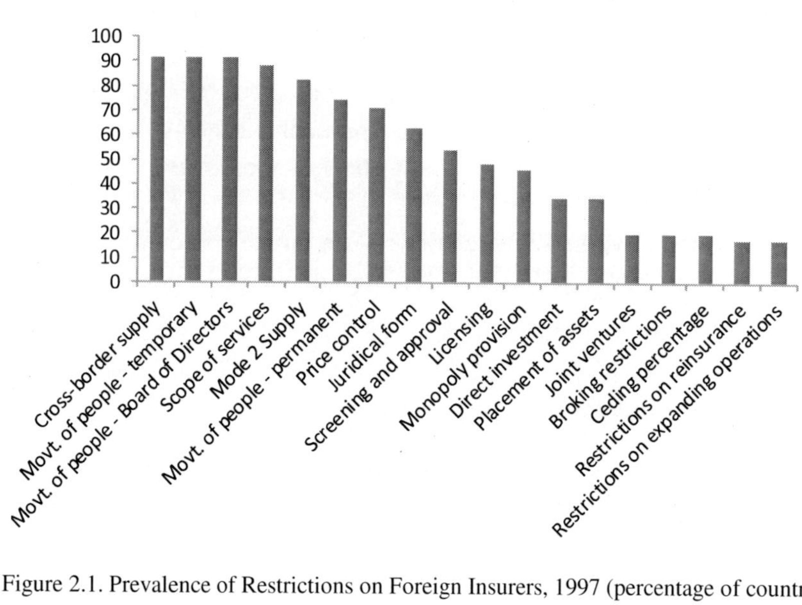

Figure 2.1. Prevalence of Restrictions on Foreign Insurers, 1997 (percentage of countries)

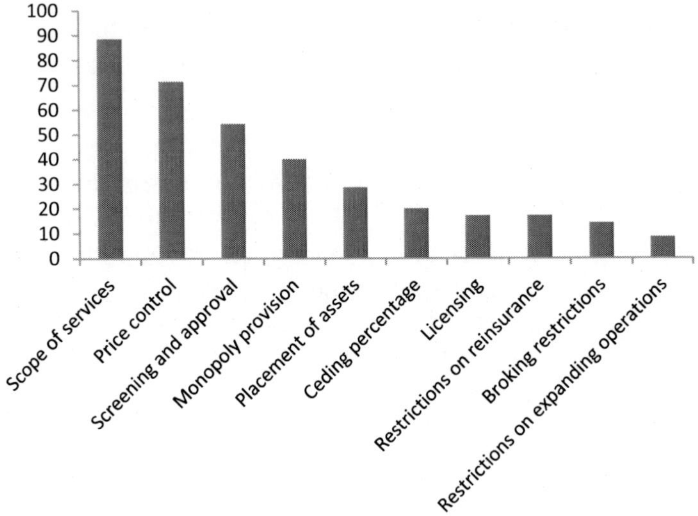

Figure 2.2. Prevalence of Restrictions on Domestic Insurers, 1997 (percentage of countries)

contentious subjects of negotiations in multilateral and bilateral forums (Mattoo and Wunsch 2004). The most prevalent restrictions on mode 3 delivery by foreign operators are those on scope of services, price control, juridical form, screening and approval, licensing, and services reserved for monopolies. Interestingly, half of these are restrictions on ongoing operations.

Not surprisingly, the same restrictions on ongoing operations are also the most prevalent restrictions affecting domestic services suppliers (Figure 2.2).

Extent of discrimination against foreign suppliers

The detailed scoring shows that locally-incorporated foreign entities are only slightly discriminated against, relative to their domestic counterparts, in the application of common restrictions. However, such discrimination is more significant in China, India and Brazil. In China, foreign insurance firms complained that the licensing requirements were complex and cumbersome (USTR 2002), and only they were subject to economic need tests and quantitative restrictions (USTR 2000). Before 2000, the Indian market was not open to foreign insurers (WTO 1998c). In Brazil, access for new foreign financial firms took place on a case-by-case basis, subject to Presidential approval, as a result of international agreements or where there was an express Presidential finding of public interest (WTO 2000).

The overall extent of discrimination against foreign suppliers is substantial, once account is also taken of the restrictions that only affect foreign providers. This is evident in Figures 2.3 and 2.4 by a large discrepancy between TRI_F and TRI_D, where TRI_F is the index of all the restrictions affecting foreign suppliers (across all modes) while TRI_D is the index of the restrictions affecting domestic providers. Combined with the above finding that discrimination in the application of potentially common restrictions is generally small, it can be concluded that overall discrimination against foreign insurers is mainly because of the higher number of restrictions applying to them.

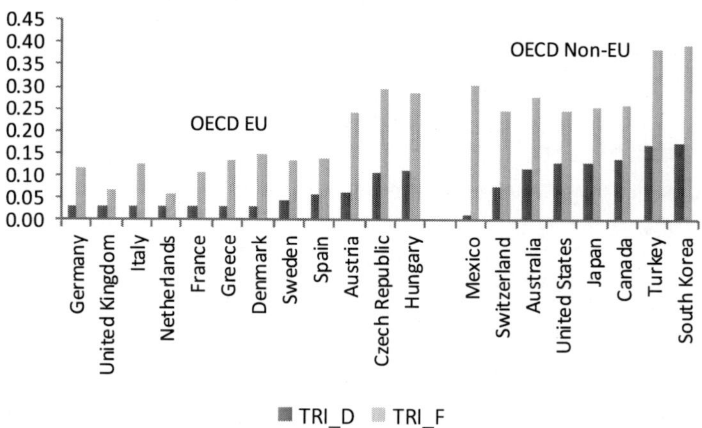

Figure 2.3. Indexes of Restrictions on Trade in Insurance in OECD Countries, Average 1997 to 2004

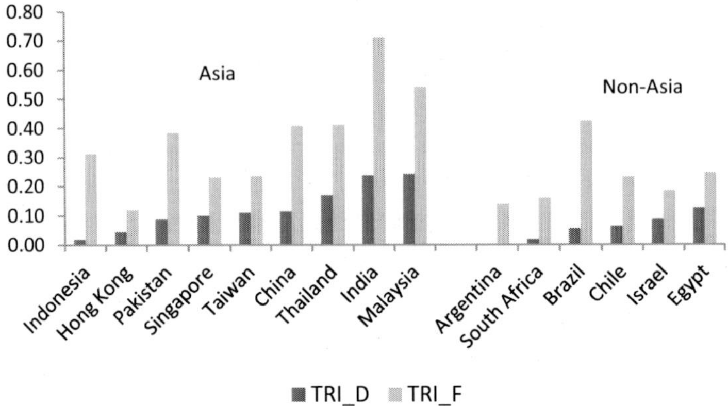

Figure 2.4. Indexes of Restrictions on Trade in Insurance Outside of OECD, Average 1997 to 2004

Extent of reform over time

Only 13 of the 35 countries in the sample show any variation in their restrictiveness index over the period 1997–2004. These countries include eight in Asia (Indonesia, Pakistan, Singapore, Taiwan, China, Thailand, India and Malaysia), one in the EU (Czech Republic), two in the OECD (Mexico and Japan), and two elsewhere (Argentina and Egypt).

In general there was a gradual reduction in restrictions on trade in insurance services in the Asian countries. More dramatic reductions occurred in China and India. These were two of the three countries with the highest average barriers over the period. For China, as for Taiwan, the liberalization was driven by WTO accession. For India, the liberalization was the result of unilateral reform. Other countries with non-trivial reductions in barriers to trade in insurance services were Singapore, Pakistan and Argentina. In all cases, these reductions were the result of unilateral domestic reforms. Pakistan's reduction was driven primarily by the privatization of a few of its biggest insurers.

Two countries actually showed slight increases in trade barriers over the period — Malaysia and Thailand. Malaysia also had the second highest average barriers to trade over the period, casting doubt on the existence of any automatic mechanism to reduce trade barriers in the most restrictive countries. In Malaysia, a law enacted in mid-1998 required the branches of foreign insurance companies to incorporate locally, raising its restrictions on joint venture requirements. In Thailand, there was a drought on issuing new licences in the second half of the period, and those 'composite' companies undertaking both life and non-life insurance were required to separate. Thus the scores for both licensing and scope of business rose over time.

Figures 2.5 and 2.6 show which particular restrictions were liberalized for domestic and foreign insurance companies, respectively, among those countries that did so over the period. These figures show the share of countries loosening each type of restriction between 1997 and 2004. For foreign insurers, the most prevalent restrictions selected for easing were foreign equity limits, licensing restrictions, ceding percentages and price control. For domestic insurers, licensing restrictions, ceding percentages and price controls were also the restrictions most often eased. Interestingly, most of the liberalization effort was directed towards restrictions affecting commercial presence, even though this has been seen as more contentious than liberalization of mode 1 and mode 2 trade.

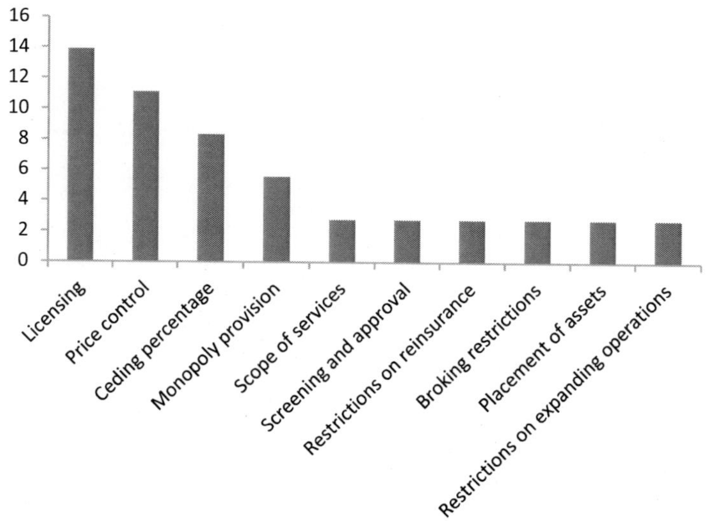

Figure 2.5. Share of Countries Easing Restrictions on Domestic Insurers, 1997 to 2004 (percentage of countries)

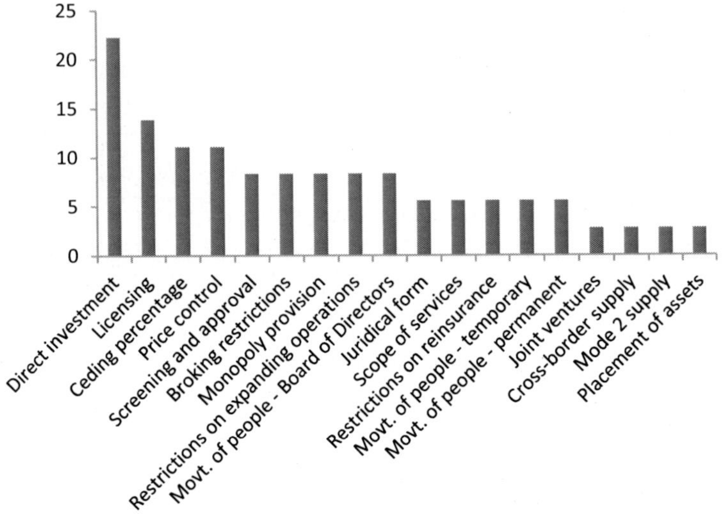

Figure 2.6. Share of Countries Easing Restrictions on Foreign Insurers, 1997 to 2004 (percentage of countries)

2.4 Estimating the Effects of Trade Barriers on Insurers' Economic Performance

Regulatory trade barriers can potentially give rise to artificial scarcity, for example by limiting the number of insurers. This can allow incumbent insurers to inflate premiums and thereby profits, even though real resource costs are unchanged. Alternatively, regulatory trade barriers may increase the real cost for insurers, perhaps by preventing them from attaining economies of scale and scope. Liberalization of trade in insurance services would have different effects, depending on whether the barriers to trade in insurance had inflated profits or raised costs. It is therefore important that any empirical investigation of the effects of barriers on economic performance be able to distinguish which of these effects has occurred.

In this section, both profit and cost are used as measures of economic performance in order to identify whether trade barriers inflate profits or raise costs. Both cost and profit functions are estimated from a firm-level panel dataset, in specifications that include index measures of regulatory barriers to trade in insurance services. Because the estimated cost and profit functions are structural, the analysis avoids the possible understatement of effects associated with estimating reduced forms. In the current analysis, both the cost and profit functions are corrected for quantities, so that the estimated effects of trade barriers can be interpreted as giving the vertical shifts in the supply curves that occur when trade barriers raise costs and/or profits. These vertical shifts can then be used as inputs into computable general equilibrium assessments of the economy-wide effects of liberalizing barriers to trade in insurance services (Chapter 10), although such economy-wide assessment is beyond the scope of this chapter.

Data

The panel dataset comes from two main sources. The Worldscope database (produced by Thomson Reuters) provides standardized accounting data for listed insurance firms on a consolidated basis. And the above analysis provides trade restrictiveness indexes for insurance services. Other data come from International Financial Statistics of the International Monetary Fund, the International Labour Organization, and Freeman and Oostendorp (2005).

The Worldscope database provides financial statements of insurance firms compiled from the balance sheets, income statements and applicable notes found in audited annual reports. These data are converted from a country-specific to a globally standardized format, although some differences in reporting and accounting conventions are likely to remain. This analysis takes into account these and other differences by controlling for country-specific fixed effects in the econometric analysis. All Worldscope data are converted into real 1997 USD using annual consumer price index and USD exchange rate data from the International Financial Statistics of the International Monetary Fund.

The resulting dataset is an unbalanced panel with 2,415 observations for 369 firms in 29 countries over the period 1997 to 2004. US insurance firms dominate, accounting for roughly 50 per cent of the total sample. There are 158 firms whose main line of business is Life Insurance, 43 mainly in Medical and Health Insurance and 168 mainly in Fire, Marine and Casualty Insurance. By income level, there are 307 firms in high income countries, 28 in upper middle income countries and 34 in lower middle income countries.

Table 2.3 presents four measures of firm performance by type of insurance and level of country income. The first performance indicator is total operating expenses, which are the sum of selling, general and administration expenses (of which salaries are a part, and are also provided separately), long-term insurance reserves, total claims expenses (including investigating expenses) and other operating expenses. Note that according to Berger, Cummins and Weiss (1997), the cost of physical capital is small relative to these other inputs. The second performance indicator is total profit, which is the gap between total revenue and total cost. Total revenue is the sum of premiums earned, investment income, other operating income, and gains/losses on the sale of securities. Two other performance indicators are unit cost and unit profit, which are defined as the ratios of total cost and total profit to total fixed capital, respectively. Total fixed capital is the sum of debt capital and equity capital, which is discussed shortly.

As can be seen, insurance firms in higher income countries tend to have higher total costs and total profits. For example, firms in the Netherlands, France and Japan have substantially larger costs and profits than those in Thailand, Pakistan, and Indonesia. In part, this may reflect relative market size. However, firms in higher income countries tend to have lower unit costs that those in developing countries. For example, firms in Denmark, Austria and Israel have unit costs that are much lower than in Brazil and Pakistan. This may reflect the differences in expertise, and possibly in market size and the extent of scale economies. Exceptional cases are Sweden, South Korea and to a lesser extent the United Kingdom, where unit costs are high. Finally, firms in developed countries tend to have the lowest unit profit. For example, the unit profit in Austria, Germany, Japan and Switzerland is less than one-fifth the average level, while that in Thailand, Pakistan and Mexico is among the highest. The profitability difference may reflect different competitiveness — a lack of competition in developing countries may allow incumbent insurers to earn high unit profits.

Table 2.3. Performance Indicators of Insurance Companies, Average 1997 to 2006

	Number of firms	*Number of observations*	*Total cost per firm (USD m)*	*Total profit per firm (USD m)*	*Unit cost per firm*	*Unit profit per firm*
Australia	6	34	3,551	405	0.43	0.04
Austria	3	24	2,931	32	0.35	0.00
Brazil	2	14	2,217	17	2.07	0.03
Canada	10	63	5,865	711	0.38	0.04
China	4	11	6,375	532	0.45	0.02
Denmark	4	23	1,619	−11	0.28	0.02
France	9	47	25,612	1,504	0.37	0.03
Germany	23	150	11,904	508	0.35	0.00
Greece	5	21	257	12	0.61	0.04
Hong Kong	2	10	249	19	0.47	0.05
Indonesia	9	61	21	−0	0.59	0.04
Israel	3	23	1,361	122	0.26	0.02
Italy	12	92	8,372	309	0.48	0.02
Japan	13	79	14,175	550	0.34	0.01
Malaysia	10	64	148	15	0.38	0.06
Mexico	2	10	684	80	0.52	0.07
Netherlands	4	21	37,098	9,443	0.40	0.10
Pakistan	2	10	49	3	0.86	0.11
Singapore	3	24	996	77	0.62	0.07
South Africa	10	63	2,627	310	1.04	0.13
South Korea	9	64	1,663	21	1.32	0.01
Spain	4	29	2,786	158	0.43	0.02
Sweden	2	11	10,179	410	2.41	0.07
Switzerland	11	79	11,053	770	0.32	0.01
Taiwan	6	33	1,360	61	0.30	0.01
Thailand	19	140	29	5	0.81	0.18
Turkey	4	15	161	30	1.49	0.19
United Kingdom	27	167	11,117	462	0.72	0.02
United States	151	1,033	2,727	368	0.66	0.06
Income groups						
Lower middle income	34	222	342	30	0.74	0.13
Upper middle income	28	166	1,297	132	0.88	0.09
High income	307	2,027	6,024	499	0.59	0.04
Insurance types						
Life insurance	158	1,014	7,268	598	0.55	0.05
Medical and Health	43	286	2,488	200	1.10	0.07
Fire, Marine, Casualty	168	1,115	3,964	338	0.57	0.05

Table 2.3. Continued.

The whole sample	369	2,415				
Mean	12.7	83.3	5,176	431	0.63	0.05
Minimum	2	10	0.2	−11,211	0.02	–4.88
Maximum	151	1,033	97,453	29,267	35.23	2.03
Standard deviation	27.3	187.7	11,491	1,711	1.31	0.17

Note: Unit cost and unit profit are defined as the ratios of total cost and profit to total fixed capital.
Source: Authors' calculations from Worldscope.

Table 2.3 also shows that the total cost and profit per firm in life insurance are roughly twice as high as in fire, marine and casualty insurance. The total cost and profit per firm are lowest in medical and health insurance. But medical and health insurance has the highest unit cost and unit profit. The unit cost and unit profit in life insurance are comparable to those in fire, marine and casualty insurance.

The estimation of cost and profit functions requires data on the key economic determinants of costs and profits. These are the quantities of the various outputs, the prices of key variable inputs, and the quantities of key fixed inputs.[3] For the current purposes, we identify two insurance outputs (risk pooling, risk bearing and real services to insured losses; and intermediation), one variable input (labour), and two fixed inputs (debt capital and equity capital).

According to Berger, Cummins and Weiss (1997), risk pooling and risk bearing is the service that insurers provide to policy holders to reduce risk through pooling and to share risk by holding equity capital. Real services include risk surveys, coverage design, loss-prevention services and loss-settlement services. In principle, risk pooling, risk bearing and real services should be measured based on the number of applications processed, the number of policies issued, or the number of claims settled. In practice, without such transaction flow data, an appropriate proxy measure for these outputs is required. This measure is the present value of real losses incurred, since the function of risk pooling/bearing and real services is to collect funds from policyholders

[3] In theory, profit functions require output prices rather than quantities. As shown in the next subsection, in order to measure vertical shifts in supply curves, we estimate an 'alternative' profit function in which output quantities rather than prices are fixed.

and equity holders and redistribute them to those who incur losses. Losses incurred are the value of claims that are expected to be paid as a result of providing insurance coverage. As in other studies (Berger, Cummins and Weiss 1997, Winter 1994), the present value of such losses incurred is proxied by the claims paid in the current year, plus the increase in reserves representing future claims to be paid from policies already written. Both are available from the expenses side of the Worldscope income statement.[4]

The second main insurance service is intermediation, where insurance companies collect premiums from policy holders and invest them in securities markets. The corresponding output quantity measure is total real invested assets, equal to the sum of bonds, mortgages, and equities. This is available from the asset side of the Worldscope balance sheet.

In principle, the main variable inputs for insurance firms are labour and business services (such as loss settlement services from lawyers and loss settlement firms). In practice, most firms in Worldscope report either salaries, or numbers of employees, but not both. Because wage data cannot be calculated from Worldscope, they are imputed from International Labour Organization and Freeman and Oostendorp (2005). These sources do not provide data at a sufficient level of disaggregation to give separate wages for insurance labour and business services, so labour and business services have been collapsed into a single variable input, and the wage for the insurance industry has been used as the single price of labour. The wage therefore gives labour expenses at the industry level rather than at the firm level.

Debt capital and equity capital are treated as fixed inputs since in the short run (a period of less than 10 years), small firms are unable to accumulate nearly as much debt capital or equity capital as large firms. Debt capital consists mainly of funds borrowed from policyholders and is measured as the sum of loss reserves and unearned premium reserves, both from the liabilities side of the Worldscope balance sheet. Loss reserves represent the present value of future benefits to be paid on

---

4 The increase in reserves is measured by the expense item 'long-term insurance reserves', which is defined in Worldscope as 'the expected discounted future payments for long term policies usually determined by regulatory agencies in each country'. Because it is an expense item, it logically measures the changes in such reserves.

behalf of or to policyholders. Unearned premiums represent premiums on policies written but not yet earned. Equity capital is measured as the sum of common stock, preferred stock, and retained earnings, available from the liabilities and net worth side of the Worldscope balance sheet. Typically, equity capital is much lower than debt capital, and much less variable.

Table 2.4 gives summary measures of this input and output data by type of insurance and level of country income. It also gives summary measures of the index of barriers to trade in insurance services used in the econometric estimation. Although indexes can be computed by mode of supply, Worldcope does not provide data on this basis, so it is hard to separate the impact of trade barriers in insurance by services delivery mode. In addition, Worldscope provides data mostly on a consolidated basis, so it is difficult to differentiate the impact of trade barriers by ownership. As a result, this current study examines the effects of trade barriers on all firms in a country using the restrictiveness index for foreign affiliate operations in that country, representing the barriers against commercial presence and the movement of natural persons (TRI_FA). As shown in Table 2.4, lower middle income countries, especially Brazil, China and Mexico, bear the highest level of restriction. Middle income countries face a slightly lower level of restriction while high income countries bear the least restriction.

Model specification

The cost and profit function specifications trace changes in cost and price mark-up, respectively, caused by trade barriers, while controlling for the other economic determinants of cost and profit. In order to estimate the vertical shifts in the supply curve, it is necessary to control for output quantities. Accordingly, an alternative profit function is estimated, which controls for output quantities rather than prices (see also Berger, Cummins and Weiss 1997). This can be seen as the result of short-term optimization, where insurers take their quantities rather than their prices as given. Thus both the cost and alternative profit functions take as exogenous output quantities, input prices and fixed input quantities.

Table 2.4. Economic Determinants of Costs and Profits of Insurance Companies, Average 1997 to 2006

	Real insurance wage (USD '000)	*Real risk pooling per firm (USD b)*	*Real inter-mediation per firm (USD b)*	*Real debt capital per firm (USD b)*	*Real equity capital per firm (USD b)*	*TRI_FA*
Australia	28.91	2.64	11.10	8.28	1.85	0.21
Austria	23.78	2.05	7.48	8.28	0.40	0.18
Brazil	14.21	1.54	0.99	0.72	0.24	0.32
Canada	29.57	4.39	22.93	19.87	2.61	0.21
China	1.47	5.01	7.97	19.43	2.06	0.28
Denmark	72.44	1.34	6.50	6.45	0.51	0.08
France	28.11	19.25	77.11	81.35	1.78	0.09
Germany	37.93	8.72	56.35	43.72	1.68	0.11
Greece	27.24	0.17	0.32	0.42	0.04	0.13
Hong Kong	31.02	0.15	0.57	0.64	0.16	0.07
Indonesia	1.61	0.01	0.02	0.02	0.05	0.19
Israel	36.50	1.05	4.43	5.26	0.25	0.13
Italy	19.25	6.06	19.05	21.88	0.55	0.09
Japan	31.44	9.96	50.85	55.53	2.10	0.18
Malaysia	14.24	0.10	0.29	0.31	0.10	0.43
Mexico	5.40	0.45	0.88	0.94	0.25	0.18
Netherlands	34.40	25.73	252.68	93.58	1.53	0.06
Pakistan	1.54	0.04	0.03	0.05	0.01	0.27
Singapore	18.80	0.90	3.15	1.07	0.25	0.18
South Africa	20.18	1.61	6.07	6.43	0.39	0.10
South Korea	17.21	1.17	1.38	1.38	0.06	0.28
Spain	30.95	2.23	4.86	6.11	0.43	0.13
Sweden	45.93	3.88	5.80	5.04	0.60	0.10
Switzerland	67.39	7.96	35.00	35.65	2.62	0.18
Taiwan	17.48	0.91	7.74	8.57	0.58	0.15
Thailand	4.28	0.02	0.04	0.03	0.01	0.38
Turkey	17.11	0.12	0.05	0.09	0.06	0.31
United Kingdom	47.58	7.42	35.14	32.27	1.93	0.07
United States	40.47	1.87	9.91	6.97	1.62	0.21
Income groups						
Lower middle income	3.28	0.26	0.42	0.99	0.12	0.32
Upper middle income	16.22	0.81	2.56	2.69	0.23	0.27
High income	38.18	4.25	22.16	18.16	1.52	0.17
Insurance types						
Life insurance	35.89	5.18	28.96	24.23	1.24	0.17
Medical and Health	38.83	1.84	5.06	4.53	0.79	0.19
Fire, Marine, Casualty	29.88	2.71	13.11	10.41	1.50	0.22

Table 2.4. Continued.

The whole sample						
Mean	33.46	3.64	18.81	15.51	1.31	0.19
Minimum	1.47	0.00	0.00	0.00	–2.02	0.06
Maximum	77.58	70.10	848.20	342.90	60.74	0.45
Standard deviation	15.24	8.19	55.58	37.70	3.56	0.08

Source: Authors' calculations from Worldscope.

Among different structural function forms,[5] the Symmetric McFadden function is chosen for this study because it is not only flexible[6] and rather parsimonious,[7] but also meets global curvature conditions without losing its flexibility. In addition, this functional form is relevant for multiple outputs, especially when some outputs have zero quantity. Negative profit data account for a significant share of the total sample. If such data are dropped, a problem of selectivity bias may arise. Although these data can be kept by adding their largest absolute value to the whole profit data and taking the logarithm of these adjusted data (as done in some studies), a new problem of measurement error arises. Thus, the ability to keep negative profit data without converting them is another justification for using the Symmetric McFadden.

The Symmetric McFadden functional form for the cost and profit functions with two outputs q_1 (risk pooling/bearing and real services) and q_2 (intermediation), one variable input (with wage w) and two fixed inputs k_1 (debt capital) and k_2 (equity capital) is shown in (2.1).

---

[5] They include the Translog (Christensen, Jorgensom and Lau 1973), the Generalized Leontief (Diewert 1971), and the Generalized McFadden and Generalized Barnett (Diewert and Wales 1987).

[6] A functional form is flexible if it either provides a second-order approximation to an arbitrary twice continuously differentiable function (which satisfies the appropriate regularity conditions), or it can be formulated to represent a second-order Taylor series approximation to an arbitrary function. In other words, a flexible functional form enables all of the effects in parameters to be portrayed, without imposing prior constraints across effects. As Chambers (1988) indicates, a flexible functional form with fewer restrictions increases the validity of any resulting inferences from the statistical tests, which are nested within the confines of the function forms.

[7] A functional form is parsimonious if it can provide a second-order approximation using a minimum number of parameters. Using many parameters reduces the degrees of freedom (Lawrence 1988, Diewert and Wales 1995).

$$\begin{aligned} PI_{ijt} &= \alpha + \chi w + \delta_1 w q_1 + \delta_2 w q_2 + \phi_1 w q_1 q_2 + \phi_2 w (q_1)^2 + \phi_3 w (q_2)^2 \\ &\quad + \rho_1 k_1 + \rho_2 k_2 + a_z TRI_{jt} + u_i + \kappa_r + \lambda_j + \eta_t + \varepsilon_{ijt} \\ &= \alpha + a_z TRI_{jt} + X_{it}^{'} \beta + u_i + \kappa_r + \lambda_j + \eta_t + \varepsilon_{ijt} \end{aligned} \quad (2.1)$$

where the performance indicator *PI* is cost or profit for firm *i* in country *j* at time *t*. Firm-specific fixed effects u_i are included to control for effects such as managerial capacities or ownership. Insurance-type fixed effects κ_r capture the impact of main business line (life insurance, medical and health insurance, or fire, marine and casualty insurance). Country-specific effects λ_j represent the effects of factors such as business environment, political system and history. Time-varying effects are captured by η_t. The Hausman test confirms that these fixed effects are needed in both the cost and profit functions. The factors that change across firms, across countries and over time are captured in the idiosyncratic term ε_{ijt}.

Estimation technique

Apart from general time-varying effects, current performance may also depend on immediate past performance. Failure to take such dynamic effects into account can lead to biased and inconsistent estimates. The Arellano-Bond linear dynamic panel data (or System Generalized Method of Moments) estimator takes account of this dependence by including lagged dependent variables as explanators. Because these variables are pre-determined, they can also be used as instruments to control for potential endogeneity of other regressors (particularly the outputs). The Arellano-Bond linear dynamic panel data estimator is particularly suitable for panels with a large cross-sectional dimension (in this case, 369 firms) and a small time dimension (in this case, 8 years). The number of lags of the dependent variable is selected by step-wise regression methods. In addition, the trade restrictiveness index is interacted with total fixed capital, the insurance type dummy or the time dummy, in order to test whether the effects of trade restrictions vary systematically by firm size, insurance type or over time. Thus the final estimating equation is shown in (2.2).

$$PI_{ijt} = \alpha_c + \sum_{n=1}^{k} \delta_n PI_{ijt-n} + \sum_{t=1}^{T} a_{zh} TRI_{jt} \times Y_t + X_{it}^{'} \beta + u_i + \kappa_r + \lambda_j + \eta_t + \varepsilon_{ijt} \tag{2.2}$$

where Y_t is either total capital (*tk*), the insurance-type dummy (*is*) or the time dummy (*y*).

As the problem of heteroskedasticity is common in panel data, unit cost and unit profit are used as dependent variables. These corresponding unit variables are the ratios of total cost and total profit to total fixed capital. In addition, US insurance firms dominate the sample. Following Claessens *et al.* (2001), the study uses the inverse of the number of firms in a country in a given year as the weights to correct for varying numbers of firms across countries. This weighted estimation approach can also correct for the problem of heteroskedasticity.

Five different models are estimated for each performance indicator. The first model includes no fixed effects or interaction terms. The second model allows for heterogenous time effects. If the joint test on the time dummy variables cannot reject the null hypothesis of homogenous time effects, time dummy variables are omitted from the last three models. The third model allows the impacts of trade barriers to vary over time. The fourth model allows the impacts of trade barriers to vary over business size. The last model allows the impacts of trade barriers to vary by type of insurance business.

Tables 2.5 and 2.6 report the regression results for these estimations of unit cost and unit profit, respectively. As can be seen, heterogeneous time effects are jointly significant in the unit profit but not the unit cost function. One lag of the dependent variable is selected for the unit cost function, while two are selected for the unit profit function. The positive coefficients of the lagged dependent variables indicate that the models are correctly specified (McKinnish 2004). In both the unit cost and profit function, the M2 tests fail to reject the hypothesis that there is no second-order serial correlation, confirming that the use of System Generalized Method of Moments estimator is justified. Sargan tests for over-identifying restrictions examine the validity of the instruments that are used to treat the endogeneity. In all specifications of the unit profit function, the over-identifying restrictions are satisfied. However, for the unit cost function, only model 4 meets these requirements.

Table 2.5. Regression Results for Unit Cost Function in Insurance

Dependent variable = Unitcost

Explanatory variable	*Model (1)*	*Model (2)*	*Model (3)*	*Model (4)*	*Model (5)*
Unitcost(–1)	0.504***	0.562***	0.535***	0.502***	0.505***
w	–0.000198	0.00271	–0.00571	–0.000257	–0.00217
wq_1	0.000894	0.000768	0.000993	0.000891	0.000818
wq_2	–6.35e–05	–7.02e–05	–6.44e–05	–6.10e–05	–5.70e–05
wq_1q_1	1.73e–06	–1.43e–06	–1.40e–07	2.23e–06	3.00e–06
wq_1q_2	–7.42e–07	–2.07e–07	–6.84e–07	–7.73e–07	–7.53e–07
wq_2q_2	1.62e–07	1.16e–07	1.52e–07	1.63e–07	1.55e–07
debt_capital	–0.00237**	–0.00165	–0.00323***	–0.00294	–0.00280**
equity_capital	–0.0693	–0.0562	–0.0468	–0.0724	–0.0664
tri_fa	0.478	0.660		0.546	
y99		0.233			
y00		–0.291			
y01		–0.292			
y02		–0.176			
y03		–0.228			
y04		–0.230			
tri_y99			2.064		
tri_y00			–1.040		
tri_y01			–0.875		
tri_y02			–0.258		
tri_y03			–0.456		
tri_y04			–0.509		
zk				0.00457	
tri_ins2					–2.061
tri_ins3					0.730
Constant	0.268*	0.251	0.517***	0.273*	0.406***
Specification tests					
M2					
Z	–1.09	–1.28	–1.19	–1.09	–1.09
Pr>z	0.278	0.202	0.235	0.277	0.278
Sargan tests					
Chi2	454.33	335	353	42.35	453
Pr>Chi2	0	0	0	0.289	0
Observations	2028	2028	2028	2028	2028
Number of firms	364	364	364	364	364

Notes: *** p<0.01, ** p<0.05, * p<0.1.

Source: Authors' calculations.

Table 2.6. Regression Results for Unit Profit Function in Insurance

Dependent variable = Unitprofit

Explanatory variable	*Model (1)*	*Model (2)*	*Model (3)*	*Model (4)*	*Model (5)*
Unitprofit(–1)	0.290***	0.281**	0.294***	0.279**	0.298***
Unitprofit(–2)	0.103	0.180**	0.146	0.194**	0.185**
w	7.10e–05	0.000159	0.000394	0.000109	0.000101
wq_1	–6.11e–05**	–5.46e–05**	–5.94e–05**	–5.47e–05**	–5.64e–05**
wq_2	1.84e–05***	1.55e–05***	1.50e–05***	1.59e–05***	1.53e–05***
wq_1q_1	1.96e–06***	1.53e–06***	1.58e–06***	1.64e–06***	1.51e–06***
wq_1q_2	–1.99e–07***	–1.45e–07***	–1.40e–07**	–1.53e–07***	–1.46e–07***
wq_1q_2	3.63e–09	1.04e–09	1.63e–09	1.42e–09	8.51e–10
debt_capital	–0.000229*	–0.000164	–0.000136	–0.000290*	–0.000146
equity_capital	–0.00253	–0.00300	–0.00338	–0.00381	–0.00280
tri_y00			0.0679		
tri_y01			0.200		
tri_y02			0.111		
tri_y03			0.0347		
tri_y04			0.376**		
y00		0.00650	–0.00452	0.00729	0.00652
y01		–0.0161	–0.0460*	–0.0151	–0.0160
y02		–0.0176	–0.0343	–0.0168	–0.0175
y03		–0.00608	–0.00958	–0.00512	–0.00560
y04		0.00634	–0.0503**	0.00742	0.00654
tri_fa	0.111**	0.111**		0.101**	
zk				0.00116	
tri_ins2					0.0215
tri_ins3					0.112
Constant	0.00560	0.00537	0.0148	0.00738	0.0151
Specification tests					
M2					
Z	–0.19	–0.76	–0.77	–0.84	–0.79
Pr>z	0.850	0.447	0.439	0.402	0.427
Sargan tests					
Chi2	41.63	33.8	29.58	33.61	33.7
Pr>Chi2	1	1	1	1	1
Observations	1653	1653	1653	1653	1653
Number of firms	340	340	340	340	340

Notes: *** p<0.01, ** p<0.05, * p<0.1.
Source: Authors' calculations.

2.5 Estimation Results

The impacts of trade barriers on cost and profit are represented by the coefficients of the trade restrictiveness index (TRI) in models (1), (2) and (4). These impacts are also reflected in the coefficients on the interaction terms between TRI and the (a) year dummy variables in model (3), (b) total fixed capital in model (4), and (c) main line of insurance business in model (5). These interactions are used to check whether the impacts of trade barriers are homogenous over time, across business size, or across line of insurance.

It is found that trade barriers have no statistically significant effect on cost. In Table 2.5, the coefficient of TRI is not statistically significant in models (1), (2) and (4), while the coefficients of the interaction terms are jointly insignificant in models (3), (4) and (5).

By contrast, trade barriers are statistically significantly associated with an improvement in insurance profitability. This result suggests trade barriers in insurance have a rent-creating effect. The coefficient of the interaction term between TRI and the year dummy variable for year 2004 in model (3), Table 2.6 is statistically significant at the 5 per cent level of significance. However, the test of the joint significance of all interaction terms between trade barriers and year dummy variables cannot reject the hypothesis of homogeneous impacts of trade barriers on unit profit over time. Model (4) in Table 2.6 shows that the impacts of trade barriers do not depend on business size. Model (5) in Table 2.6 shows that the impacts of trade barriers can vary by line of insurance business. The test of the joint significance of all interaction terms between TRI and business type rejects the null hypothesis of homogenous effects. The estimated coefficients of these interactions terms indicate that the same level of restriction creates the highest rent for casualty, fire, and marine insurance but the lowest for life insurance.

Turning to control variables, debt capital is shown to be significantly associated with a reduction in unit cost in models (1), (3) and (5), Table 2.5. In other words, there are economies of scale in insurance. This is in line with other studies that have found both economies of scale and scope in insurance (eg Geehan 1986, Grace and Timme 1992, Yuengert 1993, Cummins and Zi 1998, and Cummins, Tennyson, and Weiss 1999). Debt capital is also found to negatively affect unit profit in two models, (1) and (4), in Table 2.6. This finding is unexpected, as higher fixed capital is expected to reduce unit cost and thus improve unit profit. This puzzle can be explained as follows. Higher fixed capital leads to lower unit cost, enabling insurance firms to lower the price of their services. If the output price drops more than unit cost, then unit profit may also fall, given other factors constant.

By construction, the impact of the insurance wage on performance indicators depends on the current level of output. Evaluating the impact on unit cost at the median value of q_1 and q_2, wages have a positive effect on unit cost in both the short and long run, as expected (using the usual formula to calculate the long-run marginal effect in a distributed lag model). Wages are also estimated to have a positive effect on unit profit. This unexpected result can perhaps be explained by the fact that the models in this study do not control for the quality of labour. An increase in wage may encourage firms to use better-quality labour, improving labour productivity and thus profitability.

2.6 Impact Analysis

The previous section showed that barriers to trade in insurance services do not affect unit costs. However, these barriers are found to create rents for incumbent insurance firms. It was also found that these rent-creating effects can change over time. This section evaluates tax equivalents, which measure the percentage change in price mark-up caused by trade barriers in insurance. This impact measure is a required input for measuring the economy-wide effects of trade liberalization in the insurance sector. The formula is shown in (2.3).

$$tax\_equivalent = \frac{\frac{p_1}{v_1} - \frac{p_0}{v_0}}{\frac{p_0}{v_0}} \times 100\% = \frac{\frac{p_1 \times q_1}{v_1 \times q_1} - \frac{p_0 \times q_0}{v_0 \times q_0}}{\frac{p_0 \times q_0}{v_0 \times q_0}} \times 100\%$$

$$= \frac{\frac{TR_1}{TC_1} - \frac{TR_0}{TC_0}}{\frac{TR_0}{TC_0}} \times 100\% \tag{2.3}$$

where v_0, p_0, q_0, TC_0, TR_0 are the unit cost, unit price, output quantity, total cost, and total revenue when there are no trade barriers in insurance services; and v_1, p_1, q_1, TC_1, TR_1 are the unit cost, unit price, output quantity, total cost, and total revenue when there are trade barriers in insurance services.

The evaluation is done at $q_1=q_0$, and because the impact on cost is not significant, $TC_1=TC_0$.

As shown above, both cost and profit estimates are needed to calculate the value of total revenue required for the tax equivalent. Model (4) from Table 2.5 is used to estimate cost, as only this model satisfies the Sargan test. While both models (2) and (4) from Table 2.6 can be used estimate profit, the estimated coefficient on the trade restrictiveness index does not differ greatly between them and model (2) is selected for convenience. The evaluation is undertaken at the median values of prices, quantities and fixed capital for 2004, the most recent year for which data on trade barriers are available.[8]

Figures 2.7 and 2.8 show the tax equivalents for different country groups in 2004. As can be seen, European members of the OECD have the lowest tax equivalent. For this country group, the value of this impact measure ranges from 1.4 to 4.8 per cent. The tax equivalent is particularly low in long-standing EU members such as the Netherlands, the United Kingdom, Demark and France. However, this measure is higher in new EU members, Hungary and Czech Republic, as well as in Austria.

---

[8] At these values, the tax equivalent is calculated as 100*TRI_FA*0.1114958/0.471261.

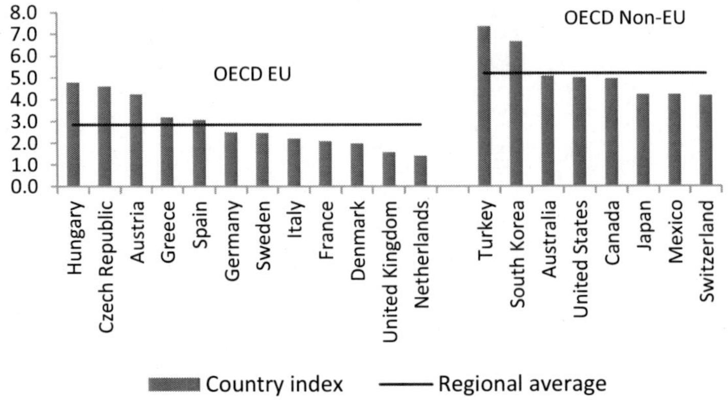

Figure 2.7. Tax Equivalents of Barriers to Trade in Insurance in OECD Countries, 2004 (per cent)

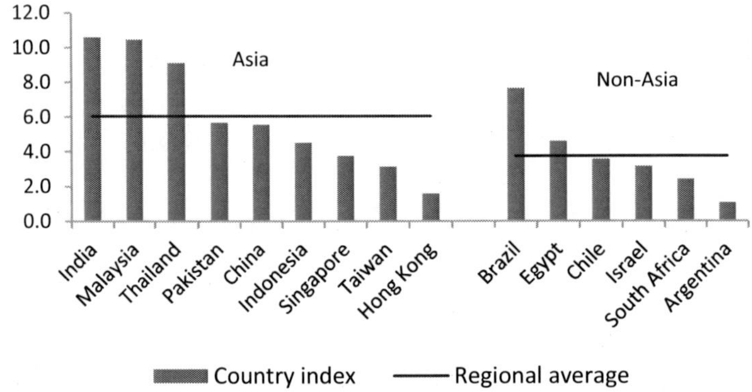

Figure 2.8. Tax Equivalents of Barriers to Trade in Insurance Outside of OECD, 2004 (per cent)

Asian countries are shown to have the highest tax equivalent. Their tax equivalent ranges from 1.6 to 10.6 per cent. The tax equivalent is especially high in India, Malaysia and Thailand while rather low in Hong Kong. Non-European members of the OECD have the second highest tax equivalent. However, there is less variation in their tax equivalent than in Asia. Although non-Asian countries have the second lowest tax equivalent on average, the variation in their tax equivalent is higher than in any other country group.

2.7 Conclusion

There are several important findings in this chapter with meaningful policy implications. First, trade barriers in insurance are found to create rents for incumbent insurers, but not to raise costs. Second, the impacts of trade barriers on firm profitability are found to vary by line of business, but do not depend on time or business size. Third, the tax equivalents tend to be higher in the developing than the developed countries. It is therefore expected that the trade liberalization in insurance in developing countries could have more profound effects on the whole economy than that in developed world.

In this study, prudential regulation is not controlled for when assessing the impact of barriers to trade in insurance. Although prudential regulation is aimed at preserving the stability of the whole system, it may also have influence on firms' performance. Thus, controlling for prudential regulation may be worth doing in further research.

Table 2.A.1. Trade Restrictiveness Index for Foreign Insurers (TRI_F), 1997 to 2004

	1997	*1998*	*1999*	*2000*	*2001*	*2002*	*2003*	*2004*
Australia	0.28	0.28	0.28	0.28	0.28	0.28	0.28	0.28
Austria	0.24	0.24	0.24	0.24	0.24	0.24	0.24	0.24
Argentina	0.21	0.14	0.14	0.14	0.14	0.14	0.14	0.14
Brazil	0.43	0.43	0.43	0.43	0.43	0.43	0.43	0.43
Canada	0.26	0.26	0.26	0.26	0.26	0.26	0.26	0.26
Chile	0.23	0.23	0.23	0.23	0.23	0.23	0.23	0.23
China	0.48	0.48	0.48	0.48	0.36	0.36	0.34	0.29
Czech	0.31	0.31	0.31	0.29	0.29	0.29	0.29	0.29
Denmark	0.15	0.15	0.15	0.15	0.15	0.15	0.15	0.15
Egypt	0.31	0.24	0.24	0.24	0.24	0.24	0.24	0.24
France	0.11	0.11	0.11	0.11	0.11	0.11	0.11	0.11
Germany	0.12	0.12	0.12	0.12	0.12	0.12	0.12	0.12
Greece	0.13	0.13	0.13	0.13	0.13	0.13	0.13	0.13
Hong Kong	0.12	0.12	0.12	0.12	0.12	0.12	0.12	0.12
Hungary	0.29	0.29	0.29	0.29	0.29	0.29	0.29	0.29
India	0.96	0.96	0.96	0.57	0.56	0.56	0.56	0.56
Indonesia	0.32	0.31	0.31	0.31	0.31	0.31	0.31	0.31
Israel	0.19	0.19	0.19	0.19	0.19	0.19	0.19	0.19
Italy	0.13	0.13	0.13	0.13	0.13	0.13	0.13	0.13
Japan	0.26	0.26	0.26	0.25	0.25	0.25	0.25	0.25
Korea	0.39	0.39	0.39	0.39	0.39	0.39	0.39	0.39
Malaysia	0.47	0.56	0.55	0.55	0.55	0.55	0.55	0.55
Mexico	0.34	0.32	0.32	0.29	0.29	0.29	0.29	0.29
Netherlands	0.06	0.06	0.06	0.06	0.06	0.06	0.06	0.06
Pakistan	0.39	0.39	0.39	0.39	0.39	0.39	0.39	0.36
Singapore	0.26	0.26	0.26	0.21	0.21	0.21	0.21	0.21
South Africa	0.16	0.16	0.16	0.16	0.16	0.16	0.16	0.16
Spain	0.14	0.14	0.14	0.14	0.14	0.14	0.14	0.14
Sweden	0.13	0.13	0.13	0.13	0.13	0.13	0.13	0.13
Switzerland	0.25	0.25	0.25	0.25	0.25	0.25	0.25	0.25
Taiwan	0.27	0.27	0.25	0.25	0.22	0.21	0.21	0.21
Thailand	0.40	0.40	0.40	0.42	0.42	0.42	0.42	0.42
Turkey	0.39	0.39	0.39	0.39	0.39	0.39	0.39	0.39
United Kingdom	0.07	0.07	0.07	0.07	0.07	0.07	0.07	0.07
United States	0.25	0.25	0.25	0.25	0.25	0.25	0.25	0.25

Source: Authors' calculations.

Table 2.A.2. Trade Restrictiveness Index for Domestic Insurers (TRI_D), 1997 to 2004

	1997	*1998*	*1999*	*2000*	*2001*	*2002*	*2003*	*2004*
Australia	0.12	0.12	0.12	0.12	0.12	0.12	0.12	0.12
Austria	0.06	0.06	0.06	0.06	0.06	0.06	0.06	0.06
Argentina	0.07	0.00	0.00	0.00	0.00	0.00	0.00	0.00
Brazil	0.06	0.06	0.06	0.06	0.06	0.06	0.06	0.06
Canada	0.14	0.14	0.14	0.14	0.14	0.14	0.14	0.14
Chile	0.06	0.06	0.06	0.06	0.06	0.06	0.06	0.06
China	0.13	0.13	0.13	0.13	0.11	0.10	0.10	0.10
Czech	0.12	0.12	0.12	0.10	0.10	0.10	0.10	0.10
Denmark	0.03	0.03	0.03	0.03	0.03	0.03	0.03	0.03
Egypt	0.12	0.12	0.12	0.12	0.12	0.12	0.12	0.12
France	0.03	0.03	0.03	0.03	0.03	0.03	0.03	0.03
Germany	0.03	0.03	0.03	0.03	0.03	0.03	0.03	0.03
Greece	0.03	0.03	0.03	0.03	0.03	0.03	0.03	0.03
Hong Kong	0.04	0.04	0.04	0.04	0.04	0.04	0.04	0.04
Hungary	0.11	0.11	0.11	0.11	0.11	0.11	0.11	0.11
India	0.27	0.27	0.27	0.23	0.21	0.21	0.21	0.21
Indonesia	0.02	0.02	0.02	0.02	0.02	0.02	0.02	0.02
Israel	0.09	0.09	0.09	0.09	0.09	0.09	0.09	0.09
Italy	0.03	0.03	0.03	0.03	0.03	0.03	0.03	0.03
Japan	0.14	0.14	0.14	0.13	0.13	0.13	0.13	0.13
Korea	0.18	0.18	0.18	0.18	0.18	0.18	0.18	0.18
Malaysia	0.25	0.25	0.24	0.24	0.24	0.24	0.24	0.24
Mexico	0.01	0.01	0.01	0.01	0.01	0.01	0.01	0.01
Netherlands	0.03	0.03	0.03	0.03	0.03	0.03	0.03	0.03
Pakistan	0.09	0.09	0.09	0.09	0.09	0.09	0.09	0.09
Singapore	0.11	0.11	0.11	0.09	0.09	0.09	0.09	0.09
South Africa	0.02	0.02	0.02	0.02	0.02	0.02	0.02	0.02
Spain	0.06	0.06	0.06	0.06	0.06	0.06	0.06	0.06
Sweden	0.04	0.04	0.04	0.04	0.04	0.04	0.04	0.04
Switzerland	0.08	0.08	0.08	0.08	0.08	0.08	0.08	0.08
Taiwan	0.11	0.11	0.11	0.11	0.11	0.10	0.10	0.10
Thailand	0.15	0.15	0.15	0.17	0.18	0.18	0.18	0.18
Turkey	0.17	0.17	0.17	0.17	0.17	0.17	0.17	0.17
United Kingdom	0.03	0.03	0.03	0.03	0.03	0.03	0.03	0.03
United States	0.13	0.13	0.13	0.13	0.13	0.13	0.13	0.13

Source: Authors' calculations.

Table 2.A.3. Trade Restrictiveness Index for Locally-Incorporated Foreign Insurers (TRI_FA), 1997 to 2004

	1997	*1998*	*1999*	*2000*	*2001*	*2002*	*2003*	*2004*
Australia	0.21	0.21	0.21	0.21	0.21	0.21	0.21	0.21
Austria	0.18	0.18	0.18	0.18	0.18	0.18	0.18	0.18
Argentina	0.11	0.04	0.04	0.04	0.04	0.04	0.04	0.04
Brazil	0.32	0.32	0.32	0.32	0.32	0.32	0.32	0.32
Canada	0.21	0.21	0.21	0.21	0.21	0.21	0.21	0.21
Chile	0.15	0.15	0.15	0.15	0.15	0.15	0.15	0.15
China	0.42	0.42	0.42	0.42	0.31	0.31	0.29	0.24
Czech	0.21	0.21	0.21	0.19	0.19	0.19	0.19	0.19
Denmark	0.08	0.08	0.08	0.08	0.08	0.08	0.08	0.08
Egypt	0.26	0.19	0.19	0.19	0.19	0.19	0.19	0.19
France	0.09	0.09	0.09	0.09	0.09	0.09	0.09	0.09
Germany	0.11	0.11	0.11	0.11	0.11	0.11	0.11	0.11
Greece	0.13	0.13	0.13	0.13	0.13	0.13	0.13	0.13
Hong Kong	0.07	0.07	0.07	0.07	0.07	0.07	0.07	0.07
Hungary	0.20	0.20	0.20	0.20	0.20	0.20	0.20	0.20
India	0.85	0.85	0.85	0.46	0.45	0.45	0.45	0.45
Indonesia	0.20	0.19	0.19	0.19	0.19	0.19	0.19	0.19
Israel	0.13	0.13	0.13	0.13	0.13	0.13	0.13	0.13
Italy	0.09	0.09	0.09	0.09	0.09	0.09	0.09	0.09
Japan	0.19	0.19	0.19	0.18	0.18	0.18	0.18	0.18
Korea	0.28	0.28	0.28	0.28	0.28	0.28	0.28	0.28
Malaysia	0.36	0.45	0.44	0.44	0.44	0.44	0.44	0.44
Mexico	0.23	0.21	0.21	0.18	0.18	0.18	0.18	0.18
Netherlands	0.06	0.06	0.06	0.06	0.06	0.06	0.06	0.06
Pakistan	0.27	0.27	0.27	0.27	0.27	0.27	0.27	0.24
Singapore	0.21	0.21	0.21	0.16	0.16	0.16	0.16	0.16
South Africa	0.10	0.10	0.10	0.10	0.10	0.10	0.10	0.10
Spain	0.13	0.13	0.13	0.13	0.13	0.13	0.13	0.13
Sweden	0.10	0.10	0.10	0.10	0.10	0.10	0.10	0.10
Switzerland	0.18	0.18	0.18	0.18	0.18	0.18	0.18	0.18
Taiwan	0.19	0.19	0.18	0.18	0.14	0.13	0.13	0.13
Thailand	0.36	0.36	0.36	0.38	0.38	0.38	0.38	0.38
Turkey	0.31	0.31	0.31	0.31	0.31	0.31	0.31	0.31
United Kingdom	0.07	0.07	0.07	0.07	0.07	0.07	0.07	0.07
United States	0.21	0.21	0.21	0.21	0.21	0.21	0.21	0.21

Source: Authors' calculations.

Chapter 3

Impact of Regulatory Barriers to Trade in Banking Services

Huong Dinh

3.1 Introduction

Services trade liberalization means removal or reduction of government rules and regulations that restrict trade in services. Although trade liberalization can lead to a reduction of some regulations in the banking sector, this process does not mean removal of all regulations — complete deregulation. A more liberalized banking sector still needs to be monitored and regulated by prudential regulation and supervision to ensure an efficient and healthy banking sector that contributes to the development and the stability of the economy. This is the main difference between trade liberalization and deregulation.

This chapter analyses the scope and first-round effects of trade liberalization in the banking sector. The study derives a panel data set of trade restrictiveness indexes for domestic banks and locally incorporated foreign banks in 36 countries over the period 1997–2006. This panel data set helps policy makers to see how restrictions on banking services are changing over time, facilitating international negotiations in banking services. It also provides an important input into a subsequent empirical evaluation of the sectoral impacts of barriers to trade in banking services on bank performance.

3.2 The Scope of Trade Liberalization in Banking

Apart from prudential measures, governments often impose other economic regulations that potentially affect all modes by which banking services are traded. Drawing on Llewellyn's (1986) study, these regulations can include:

- Geographical restrictions: banking services are geographically restricted. For example, before China's WTO accession, onshore foreign banks were confined to some big cities in China.
- Functional restrictions: each type of bank may be allowed to undertake only certain banking business, or to focus on a certain industry. For example, industrial banks may lend primarily to firms, while agricultural banks may make loans mainly to farmers. Savings and loan associations may be limited to mortgage loans. In many countries, banking, insurance, real estate, and securities business are strictly compartmentalized.
- Ownership restrictions: there may be restrictions on private ownership of banks, or on ownership of local banks by foreign banks. For example, a cap of 49 per cent on the foreign equity ownership of domestic banks is widely imposed in many developing countries.
- Pricing restrictions: banks may be subject to restrictions on the interest rates they can pay to depositors and can earn on loans. For example, instead of being able to set interest rates fully on their own, Vietnamese banks used to be subject to interest rate ceilings.
- Restrictions on business operation: regulations may be applied to banking activities. For example, onshore foreign banks may not be allowed to accept deposits in local currency from residents in the host country.
- Restrictions on entry and establishment: there may be restrictions on entry and establishment via licensing requirements. For example, market entry may be controlled by financial and managerial competence, or even an annual quota of licences. Establishment may also be constrained by the legal forms that foreign banks can take. For

example, foreign banks might not be allowed to set up branches in the host country, but may have to incorporate locally.

When restrictions on market entry of both foreign and domestic banks are lifted, more banks can enter the local market, creating pressure of competition between incumbent and new banks. Competitive pressure can force existing banks to be more innovative in order to sustain their existing market niches, while the new entrants must show their competitiveness in order to position themselves in the banking market. The higher competition can contribute to increased availability of financial services, improvement in the quality and productivity of financial services, and a reduction in their prices. The reduced prices and improved quality can, in turn, lower the costs of financial services for other sectors and households, especially those with relatively close linkages with the banking sector.

Trade liberalization can also stimulate the recapitalization and technology transfer from foreign to domestic banks. In developing countries, most commercial banks are undercapitalized and lack expertise in banking operations. The removal of foreign ownership limits in local banks, for example, can be seen as a quick way of building up the equity capital of local banks. This relaxation can also enable greater application of skills and technologies in banking operations through technology transfer from foreign to domestic banks.

This section canvasses non-prudential economic regulations that can be considered barriers to trade in commercial banking services, of the type outlined above. Adapting McGuire and Schuele (2000) and Dihel and Shepherd (2007), Table 3.1 presents a detailed template of such barriers to trade. It identifies 13 common restrictions affecting both domestic and foreign banks, though perhaps to differing degrees, and 11 restrictions affecting only foreign banks. Restrictions that affect only foreign banks have a name ending with F while those restricting both domestic and foreign banks have a name ending with B. Restrictions that affect cross-border supply, consumption abroad, commercial presence, and presence of natural persons are prefixed with M1_ to M4_, respectively.

Table 3.1. Template for Scoring Restrictions on Trade in Banking Services

Restriction name	*Weight*	*Score*	*Restriction category*
			Restrictions on cross border trade
M1_RAISINGF	0.06		**Cross-border fund raising — foreign**
		1	Foreign banks located abroad are not permitted to raise funds in the analysed country
		0.66	Foreign banks located abroad are permitted to raise funds in the analysed country with a specific amount
		0.33	Foreign banks located abroad are permitted to raise funds in the analysed country with a specific form of raising (for example only through deposits) or from a specific group of people (for example, only from non-residents in the analysed country)
		0	Foreign banks located abroad are permitted to raise funds in the analysed country without non-prudential restrictions
M1_LENDINGF	0.06		**Cross-border fund lending — foreign**
		1	Foreign banks located abroad are not permitted to lend in the analysed country
		0.66	Foreign banks located abroad are permitted to lend in the analysed country with a specific amount
		0.33	Foreign banks located abroad are permitted to lend in the analysed country with a specific form of lending (for example only through credit card service), or to a specific group of borrowers (for example, only to non-residents in the analysed country)
		0	Foreign banks located abroad are permitted to lend in the analysed country without non-prudential restrictions
M1_SETSERF	0.05		**Cross-border settlement services (eg collection, payment) — foreign**
		1	Foreign banks located abroad are not permitted to do cross-border settlement services in the analysed country
		0.5	Foreign banks located abroad are permitted, with some restrictions, to do cross-border settlement services in the analysed country
		0	Foreign banks located abroad are permitted to do cross-border settlement services in the analysed country, without non-prudential restrictions

Table 3.1. Continued.

M1_FOREXF	0.05		**Cross-border foreign exchange business — foreign**
		1	Foreign banks located abroad are not permitted to do foreign exchange business in the analysed country
		0.5	Foreign banks located abroad are permitted, with some restrictions, to do foreign exchange business in the analysed country
		0	Foreign banks located abroad are permitted to do a full range of foreign exchange business in the analysed country without non-prudential restrictions
			Restrictions on consumption abroad
M2_CONSF	0.04		**Consumption abroad — foreign**
		1	Residents are not authorized to purchase any financial services abroad
		0.66	Quotas related to the value of transaction, number of operations between foreign banks abroad and residents travelling abroad, or number of nationals travelling abroad (visas)
		0.33	Taxes or registration/authorization requirements on consumers travelling abroad
		0	No restrictions
			Restrictions on commercial presence
M3_DIF	0.03		**Foreign equity limit in a joint-venture bank — foreign**
			The score will be the difference between 1 and the maximum foreign equity participation permitted in a domestic bank, with or without approval. For example, ownership to a maximum of 49 per cent of a bank would receive a score of 0.51.
M3_FOCF	0.05		**Form of commercial presence — foreign**
		1	No commercial presence permitted
		0.75	Only representatives/agencies allowed
		0.5	Legal business forms except branches, in addition to representatives allowed
		0.25	Restricted branches (required to lend against local capital) and/or other legal business forms in addition to representatives allowed
		0	Unrestricted branches (able to lend against parent capital) and/or other legal business forms in addition to representatives allowed

Table 3.1. Continued.

M3_RECIPF	0.02		**Reciprocity requirement — foreign**
		1	Licensing is granted on a reciprocal basis
		0	No reciprocity requirement
M3_LICENSINGB	0.04		**Licensing — foreign/domestic**
			The score will be equal to (1–0.1*the number of approved applications + the percentage of declined applications over the total submitted applications)/2. The score would be 1 if there is a blanket ban. If the number of approved applications is greater than 10 then the score will be equal to the percentage of declined applications over the total submitted applications
M3_SCREENB	0.02		**Screening and approval — foreign/domestic**
		1	Investors must show economic benefits
		0.66	Approval unless contrary to national interest
		0.33	Notification (pre or post) requirements
		0	No screening or approval requirements
M3_DIB	0.04		**Ownership share of the government in the banking system — foreign/domestic**
			It is represented by the share of government assets in the banking system
M3_RAISINGB	0.04		**Fund raising — foreign/domestic**
		1	Banks are unable to raise funds from domestic sources
		0.75	Banks are permitted to raise funds from domestic sources with a specific amount
		0.5	Banks are permitted to raise funds from domestic sources with a specific form of raising (for example, only through deposits or local currency) or from a specific group of people (for example, only from non-residents in the analysed country)
		0.25	Banks are permitted to do a full range of raising forms, but all or some must be conducted in subsidiaries (eg branches are limited to wholesale banking services)
		0	Banks can raise funds from any domestic source with only prudential restrictions
			Lending — foreign/domestic
M3_LENDINGB	0.05	1	Banks are not allowed to lend to domestic borrowers
		0.75	Banks are restricted to a specified lending size or lending to government projects

Table 3.1. Continued.

		0.5	Banks are restricted in providing certain lending services such as leasing, credit card services, or consumer finance
		0.25	Banks are directed to lend to housing, small business, natural persons, and or businesses in certain regions
		0.1	Banks are permitted to do a full range of lending activities, but all or some must be conducted in subsidiaries
		0	Banks can lend to any domestic source with only prudential restrictions
M3_SETSERB	0.04		**Settlement services (eg collection, payment) — foreign/domestic**
		1	Banks are not permitted to do settlement services
		0.5	Banks are permitted to do settlement services with some restrictions
		0	Banks are permitted to do settlement services without non-prudential restrictions
M3_FOREXB	0.03		**Foreign exchange business — foreign/domestic**
		1	Banks are not permitted to do foreign exchange business
		0.66	Banks are limited to some foreign exchange business
		0.33	Banks are permitted to do a full range of activities, but all or some must be conducted in subsidiaries
		0	Banks are permitted to do a full range of activities without non-prudential restrictions
M3_OPERATIONB	0.03		**Expanding operations — street branches, offices and ATMs — foreign/domestic**
		1	One banking outlet with no new banking outlets is permitted
		0.66	Number of bank outlets is limited in number and location
		0.33	Expansion of bank outlets is subject to non-prudential regulatory approval
		0	No restrictions on banks expanding operations
M3_INTERESTB	0.03		**Price control — foreign/domestic**
		1	Interest rates are fully set by the government
		0.66	Some interest rates are set by the government

Table 3.1. Continued.

		0.33	Interest gap (between lending and borrowing) is restricted
		0	No restriction on interest
M3_SECUSERB	0.04		**Securities activities (eg underwriting, dealing, brokering) — foreign/domestic**
		1	Banks are not permitted to do securities business
		0.66	Banks are limited to some securities business
		0.33	Banks are permitted to do a full range of activities, but all or some must be conducted in separate subsidiaries
		0	Banks are permitted to do a full range of activities without non-prudential restrictions
M3_REESTATEB	0.04		**Real estate business (real estate investment, development, and management) — foreign/domestic**
		1	Banks are not permitted to do real estate business
		0.66	Banks are limited to some real estate business
		0.33	Banks are permitted to do a full range of activities, but all or some must be conducted in separate subsidiaries
		0	Banks are permitted to do a full range of activities without non-prudential restrictions
M3_INSURANCEB	0.04		**Insurance — foreign/domestic**
		1	Banks are not permitted to do insurance
		0.66	Banks are permitted to insure domestically but limited to some specific amount or some insurance services
		0.33	Banks are permitted to insure domestically, but all or some must be conducted in separate subsidiaries
		0	Banks are permitted to provide insurance domestically without non-prudential restrictions
M3_NONFINOWNB	0.04		**Ownership of non-financial firms — foreign/domestic**
		1	Banks are not allowed to own non-financial firms
		0.66	Banks are allowed to own less than 100 per cent of non-financial firms
		0.33	Banks may own 100 per cent of the equity in a non-financial firm but ownership is limited based on a bank's equity capital
		0	Banks are allowed to own non-financial firms without restrictions

Table 3.1. Continued.

			Restrictions on natural persons
M4_MOPPERF	0.04		**Movement of people — Permanent — foreign**
		1	No entry of executives, senior managers and/or specialists
		0.8	Executives, senior managers or specialists can stay up to 1 year
		0.6	Executives, senior managers or specialists can stay up to 2 years
		0.4	Executives, senior managers or specialists can stay up to 3 years
		0.2	Executives, senior managers or specialists can stay up to 4 years
		0	Executives, senior managers or specialists can stay more than 4 years
M4_MOPTEMF	0.05		**Movement of people — Temporary — foreign**
		1	No temporary entry of sales persons or business people
		0.75	Temporary entry of sales persons or business people up to 30 days
		0.5	Temporary entry of sales persons or business people up to 60 days
		0.25	Temporary entry of sales persons or business people up to 90 days
		0	Temporary entry of sales persons or business people over 120 days
M4_BODF	0.05		**Movement of people — Board of Directors — foreign**
		1	Board cannot comprise foreigners
		0	No restrictions on the composition of the board of directors
			The score is inversely related to the percentage of the Board which can comprise foreigners. For example, if 20% of a BOD can comprise foreigners this would receive a score of 0.80.

Source: Author.

The common restrictions consist of limitations on establishment (restrictions on licensing, screening and approval requirements, and government ownership), restrictions on traditional banking operations (limitations on lending or fund raising, restrictions on undertaking settlement services or foreign exchange business, restrictions on network expansion, and interest rate controls), and restrictions on non-traditional banking activities (restrictions on banks' ability to undertake insurance, securities, and real estate business and to own non-financial firms).

In addition to these common restrictions, foreign banks may also face limitations on the foreign ownership share in joint-venture banks, legal forms of establishment, reciprocity requirements, restrictions on the temporary and permanent movement of natural persons and the composition of the board of directors. They may also face limitations on delivering various services via cross-border supply and consumption abroad.

Given the experience during the 2008 global financial crisis, restrictions on banks' ability to undertake non-traditional activities (insurance, securities, and real estate business and to own non-financial firms) can be considered as 'grey area measures' because they may have a legitimate prudential role. As surveyed by Barth *et al.* (2004), many empirical studies found it beneficial for banks to undertake such non-traditional activities, in part because of the opportunity they provided for risk spreading. However, there are also a number of arguments against non-traditional banking activities. They may create conflicts of interest, which can induce the problem of moral hazard (John *et al.* 1994, Boyd *et al.* 1998). Diversification of activities may also generate a concentration of financial power, which may lead to 'too big to monitor', 'too big to discipline' and 'too big to fail' problems, and reduce competition and hence efficiency in the financial sector (Camdessus 1997). The global financial crisis reinforced these arguments (Blundell-Wignall *et al.* 2009, Stiglitz 2010). Whether restrictions on non-traditional activities should continue to be seen as barriers to trade is examined later in the chapter.

The template used in this chapter is more detailed than that used by Dihel and Shepherd (2007). While covering restrictions by modes of supply, as in Dihel and Shepherd (2007), the current template also differentiates barriers to trade via commercial presence affecting domestic and foreign banks. This treatment helps to identify pure discrimination against foreigners. In addition, the current template not only considers restrictions on lending and fund raising, which are captured in Dihel and Shepherd (2007), but also extends to other barriers including restrictions on settlement services, foreign exchange business, non-traditional banking services, and interest rate controls.

The current template is not as detailed as the questionnaire developed by Barth *et al.* (2001) in terms of coverage. Their questionnaire would be completed effectively only by government officials with detailed knowledge of the legislation affecting the banking sector in each country, whereas the current template relies on secondary sources. Since prudential regulation has been considered legitimate for the safety of the system, the current template also neglects information on prudential regulation. Although Barth *et al.* (2001) provide a rich dataset of bank regulation and supervision, they do not look at barriers to trade in any mode of supply other than commercial presence. Also, Barth *et al.* (2001) do not distinguish barriers against foreign banks from those against domestic banks.

The current template is used to collect information for 36 countries in the period from 1997 to 2006. Information for quantification comes from country schedules of the General Agreement on Trade in Services (GATS) under the World Trade Organization (WTO), the WTO Trade Policy Reviews, APEC Individual Action Plans, and the National Trade Estimates Reports on Foreign Trade Barriers from the Office of the United States Trade Representative, various editions of the International Financial Law Review, country-specific legal documents, and other publications. This study also uses the 1999, 2003, and 2007 databases on bank regulation and supervision by Barth *et al.* (2007), which are available on the World Bank website, and La Porta's (1999) database on government ownership.

The indexing technique

In order to present the degree of restrictiveness in a summary form convenient for cross-country and over-time comparisons, various summary restrictiveness indexes are constructed using the weights shown in the second column of Table 3.1. The weights were constructed by applying principal component analysis to all possible restrictions — the common restrictions as they affect both domestic and foreign banks, and the restrictions that affect only foreign banks.[1] These weights, or appropriate subsets of them, are then used to construct the following summary trade indexes. For foreign banks, a summary index (TRI_F) is constructed using the restrictions affecting all modes of foreign supply. For locally-incorporated foreign banks, a summary index (TRI_FA) is constructed using the restrictions affecting foreign banking services delivered via commercial presence and the presence of natural persons. Two other summary indexes, TRI_FB and TRI_D, are constructed for domestic and foreign banks, respectively, using the common restrictions as they affect each type of bank.

The two summary trade restrictiveness indexes, TRI_FB and TRI_D, are constructed to examine the extent to which potentially common restrictions are applied in a way that discriminates against foreign banks. But foreign banks also face more restrictions in total. The two summary indexes for domestic banks and locally-incorporated foreign banks, TRI_D and TRI_FA, capture both sorts of discrimination against locally-incorporated foreign banks. They are essential inputs for accurately differentiating the first-round impacts of trade barriers on bank performance by bank ownership. These first-round impacts will be explored in the next section. Summary indexes are presented in appendix Tables 3.A.1 to 3.A.3 at the end of this chapter.

Extent of restrictions

Figures 3.1 and 3.2 show the variation in restrictions affecting banking services of domestic banks and foreign banks across countries and different country groups over the decade. The difference between TRI_FA and TRI_D indicates the overall discrimination against locally-incorporated foreign banks, taking into account both the differential application of the common restrictions, and the additional restrictions that apply only to foreign banks. A comparison of TRI_D and TRI_FB shows whether the common restrictions are applied differently to

[1] The principal component technique gives a weight for each individual restriction category defined by its variance as a percentage of the total variance in the dataset explained by all selected principal components.

domestic and locally-incorporated foreign banks. The difference between TRI_F and TRI_D shows the overall discrimination against foreign banks, taking into account the restrictions on cross-border trade and consumption abroad.

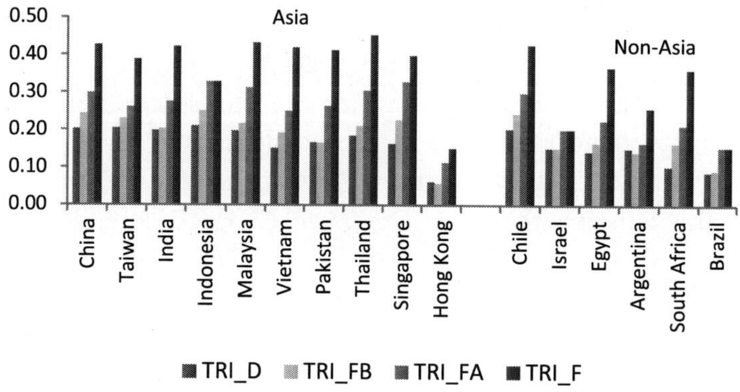

Figure 3.1. Trade Restrictiveness of Banking Services Outside of OECD, Average 1997 to 2006

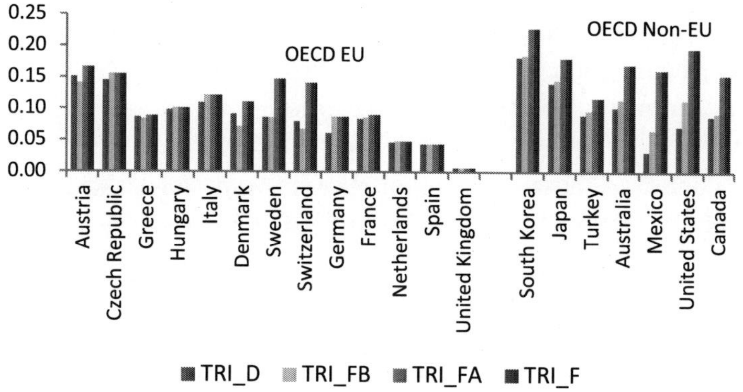

Figure 3.2. Trade Restrictiveness of Banking Services in OECD Countries, Average 1997 to 2006

For most countries, locally-incorporated foreign banks were discriminated against in the application of the common restrictions, as shown by the difference between TRI_FB and TRI_D. However, there are some exceptional cases where domestic banks were discriminated against — Greece, Taiwan, the Czech Republic, South Korea, and Turkey. This situation arises because in these countries, domestic banks found it more difficult to obtain licences than locally-incorporated foreign banks. In all countries, locally-incorporated foreign banks were subject to a higher level of overall restriction than domestic banks.

In the 36 countries studied, Asian countries dominated the top-ten countries with the highest degree of restrictiveness on both domestic banks and locally-incorporated foreign banks. OECD countries in the EU had the lowest restrictiveness compared to other groups. In particular, nine countries in this region belonged to the top-ten least restrictive countries.

Asian countries such as China, India, Malaysia and Viet Nam used a number of discriminatory restrictions, as shown by the sizable difference between TRI_FA and TRI_D. Foreign banks were discriminated against in terms of both entry and operation. For example, in Viet Nam, Thailand, Pakistan, and Malaysia, foreign ownership was capped at 49 per cent in a joint-venture bank. In Viet Nam and China, foreign banks were not allowed to take local currency deposits from residents. For both domestic banks and locally-incorporated foreign banks, Viet Nam applied administrative measures to control interest rates and foreign exchange business.

By contrast, most EU countries did not apply discriminatory restrictions, as shown by the lack of difference between TRI_FA, TRI_F, and TRI_D. The EU applies the single passport system which is a single licence allowing foreign banks to set up their branches and to offer services through the Union. However, if the principle of reciprocity is observed by the country in which the head office of the foreign bank branch is based, the EU may agree to apply identical provisions to that foreign bank branch (Directive 2000/12/EC 2000). The EU also imposed a very low degree of restrictiveness in every other restriction category.

Extend of reform over time

Figures 3.3 and 3.4 show the cross-country variation in changes (between 1997 and 2006) in the trade restrictiveness indexes of domestic and foreign banks. In all country groups, foreign banks were subject to a greater relaxation of restrictions on banking services than domestic banks. For example, 85 per cent of the OECD countries eased restrictions on foreign banks, whereas only 50 per cent of these countries eased restrictions on domestic banks. In Asian countries, these figures were 67 per cent for foreign banks and 44 per cent for domestic banks.

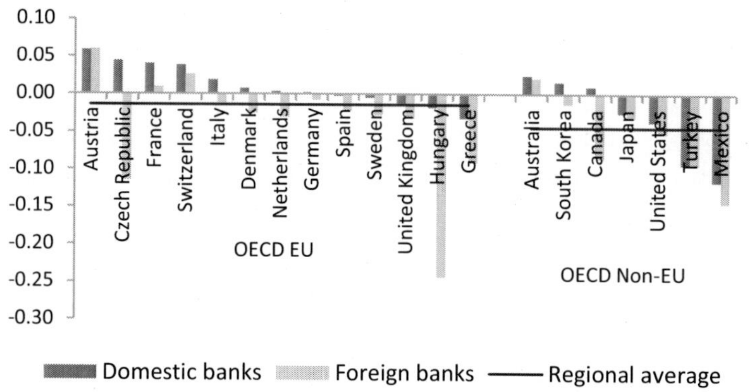

Figure 3.3. Change in Degree of Restrictiveness in OECD Countries, 1997 to 2006

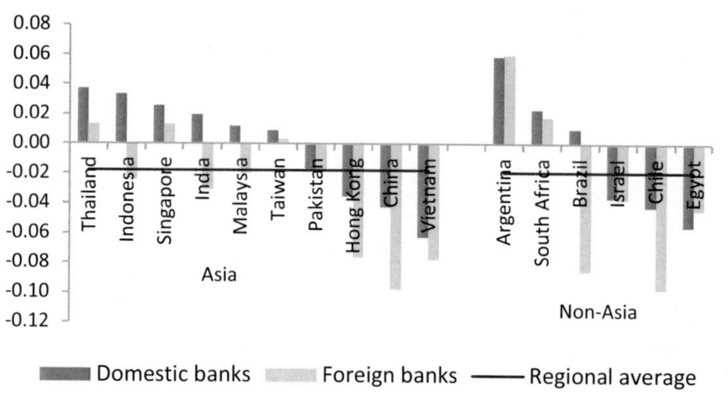

Figure 3.4. Change in Degree of Restrictiveness Outside of OECD, 1997 to 2006

There were 16 countries (44 per cent of the total sample) that reduced restrictions on both domestic and foreign banks. These countries included ten countries from the OECD, three from Asia, and three from other regions. Interestingly, however, nine countries tightened their restrictions on both domestic and foreign banks. These were Argentina, Switzerland, Austria, France, Australia, South Africa, Thailand, Taiwan, and Singapore. There were 11 countries that tightened restrictions on domestic banks but eased restrictions on foreign banks — seven OECD countries, three Asian countries, and one Latin America country. Figures 3.5 to 3.8 show the prevalence of both the easing and tightening of restrictions affecting domestic and foreign banks.

Figures 3.5 and 3.6 show the prevalence across the countries in the sample of changes in individual restrictions affecting domestic banks. Among the 13 possible restrictions affecting domestic banks, the restriction most frequently eased was the one that preserved government ownership of the banking sector. More than two thirds of the sample countries reduced the participation of the government in the banking system, while only Chile increased government ownership. In many countries, the reduction of the government in the banking sector was a result of the privatization process in this sector.

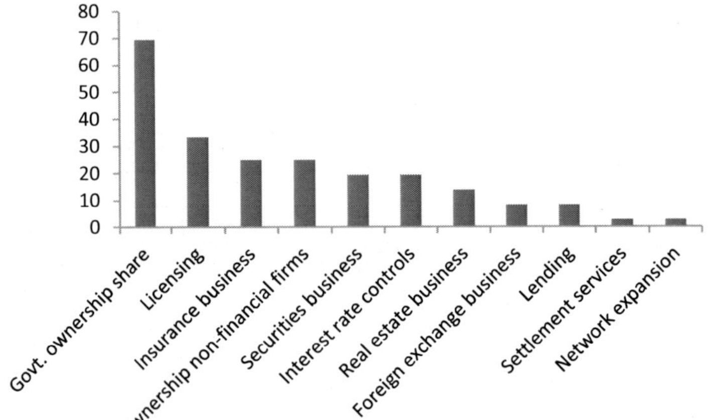

Figure 3.5. Share of Countries Easing Restrictions on Domestic Banks, 1997 to 2006 (percentage of countries)

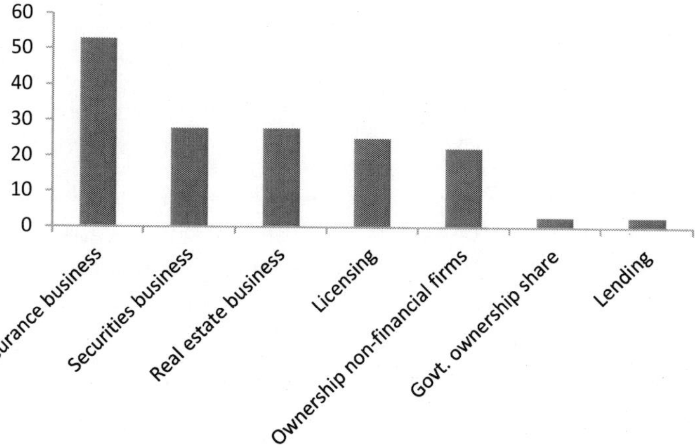

Figure 3.6. Share of Countries Tightening Restrictions on Domestic Banks, 1997 to 2006 (percentage of countries)

The second most frequently loosened restriction on domestic banks was that on licensing, which was reduced in one third of the sample countries. However, this restriction was also tightened in a further quarter of the sample countries.

Restrictions on domestic banks' ability to undertake non-traditional activities were among the top-five most frequently tightened restrictions. The share of countries tightening these restrictions was significantly greater than the share of countries easing them, suggesting that non-traditional banking activities have tended to be curtailed over time.

Viet Nam and Mexico were the two countries that eased the highest number of restrictions on domestic banks. Viet Nam and Taiwan were the two countries that loosened restrictions on domestic banks undertaking settlement services, and setting up additional branches. In general, nearly all countries reduced the degree of restrictiveness of at least three restrictions on domestic banks.

Figures 3.7 and 3.8 show the prevalence of changes in restrictions on foreign banks. A third of the sample countries eased restrictions on licensing of foreign banks, provision of cross-border banking services, and foreign ownership of local banks. By contrast, only one fifth of countries tightened restrictions on the licensing of foreign banks, less than a tenth tightened the provision of cross-border banking services and no country tightened the foreign equity ownership cap. These facts suggest that foreign banks were increasingly encouraged to enter the host market through all modes of supply, and to provide a full range of traditional banking services.

As with domestic banks, foreign banks were increasingly discouraged from undertaking non-traditional banking activities. Specifically, just over half of the sample countries tightened restrictions on banks' ability to undertake insurance — banks were either not allowed to engage in insurance business, or were required to set up separate subsidiaries to provide insurance. This occurred in Australia, Austria, Argentina, Chile, the Czech Republic, Denmark, France, Germany, Hungary, Indonesia, Italy, South Korea, Malaysia, Singapore, South Africa, Spain, Sweden, Switzerland, and Thailand. Meanwhile, only a quarter of the sample countries loosened this type of restriction. Thus, non-traditional banking

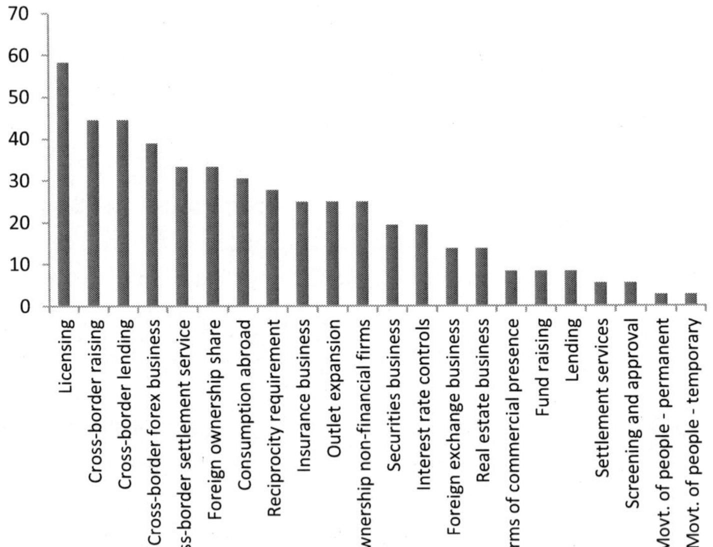

Figure 3.7. Share of Countries Easing Restrictions on Foreign Banks, 1997 to 2006 (percentage of countries)

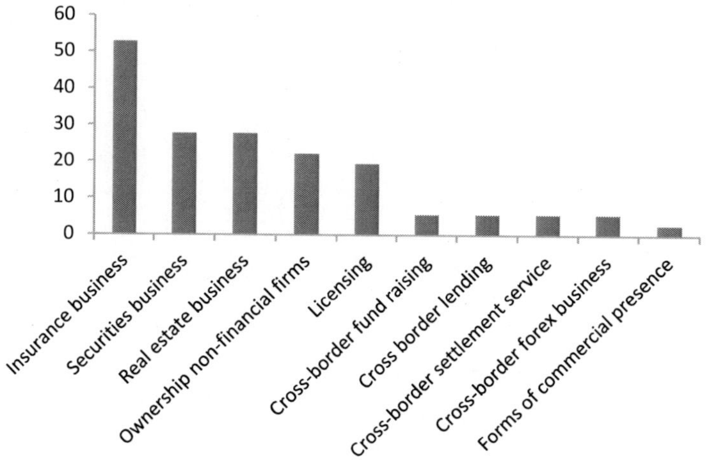

Figure 3.8. Share of Countries Tightening Restrictions on Foreign Banks, 1997 to 2006 (percentage of countries)

activities are becoming increasingly discouraged, regardless of ownership. This supports the idea that restrictions on non-traditional banking activities are being recognized as serving a prudential purpose, and should not be treated as barriers to trade in banking services. This argument is tested in the next section.

3.3 The Sectoral Effects of Trade Liberalization in Banking

This section measures the first-round impacts of restrictions on trade in banking services, using the trade restrictiveness indexes calculated in the previous section. This analysis uses both cost and profit as measures of economic performance in banking, in order to distinguish whether trade barriers have raised prices by raising costs or profits. This issue is under-researched in the current literature.[2] The analysis involves estimating cost and profit functions that are structural and corrected for quantities,

[2] Studies by Saunders and Schumacher (2000), Kalirajan *et al.* (2000), Barth *et al.* (2004), Dihel and Shepherd (2007) and Pasiouras *et al.* (2009) look at the impact of trade barriers on bank net interest margins, which represent economic rents. There are only a few studies (eg Barth *et al.* 2004, Pasiouras *et al.* 2009) that have examined the impacts of regulatory restrictions in costs.

allowing identification of the extent to which trade barriers have led to vertical shifts in the supply curve. This is something that has not been measured in most previous studies using reduced functional forms.

This section makes use of panel accounting data on the economic performance of 7,314 commercial banks in 28 countries over the period 1997 to 2006 from Bankscope (produced by Fitch IBCA) to construct measures of banking inputs and outputs.[3] This panel dataset makes it possible to control for country- and time-specific effects, which may improve the accuracy of estimation of the sectoral impacts of trade barriers in banking services.

While following a similar approach to that in Chapter 2 for insurance, this chapter differs in several important aspects. First, the analysis controls for prudential regulation. Second, the Bankscope data are available on an unconsolidated basis, meaning that the domestic banking services of a locally-established bank can be separated from the offshore banking services of its overseas branches or subsidiaries. This makes it possible to estimate the effects of services trade barriers on domestically-owned and foreign-invested banks separately.

As in Chapter 2, the Symmetric McFadden functional form is chosen to meet three criteria: flexibility, parsimony, and regularity conditions (Lawrence 1988, Diewert and Wales 1995). It is relevant for multiple outputs, especially when some output is zero-quantity, and allows negative profit data to be retained without rescaling.

Normally, the profit function is a function of input prices and output prices. However, in order to trace the vertical shifts in the supply curve, it is necessary to keep output quantities constant. As such, in this chapter, a constrained profit function is used (see, for example, Varian 1992, Berger *et al.* 1997). This alternative profit function is a function of input prices and output quantities. In this case, output quantities are taken as fixed but output prices are varied, suggesting that the alternative profit function is the result of short-run profit maximization.

Apart from input prices (w) and output quantities (q), total fixed capital (tk) is also included in the model to control for differences in

---

[3] During the period 1997–2006, some banks were merged or closed and new banks were established, so the panel is unbalanced.

bank size. The trade restrictiveness indexes (*TRI*) are entered into the model to evaluate the impacts of trade barriers in banking services on bank performance. The prudential measures, the capital adequacy ratio (*CAP*) and liquidity ratio (*LIQ*), are also included in the estimations to distinguish the impacts of prudential regulation from those of trade barriers on bank performance. Time dummy variables (*YEAR*) are included to control for unobservable effects that vary over time but stay unchanged across countries and banks. Country dummy variables (*D*) are used to capture the effect of country-specific characteristics such as the political system, geography, and history. These country-specific characteristics are considered to be time- and firm-invariant but country-variant. The models also account for additional unobservable differences in the cost/profit structure of domestic and foreign banks by including a foreign bank dummy variable (*FOR*). The models take into account the effects of bank-specific factors (u), including managerial skills and reputation, which do not change over time and across countries, but vary across banks. The factors that vary across banks, countries and time are captured in the idiosyncratic error terms (ε).

Bankscope is a rich dataset of commercial banks' economic performance. It divides total assets into liquid assets, risk assets, and fixed assets. It also allows total assets to be broken down into loans and investment assets. In addition, the data divide liabilities into different sources: deposits and other borrowed funds such as certificates of deposit, commercial paper, debt securities, and securities loaned. In the income statements, Bankscope gives the total revenue as the sum of interest income, commission income, fee income, trading income, and other operating income. It gives total expenses as the sum of interest expenses, commission expenses, fee expenses, trading expenses, personnel expenses, and other operating expenses.

Measures of bank characteristics

Following the intermediation approach where banks are considered as intermediaries between savers and investors (Sealey and Lindley 1977), this study defines three inputs (two variable inputs and one fixed input) and two outputs. The three inputs are total deposits and borrowed funds, labour, and fixed capital, where fixed capital is the sum of equity capital and fixed assets. The outputs consist of total loans and investments. Given the high correlation between the two output quantities,[4] an aggregate output quantity is used in the regressions.

The price of total deposits and borrowed funds is measured by dividing the sum of interest, commission, fee, and trading expenses by the sum of deposits and borrowed funds. The price of labour is obtained by dividing personnel expenses by the number of employees (also from Bankscope). The price of investment is defined as the ratio of the sum of commission income, fee income, and trading income to the value of investments. The price of loans is measured by dividing interest income by the value of loans.

In general, firms use depreciation as the cost of fixed capital. However, depreciation neither reflects the opportunity cost of capital nor captures the economic depreciation (or appreciation) in the market value of the firms' assets. Consequently, it does not reveal the true cost of fixed capital (Kalirajan *et al.* 2000). In this study, the opportunity cost is the expected return on an alternative investment other than fixed capital, measured by the risk-free bond rate. The true cost of capital is thus measured by this opportunity cost plus the change in the market value of bank assets. The proxy variables for the risk-free bond rate and the change in market value of bank assets are, respectively, the government bond rate from the International Financial Statistics (IFS) of the International Monetary Fund, and the relative year-on-year change in the market value of equity capital from Bankscope.

In this study, the definition of total cost uses economic rather than accounting concepts. Total cost is accordingly defined as the interest expenses paid on deposits and borrowed funds, plus the economic costs of other purchased inputs — labour and fixed capital. The economic cost of fixed capital is measured using the above imputed price of capital, namely, the sum of the risk-free bond rate and the relative year-on-year change in equity capital. Total revenue is defined as the sum of interest

[4] The correlation coefficient between loans and investments across banks in all countries and over time is 0.91.

income, commission income, fee income, and trading income. Total profit is the gap between total revenue and the imputed total cost.

In order to correct for the problem of heteroscedasticity, which is common in cross-section and time-series data, the chapter takes unit cost and unit profit as the dependent variables. These corresponding unit variables are the ratio of total cost and total profit to total fixed capital.[5]

All prices and quantities of inputs and outputs are expressed in 1997 USD to remove the influence of inflation as well as to facilitate cross-country comparison. The annual producer and consumer price indexes from the IFS are used to deflate nominal items to real ones.[6] All data are converted into USD using the exchange rate from the IFS, where the 1997 exchange rate is used for real-term data and the current exchange rate is used for nominal-term data.

In order to map the impact of trade barriers by bank ownership, a foreign bank dummy variable is constructed. In this study, a bank is classified as a foreign bank if, in aggregate, foreigners own at least 51 per cent of its total equity. The ownership data come from Bankscope. Because US banks outnumber non-US banks, a US dummy variable is constructed and interacted with price and quantity variables.

For prudential measures, this chapter uses bank-specific total capital and liquidity ratios. The total capital ratio is defined by Bankscope as the ratio of Tier 1 and Tier 2 capital to total risk-weighted assets. The liquidity ratio is defined as the ratio of liquid assets to total assets. These bank-specific prudential ratios reflect the actual responsiveness of banks to the prudential regulation that directly affects bank operation. These measures also provide enough sample variation for conducting econometric exercises, thus improving the accuracy of estimation.

The present chapter focuses on the impacts of trade barriers on domestic and locally-incorporated foreign banks. For domestic banks, restrictions on domestic banking activities are used. For locally-incorporated foreign banks, the restrictions that directly affect them are

---

[5] In the short run, it is reasonably assumed that total fixed capital is exogenous while total revenue is not, so total fixed capital is chosen as a denominator.

[6] When the producer price index is not available, the consumer price index is used to convert nominal prices and values to real ones.

included, namely, restrictions on commercial presence and the presence of natural persons.

In order to test whether restrictions on banks' ability to undertake non-traditional activities should be treated as barriers to trade in banking services, these restrictions are separated from restrictions on establishment and operation. Two summary sub-indices of trade restrictiveness are thus constructed separately for domestic and foreign banks: a trade restrictiveness index on the establishment and on-going operation of traditional banking services and network expansion *(TRI_EO);* and a trade restrictiveness index on non-traditional banking activities *(TRI_SC).* Restrictions on establishment and operation include restrictions that may restrict new entry, indirectly creating more market power for incumbent banks. So it is expected that this type of restriction will allow the price-cost margins of incumbent banks to be inflated. Restrictions on establishment and operation also include restrictions that may restrict the banking operations of incumbent banks, directly affecting their cost structures. So it is expected that this type of restriction will also escalate real resource costs for incumbent banks. Restrictions on non-traditional banking activities have tended to be tightened over time, tentatively suggesting that these restrictions may have a legitimate prudential function.

Table 3.2 presents a summary of variable definitions and data sources, while Tables 3.3 and 3.4 report the summary statistics of important variables.

Estimation technique

Because of the multicollinearity between the interaction terms, the chapter applies the data-centering method, which de-means the data. First order serial correlation is detected in the regression, which can bias the standard errors and cause the results to be less efficient. The Hausman tests confirm that latent fixed effects influence bank performance, so that fixed-effects models are needed.

Table 3.2. Variable Definitions

Variable name	*Description*
Dependent variables	
Unit_cost	Ratio of total economic cost (as the sum of interest expenses, wages, and the imputed economic cost of capital) to total fixed capital
Unit_profit	Ratio of total profit (the gap between total revenue, as the sum of interest income, commission income, fee income, and trading income, and total economic cost) to total fixed capital
Explanatory variables	
Bank characteristics	
q1	Total loans (billions of USD)
q2	Total investments (billions of USD)
q	The total output quantities (billions of USD), where q = q1 + q2
p1	Borrowing rate measured by dividing the sum of interest, commission, fee, and trading expenses by the sum of deposits and borrowed funds
p2	Wage measured by dividing personnel expenses by the number of employees
tk	Total fixed capital as the sum of total physical fixed assets and equity capital (billions of USD)
for	Foreign bank dummy variable (1 if a bank has at least 51% foreign ownership, 0 otherwise)
US	US dummy variable (1 if a bank is located in the US, 0 otherwise)
Prudential measures	
cap	Total capital ratio (%)
liq	Liquidity ratio as measured by dividing total liquid assets by total assets (%)
Trade restrictiveness in banking services	
TRI_EO	Trade restrictiveness index covering bank establishment and operation
TRI_SC	Trade restrictiveness index covering non-traditional banking operation
Interaction terms	
p1p2	The interaction term between squared input price gap and output quantities, where $p1p2 = [(p1 - p2)^2 q]/(\theta 1 p1 + \theta 2 p2)$ and θ1, θ2 are the corresponding mean values of q1, q2
US_p1p2_1	Interaction term between p1p2 and US, where US_p1p2_1 = p1p2US
US_p1_1	Interaction term between p1 and US, where US_p1_1 = p1US
US_p2_1	Interaction term between p2 and US, where US_p2_1 = p2US
p1out	Interaction term between p1 and total output quantity, where p1out = p1q
US_p1out_1	Interaction term between p1out and US, where US_p1out_1 = p1qUS
p2out	Interaction term between p1 and total output quantity, where p2out = p2q
US_p2out_1	Interaction term between p1out and US, where US_p2out_1 = p2qUS
p1out2	Interaction term between p1 and square of total output quantity, where p1out2 = $p1q^2$
US_p1outa1	Interaction term between p1out2 and US, where US_p1outa1 = $p1q^2US$
p2out2	Interaction term between p2 and square of total output quantity, where p2out2 = $p2q^2$
US_p2outa1	Interaction term between p2out2 and US, where US_p2outa1 = $p2q^2US$

Source: Author.

Table 3.3. Data Summary, Average 1997 to 2006

Country	*Number of banks*	*Number of observations*	*Unit_cost*	*Unit_profit*	*Borrowing rate*	*Wage (USD '000)*
Argentina	9	10	0.66	0.20	5.24	28.47
Australia	2	2	1.24	0.30	5.55	185.27
Austria	17	65	0.70	0.15	4.00	77.58
Brazil	13	20	1.61	0.23	15.73	49.20
Chile	1	2	0.83	0.02	8.32	51.55
China	8	18	0.58	0.31	1.86	23.85
Czech Republic	13	27	0.51	0.12	3.20	20.68
Denmark	10	31	0.55	0.12	2.95	73.83
France	131	690	0.94	0.25	4.43	77.09
Germany	70	320	1.01	0.22	3.90	89.79
Greece	8	14	0.80	0.09	4.20	46.32
Hungary	3	6	1.07	0.18	7.08	19.45
India	50	152	1.27	0.14	7.34	5.34
Indonesia	10	15	0.52	0.10	6.64	21.86
Israel	3	5	0.82	0.07	5.63	76.60
Italy	126	252	0.50	0.17	3.17	65.71
Japan	113	322	0.32	0.08	1.09	79.28
Korea	3	3	0.87	0.17	6.67	41.79
Netherlands	3	6	0.71	0.05	6.79	87.74
Singapore	4	6	0.59	0.19	2.71	48.34
South Africa	2	6	0.48	0.08	10.14	91.25
Spain	5	5	0.33	0.13	2.20	52.31
Sweden	4	21	0.96	0.22	3.98	88.18
Switzerland	92	457	0.37	0.15	2.58	96.85
Taiwan	27	43	0.35	0.11	1.83	43.32
Thailand	13	24	0.43	0.08	3.47	17.97
United States	6,572	34,668	0.41	0.15	2.66	43.43
Viet Nam	2	5	0.39	0.03	3.71	6.20
Whole sample						
Total	7,314	37,195				
Mean			0.43	0.16	2.73	45.50
Std. deviation			0.21	0.10	1.31	17.22
Min			0.01	0.00	1.00	1.10
Max			2.77	1.00	37.85	292.88

Table 3.3. Continued

Country	*Loans (USD '000)*	*Investment (USD '000)*	*Total fixed capital (USD '000)*	*Total capital ratio (per cent)*	*Liquidity ratio (per cent)*
Argentina	2,343,862	826,369	575,617	11.74	45.37
Australia	4,348,622	914,213	391,555	5.54	10.20
Austria	3,469,522	1,369,319	285,418	9.82	28.70
Brazil	5,609,674	5,771,867	1,978,730	16.03	60.36
Chile	1,367,384	220,095	194,357	12.11	15.11
China	55,400,000	32,700,000	7,217,563	10.02	24.97
Czech Republic	1,369,469	537,994	308,675	14.26	50.57
Denmark	18,700,000	12,600,000	2,719,901	12.32	23.34
France	8,465,306	6,034,228	946,870	8.47	37.17
Germany	26,700,000	15,700,000	2,133,287	5.34	33.29
Greece	11,400,000	4,096,181	1,511,772	8.82	35.32
Hungary	1,230,078	507,391	235,311	10.49	28.54
India	1,870,923	1,575,787	307,152	13.04	54.56
Indonesia	586,779	82,747	78,401	38.50	59.75
Israel	10,000,000	1,535,998	1,216,617	13.34	29.11
Italy	6,493,582	2,071,596	995,356	16.55	41.38
Japan	45,200,000	24,900,000	4,023,583	10.34	20.63
Korea	3,924,937	2,360,932	696,534	10.47	20.40
Netherlands	555,619	415,432	180,119	21.67	54.42
Singapore	13,100,000	6,656,188	3,350,295	14.31	55.14
South Africa	225,602	178,769	104,225	26.54	42.55
Spain	4,012,225	66,470	426,858	9.47	5.40
Sweden	27,200,000	32,600,000	2,702,433	22.26	65.10
Switzerland	3,090,504	2,313,997	389,719	10.32	24.33
Taiwan	16,000,000	4,896,894	2,377,485	12.32	17.55
Thailand	9,987,830	1,946,742	1,658,593	13.74	21.93
United States	651,958	309,439	112,069	15.35	8.46
Viet Nam	215,379	13,353	37,587	11.38	33.32
Whole sample					
Total					
Mean	1,577,816	860,313	202,577	15.02	10.16
Std. deviation	14,400,000	10,600,000	1,604,057	6.31	11.15
Min	392.19	0.81	604.10	0.61	0.04
Max	698,000,000	476,000,000	81,900,000	99.94	431.29

Note: For each country, the value is the mean value across banks over the period 1997 to 2006.

Source: See text.

Table 3.4. Trade Restrictiveness Indexes of Locally-Incorporated Banks, Average 1997 to 2006

Country	*Domestic banks*		*Foreign banks*	
	TRI_EO	*TRI_SC*	*TRI_EO*	*TRI_SC*
Argentina	0.05	0.07	0.07	0.07
Australia	0.02	0.07	0.09	0.07
Austria	0.01	0.03	0.05	0.03
Brazil	0.05	0.07	0.19	0.07
Chile	0.04	0.11	0.14	0.11
China	0.08	0.14	0.20	0.14
Czech Republic	0.04	0.08	0.05	0.08
Denmark	0.03	0.06	0.06	0.06
France	0.02	0.04	0.03	0.04
Germany	0.03	0.03	0.06	0.03
Greece	0.04	0.06	0.06	0.06
Hungary	0.02	0.08	0.08	0.08
India	0.11	0.09	0.20	0.09
Indonesia	0.06	0.14	0.19	0.14
Israel	0.06	0.11	0.11	0.11
Italy	0.01	0.09	0.03	0.09
Japan	0.05	0.10	0.09	0.10
Korea	0.10	0.08	0.15	0.08
Netherlands	0.02	0.02	0.03	0.02
Singapore	0.08	0.07	0.25	0.07
South Africa	0.03	0.06	0.14	0.06
Spain	0.01	0.03	0.01	0.03
Sweden	0.01	0.07	0.08	0.07
Switzerland	0.03	0.03	0.10	0.03
Taiwan	0.09	0.11	0.15	0.11
Thailand	0.07	0.09	0.21	0.09
United Kingdom	0.01	0.01	0.01	0.01
United States	0.01	0.08	0.14	0.08
Viet Nam	0.13	0.05	0.23	0.05
Whole sample				
Mean	0.04	0.07	0.11	0.07
Std. deviation	0.03	0.03	0.07	0.03
Min	0.00	0.01	0.01	0.01
Max	0.16	0.16	0.28	0.16

Note: United Kingdom was not included in the econometric estimation because data on some explanatory variables was incomplete. It is included in the subsequent impact analysis, so its trade restrictiveness index values are presented in this table.
Source: See text.

In order to correct for these problems, this chapter applies fixed-effects models that allow for bank-specific fixed effects and incorporate Baltagi and Wu's (1999) method to correct for the first-order serial correlation. Ideally, the unit cost and unit profit functions should also be estimated using seemingly unrelated regression techniques, to take account of common shocks affecting both error terms. However, it has not been possible to do this while also allowing for latent bank-specific fixed effects and correcting for serial correlation. The regression summary of the estimated unit cost and unit profit functions is presented in Table 3.5.

Econometric results

The concavity condition requires that the second derivative of the unit cost function with respect to the wage variable be negative. As shown in Table 3.5, the regression results from the estimated cost function show that the coefficients of the interaction terms, *p1p2* and *US_p1p2,* are of an unexpected sign and statistically significant at the 0.01 per cent level of significance. The curvature condition also requires the second derivative of the profit function with respect to the wage variable be positive. In the estimated profit function, the coefficient *p1p2* has an unexpected sign but the coefficient of *US_p1p2* is of the right sign and statistically significant at the 1 per cent level of significance. These results suggest non-US banks are neither cost-minimizers nor profit-maximizers but US banks are profit-maximizers.

Bikker and Bos (2008) give several reasons why banks may not minimize their costs and maximize their profits. First, highly risk-averse banks are willing to forgo the investments with big returns but high risk opportunities in exchange for those with stable but moderate income. Given that studies on modelling banks' risk-return trade-off are still in their infancy and there is a lack of data on risk, this study does not take risk into account. Second, because of the information asymmetry between the principal and agent, managers may be induced to make discretionary decisions that are contrary to shareholder interests, resulting in departures from cost minimization and profit maximization.

Table 3.5. Regression Summary for Banking Services

Variable	*Unit cost*		*Unit profit*	
	Coefficient	*Robust standard error*	*Coefficient*	*Robust standard error*
p1p2	1.69	0.18***	–0.07	0.14
US_p1p2_1	0.98	0.16***	0.27	0.12**
p1	12.31	0.14***	–1.86	0.12***
US_p1_1	–0.78	0.13***	–1.31	0.11***
p2	3.91	0.13***	0.97	0.12***
US_p2_1	1.61	0.14***	0.39	0.12
p1out	0.76	0.13***	0.17	0.11
US_p1out_1	–0.30	0.06***	–0.01	0.05
p2out	1.58	0.34***	–0.62	0.26**
US_p2out_1	–0.31	0.16***	0.36	0.12***
p1out2	–0.48	0.17***	0.42	0.14***
US_p1outa1	–0.04	0.05	–0.12	0.04***
p2out2	0.18	0.09***	0.01	0.07
US_p2outa1	0.81	0.08***	0.09	0.06
cap	–0.71	0.02***	0.03	0.02*
liq	0.02	0.01*	–0.04	0.01***
tk	–21.21	1.49*	–2.81	1.13***
TRI_EO	0.007	0.003***	0.008	0.002***
TRI_SC	–0.002	0.001***	0.007	0.001***
year98	24.42	0.75*	10.02	0.82***
Year99	37.81	1.11***	12.63	1.09***
Year00	46.04	1.21***	12.70	1.10***
Year01	48.33	1.24***	9.06	1.08***
Year02	49.89	1.31***	6.40	1.10***
Year03	49.99	1.36***	3.45	1.12***
Year04	49.95	1.39***	1.58	1.12***
Year05	49.29	1.40***	1.07	1.12
Year06	48.58	1.41***	–0.40	1.11
Constant	3.07	0.46***	5.23	0.54
Within R_sq.	0.55		0.18	
No. of observations	29881		29881	
No. of groups	6598		6598	

Notes: *** p<0.01, ** p<0.05, * p<0.1. For convenience in reporting and interpretation, all dependent variables (unit cost and unit profit) and the trade restrictiveness index are multiplied by 100 in the regressions. The fixed-effects estimation dropped out time-invariant variables, namely, the foreign bank dummy variable (FOR) and the country dummy variables (D).

Source: Author's calculations.

Although the incentive structure might explain the suboptimal problem, it is difficult to test this argument empirically, thus it is excluded from the estimation. Third, exogenous factors such as regulations or shocks can cause suboptimal performance. These factors may be the main reason for the inefficient use of inputs and incorrect setting of output prices. In this study, restrictions on banking services are controlled for, partly explaining imperfect competition which drives a wedge between cost minimization and profit maximization, and partially explaining the suboptimal performance.

Based on the estimated unit cost and unit profit functions, the elasticities and semi-elasticities of total cost and total profit can be derived with respect to total fixed capital, prudential ratios, and trade restrictiveness indexes, and then evaluated at the world median values of input prices, output quantities, and trade restrictiveness indexes across 28 countries and over the 1997–2006 period (see Dinh 2011 for details). The results are shown in Table 3.6.

It is estimated that a one per cent increase in total fixed capital generates slightly less than a one per cent increase in total cost. The same effect also occurs on total profit. These results indicate slight economies of scale for the commercial banks in the sample. In other words, the chapter finds no evidence against removing restrictions on bank network expansion.

It is estimated that a one percentage point increase in the total capital ratio cuts total cost by 1.9 per cent and improves total profit by 0.2 per cent, holding other variables constant. The higher capital adequacy means that banks can use fewer borrowed inputs to provide the same lending outputs as before, leading to lower total cost. This reduction might also come from the fact that depositors feel more confident in

Table 3.6. Elasticities and Semi-Elasticities of Bank Performance with Respect to Bank Characteristics

	Total cost	*Total profit*
Total fixed capital	0.9997	0.9998
Total capital ratio	–1.9	0.2
Liquidity ratio	0.05	–0.3

Source: Author's calculations.

banks with a higher capital adequacy; they are willing to put their deposits into such banks at lower interest rates. The cost reduction thus enables banks to improve their profit. A one percentage point increase in the liquidity ratio is estimated to increase total cost by 0.05 per cent and reduce profit by 0.3 per cent. These results may indicate that a higher liquidity ratio leads to a reduction in the funds used for lending and investment purposes. In this situation, in order to keep output quantity unchanged, banks need to use more borrowed inputs, thus increasing their total cost. The cost escalation thus reduces bank profit.

The regression results presented in Table 3.5 show that restrictions on bank establishment and operation, such as licensing requirements, government ownership, and restrictions on lending and fund raising, are statistically positive determinants of both cost and profit, at the 1 per cent level of significance. This result suggests that restrictions on establishment and operation are both cost-escalating and rent-creating. As shown in Table 3.7, a one percentage point increase the trade restrictiveness index on establishment and operation is estimated to raise total cost by 1.9 per cent and to improve profit by 4.8 per cent.

It is reasonable that restrictions on bank establishment and operation are cost-escalating, as these restrictions include measures that affect operation. For example, in many countries, the government still owns a significant part of the banking system, thus directly or indirectly imposing extra real resource costs for incumbent banks. Non-state owned banks also find it difficult to compete with state-owned banks in gaining business from state economic corporations. In nearly a quarter of the sample countries, reciprocity requirements are still applied. These requirements may force foreign banks to establish themselves in higher

Table 3.7. Semi-Elasticities of Bank Performance with Respect to Trade Restrictions

	Total cost	*Total profit*
Restrictions on establishment and operation	1.92	4.77
Restrictions on non-traditional banking activities	–0.61	4.20

Source: Author's calculations.

cost environments than otherwise, because these are where reciprocal rights of establishment are granted.

It is also reasonable that restrictions on establishment and operation are rent-creating, as the restrictions on operation include some measures that may create greater market power for incumbent banks. This may happen when the establishment of new banks is restricted, thus enabling incumbent banks to inflate the price of their services. Similarly, interest rate ceilings may generate an artificial scarcity of credit supply, encouraging banks to charge borrowers extra fees in addition to interest rates, thereby creating a rent for banks.

Restrictions on banks' ability to undertake insurance, securities, and real estate business and to own non-financial companies are shown to reduce banks' costs and to increase profit. As shown in Table 3.7, a percentage point increase in the trade restrictiveness index on non-traditional banking activities is estimated to reduce banks' costs by 0.61 per cent and to help banks gain 4.2 per cent more profit. This suggests there are diseconomies of scope in non-traditional banking activities.

This finding of a cost-reducing effect of restrictions on non-traditional banking activities is the opposite of that found by Barth *et al.* (2004). They found that this type of restriction had no statistically significant effects on total overhead cost. However, the current finding is consistent with the global trend of tightening restrictions on non-traditional banking activities. The finding also supports the earlier arguments against allowing banks to undertake non-traditional activities. The current finding implies that it is beneficial to banks if non-traditional banking activities are restricted. In other words, restrictions on such activities should not be treated as significant barriers to trade in banking services.

3.4 Impact Analysis for 36 Countries

The previous section provides a useful look at the impacts of trade barriers on bank performance. In order to facilitate an economy-wide assessment of the effects of trade liberalization in banking services, two measures of impact are constructed for each country, namely, a productivity equivalent and a tax equivalent. The productivity equivalent is defined as the percentage change in total cost arising from impediments to trade in banking services. The tax equivalent is measured as the percentage change in the price markup arising from trade restrictions. Productivity and tax equivalents measure vertical shifts in the supply curve, and can be modelled as such in a computable general equilibrium model to trace the economy-wide effects of trade liberalization on banking services.

The formulas for evaluating the productivity and tax equivalents in banking services are as follows:

$$productivity\_equivalent = \frac{v_1 - v_0}{v_0} \times 100\% = \frac{v_1 q_1 - v_0 q_0}{v_0 q_0} \times 100\% = \frac{TC_1 - TC_0}{TC_0} \times 100\% \tag{3.1}$$

$$tax\_equivalent = \frac{\frac{p_1}{v_1} - \frac{p_0}{v_0}}{\frac{p_0}{v_0}} \times 100\% = \frac{\frac{p_1 \times q_1}{v_1 \times q_1} - \frac{p_0 \times q_0}{v_0 \times q_0}}{\frac{p_0 \times q_0}{v_0 \times q_0}} \times 100\% = \frac{\frac{TR_1}{TC_1} - \frac{TR_0}{TC_0}}{\frac{TR_0}{TC_0}} \times 100\% = \left(\frac{TR_1}{TR_0} \times \frac{TC_0}{TC_1} - 1 \right) \times 100\% \tag{3.2}$$

where $q_1 = q_0$; v_0, p_0, q_0, TC_0, TR_0 are respectively the unit variable cost, unit price, output quantity, total cost, and total revenue when there are no trade barriers in banking services; and v_1, p_1, q_1, TC_1, TR_1 are respectively the unit variable cost, unit price, output quantity, total cost, and total revenue when there are trade barriers in banking services. The cost, profit, and revenue are predicted from the estimated unit cost and unit profit functions.[7]

[7] The estimated total revenue equals the sum of the estimated total cost and the estimated total profit.

A positive productivity equivalent means a productivity loss for incumbent banks because of restrictions in banking services. In other words, banks would gain in terms of productivity if these restrictions were removed. Similarly, a positive tax equivalent implies an economic rent for banks because of trade barriers. This also means a loss of bank rent if these barriers were removed. However, in both cases, the productivity and tax equivalents create a welfare loss to the economy as a whole.

In order to examine the cross-country pattern of productivity and tax equivalents, it would be ideal for these impact estimates to be evaluated for a typical firm in each country. However, country data are unbalanced, so not all country sub-samples are fully representative of a particular country. This chapter uses the world median value of prices, quantities and time-specific effects in order to facilitate out-of-sample forecasting.[8] For cross-country comparison, the evaluation also uses the 2006 trade restrictiveness indexes of all 36 countries (including 28 sample and 8 out-of-sample countries). As noted earlier, restrictions on non-traditional banking activities should not be considered as significant barriers to trade in banking services. So this type of restriction is excluded from the calculation of productivity and tax equivalents.

Tables 3.8 and 3.9 show the estimates of productivity and tax equivalents for domestic and foreign banks in 36 economies. The estimation of each restriction category is found by applying its index value and the above formulas for calculating the productivity and tax equivalents.

The productivity equivalents of trade barriers in banking services

As expected, in 2006, EU countries in the OECD bore the smallest cost burden from barriers to trade in banking services. Most of them incurred

---

[8] At these values, the productivity equivalent is calculated as 100*100*TRI_EO*0.0072765/0.3891625 and the tax equivalent is calculated as {((0.5088183+0.0072765*TRI_EO*100+0.00826* TRI_EO *100)* 0.3891625)/ [(0.3891625 + 0.0072765*TRI_EO*100)* 0.5088183]–1}*100.

Table 3.8. Productivity Equivalents of Barriers to Trade in Banking, 2006 (per cent)

	Domestic banks	*Foreign Banks*
OECD — EU	**3.1**	**6.0**
Germany	4.3	9.2
United Kingdom	1.1	1.1
Hungary	1.1	1.7
Italy	0.7	3.0
Spain	1.1	1.1
Netherlands	4.4	4.7
France	3.4	4.7
Greece	6.5	6.9
Denmark	4.8	8.4
Czech Republic	7.3	9.2
Sweden	1.1	12.7
Austria	1.1	9.8
OECD — Non-EU	**7.2**	**20.4**
Japan	8.8	16.3
South Korea	17.3	26.0
Turkey	12.1	17.0
United States	1.3	24.4
Australia	4.6	17.5
Mexico	1.1	25.5
Switzerland	5.5	17.1
Canada	6.8	19.2
ASIA	**14.3**	**32.9**
Taiwan	16.4	26.9
Hong Kong	9.0	18.6
China	11.1	29.2
Indonesia	10.3	32.3
India	19.6	34.1
Thailand	13.1	35.6
Viet Nam	18.8	37.1
Malaysia	19.8	41.5
Pakistan	9.3	27.4
Singapore	15.7	46.7
Non-ASIA	**8.6**	**23.8**
Argentina	10.7	13.5
South Africa	4.9	25.3
Israel	8.6	17.9
Egypt	11.9	27.3
Chile	7.3	26.6
Brazil	8.3	32.0

Source: Author's calculations.

Table 3.9. Tax Equivalents of Barriers to Trade in Banking, 2006 (per cent)

	Domestic banks	*Foreign Banks*
OECD — EU	**1.9**	**3.5**
Germany	2.6	5.4
United Kingdom	0.7	0.7
Hungary	0.7	1.0
Italy	0.5	1.9
Spain	0.7	0.7
Netherlands	2.6	2.8
France	2.1	2.8
Greece	3.9	4.1
Denmark	2.9	4.9
Czech Republic	4.3	5.3
Sweden	0.7	7.1
Austria	0.7	5.7
OECD — Non-EU	**4.1**	**10.7**
Japan	5.1	8.9
South Korea	9.3	13.1
Turkey	6.8	9.2
United States	0.8	12.4
Australia	2.8	9.4
Mexico	0.7	12.9
Switzerland	3.3	9.2
Canada	4.1	10.2
ASIA	**7.9**	**15.5**
Taiwan	8.9	13.4
Hong Kong	5.2	9.9
China	6.3	14.3
Indonesia	5.9	15.5
India	10.4	16.1
Thailand	7.3	16.6
Viet Nam	10.0	17.1
Malaysia	10.5	18.6
Pakistan	5.4	13.6
Singapore	8.6	20.1
Non-ASIA	**5.0**	**12.0**
Argentina	6.1	7.5
South Africa	3.0	12.8
Israel	5.0	9.6
Egypt	6.7	13.6
Chile	4.3	13.3
Brazil	4.9	15.4

Source: Author's calculations.

a cost impost of less than 5 per cent for domestic banks and 10 per cent for foreign banks. As discussed earlier, this country group imposes the fewest restrictions on banking services. Non-EU countries in the OECD bore the second smallest cost burden, followed by Latin American countries. The biggest cost burden from trade barriers in banking services was incurred by Asian countries. On average, their cost impost was 14.3 per cent for foreign banks and 32.9 per cent for domestic banks.

Foreign banks incurred a higher cost than their domestic counterparts across all countries. The cost escalation ranged from 1.1 to 46.7 per cent for foreign banks, and from 0.7 to 19.8 per cent for domestic banks. These results also indicate a large variation in the cost impact measures across countries.

In 2006, the top-five countries with the highest productivity loss were Singapore, Malaysia, Viet Nam, Thailand, and India. This reflects that these countries imposed the highest barriers on the licensing of foreign banks. For instance, Malaysia deferred issuing new licenses to foreign banks in an effort to restructure the banking system after the economic crisis occurred in 2001.[9] Singapore had not granted any new licences from 2001 to 2006. Viet Nam raised the minimum capital requirement as a way of restricting new entry and restructuring the banking system.

The tax equivalents of trade barriers in banking services

Across 36 countries, in 2006, the tax equivalent ranged from 0.5 to 10.5 per cent for foreign banks and from 0.7 to 20.1 per cent for domestic banks. As noted before, this tax equivalent means a welfare loss to the economy as a whole. This loss would be even higher if the rents of foreign banks were repatriated overseas.

---

[9] Recently, however, there has been some liberalization. In April 2009, the Bank Negara Malaysia announced a liberalization package for the conventional and Islamic financial sectors. Foreign equity limits were increased from 49 to 70 per cent for domestic Islamic banks (provided they maintain paid-up capital of at least USD 1 billion), investment banks, insurance companies, and *takaful* (Islamic insurance) operators. Locally incorporated foreign commercial banks were given more operational flexibilities: they were allowed to open up to ten microfinance branches from 2009 and up to four new branches in 2010 (WTO 2009).

As expected, in 2006, EU countries in the OECD had the lowest tax equivalents, since this group imposed the fewest restrictions. On average, in this country group, domestic banks received an economic rent of 1.9 per cent while foreign banks obtained a substantially higher rent of 3.5 per cent because of trade barriers in banking services. Non-EU countries in the OECD had a higher tax equivalent, at 4.1 per cent for domestic banks and 10.7 per cent for domestic banks. This group was followed by Latin American and other unclassified countries, where the tax equivalent was 5 per cent for domestic banks and 12 per cent for foreign banks. Asian countries had the highest tax equivalent, 7.9 per cent for domestic banks and 15.5 per cent for foreign banks. Banks in Singapore, Viet Nam, India, and Taiwan were the highest receivers of economic rents created by barriers to trade in banking services.

3.5 Conclusion

This chapter has uncovered important findings about the pattern of trade restrictiveness in banking services across countries and over time. Banks in developing countries had more restrictions imposed on them than those in the developed world. In most of the sample countries, locally-incorporated foreign banks were more restricted than domestic banks. Foreign banks were highly restricted in providing banking services via cross-border supply and commercial presence.

Both domestic and foreign banks have been facing a lower degree of restriction over time, though the reduction has been larger for foreign banks. For domestic banks, the reduction resulted from the decreasing government ownership in the banking sector and relaxation of restrictions on licensing. For foreign banks, the reduction in their restrictiveness came from relaxations of restrictions on all modes of supply, as well as on their traditional banking activities.

Restrictions on non-traditional banking activities have tended to be tightened over time, regardless of bank ownership. Tentatively, this finding suggests that these restrictions may serve a prudential purpose, and should not be treated purely as barriers to trade in banking services.

Using cost and profit as measures of bank performance in structurally-specified cost and profit functions, the chapter has found that restrictions on trade in banking services escalate real resource costs and create economic rents for banks. These effects are expected. Some barriers affect operation, thus raising bank cost. Some barriers limit entry or output, thus creating more power for incumbent banks and generating bank rents.

Restrictions on banks' ability to do non-traditional banking services are shown to reduce cost and increase bank rent. This implies that this type of restriction is beneficial to banks. It helps to confirm the impression that restrictions on undertaking insurance, securities, or real estate business and owning non-financial firms should not be treated as significant barriers to trade in banking services.

The estimates suggest that commercial banks in Asian countries were the most affected by restrictions in banking services. They incurred the highest loss of productivity through restrictions on both establishment and operation. The incumbent banks in Asia also received the largest gain in terms of economic rents created by barriers to operation. By comparison, the productivity loss and rent gain for banks in European countries were trivial. Removing restrictions affecting banking services in Asian countries could be expected to reduce the price of banking services significantly.

Table 3.A.1. Trade Restrictiveness Index for Foreign Banks Operating via All Modes of Supply

	1997	*1998*	*1999*	*2000*	*2001*	*2002*	*2003*	*2004*	*2005*	*2006*
Argentina	0.22	0.20	0.20	0.19	0.22	0.24	0.25	0.25	0.26	0.26
Australia	0.28	0.26	0.26	0.26	0.30	0.30	0.30	0.28	0.28	0.28
Austria	0.06	0.08	0.07	0.07	0.09	0.09	0.09	0.09	0.09	0.09
Brazil	0.47	0.49	0.48	0.45	0.38	0.39	0.40	0.43	0.42	0.42
Canada	0.26	0.24	0.23	0.18	0.14	0.14	0.14	0.16	0.16	0.15
Chile	0.37	0.38	0.38	0.37	0.36	0.36	0.36	0.37	0.36	0.36
China	0.50	0.52	0.52	0.52	0.48	0.47	0.46	0.44	0.42	0.42
Czech Republic	0.28	0.27	0.25	0.25	0.26	0.25	0.25	0.25	0.14	0.16
Denmark	0.15	0.14	0.12	0.12	0.12	0.12	0.12	0.11	0.11	0.11
Egypt	0.38	0.41	0.41	0.43	0.39	0.39	0.38	0.38	0.37	0.37
France	0.09	0.08	0.06	0.06	0.05	0.05	0.05	0.09	0.09	0.09
Germany	0.08	0.09	0.08	0.07	0.09	0.09	0.09	0.09	0.09	0.09
Greece	0.17	0.18	0.15	0.12	0.12	0.11	0.12	0.09	0.09	0.09
Hong Kong	0.24	0.23	0.23	0.23	0.21	0.18	0.17	0.15	0.15	0.15
Hungary	0.33	0.33	0.33	0.33	0.35	0.35	0.35	0.24	0.10	0.10
India	0.42	0.45	0.45	0.45	0.47	0.45	0.44	0.43	0.42	0.42
Indonesia	0.36	0.34	0.31	0.32	0.32	0.32	0.32	0.33	0.33	0.33
Israel	0.23	0.24	0.24	0.23	0.23	0.22	0.22	0.20	0.20	0.20
Italy	0.13	0.13	0.12	0.11	0.11	0.11	0.11	0.12	0.12	0.12
Japan	0.22	0.21	0.21	0.21	0.20	0.18	0.18	0.18	0.18	0.18
South Korea	0.34	0.33	0.33	0.33	0.37	0.37	0.37	0.35	0.34	0.34
Malaysia	0.46	0.45	0.45	0.45	0.46	0.46	0.42	0.46	0.44	0.43
Mexico	0.35	0.36	0.34	0.33	0.28	0.27	0.27	0.22	0.21	0.21
Netherlands	0.08	0.08	0.05	0.05	0.05	0.05	0.05	0.05	0.05	0.05
Pakistan	0.40	0.45	0.44	0.44	0.42	0.42	0.42	0.43	0.41	0.41
Singapore	0.40	0.38	0.38	0.38	0.38	0.41	0.41	0.40	0.40	0.40
South Africa	0.34	0.34	0.34	0.34	0.34	0.34	0.34	0.36	0.36	0.36
Spain	0.07	0.07	0.05	0.05	0.03	0.03	0.03	0.04	0.04	0.04
Sweden	0.18	0.18	0.16	0.16	0.12	0.12	0.12	0.16	0.15	0.15
Switzerland	0.11	0.11	0.11	0.11	0.13	0.13	0.13	0.14	0.14	0.14
Taiwan	0.37	0.39	0.39	0.39	0.40	0.39	0.39	0.40	0.39	0.39
Thailand	0.43	0.44	0.43	0.43	0.46	0.46	0.46	0.46	0.45	0.45
Turkey	0.20	0.21	0.20	0.20	0.15	0.15	0.15	0.15	0.12	0.12
United Kingdom	0.04	0.04	0.02	0.02	0.02	0.02	0.02	0.01	0.01	0.01
United States	0.25	0.25	0.25	0.22	0.20	0.20	0.20	0.20	0.20	0.20
Viet Nam	0.46	0.48	0.48	0.46	0.45	0.44	0.43	0.43	0.42	0.42

Source: Author's calculations.

Table 3.A.2. Trade Restrictiveness Index for Locally-Incorporated Foreign Banks

	1997	*1998*	*1999*	*2000*	*2001*	*2002*	*2003*	*2004*	*2005*	*2006*
Argentina	0.11	0.11	0.11	0.10	0.14	0.15	0.15	0.17	0.17	0.17
Australia	0.15	0.15	0.15	0.15	0.19	0.19	0.19	0.17	0.17	0.17
Austria	0.08	0.07	0.07	0.07	0.09	0.09	0.09	0.09	0.09	0.09
Brazil	0.31	0.31	0.30	0.27	0.19	0.21	0.22	0.25	0.24	0.24
Canada	0.24	0.24	0.23	0.18	0.14	0.14	0.14	0.16	0.16	0.15
Chile	0.23	0.23	0.23	0.23	0.26	0.26	0.26	0.27	0.27	0.27
China	0.37	0.37	0.37	0.37	0.35	0.34	0.33	0.30	0.30	0.30
Czech Republic	0.13	0.12	0.10	0.10	0.14	0.14	0.14	0.14	0.16	0.16
Denmark	0.14	0.14	0.12	0.12	0.12	0.12	0.12	0.11	0.11	0.11
Egypt	0.27	0.27	0.26	0.29	0.25	0.25	0.24	0.23	0.23	0.23
France	0.08	0.08	0.06	0.06	0.05	0.05	0.05	0.09	0.09	0.09
Germany	0.09	0.09	0.08	0.07	0.09	0.09	0.09	0.09	0.09	0.09
Greece	0.18	0.18	0.14	0.12	0.11	0.11	0.12	0.09	0.09	0.09
Hong Kong	0.19	0.19	0.19	0.19	0.17	0.14	0.13	0.11	0.11	0.11
Hungary	0.19	0.17	0.17	0.17	0.19	0.19	0.19	0.15	0.10	0.10
India	0.30	0.30	0.30	0.30	0.31	0.30	0.29	0.28	0.28	0.28
Indonesia	0.35	0.34	0.31	0.32	0.32	0.32	0.32	0.33	0.33	0.33
Israel	0.24	0.24	0.23	0.23	0.23	0.22	0.22	0.20	0.20	0.20
Italy	0.13	0.13	0.12	0.11	0.11	0.11	0.11	0.12	0.12	0.12
Japan	0.21	0.21	0.21	0.21	0.20	0.18	0.18	0.18	0.18	0.18
South Korea	0.24	0.22	0.22	0.22	0.26	0.26	0.26	0.23	0.23	0.23
Malaysia	0.33	0.33	0.33	0.33	0.34	0.34	0.30	0.34	0.32	0.31
Mexico	0.30	0.29	0.28	0.28	0.21	0.21	0.21	0.16	0.16	0.16
Netherlands	0.08	0.08	0.05	0.05	0.05	0.05	0.05	0.05	0.05	0.05
Pakistan	0.28	0.30	0.29	0.29	0.27	0.27	0.27	0.26	0.26	0.26
Singapore	0.31	0.31	0.30	0.30	0.30	0.33	0.33	0.33	0.33	0.33
South Africa	0.19	0.19	0.19	0.19	0.19	0.19	0.19	0.21	0.21	0.21
Spain	0.07	0.07	0.05	0.05	0.03	0.03	0.03	0.04	0.04	0.04
Sweden	0.18	0.18	0.16	0.16	0.12	0.12	0.12	0.16	0.15	0.15
Switzerland	0.11	0.11	0.11	0.11	0.13	0.13	0.13	0.14	0.14	0.14
Taiwan	0.26	0.26	0.26	0.26	0.26	0.26	0.26	0.26	0.26	0.26
Thailand	0.29	0.29	0.28	0.28	0.31	0.31	0.31	0.31	0.31	0.31
Turkey	0.21	0.20	0.20	0.20	0.15	0.15	0.15	0.14	0.12	0.12
United Kingdom	0.04	0.04	0.02	0.02	0.02	0.02	0.02	0.01	0.01	0.01
United States	0.25	0.25	0.25	0.22	0.20	0.20	0.20	0.20	0.20	0.20
Viet Nam	0.33	0.31	0.31	0.29	0.28	0.27	0.26	0.25	0.25	0.25

Source: Author's calculations.

Table 3.A.3. Trade Restrictiveness Index for Domestic Banks

	1997	*1998*	*1999*	*2000*	*2001*	*2002*	*2003*	*2004*	*2005*	*2006*
Argentina	0.09	0.09	0.09	0.08	0.15	0.15	0.15	0.15	0.15	0.15
Australia	0.08	0.08	0.08	0.08	0.12	0.12	0.12	0.10	0.10	0.10
Austria	0.03	0.02	0.02	0.02	0.05	0.04	0.04	0.04	0.04	0.04
Brazil	0.14	0.14	0.14	0.13	0.08	0.09	0.10	0.12	0.11	0.11
Canada	0.08	0.08	0.08	0.08	0.07	0.07	0.07	0.09	0.09	0.09
Chile	0.13	0.13	0.13	0.13	0.16	0.16	0.16	0.17	0.17	0.17
China	0.25	0.25	0.22	0.22	0.22	0.22	0.22	0.20	0.20	0.20
Czech Republic	0.10	0.10	0.10	0.09	0.14	0.14	0.13	0.13	0.15	0.15
Denmark	0.08	0.08	0.08	0.08	0.10	0.10	0.10	0.09	0.09	0.09
Egypt	0.20	0.20	0.19	0.19	0.15	0.15	0.15	0.15	0.14	0.14
France	0.04	0.04	0.04	0.04	0.04	0.04	0.04	0.08	0.08	0.08
Germany	0.06	0.06	0.06	0.06	0.06	0.06	0.06	0.06	0.06	0.06
Greece	0.12	0.12	0.11	0.11	0.11	0.10	0.11	0.09	0.09	0.09
Hong Kong	0.10	0.10	0.10	0.10	0.09	0.08	0.07	0.06	0.06	0.06
Hungary	0.12	0.10	0.10	0.10	0.10	0.10	0.10	0.10	0.10	0.10
India	0.18	0.18	0.18	0.18	0.23	0.23	0.23	0.20	0.20	0.20
Indonesia	0.18	0.18	0.18	0.19	0.20	0.20	0.20	0.21	0.21	0.21
Israel	0.19	0.19	0.18	0.18	0.18	0.17	0.17	0.15	0.15	0.15
Italy	0.09	0.09	0.09	0.09	0.09	0.09	0.08	0.11	0.11	0.11
Japan	0.17	0.17	0.17	0.17	0.17	0.15	0.15	0.15	0.14	0.14
South Korea	0.17	0.17	0.16	0.16	0.21	0.21	0.21	0.18	0.18	0.18
Malaysia	0.19	0.19	0.19	0.19	0.20	0.20	0.20	0.20	0.20	0.20
Mexico	0.15	0.15	0.15	0.15	0.08	0.08	0.08	0.03	0.03	0.03
Netherlands	0.04	0.04	0.04	0.04	0.04	0.04	0.04	0.05	0.05	0.05
Pakistan	0.18	0.18	0.17	0.17	0.17	0.17	0.17	0.16	0.16	0.17
Singapore	0.14	0.14	0.14	0.14	0.17	0.17	0.17	0.16	0.16	0.16
South Africa	0.08	0.08	0.08	0.08	0.08	0.08	0.08	0.10	0.10	0.10
Spain	0.05	0.05	0.05	0.05	0.03	0.03	0.03	0.04	0.04	0.04
Sweden	0.09	0.09	0.09	0.09	0.06	0.06	0.06	0.10	0.09	0.09
Switzerland	0.04	0.04	0.04	0.04	0.07	0.07	0.07	0.08	0.08	0.08
Taiwan	0.20	0.20	0.19	0.19	0.21	0.21	0.21	0.20	0.20	0.20
Thailand	0.15	0.15	0.15	0.15	0.15	0.15	0.15	0.16	0.18	0.18
Turkey	0.18	0.18	0.18	0.18	0.12	0.12	0.12	0.12	0.09	0.09
United Kingdom	0.02	0.02	0.02	0.02	0.02	0.02	0.02	0.01	0.01	0.01
United States	0.11	0.11	0.11	0.08	0.07	0.07	0.07	0.07	0.07	0.07
Viet Nam	0.21	0.21	0.20	0.18	0.18	0.16	0.16	0.16	0.15	0.15

Source: Author's calculations.

Chapter 4

Regulatory Restrictions in Logistics Services

Claire Hollweg and Marn-Heong Wong

4.1 Introduction

Logistics is the part of the supply chain process that plans, implements, and controls the efficient, effective flow and storage of goods, services, and related information from the point of origin to the point of consumption in order to meet consumers' requirements (de Souza *et al.* 2007). Thus efficient delivery of logistics services is the ability to move goods expeditiously, reliably and cheaply. The costs of delays are high and ultimately passed on to consumers. A competitive and efficient logistics sector is therefore vital for all economies and is an essential component of all trade.

Logistics involves a range of sub-sectors, which can be classified into three tiers (United States International Trade Commission 2005). Tier 1 services are transport management and supply chain consulting services, including network design, the development of distribution strategies, storage, warehousing, cargo handling, transport agency services and customs brokerage. Tier 2 services are freight services, including maritime, inland waterways, air, rail and road transport services. Tier 3 services cover a large number of other inputs or value added services, including wholesale and retail trade services, packaging services, real estate services, and management consulting services. These may or may not be associated directly with revenue flows to logistics providers, but this tier includes services that must be available to logistics firms.

Government restrictions imposed on logistics services providers (LSPs) can adversely affect the price, reliability and quality of these services, and limit competition in their provision. Many such regulatory restrictions can be considered barriers to trade in these services. This study focuses on government regulations affecting the provision of Tier 1 and Tier 2 logistics services. As the main modes of international transport, these are the critical inputs to the efficient supply of logistics services across borders.

This chapter aims to measure the extent of restrictions on trade in these logistics services in the 16 economies of the ASEAN+6 group, through the construction of a logistics regulatory restrictiveness index. The ASEAN+6 group comprises the ten members of the Association of South East Asian Nations (ASEAN) — Brunei Darussalam, Cambodia, Indonesia, Lao People's Democratic Republic (PDR), Malaysia, Myanmar, Philippines, Singapore, Thailand and Viet Nam — plus Australia, China, India, Japan, the Republic of Korea and New Zealand. The chapter reviews the types of restrictions faced by the logistics sector, details the index methodology used to construct the logistics sector restrictiveness index, and analyses the results for the ASEAN+6 economies.

A positive relationship is shown to exist between actual restrictions and perceived performance — the fewer the restrictions according to the logistics sector restrictiveness index of this study, the better the perceived performance of the logistics sector, as measured by the World Bank's Logistics Performance Index. Thus poor logistics performance could be expected to create pressure from traders and logistics operators for governments to ease the regulatory constraints. This chapter documents how such pressure has led to recent logistics reforms in Indonesia and Thailand. The case studies confirm that traders themselves can become important sources of pressure for liberalization of trade in logistics services.

4.2 Types of Restrictions

Restrictions on trade in logistics services are barriers that inhibit LSPs from entering or operating in a market. Although restrictions on trade can arise from many sources, including the poor quality of infrastructure, which can act to slow the transport of goods, this study focuses on government regulation of entry and operations. Some of this regulation treats foreign services suppliers less favourably than their domestic counterparts. Some applies to both domestic and foreign providers, but still restricts activity.

Many of the restrictions that this study uses in the restrictiveness index have been identified in previous studies by actors within the logistics industry. As a starting point, a list of government regulations or restrictions on the entry and operations of logistics service suppliers was compiled by the Regional Economic Policy Support Facility (REPSF) Project of the ASEAN Secretariat and the Logistics Institute of Asia Pacific (de Souza *et al.* 2007). The project identified in-country policies, measures and regulations that directly and indirectly influenced the efficient door-to-door delivery of goods with ASEAN. Supported by a survey questionnaire of interviews of various players in the logistics supply chain, the project constructed a database of policies and performance measures that impede free trade in logistics services worldwide. Those regulatory barriers are incorporated into the framework for this study. The framework also draws on other studies of barriers to trade in logistics services, primarily maritime and air transport (Doove *et al.* 2001, Zhang and Findlay 2011, McGuire *et al.* 2000), as well as Arvis *et al.* (2007) and Asia Pacific Foundation of Canada (2000).

The approach taken is to quantify restrictions on LSPs regardless of whether they are specific to logistics or not. Thus the coverage includes major horizontal restrictions on the movement of people and on direct investment. Table 4.1 gives a summary of the coverage of the logistics sector restrictiveness index developed in this chapter. This table also shows whether the identified restrictions affect only foreign LSPs, or also affect their domestic counterparts.

Table 4.1. Logistics Restriction Categories and Relevance for Foreign and Domestic Providers

	Foreign?	*Domestic?*
Customs		
Number of customs documents	Yes	Yes
Number of customs signatures	Yes	Yes
Import licensing	Yes	Yes
Local language used on customs documents	Yes	Yes
Customs inspections	Yes	Yes
Import restrictions	Yes	Yes
Unavailability of Electronic Data Interchange (EDI)	Yes	Yes
Non-use of Harmonized Commodity Description and Coding System	Yes	Yes
Possibility of a review	Yes	Yes
Limited customs operating hours	Yes	Yes
Restrictions on customs brokerage services	Yes	Yes
Customs clearance times	Yes	Yes
Customs procedures time	Yes	Yes
Customs charges or fees	Yes	Yes
Improper penalties or fees	Yes	Yes
Discriminatory fees or inspection practices	Yes	No
Small *de minimis* level (threshold value below which there is a waiver of duty)	Yes	Yes
Investment		
Restrictions on commercial presence	Yes	No
Foreign equity limits	Yes	Yes
Licensing requirements	Yes	Yes
Discriminatory licensing	Yes	No
Factors affecting investment (eg screening, needs tests)	Yes	Yes
Movement of people		
Licensing requirements on management	Yes	No
Limitations on movement of people — permanent	Yes	No
Limitations on movement of people — temporary	Yes	No
Local employment requirements	Yes	Yes
Difficulty in firing	Yes	Yes
Maritime transport		
Cabotage restrictions (limit domestic movements by foreign carriers)	Yes	No
Cargo reservation	Yes	Yes
Cargo handling restrictions	Yes	No
Storage and warehousing restrictions	Yes	No
Restrictions on container station and depot services	Yes	No
Lack of general competition legislation to govern shipping	Yes	Yes
Monopolized handling of port-related services	Yes	Yes

Table. 4.1. Continued.

Aviation transport		
Limited allocation of take-off and landing slots	Yes	Yes
Ground-handling restrictions	Yes	No
Cargo-handling and warehousing restrictions	Yes	No
Foreign investment limits in domestic airlines	Yes	Yes
Absence of open skies agreements	Yes	No
Absence of seventh freedom rights (to carry passengers/ cargo between two economies by an airline of a third economy)	Yes	No
Cabotage restrictions (limit domestic movements by foreign carriers)	Yes	No
Lack of multiple designation on international routes	Yes	No
Road transport		
Equipment usage restrictions	Yes	No
Restricted hours of operation	Yes	Yes
Other		
Statutory monopolies	Yes	Yes

Burdensome customs procedures are reported to pose the most significant barrier to trade (de Souza *et al.* 2007). Regulatory customs procedures include time-consuming documentation, customs inspections, and lack of border coordination and clearance. Trade barriers to investment arise through licensing requirements for the provision of transportation services and cross-sectoral investment regulations that either limit the foreign equity participation in a firm or regulate the form of establishment. Labour regulations refer to policies or measures that limit the movement or hiring of key personnel. For example, most countries require the hiring of local residents by foreign firms.

Whereas customs barriers and restrictions on investment and the movement of people generally apply to all LSPs, other sector-specific regulatory barriers only affect LSPs dealing specifically with maritime, aviation or road transport. These barriers may impede the operational efficiency and the quality of services provided by these LSPs.

4.3 Index Methodology

The full template for the restrictiveness index is given in Table 4.2. It has been used to quantify the overall logistics restrictiveness environment faced by LSPs in each of the 16 economies of the ASEAN+6 group.

Table 4.2. Restrictiveness Index for Logistics Services

Category weightings *R*	*MFN*	*Total*	*Score*	*Restriction category*
				RESTRICTION ON CUSTOMS:
0.0388	na	0.0388		**Customs documents** The score will be proportional to the average number of customs documents required for exports and imports over the number of customs documents of the economy with the greatest number.
0.0388	na	0.0388		**Customs signatures** The score will be proportional to the average number of customs signatures required for exports and imports over the number of customs signatures of the economy with the greatest number.
0.0388	na	0.0388		**Import licensing**
			0.00	Import licences are not required.
			0.50	Some goods require import licences.
			1.00	All goods require import licences.
0.0065	na	0.0065		**Local language**
			0.00	Local language is not used on customs documents.
			1.00	Local language is used on customs documents.
0.0388	na	0.0388		**Customs inspections** The score will be equivalent to the average percentage of goods inspected during shipment. For example, an average rate of physical inspection of 25 per cent of goods receives a score of 0.25.
0.0065	na	0.0065		**Import restrictions (scores additive)**
			0.25	Restrictions on weight.
			0.25	Restrictions on value of shipment.
			0.25	Restrictions on certain goods.
			0.25	Requirement that imports and exports be balanced.
0.0388	na	0.0388		**Customs Electronic Data Interchange (EDI)**
			0.00	EDI processing for customs documentation is fully functional.
			0.50	EDI processing for customs documentation is available but not fully functional.
			1.00	EDI processing for customs documentation is not available.

Table. 4.2. Continued.

0.0356	na	0.0356		**Harmonized Commodity Description and Coding System (HS)**
			0.00	HS for customs classification is fully functional.
			0.50	Use HS for customs classification, but customs officials can change the classification codes arbitrarily and intentionally.
			1.00	HS for customs classification is not used.
0.0324	na	0.0324		**Possibility of a review for imports** The score (from 0 to 1) measures the possibility that a simple and inexpensive review procedure for imports is available, where 0 indicates the highest possibility.
0.0194	na	0.0194		**Customs operating hours**
			0.00	Customs facilities are open 24 hours.
			0.50	Limited hours of operation at customs facilities, but open extended hours if requested.
			1.00	Limited hours of operation at customs facilities, such as closure on weekends or public holidays.
0.0129	na	0.0129		**Customs brokerage services**
			0.00	Firms are allowed to freely provide customs brokerage services.
			0.50	Customs brokerage services can only be provided in restricted areas or limited to individual citizens or a few firms.
			1.00	Regulations do not allow firms to freely provide customs brokerage services.
0.0324	na	0.0324		**Customs clearance** The score will be proportional to the average number of days of border waiting time required to clear customs over the number of days of the economy with the highest number.
0.0324	na	0.0324		**Customs procedures time** The score will be proportional to the average number of days necessary to comply with all customs procedures to import or export goods over the number of days of the economy with the highest number.
0.0194	na	0.0194		**Customs charges or fees** The score will be proportional to the average customs charges or fees per container to import or export goods over the cost of the economy with the highest value.

Table. 4.2. Continued.

0.0259	na	0.0259		**Improper penalties or fees**
			0.00	Improper penalties or fees are rare or non-existent.
			0.50	Improper penalties or fees are noted.
			1.00	Improper penalties or fees are common.
0.0194	na	0.0194		**Discriminatory fees or inspection practices**
			0.00	Discriminatory fees or inspection practices are rare or non-existent.
			0.50	Discriminatory fees or inspection practices are noted.
			1.00	Discriminatory fees or inspection practices are common.
0.0388	na	0.0388		**De *minimis* level**
				The score will be 1 minus the proportion of the *de minimis* level over the *de minimis* level of the economy with the highest value.
				RESTRICTIONS ON INVESTMENT:
0.0259	na	0.0259		**Commercial presence**
			0.00	No restrictions on establishment.
			0.50	Logistics service suppliers must be represented by a local agent.
			1.00	Form of commercial presence is restricted through a specific type of legal entity or joint venture arrangement.
0.0246	0.0013	0.0259		**Foreign equity participation**
				The score will be inversely proportional to the maximum foreign equity participation permitted in a domestic logistics firm.
0.0194	na	0.0194		**Licensing**
			0.00	No licensing requirements for the provision of transportation services.
			1.00	Licensing requirements for the provision of transportation services.
0.0259	na	0.0259		**Discriminatory licensing**
			0.00	No discriminatory licensing for the provision of transportation services.
			1.00	Discriminatory licensing for the provision of transportation services.

Table. 4.2. Continued.

0.0259	na	0.0259		**Factors affecting investment (scores additive)**
			0.30	Takeovers are hindered by regulation.
			0.30	Investors must meet performance requirements.
			0.20	Establishment subject to an economic needs test.
			0.20	Government screening of investment.
				RESTRICTIONS ON MOVEMENT OF PEOPLE:
0.0123	0.0006	0.0129		**Licensing requirements on management**
			0.00	No licensing requirements on directors and managers.
			0.25	Directors and managers must be domiciled in the foreign economy.
			0.50	Directors and managers must be locally licensed.
			0.75	At least 1 director or manager must be a national or resident.
			1.00	All directors or mangers or at least a majority of them must be nationals or residents.
0.0123	0.0006	0.0129		**Movement of people – Permanent**
			0.00	Executives, senior managers or staff can stay a period of more than 4 years.
			0.20	Executives, senior managers or staff can stay a period of up to 4 years.
			0.40	Executives, senior managers or staff can stay a period of up to 3 years.
			0.60	Executives, senior managers or staff can stay a period of up to 2 years.
			0.80	Executives, senior managers or staff can stay a period of up to 1 year.
			1.00	No entry of executives, senior management or staff.
0.0123	0.0006	0.0129		**Movement of people – Temporary**
			0.00	Temporary entry of executives, senior managers and/or specialists over 90 days.
			0.25	Temporary entry of executives, senior managers and/or specialists up to 90 days.
			0.50	Temporary entry of executives, senior managers and/or specialists up to 60 days.
			0.75	Temporary entry of executives, senior managers and/or specialists up to 30 days.
			1.00	No temporary entry of executives, senior managers and/or specialists.

Table. 4.2. Continued.

0.0129	na	0.0129		**Local employment requirements**
			0.00	No local employment requirements of hiring of local residents.
			1.00	Local employment requirements of hiring of local residents.
0.0194	na	0.0194		**Difficulty in firing**
			0.00	No noted burdensome practices required to layoff, severance packages, *etc.*
			1.00	Noted burdensome practices required to layoff, severance packages, *etc.*
				RESTRICTIONS ON MARITIME TRANSPORT:
0.0184	0.0010	0.0194		**Cabotage restrictions**
			0.00	No cabotage restrictions.
			0.50	Restrictions on length of time cargoes can be carried.
			0.75	Foreigners that fly the national flag can provide domestic maritime services.
			1.00	Foreigners generally cannot provide domestic services.
0.0123	0.0006	0.0129		**Cargo reservation**
			0.00	No restrictions on types of cargo that may be carried.
			1.00	Restrictions on types of cargo that may be carried.
0.0129	na	0.0129		**Cargo handling**
			0.00	No restrictions on foreign maritime firms to provide own or third-party cargo handling services.
			0.50	Foreign maritime firms are subject to foreign equity, nationality or licensing requirements to provide cargo handling services.
			1.00	Foreign maritime firms have no access to provide cargo handling services.
0.0123	0.0006	0.0129		**Storage and warehousing**
			0.00	No restrictions on foreign maritime firms to provide own or third-party storage and warehousing services.
			0.50	Foreign maritime firms are subject to foreign equity, nationality or licensing requirements to provide storage and warehousing.
			1.00	Foreign maritime firms have no access to provide storage and warehousing services.

Table. 4.2. Continued.

0.0123	0.0006	0.0129	**Container station and depot services**
		0.00	No restrictions on foreign maritime firms to provide own or third-party container station and depot services.
		0.50	Foreign maritime firms are subject to foreign equity, nationality or licensing requirements to provide container station and depot services.
		1.00	Foreign maritime firms have no access to provide container station and depot services.
0.0194	na	0.0194	**General competition legislation**
		0.00	Existence of a legislative framework to regulate the behavior of shipping conferences or domestic shipping lines.
		1.00	Absence of a legislative framework to regulate the behavior of shipping conferences or domestic shipping lines.
0.0129	na	0.0129	**Monopolized handling of port-related services**
		0.00	No existence of port monopoly of port-related services.
		0.50	Licences granted to limit number of cargo handlers.
		1.00	Ports controlled by one authority.
			RESTRICTIONS ON AVIATION TRANSPORT:
0.0065	na	0.0065	**Take-off and landing slots**
		0.00	Sufficient allocation of take-off and landing slots.
		1.00	No or limited allocation of take-off and landing slots.
0.0065	na	0.0065	**Ground-handling**
		0.00	No restrictions on foreign aviation firms to provide own or third-party ground-handling services such as aircraft parking, refuelling or passenger handling.
		0.50	Foreign aviation firms are subject to foreign equity, nationality or licensing requirements to provide ground-handling services such as aircraft parking, refuelling or passenger handling.
		1.00	Foreign aviation firms have no access to provide ground-handling services such as aircraft parking, refuelling or passenger handling.
0.0259	na	0.0259	**Cargo-handling and warehousing**
		0.00	No restrictions on foreign aviation firms to provide own or third-party cargo-handling and warehousing facilities.

Table. 4.2. Continued.

			0.50	Foreign aviation firms are subject to foreign equity, nationality or licensing requirements to provide cargo-handling and warehousing facilities.
			1.00	Foreign aviation firms have no access to provide cargo-handling and warehousing facilities.
0.0065	na	0.0065		**Foreign investment in domestic airlines**
			0.00	Investment in domestic airlines by foreign airlines is allowed.
			1.00	Investment in domestic airlines by foreign airlines is not allowed.
0.0259	na	0.0259		**Open skies agreement**
			0.00	Have signed an open skies agreement with more than 5 countries.
			0.50	Have signed an open skies agreement with 3 to 5 countries.
			1.00	Have signed an open skies agreement with 2 or fewer countries.
0.0259	na	0.0259		**Seventh freedom rights**
			0.00	Seventh freedom rights are granted to some foreign carriers.
			1.00	The open skies policy does not include seventh freedom rights.
0.0259	na	0.0259		**Cabotage restrictions**
			0.00	Cabotage or eighth freedom rights are granted to some foreign carriers.
			1.00	The open skies policy does not include eighth freedom rights.
0.0259	na	0.0259		**Multiple designation on international routes**
			0.00	Two or more carriers including the private carriers roughly have the equal right in being designated for flying international routes.
			0.50	The national carrier has the priority in gaining international rights over the domestic private carriers, or domestic private carriers are not eligible to fly international routes before fulfilling some conditions such as servicing domestic market for a certain period of time.
			1.00	The national carrier is predominantly the designated airline servicing international routes.

Table. 4.2. Continued.

				RESTRICTIONS ON ROAD TRANSPORT:
0.0307	0.0016	0.0324		**Equipment usage**
			0.00	No restrictions on equipment usage, rental of vehicles or fleet size.
			1.00	Restrictions on equipment usage, rental of vehicles or fleet size.
0.0324	na	0.0324		**Hours of operation**
			0.00	No restrictions on hours of operation.
			1.00	Restrictions on hours of operation.
				OTHER:
0.0129	na	0.0129		**Statutory government monopolies** Average score for 5 categories in which logistics services occur through statutory government monopolies (see text for details).
0.9922	0.0078	1.00		**Total**

Notes: na = not applicable. R is the restriction category weighting. MFN is the most-favoured-nation category weighting.

The qualitative information on existing policies restricting logistics services in the ASEAN+6 economies has been taken from a number of sources:

- De Souza *et al.* (2007);
- WTO Trade Policy Reviews;
- US State Department Country Commercial Guides;
- the National Trade Estimate Reports on Foreign Trade Barriers from the Office of the United States Trade Representative;
- the APEC Investment Guide;
- APEC Individual Action Plans;
- the APEC Business Travel Handbook;
- UPS's Trade Barrier Survey Reports;
- ASEAN Customs for Business reports;
- the ASEAN Express Delivery Services Regulatory Matrix;

- the World Bank's Doing Business Reports;
- Arvis *et al.* (2007); and
- country-specific sources.

The information reflects, as best as possible, restrictions applying to logistics services as of December 2008. The validity and reliability of the restrictiveness index score for different economies depends in part on the depth and quality of information. The sources used here are the best-known sources of data on logistics services.

Some restrictions may not necessarily fit within a restriction category. This may be because, for example, certain restrictions apply only in one economy and are not covered by a restriction category in the restrictiveness index. These restrictions are not directly assigned a score but are used as background information in assigning appropriate scores in some other restriction categories.

Each restriction category receives a score that ranges from 0 (least restrictive) to 1 (most restrictive) based on the stringency of the existing policy — the more stringent the restriction, the higher the score. Each restriction category's score is then weighted to reflect how restrictive that category is relative to other types of restrictions — the more restrictive the category, the higher the weighting. The weights take six different values, ranging from 0.0065 (least restrictive) to 0.0388 (most restrictive). These values are normalized values that correspond to a scale of 1 to 6 that the REPSF Report (de Souza *et al.* 2007) used to classify the restrictiveness of a regulation.[1] These were in turn based on survey responses. As such, the weighting, although based on informed judgment, is subjective.[2] The scores and weights associated with the full list of restriction categories are given in Table 4.2.

---

[1] Each restriction category was assigned a score of between 1 and 6. Restriction categories not included in the REPSF Report are assigned a score using best judgment. Then the sum of all the restriction category scores was obtained, and each restriction category's weight was calculated as a proportion of the total.

[2] As a sensitivity test, restrictiveness indices were also calculated using weights derived from factor analysis. The results are given in Hollweg and Wong (2009). It was found that these indices yielded similar results on the relative regulatory restrictiveness in the logistics sectors across the ASEAN+6 economies as the indices that are based on subjective weights.

If selected logistics services are controlled by a statutory government-owned monopoly, this limits other domestic and foreign firms from entering the market. The statutory government monopolies category score is based on the presence of government monopolies in five logistics services categories — cargo handling, postal service, state trading rights, container trucking and ground handling services. The presence of a government monopoly in any category receives a score of 1, and the scores from each category are totalled and divided by 5 to show the extent of the restrictions for all categories.

An issue arises when scoring economies that allow reciprocal or preferential treatment with a particular set of partner economies through most-favoured-nation (MFN) exemptions. If the details of the reciprocal or preferential treatment were known, this information could be built directly into the computation of the restrictiveness index on a bilateral basis. For example, if an economy granted preferential treatment on the temporary movement of people with a partner economy, and the extent of the preferential treatment was known, its restrictiveness index score for this restriction category could be computed separately for that partner economy and would be lower than against other economies. However, such details are not available.

Information on MFN exemptions for any relevant restriction category is drawn from the Article II MFN Exemptions listed in the country schedules of the General Agreement on Trade in Services (GATS) under the World Trade Organization (WTO), accessed from the online WTO Services Database. These exemptions specify the sector coverage, the economies to which they apply and the intended duration, but not the nature or extent of the reciprocal or preferential treatment needed to disentangle such details.

The approach taken in this study to scoring economies that have MFN exemptions is similar to that in McGuire *et al.* (2000) and Kalirajan (2000). Each type of exemption is scored, rather than adjusting each restriction category for any reciprocal or preferential arrangement between two economies. The scoring still recognizes that an economy that applies an MFN exemption to one or a number of economies has lower restrictions overall than an economy without such an arrangement. Thus, economies with MFN exemptions receive a lower score than

Table 4.3. Scores for MFN Exemptions

Score	*Type of MFN exemption*
1.00	No MFN exemption.
0.50	MFN exemption with reciprocity with selected or all economies.
0.00	MFN exemption with preferential treatment with selected or all economies.

economies without these arrangements. The relevant restriction categories to which MFN exemptions might apply are noted in Table 4.2. The scores for the MFN exemptions are outlined in Table 4.3.

MFN exemptions are assigned scores in a matrix to measure how the 16 economies treat each other. For example, Brunei Darussalam has a preferential treatment MFN exemption with Indonesia, Malaysia and Singapore on entry and temporary stay of workers. In the matrix for temporary movement of people, Indonesia, Malaysia and Singapore receive a score of 0 and the 12 remaining economies receive a score of 1. The total score of 12 is divided by 15 to obtain a *pro rata* score for the number of economies to which the MFN exemption is not applicable. The denominator of 15 reflects the number of economies in the sample that Brunei Darussalam can potentially trade with, since it cannot have a MFN exemption with itself. Thus, Brunei Darussalam scores 0.8 for the temporary movement of people. This score is then multiplied by the respective MFN weighting in Table 4.2, where the MFN weighting represents five per cent of the total category weighting.[3]

The methodology of the logistics sector restrictiveness index has been developed to assess the overall restrictiveness of the regulatory environment across economies — the greater the restrictions on LSPs, the greater the logistics sector restrictiveness index score. But governments do not apply the same set of restrictions to foreign and domestic logistics firms. Thus a score has been calculated separately for domestic and foreign services suppliers. The foreign restrictiveness index covers restrictions that are relevant to foreign logistics service suppliers. The domestic restrictiveness index covers restrictions that are relevant to both domestic and foreign services suppliers. The restriction categories

[3] The MFN weighting follows McGuire *et al.* (2000).

used in the domestic index are noted in Table 4.1. The weights used are a corresponding subset of the weights shown in Table 4.2. Thus the maximum possible foreign restrictiveness index score is 1 and the maximum possible domestic restrictiveness index score is 0.6634. The values for the domestic and foreign indexes and their subcomponents are shown in Tables 4.A.1 and 4.A.2 at the end of this chapter. The difference between the foreign and domestic restrictiveness indices represents a measure of the discrimination against foreigners.

4.4 Results for ASEAN+6 Economies

As shown in Figure 4.1, Malaysia, China, Indonesia, Lao PDR, the Philippines and Viet Nam are the most restricted economies for logistics services in this region, according to both the domestic and foreign indices. These economies have a broad range of restrictions on LSPs.

- In Lao PDR, a number of licences are required for the importation of all goods, and the importer must apply for an import licence from the Ministry of Commerce. Lao PDR also has the highest costs associated with all procedures to import and export.

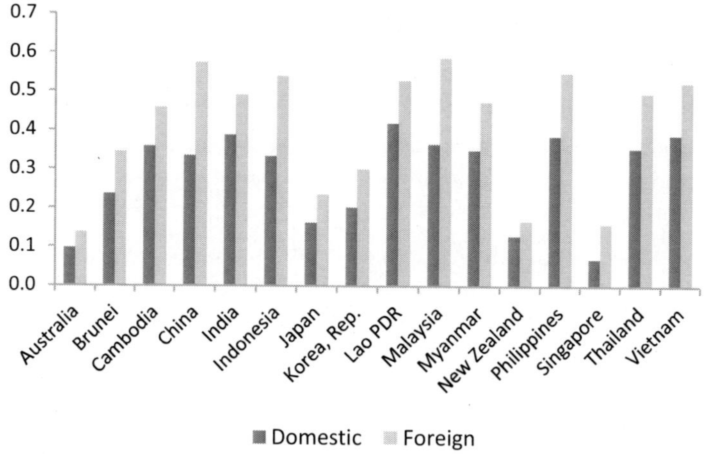

Figure 4.1. Restrictiveness Indices for Logistics Services in ASEAN+6 Economies

- Viet Nam maintains high restrictions within its maritime services. Port services are provided exclusively by Vietnamese enterprises, resulting in a high degree of discrimination. Cabotage restrictions exist where Viet Nam shipping does not allow direct sailing of foreign flags, meaning foreign flags can only go to the gateway ports. Viet Nam is also one of the few economies that practices cargo reservation, along with Indonesia, Malaysia and the Philippines.
- The network of public ports in the Philippines is controlled by the Philippines Ports Authority (PPA), which acts as both landlord and regulator. It leases selected berths and storage facilities to private operators and grants cargo-handling licences to stevedoring companies that operate on common-user facilities. There is also a policy of limiting the number of cargo handlers to at most two in any port with the exception of Manila. The monopolization of cargo handling was formalized under the Executive Order 59, which granted an exclusive contract for the handling of cargo in all ports.
- Heavy licensing requirements exist in Indonesia that also discriminate against foreign logistics firms. For warehousing and transportation, more than three different licences are required for all firms. Indonesia allows foreign investment in warehousing and distribution but not in transportation.
- In China trucks are not allowed daytime access in almost all major Chinese cities. It has been noted that China's enforcement efforts are often targeted at foreign transport and logistics firms, while local firms are permitted to operate without full compliance.
- The customs facilities of East Malaysia do not operate on Saturdays or Sundays. Goods arriving on Friday therefore have to wait till the next Monday, thus causing delays in shipment. On Fridays, since Malaysian customs do not operate 24 hours for religious reasons, a number of trucks have to queue overnight at the Singapore–Malaysian border.

Singapore and Australia are the most open economies for trade in logistics services, along with Japan and New Zealand, according to both the domestic and foreign indices. These economies have more liberal regulatory environments towards LSPs.

- Singapore has one of the most liberalized environments. Customs facilities are open around the clock in Singapore with fully functional electronic data interchange for customs documentation. Furthermore, licensing requirements are present in almost all countries but not in Singapore.
- Australia has the highest *de minimis* level of any economy in the region and does not require companies or individuals to hold import licences.
- Japan maintains a highly liberalized open investment regime. It has, in principle, no performance requirement and no restriction on foreign exchange or repatriation of funds related to foreign investment. Foreign direct investment in Japan requires only *ex post* reporting, except for a very few sectors where prior notification is required.

Malaysia, Indonesia and China are the economies that discriminate most against LSPs in this region, whereby foreign providers are treated less favourably than domestic providers.

- In most countries, except Singapore, foreign firms are not allowed to freely provide brokerage services. Malaysia, along with Indonesia, Thailand and Myanmar, do not allow foreign companies to own brokerage licences. In Malaysia, customs brokerage is much sought after. This licence, granted by the customs authorities, requires passing a 10-day course offered by the local customs and freight forwarders association. An applicant needs two referees. Once the certificate is granted, a firm can operate as a customs brokerage house.
- There is concern in China that a Postal Law includes language that could severely limit the ability of private express delivery firms to operate in China by reserving delivery of certain letters and other documents to China Post and Chinese domestic express delivery companies. The new Express Delivery Standards also may negatively affect foreign express delivery providers. In most economies express delivery is not regulated directly. On the related issue of air freight forwarding, wholly-foreign owned express delivery companies cannot qualify for an Air Transport Agency licence and therefore do not have

the ability to directly load cargo on Chinese domestic or international flights, but instead must work through a Chinese agent.

Correlation with World Bank Logistics Performance Index

The restrictiveness index developed here is an objective indicator based on hard information, albeit with subjective weights based on the perceptions of logistics operators about the relative stringency of the different restriction categories. By contrast, the World Bank's Logistics Performance Index (LPI) is a perceptions index. It is a composite index based on information from a web-based questionnaire completed by more than 800 logistics professionals worldwide on seven areas of performance (Arvis *et al.* 2007) — customs, infrastructure, international shipments, logistics competence, tracking and tracing, domestic logistics costs, and timeliness. In each area, the respondents are asked questions such as whether transport charges, the quality of infrastructure and the level of competence of various agencies is 'high' or 'low'. These perceptions are weighted together. A lower LPI score indicates a worse logistics sector performance.

Figure 4.2 shows that there is a reasonable correlation between the LPI and the logistics sector restrictiveness index for foreign LSPs constructed in this study. A similar correlation also exists between the restrictiveness index for foreign LSPs and various sub-components of the LPI — international shipments, logistics competence, tracking and tracing, and timeliness. The only exception is the domestic logistics costs component of the LPI, which has a slight positive relationship with the restrictiveness index for foreign LSPs. This result is unsurprising, as World Bank researchers have found that domestic logistics costs were uncorrelated with the other areas in the LPI, which could indicate data irregularities. This component was dropped from the composition of the LPI (Arvis *et al.* 2007).[4]

---

[4] The correlation was not tested for the LPI component 'quality transport and information technology infrastructure for logistics', as the logistics sector restrictiveness index does not include regulations that affect the quality of infrastructure.

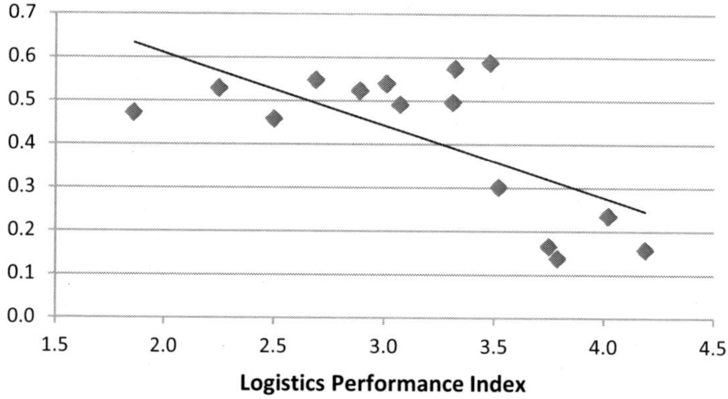

Figure 4.2. Logistics Performance Index versus Foreign Restrictiveness Index

Overall, the higher the LPI score for each component, indicating better overall logistics performance in that component, then the lower the logistics sector restrictiveness index score for foreign LSPs, indicating a less restrictive regulatory environment. The results indicate that the less restrictive the regulatory environment in which LSPs operate in each economy, then the better the perceived overall logistics performance within that economy.

Customs regulations are considered to pose the greatest barrier to trade in logistics services. Furthermore, the customs component of this study has the greatest number of identified trade restrictions. A customs restrictiveness index was constructed using the same methodology as in the previous section, using only the restrictions on customs in the top-most sections of Tables 4.1 and 4.2. In Figure 4.3 this is plotted against the customs component of the LPI.

Again, a strong correlation exists between the customs components of the LPI and the newly constructed foreign customs restrictiveness index of this study. The fewer customs restrictions faced by LSPs, then the better the perceived customs performance within that economy.

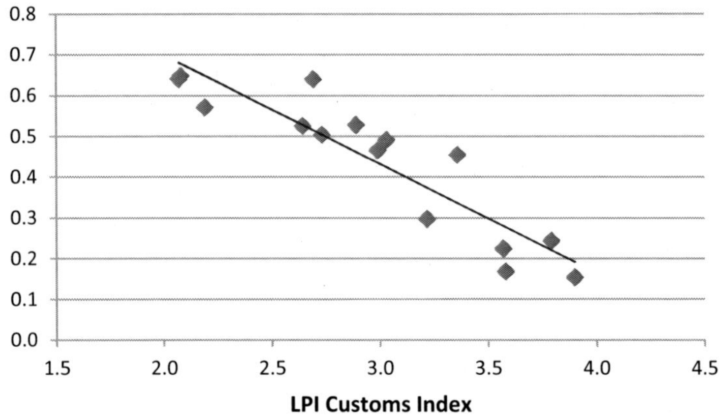

Figure 4.3. LPI Customs Index versus Foreign Customs Restrictiveness Index

4.5 Recent Logistics Sector Reforms

Indonesia[5]

Indonesia's geography and the distribution of industry and resources pose major challenges for efficient and low cost logistics. Indonesia is the world's largest archipelago spanning more than 5,000 kilometres. About 60 per cent of its population of about 240 million people live on Java but the remainder is distributed among 6,000 inhabited islands which are often very sparsely populated. Java is also the centre of manufacturing, while resources are widely spread over the archipelago. Although Indonesia has 25 strategic ports and 27 airports with international status, domestic and international transport hubs are focused on Jakarta, in Java, creating major challenges for inter-island connectivity and development. Many of the inter-island connections are conducted through small commercial and non-commercial ports and hundreds of small domestic airports.

The challenges are revealed in Indonesia's logistics performance. According to the World Bank, the cost of shipping of a 40ft container

[5] This section is based on Herliana and Parsons (2011).

from Padang on the coast of West Sumatra to Jakarta is currently USD 600, while transporting the same container from Jakarta to Singapore costs USD 185, despite the latter being further away. In addition, differences in logistics costs are an important reason why rice prices in one province can be up to 64 per cent higher than in another (World Bank 2010). The high cost differentials among regions on products like staple foods and basic products for industry and construction are constraints on development.

The issues associated with the distribution of resources, industry and people have taken on new importance in recent years, given greater regional and provincial autonomy. Popularly elected governments and officials across the economy are demanding a large share of national development. While Indonesia had a long-standing record of successful structural reforms, these were carried out either under more autocratic regimes or under International Monetary Fund conditionality associated with the economic recovery programs following the Asian economic crisis of 1997–98. Structural reforms in the logistics and transport sectors in Indonesia are now part of the wider economic reform agenda of the Yudhoyono Government. They are being undertaken in an entirely different context — one of democracy and open debate, pluralism and regional autonomy.

On the one hand this makes the policy reform agenda more complex and challenging. On the other hand it has enabled new actors to press for change in a way that they were not able to do before. The activism of some of these groups is also driven by the urgency of infrastructure reform after many years of delays in progress. The lack of quality infrastructure, especially in the transport sectors and in the provinces, is now a clear constraint to growth and improved competitiveness. It is holding back domestic and foreign investment that is critical for Indonesia's long term growth and development objectives.

The key drivers of structural reform in logistics and transport in Indonesia now are:

- *Domestic business and foreign investors,* who are concerned about the cost of doing business in Indonesia in existing areas and who believe that opportunities are being missed to expand business in the potentially lucrative regions. They stress the urgency of action and the importance of finding short-term solutions along with the longer-term programs. Foreign investors are also concerned that Indonesia cannot be integrated into their supply chains without efficient logistics.

- *The 33 provinces of Indonesia,* which often face the consequences of the high cost of domestic transport and logistics and which are constrained in their ability to attract more domestic and foreign investment in other sectors without adequate transport and logistics. Popular elections and regional autonomy mean that the provinces are much more active in domestic political debate.
- *The Ministry of Trade,* which oversees both domestic and international trade and views the poor performance in logistics as a constraint to export growth.
- *The Ministry of Industry,* which is developing an ambitious agenda for the revitalization of industry, including in the provinces. The share of manufacturing in GDP has not returned to that seen before the Asian economic crisis, and the lack of good infrastructure and logistics is seen as an impediment to markedly increasing this share. Cutting the costs of logistics and domestic transport is a pillar for the Ministry's regional development policy.
- *Obligations under the ASEAN Economic Community Blueprint* commit Indonesia, along with the other major ASEAN economies, to open the logistics sector by 2013.[6] While there is some concern about foreign competition in parts of the logistics sector, there is also pressure to prepare for the target date set by ASEAN. This commitment in ASEAN is being reinforced by the development of the Supply Chain Framework in the APEC forum.

---

[6] ASEAN initiatives include the ASEAN Framework Agreement on Multi-modal Transportation in 2005; the ASEAN Economic Community Blueprint 2007 initiatives on Single Market and Production Base, Competitive Economic Region, Equitable Economic Development, and Full Integration into Global Economy; the ASEAN Integration Protocol for the Logistics Services Sector in 2013–2015; the ASEAN Roadmap for the Integration of Logistics Services in 2007; the ASEAN Multilateral Agreement on the Full Liberalization of Air Freight Services; the ASEAN Multilateral Agreement on Air Services; and the ASEAN Framework Agreement on the Facilitation of Inter-State Transport.

- *Stronger international competition brought about through Free Trade Agreements* is already putting pressure on manufacturing sectors that are intensive users of logistics. There is a clear understanding in business and government that logistics performance remains critical to Indonesia's ability to integrate through global and regional supply chains.

There is also a fiscal dimension to the drivers of reform. State-owned enterprises and others who have enjoyed monopolies in the sectors associated with transport and logistics have often been reluctant to give up their exclusive ownership, but the government's inability to fund sufficient infrastructure from the state's budget means that they are now less active in opposition to reform.

Finally, these changes take place in an international context, as the last two items on the list above indicate. On the one hand the international context places competitive pressures on the Indonesian economy. But on the other hand it also provides various forms of international cooperation, including commitments to ASEAN and through APEC's focus on trade facilitation and connectivity through its supply chain initiative. This informational context provides both encouragement and credibility for the components of Indonesia's plan.

Indonesia has been undertaking major and simultaneous structural reforms in the logistics and transport sectors since 2007. Table 4.4 provides a summary of the legal and regulatory reforms that have been made and highlights those that are still currently underway. The foundations of these reforms were made through new laws for rail, shipping, aviation, and traffic and land transport. These changes were largely motivated by the need to increase private investment in new infrastructure and to reduce the dependency on the state budget to meet growing demand throughout the economy for more modern and efficient infrastructure and transport related services.

From 2010 new operational plans are being developed for logistics and ports and rail. The structural reforms show a trajectory away from government ownership to private sector participation and more independent regulation. This movement is ongoing, with further deregulation foreshadowed in many sectors.

Table 4.4. Indonesia's Logistics and Transport Reform Agenda

Reform	*Time frame*
National Logistics Blueprint	To be released 2010
Transportation: deregulation of transport sector	Started 1990s
New Laws	
Rail	2007
Shipping	2008
Aviation	2009
Traffic and Land Transport	2009
Master Plans	
New National Ports Master Plan	Under way
New National Rail Master Plan	Under way

Thus substantial reforms are already in progress in the component transport sectors. It has also been important to coordinate reform across these sectors. The response has been the development of a National Blueprint for the development of the logistics sector. This plan is challenging in its scope — in the number of sectors involved and the number of agencies involved. The formal plan is about to be released but a substantial amount of work has already been completed. Key principles for the design of its implementation have already been identified. The next steps are the schedule of measures of implementation. During these stages, the momentum will depend on some of the key reform champions noted above.

Thailand[7]

In general, international road transport services in Thailand are not open to competition. Cross-border transport between Thailand and neighbouring economies is allowed only between border cities (ie those up to seven kilometres from the border). Cross-border transport must be operated under bilateral agreements such as the Thailand–Malaysia and Thailand–Lao PDR Agreement or multilateral agreements such as the ASEAN Economic Cooperation Agreement and the Asian Development Bank Greater Mekong Sub-region Economic Cooperation Program. The government generally regulates international haulage by having an

[7] This section is based on Pomlaktong *et al.* (2011).

international haulage licence quota, with operators selected and approved by the Department of Land Transport.

Under these agreements an international road transport operator must be a Thai juristic person, whose head office must be located in Thai territory. Foreigners are allowed to have equity participation of no more than 49 per cent. International road transport under the Land Transport Act BE2522 (1979) is categorized as:

- Fixed Route and Non-Fixed Route International Road transport services — the providers must be either a limited company, a limited public company or a Thai government organization; and
- Private International Road Transport Service (Commercial) — the providers must be either a registered ordinary partnership, a limited company or a limited public company.

The international road transport service providers must have been domestic road transport service providers beforehand. The licence fee of THB 2,500 (USD 77.4) is for a 5-year period.

The Thailand–Lao PDR Agreement is the first bilateral agreement to be liberalized. This has been the result of pressure from transport users in the face of poor service and high charges.

From 1978 to 1990 cross-border transport between Thailand and Lao PDR was a monopoly under the Express Transportation Organization of Thailand (ETO), a government enterprise. In 1991 the ETO had its licences on this route terminated because Lao PDR appealed its expensive service fee. The Thai Cabinet approved T.L. Enterprise, a joint venture between Thailand and Lao PDR, to become the monopoly transport operator. In response to many complaints about its monopoly, the Ministry of Transport opened the market for competition in 1992. In this first year, there were five transport operators. In 2004, the governments of Thailand and Lao PDR agreed to open the market for cross-border transport of both passengers (non-fixed route) and freight without quota limitation, since previously the transport costs were very high. In the year of liberalization, the total number of international freight transport operators increased from two (who only operated on the

Thailand–Malaysia route) to 123 (including those on the Thailand–Lao PDR route).[8]

Cross-border transport between Thailand and Lao PDR is now highly competitive among domestic operators — 226 international truck licences and 57 international non-fixed route bus licences have been issued (Table 4.5). In comparison, international freight transport between Thailand and Malaysia is an oligopoly as it has a quota limitation and only allows the transport of perishable goods from Thailand to Singapore through Malaysia. Banomyong (no date) reports that as a result of the agreement, freight rates fell by 20–30 per cent between Vientiane and Thai ports. Banomyong points out some logistical constraints on the agreement's impact on routes other than between the major points. One of these is the report by Thai operators that Lao authorities continue to insist that some Thai trucks be re-loaded on to Lao trucks at the border. Also, partnership operators may have difficulty in meeting the legal requirements of the agreement (which refers to 'juristic persons').

The operation of a cross-border non-fixed or chartered route bus was also liberalized between Thailand and Lao PDR. However, the fixed route international bus service between Thailand and Lao PDR is a monopoly run by Transport Company Ltd (Thailand), a government-owned enterprise of Thailand and the government-owned Bus Enterprise

Table 4.5. Number of International Transport Operating Licences in Thailand, 2007

International licence	*Total number of licences*	*Total number of vehicles*
Non-Fixed Route Bus	57	177
Fixed Route Bus	2	–
Non-Fixed Route Truck (Transport Operators)	229	8,979
Thailand–Malaysia (only perishable goods)	3	79
Thailand–Lao PDR	226	8,900
Private Transport (Own Account)		
Truck (Thailand–Lao PDR)	84	861

Note: A non-fixed route bus is a 'for hire' vehicle.
Source: Department of Land Transport, Land Transport Promotion Centre, 2010.

[8] Note that the cross-border road transport service between Thailand and Malaysia is still an oligopoly. There are currently three transport operators under this agreement.

of Laos. Currently, there are five fixed routes of international transport between Thailand and Lao PDR: (1) Nongkhai–Vientiane, (2) Udonthani–Nongkhai–Vientiane, (3) Ubonratchathaini–Pak se, (4) Vientiane–Khon Kaen and (5) Savannakhet–Mukdahan. Fares are difficult to compare between bus routes because of the differences in service quality, but the entry of chartered buses provides consumers with more options.

4.6 Conclusion

Past studies have explored the regulatory performance within specific logistics sub-sectors such as maritime and aviation. This is the first study of its kind to measure a regulatory index of the entire logistics sector. The results of this study have illustrated that large differences exist in the regulatory environment for logistics of the ASEAN+6 economies. Many of these economies are open to trade in logistics services, while others are relatively restrictive.

Clear relationships exist between the perceived performance of the logistics sector and the regulatory environment — a less restricted trade environment results in better perceived performance for the logistics sector. This relationship has in turn created pressure for change. In Indonesia, the key champions of reform have included domestic business and foreign investors, as well as the 33 provinces, where economic development depends crucially on adequate transport and logistics links. In Thailand too, the government has responded to complaints about poor service and high costs on the Thailand–Lao PDR route with liberalization initiatives that have dramatically increased the extent of competition.

Table 4.A.1. Logistics Restrictiveness Index for Domestic Suppliers

	Customs	*Invest-ment*	*Movt. of people*	*Maritime*	*Aviation*	*Road*	*Other*	*Total*
Australia	0.0756	0.0184	0.0000	0.0000	0.0000	0.0000	0.0026	0.0966
Brunei	0.2025	0.0246	0.0000	0.0097	0.0000	0.0000	0.0000	0.2368
Cambodia	0.2817	0.0324	0.0324	0.0097	0.0000	0.0000	0.0026	0.3588
China	0.2010	0.0533	0.0194	0.0194	0.0065	0.0324	0.0026	0.3346
India	0.2812	0.0583	0.0194	0.0194	0.0065	0.0000	0.0026	0.3874
Indonesia	0.2353	0.0404	0.0194	0.0330	0.0000	0.0000	0.0052	0.3333
Japan	0.1134	0.0194	0.0194	0.0000	0.0065	0.0000	0.0026	0.1613
Korea, Rep.	0.1398	0.0430	0.0194	0.0000	0.0000	0.0000	0.0000	0.2022
Lao PDR	0.3403	0.0456	0.0324	0.0000	0.0000	0.0000	0.0000	0.4182
Malaysia	0.2060	0.0634	0.0246	0.0330	0.0000	0.0324	0.0052	0.3645
Myanmar	0.2839	0.0401	0.0129	0.0097	0.0000	0.0000	0.0026	0.3493
New Zealand	0.1096	0.0181	0.0000	0.0000	0.0000	0.0000	0.0000	0.1277
Philippines	0.2485	0.0362	0.0194	0.0459	0.0000	0.0324	0.0026	0.3851
Singapore	0.0685	0.0000	0.0000	0.0000	0.0000	0.0000	0.0000	0.0685
Thailand	0.2201	0.0505	0.0194	0.0194	0.0065	0.0324	0.0052	0.3535
Viet Nam	0.2471	0.0503	0.0194	0.0330	0.0065	0.0324	0.0000	0.3886
Australia	0.0756	0.0184	0.0000	0.0000	0.0000	0.0000	0.0026	0.0966
Brunei	0.2025	0.0246	0.0000	0.0097	0.0000	0.0000	0.0000	0.2368
Cambodia	0.2817	0.0324	0.0324	0.0097	0.0000	0.0000	0.0026	0.3588

Source: Authors' calculations.

Table 4.A.2. Logistics Restrictiveness Index for Foreign Suppliers

	Customs	*Invest-ment*	*Movt. of people*	*Maritime*	*Aviation*	*Road*	*Other*	*Total*
Australia	0.0756	0.0184	0.0155	0.0000	0.0259	0.0000	0.0026	0.1380
Brunei	0.2025	0.0375	0.0207	0.0227	0.0291	0.0324	0.0000	0.3449
Cambodia	0.2817	0.0453	0.0472	0.0356	0.0453	0.0000	0.0026	0.4578
China	0.2204	0.1051	0.0194	0.0324	0.1294	0.0647	0.0026	0.5741
India	0.3006	0.0583	0.0194	0.0453	0.0647	0.0000	0.0026	0.4909
Indonesia	0.2451	0.0922	0.0406	0.0718	0.0841	0.0000	0.0052	0.5390
Japan	0.1134	0.0194	0.0350	0.0194	0.0453	0.0000	0.0026	0.2351
Korea, Rep.	0.1398	0.0689	0.0278	0.0194	0.0453	0.0000	0.0000	0.3012
Lao PDR	0.3403	0.0585	0.0453	0.0388	0.0453	0.0000	0.0000	0.5282
Malaysia	0.2157	0.1152	0.0401	0.0718	0.0744	0.0647	0.0052	0.5872
Myanmar	0.2839	0.0531	0.0259	0.0291	0.0453	0.0324	0.0026	0.4722
New Zealand	0.1096	0.0181	0.0117	0.0000	0.0259	0.0000	0.0000	0.1653
Philippines	0.2485	0.0621	0.0258	0.0731	0.1036	0.0324	0.0026	0.5481
Singapore	0.0685	0.0259	0.0122	0.0387	0.0129	0.0000	0.0000	0.1582
Thailand	0.2298	0.0764	0.0362	0.0388	0.0453	0.0645	0.0052	0.4962
Viet Nam	0.2568	0.0632	0.0278	0.0912	0.0518	0.0324	0.0000	0.5231
Australia	0.0756	0.0184	0.0155	0.0000	0.0259	0.0000	0.0026	0.1380
Brunei	0.2025	0.0375	0.0207	0.0227	0.0291	0.0324	0.0000	0.3449
Cambodia	0.2817	0.0453	0.0472	0.0356	0.0453	0.0000	0.0026	0.4578

Source: Authors' calculations.

Chapter 5

Impact of Air and Maritime Restrictions on International Transport Margins[1]

Patricia Sourdin

5.1 Introduction

Transport costs are often viewed as technologically determined but in practice they vary considerably across different bilateral trade flows. Some of the variation is due to distance and other geographical constraints and some reflects the commodity composition of trade. However, port infrastructure and corrupt customs officials are policy-related trade barriers, while other determinants of transport costs may be indirectly policy-related. For example, a lack of competition among shippers may be due to low volumes or to the non-implementation of an anti-monopoly policy. Variations related to institutional settings such as poor law enforcement increase trade risks and hence affect insurance rates and inventory costs.

The importance of understanding better what determines trade costs stems from their impact on international trade flows. Higher trade costs significantly impede trade for some, and since the major component of trade costs is undoubtedly the transport component, a

[1] This chapter is based on a paper produced with funding from the Asia Pacific Economic Cooperation's Policy Support Unit and material from that paper is reproduced with its permission. Information is taken from The Impacts and Benefits of Structural Reforms in the Transport, Energy and Telecommunications Sectors in APEC Economies APEC#211-SE-01.1. The views expressed in this paper are those of the authors and do not necessarily represent those of the APEC Secretariat or APEC Member Economies.

better understanding of its determinants ensures policy makers are equipped with the best instruments with which to reduce them.

The purpose of this chapter is to identify the major determinants of air and maritime transport costs for merchandise exports from APEC members towards four major trading partners — Australia, Brazil, Chile and the United States — using commodity level data at the 6-digit level of aggregation of the Harmonized System (HS).[2] The chapter discusses data and methodology, econometric analysis and results, and finally presents some conclusions.

5.2 Data Description

The dataset used throughout the analysis consists of import data collected by the customs agencies of four importing economies — Australia, Brazil, Chile and the United States — at the 6-digit level of aggregation of the HS. The data contain detailed records of import value, weight, cost, insurance and freight (cif) values and free on board (fob) values and commodity codes for the years 1990–2008. The four economies are notable for compiling both cif and fob data on a comparable basis. In this section of the paper the trends in *ad valorem* transport costs over time are analysed as well as trends across exporting APEC members for 1990–2008. *Ad valorem* transport costs are calculated from the data as the difference between the cif and fob values divided by the fob value *(cif–fob)/fob* for each importer/exporter, year and 6-digit product combination.

Trends in transport costs over time are calculated and analysed in the following ways. Aggregate, *ad valorem* and import-weighted transport costs are calculated for each exporting APEC member for each year by mode of transport. In addition, and following Hummels (2007) and Moreira, Volpe and Blyde (2008), *ad valorem* transport costs are calculated and adjusted for commodity composition and changes in the

[2] The author is grateful to the Economic Research Institute for ASEAN and East Asia (ERIA) in Jakarta for generously making the data available.

value-to-weight ratio over time. This is achieved by regressing 6-digit *ad valorem* transport costs on the value-to-weight ratio and year dummies and economy-pair-product fixed effects. The exponentiated, predicted *ad valorem* transport costs by year are the adjusted values which control for changing commodity composition and trade partners over time.

The Annex Tables A1 to A3 in Sourdin (2011) reported the import-weighted *ad valorem* transport costs overall and by mode of transport for each APEC member to all four pooled importers. (The importers were pooled to alleviate the problem of a small number of transactions for some of the smaller APEC economies.) The data highlighted that in 2008, Mexico, Singapore, Malaysia, Canada and Japan had the lowest value of *ad valorem* transport costs. Low values were also evident for Brunei and Papua New Guinea, although the small number of trade flows from these two economies rendered the values less statistically reliable. Overall, several APEC members had a reduction in transport costs of over 50 per cent over the period 1990–2008. These included Chile, Mexico, New Zealand, Peru, the Russian Federation (where data were only available from 1992), Papua New Guinea and Brunei. For ocean transport, the economies with a greater than 50 per cent reduction in transport costs were Mexico, Chile, and Brunei, while for air transport they were Canada, China, Indonesia, the Republic of Korea and Chinese Taipei.

Analysing trends by importing economy, Figures 5.1 to 5.4 graph average, import-weighted *ad valorem* transport costs for each of the importing economies in the dataset. For the United States (Figure 5.1), the trend is downward for air transport costs, but otherwise there is not a great decline for sea transport or for APEC members in general. Australian imports, on the other hand, show a clear downward trend for all four series (Figure 5.2). Chilean and Brazilian imports (Figures 5.3 and 5.4) are more volatile but the trend is downward overall. Pooling the four importers in Figure 5.5 shows a clear downward trend for air freight charges and significantly less so for sea freight, APEC freight costs and overall freight charges.

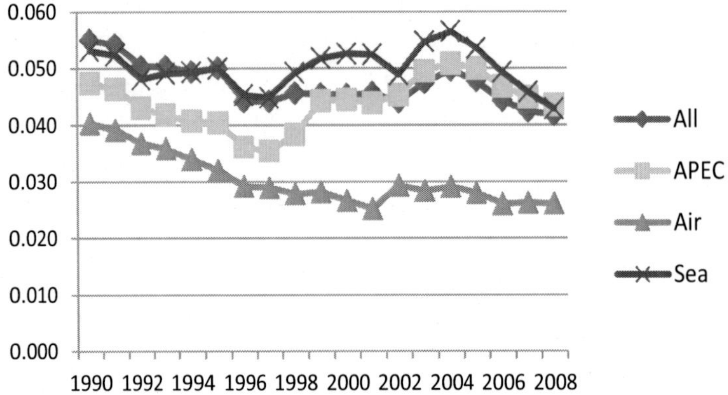

Figure 5.1. *Ad Valorem* Trade Costs on Imports to the United States (ratio)

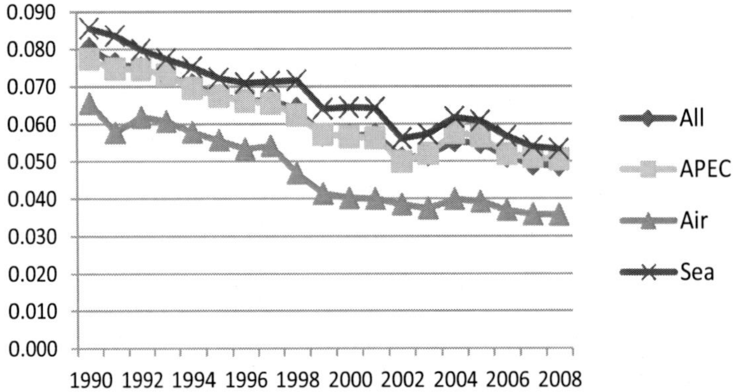

Figure 5.2. *Ad Valorem* Trade Costs on Imports to Australia (ratio)

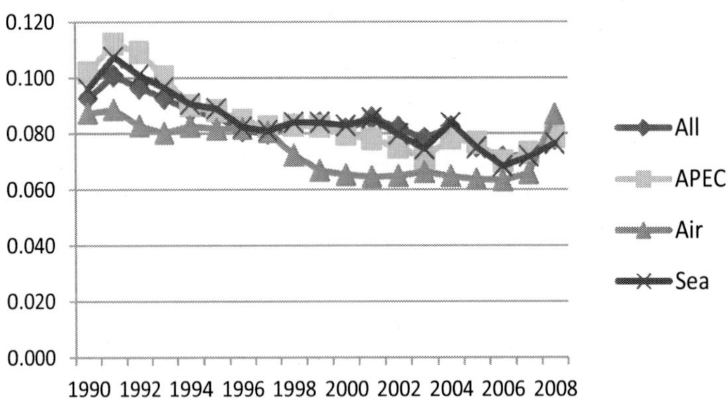

Figure 5.3. *Ad Valorem* Trade Costs on Imports to Chile (ratio)

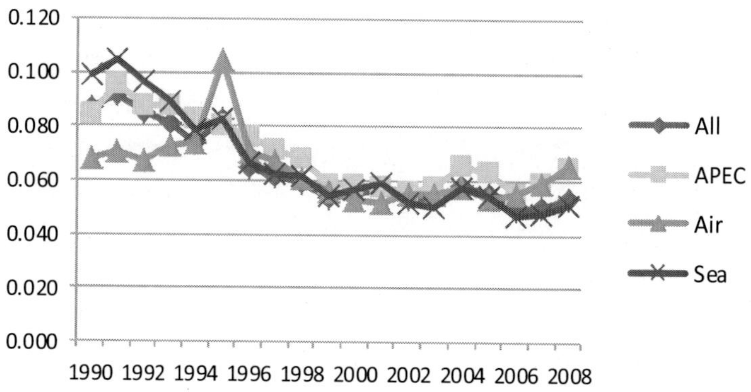

Figure 5.4. *Ad Valorem* Trade Costs on Imports to Brazil (ratio)

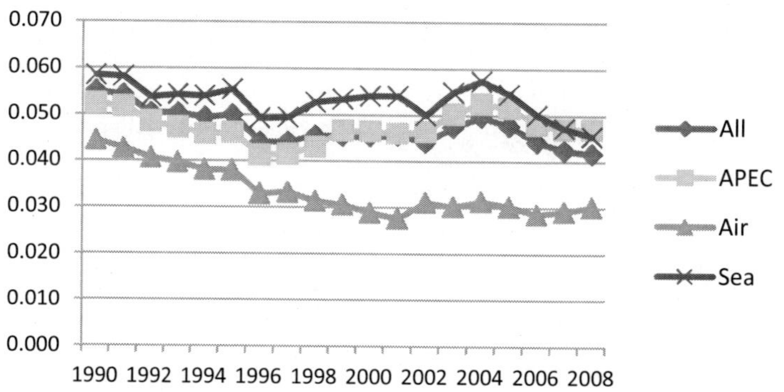

Figure 5.5. *Ad Valorem* Trade Costs on Imports to the United States, Australia, Chile and Brazil Combined (ratio)

Once we adjust for commodity composition, the changing value-to-weight ratios and changes in trading partners over time, the average overall transport costs are higher and exhibit smaller percentage declines over time (Annex Table A4 in Sourdin (2011)). The individual APEC economies' adjusted transport costs are graphed in Figure 5.6.

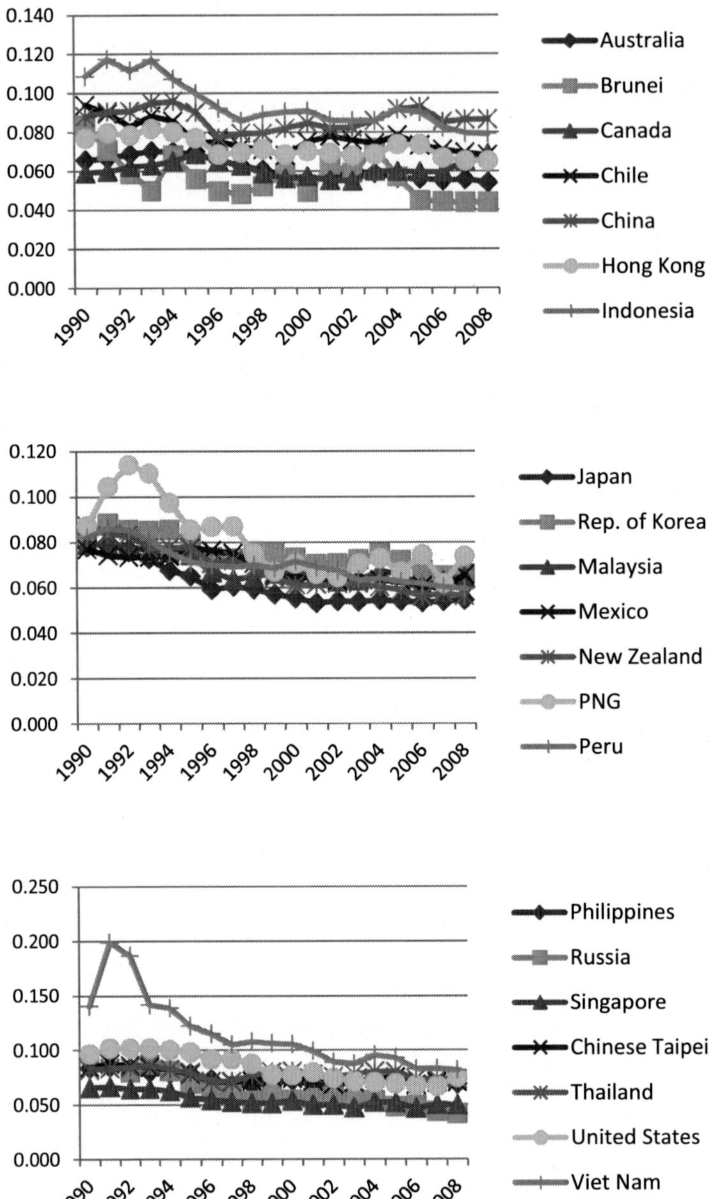

Figure 5.6. Average Adjusted *Ad Valorem* Trade Costs, Selected APEC Economies (ratio)

5.3 Determinants of Transport Costs

There is an extensive literature examining the determinants of transport costs. Several factors have been found to have a robust and significant influence.

Higher volumes of bilateral trade on routes allow shippers to take advantage of scale economies and thus lower freight charges. This is likely to influence ocean shipped goods more than air shipped goods. Related to volume are trade imbalances, where high volumes of trade in one direction are not matched by the volumes of trade on the return leg. If vessels are forced to return empty, this will be reflected in the price charged for shipping. On some routes there are significant differences in the prices of hauling containers on the eastbound or westbound direction. When the trade imbalance is very high, such as on the US–Asia and Asia–US routes, the price of transporting a container one way can be close to double that of hauling it back.[3]

An obvious determinant of transport costs is geography, especially distance. Transport costs are increasing in distance, but there are clearly non-linearities in this relation because of high fixed costs. Distance is strongly positively correlated with time, and increasingly, time costs influence the ability for exporters to fit into global supply chains, which depend crucially on timely delivery.

The presence of market power and lack of competition on routes will adversely affect freight charges. Similarly, restrictive regulatory policies related to transport services would significantly raise prices above marginal cost if they act to impede the competitive environment in which the transport sector operates. A measure of competition is the number of carriers servicing a particular economy, as well as measures of restrictive regulatory environments.

The number of carriers is obtained from UNCTAD's Liner Shipping Connectivity Index (*LSCI*) which lists the number of liner companies operating on a route. Table 5.1 shows the data on numbers of liner companies for APEC economies in 2008. China, the United States and

[3] See the Containerization International website at www.ci-online.co.uk.

Table 5.1. Number of Liner Companies

APEC Member	*Liner Companies*	*APEC Member*	*Liner Companies*
China	88	Australia	37
United States	84	Russian Federation	36
Singapore	80	Canada	35
Hong Kong	70	Mexico	30
Republic of Korea	69	New Zealand	27
Malaysia	68	Philippines	26
Japan	65	Peru	23
Chinese Taipei	49	Chile	21
Thailand	46	Brunei	6
Viet Nam	41	Papua New Guinea	6
Indonesia	38		

Source: UNCTAD Liner Shipping Connectivity Index.

Hong Kong have the highest number of liner companies, which is to be expected given the large volumes of containerized trade for these economies. The overall Liner Shipping Connectivity Index also includes other elements of connectivity: TEU deployed (where TEU stands for twenty-foot equivalent, a measure of shipping capacity), number of vessels, shipping opportunities and maximum size (TEU) of a ship on a specific route. The overall index, as well as its various components, are used in subsequent analysis.

For the general regulatory environment in the air and ocean transport sectors, two constructed indices are used — one for air and one for sea. The sea index in Table 5.2 is taken from Bertho (2011), and higher values are associated with fewer restrictions. The air index in Table 5.3 is taken from Zhang and Findlay (2011), and higher values are indicative of a greater degree of restrictiveness. The sea index covers cabotage restrictions, cargo handling restrictions, quotas for private or government cargo, the availability of exemptions for carrier agreements from competition law, and the existence of an independent regulatory authority. It also covers some direct barriers to services trade — foreign equity limits, limits on the legal form of establishment (branches, subsidiaries) of foreign greenfield operations, whether foreign operators can take a controlling stake in existing private or public entities, and whether there are nationality requirements on the employees or boards of

Table 5.2. Sea Index for APEC Economies

	Quotas for govt. or private cargo	*Exemptions of carrier agreements from competition law*	*Form of ownership (greenfield branches and subsids. allowed)*	*Percentage of foreign ownership*	*Foreign controlling stake in public and private entities allowed*	*Nationality requirement on employees*	*Nationality requirement on BOD*	*Cabotage restrictions*	*Cargo handling restrictions*	*Indep. regulatory authority*	*Simple average*
Australia	1	0	0.5	1	1	0	1	1	1	1	0.75
Canada	1	1	0.5	1	1	0	0	0	na	1	0.61
Chile	1	1	1	1	1	na	na	0	na	1	0.86
China	1	1	0.5	0.49	0	1	1	0	1	0	0.60
Hong Kong	1	1	1	1	na	na	na	nr	1	na	1.00
Indonesia	0.5	1	0.5	0.49	1	1	1	0	1	0	0.65
Japan	1	0	0.5	1	1	na	0	0	1	1	0.61
Rep. of Korea	1	0	0.5	1	1	0	1	0	na	1	0.61
Malaysia	1	1	1	0.3	0	na	na	0	na	1	0.61
Mexico	1	1	1	1	1	0	1	0	na	0	0.67
New Zealand	1	0	0.5	1	1	na	na	1	1	1	0.81
Peru	1	1	1	1	1	0	0	0	na	0	0.56
Philippines	0	1	0.5	0.4	na	1	0	0	0	1	0.43
Russia	0	1	0.5	1	1	1	1	0	1	0	0.65
Singapore	1	0	0.5	1	na	na	na	nr	1	na	0.70
Chinese Taipei	1	0	1	na	na	na	na	0.5	0	0	0.42
Thailand	0.5	1	1	0.49	0	1	0	0	0	0	0.40
United States	0	0	0.5	1	1	0	0	0	1	1	0.45
Viet Nam	1	1	0	0	0.5	0	0	0	0	0	0.25

Notes: na = not available, nr = not relevant.
Source: Bertho (2011).

Table 5.3. Air Index for APEC Economies

	Privatized	*Foreign equity*	*Low cost airline*	*Effective competitors*	*Desig-nation*	*Open skies*	*7th freedom*	*Total score*
Australia	0	0	0	0.5	0.5	0	0	1
Brunei	1	0	1	1	1	0	0	4
Canada	0	0.75	0	1	1	0	0	2.75
Chile	0	0	1	1	1	0	0	3
China	0.67	0.5	0.5	0	0.5	1	1	4.17
Hong Kong	0	0	0.5	1	1	0	1	3.5
Indonesia	1	0.5	0.5	0	0.5	0.5	0	3
Japan	0	0.75	0.5	0	0	0.5	1	2.75
Republic of Korea	0	0.5	0.5	0.5	0	0.5	1	3
Malaysia	0.67	0.5	0	0	0.5	0	0	1.67
Mexico	0	0.5	0.5	0.5	0	0	1	2.5
New Zealand	0.67	0	0.5	0.5	0.5	0	0	2.17
Peru	0	0.5	0.5	0.5	0.5	0	0	2
Philippines	0	0.5	0.5	0	0.5	1	1	3.5
Russia	0.67	0.75	0.5	0	0.5	0	1	3.42
Singapore	0.67	0	0	0.5	0	0	0	1.17
Chinese Taipei	0.67	0.5	1	0.5	0	0.5	0	3.17
Thailand	0.67	0.5	0	0	0.5	0	0	1.67
United States	0	0.75	0	0	0	0	0	0.75
Viet Nam	1	0.5	0.5	0.5	1	0.5	0	4

Source: Zhang and Findlay (2011).

directors of foreign companies. The air index covers privatization of national airlines, foreign equity participation in domestic airlines, the existence of low cost carriers, the number of effective passenger airlines (indicating ease of entry), whether there is multiple designation on international routes, whether there are more than two open skies agreements, and whether seventh freedom cargo rights are granted to at least some foreign carriers.

Higher quality infrastructure, higher quality of logistics services and improvements in and implementation of trade facilitation measures also play significant roles in lowering transport costs. Port and airport infrastructure affect transport costs in several ways. For example, technological advances mean that cargo can be loaded and unloaded more rapidly and thus create gains in efficiency. Infrastructure levels are highly correlated with economic development and GDP per capita.

The World Economic Forum's Global Competitiveness Report surveys enterprises regarding port and airport infrastructure and efficiency in 135 economies (Porter and Schwab 2008). The survey assigns economies a score on a scale of 1 to 7, with a score of 1 for underdeveloped infrastructure and 7 for infrastructure that is as developed as the world's best, and then ranks them according to the results. Among APEC members, Singapore and Hong Kong, China are ranked 1st and 2nd, respectively, with respect to port and airport infrastructure quality. Of the other APEC members, only Australia, Canada, and the United States rank in the top 20 for airport infrastructure, while Canada, Malaysia, Chinese Taipei and the United States rank in the top 20 for port infrastructure (Table 5.4).

Table 5.4. Global Competitiveness Report Infrastructure Rankings

APEC member	*Airport rank*	*Port rank*
Australia	20	42
Brunei	39	36
Canada	18	15
Chile	25	37
China	75	55
Hong Kong	2	2
Indonesia	76	105
Japan	50	26
Republic of Korea	27	30
Malaysia	21	16
Mexico	57	95
New Zealand	24	24
Papua New Guinea	n/a	n/a
Peru	95	128
Philippines	90	101
Russia	89	77
Singapore	1	1
Chinese Taipei	33	19
Thailand	29	49
United States	13	12
Viet Nam	93	113

Source: Porter and Schwab (2008).

General institutional quality and corruption is another potentially important determinant of transport costs. Where there is a known problem of bribe-taking by customs officials at port or at airport level or where there may be uncertainty or risk to the merchandise being transported, transport firms will pass some of these costs on to exporters, so transport costs will be higher from those destinations. Sequeira and Djankov (2008) provide detailed evidence from two African ports.

An indicator of corruption is the Corruption Perceptions Index (*cpi*) compiled by Transparency International.[4] This is a general perceptions index of the level of public and political sector corruption and bribe-taking, which may impact on transport costs. The index relates perceptions of the degree of corruption and ranges between 10 (highly clean) and 0 (highly corrupt). APEC members range between 2 and 9.3 for 2008 (Table 5.5). For 2008 the Corruption Perceptions Index is highly correlated with air and port infrastructure (0.82 for port and 0.79 for air).

Transport costs are influenced by a commodity's value-to-weight ratio, since heavy, low value-added items are more expensive to transport than are light, high-value-added ones. In part, this is due to higher insurance charges, which are included in the transport cost variable (*cif–*

Table 5.5. APEC Rankings in the Corruption Perceptions Index 2008

APEC member	*Ranking*	*APEC member*	*Ranking*
New Zealand	9.3	China	3.6
Singapore	9.2	Mexico	3.6
Australia	8.7	Peru	3.6
Canada	8.7	Thailand	3.5
Hong Kong	8.1	Viet Nam	2.7
Japan	7.3	Indonesia	2.6
United States	7.3	Philippines	2.3
Chile	6.9	Russian Federation	2.1
Chinese Taipei	5.7	Papua New Guinea	2.0
Republic of Korea	5.6	Brunei	na
Malaysia	5.1		

Note: na = not available.
Source: Transparency International website.

[4] This is available at http://www.transparency.org/policy_research/surveys_indices/cpi/overview.

fob)/fob, but are generally proportional to the value of the goods since higher value-added goods may also attract higher quality freight services. There is a trend for goods to become lighter with technological advances, and increases over time in the value-to-weight ratio mean that air transport becomes more attractive and less costly. Consequently, we expect the share of air shipped goods to be increasing over time.

Figure 5.7 graphs the air share of imports for Australia, Brazil, Chile and the United States between 1990 and 2008. The air share of imports from APEC members by value and by reporter does not exhibit any clear trend over the period 1990–2008. For Australia, Brazil and Chile there was an increase in the air share of imports in the mid to late 1990s, while for the United States the rise in the share commenced earlier. All four economies have experienced a reduction in the air share of their imports since around 2000.

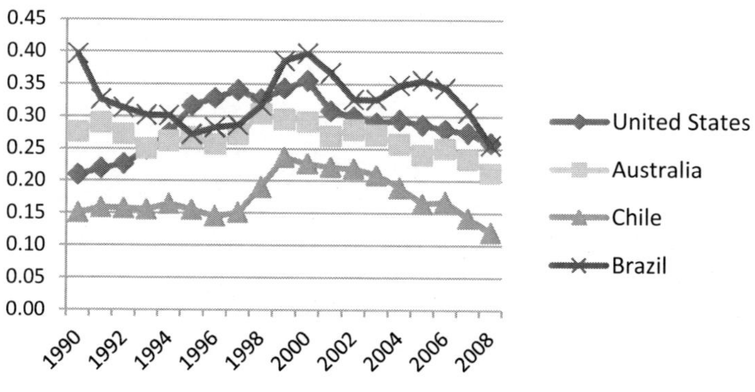

Figure 5.7. Air Share of Imports by Value for United States, Australia, Chile and Brazil (ratio)

5.4 Estimating a Model of Transport Costs

Estimating framework

In this section, the determinants of air and sea transport costs for APEC member exports to four large economies — Australia, Brazil, Chile and the United States — are analysed econometrically. The modelling approach incorporates as many of the factors identified above as possible.

As the previous discussion has highlighted, there are many factors contributing to the determination of freight costs. Our modelling strategy follows earlier studies (for example, Micco and Serebrisky 2006, Clark, Dollar and Micco 2004, Fink, Mattoo and Neagu 2002, Wilmsmeier and Hoffmann 2008, Hummels 2007, Hummels, Lygovysky and Skiba 2009, Micco and Pérez 2002, Mirza and Zitouna 2009, Moreira, Volpe and Blyde 2008 and Wilmsmeier, Hoffmann and Sanchez 2006) where we incorporate as many of the determinants as possible. Since many of the variables are highly correlated, it is not possible to include them all in one model as this leads to unstable coefficients across specifications. The modelling strategy begins with a baseline specification in which the main determinants of transport costs are considered. Several additional models are estimated which specifically control for factors such as those affecting competition on a route, factors related to infrastructure and efficiency and those which capture the general quality of the exporting economy's institutions.

For each transport mode, the baseline specification models transport costs in the following way:

$$\begin{aligned}\ln(f_{ijkt}) = \beta_0 + \beta_1 \ln(dist)_{ij} + \beta_2 \ln(imports_{ijt}) \\ + \beta_3 \ln(val/wgt)_{ijkt} + \alpha_k + \gamma_t + u_{ijkt}\end{aligned} \tag{5.1}$$

where i indexes partner economies, j indexes reporting economies, k indexes commodities imported by economy j disaggregated at the 6-digit level of the Harmonized System, and t indexes time. The dependent variable, $\ln(f_{ijkt})$, is the log of *ad valorem* freight charges. The baseline determinants of freight include $\ln(imports_{ijt})$ which is the log of the value of total imports from economy i to economy j in period t for each transport mode, $\ln(val/wgt)_{ijkt}$ is the log of the unit value of each good shipped and $\ln(dist)_{ij}$ is the log of distance between each economy pair. Distance is from Centre D'études Prospectives Et D'informations Internationales (CEPII) and is measured as the distance between two economies based on bilateral distances between the biggest cities of those two economies, those inter-city distances being weighted by the

share of the city in the overall economy's population. In addition, a product-specific fixed effect α_k is included and u_{ijkt} is the idiosyncratic error. The product fixed effects capture any commodity-specific features that influence freight costs but are difficult to quantify and not explicitly included in the models. For instance, these effects control for such things as the fact that bulky goods have higher transportation costs in every period than shipping shoes.

Freight costs are expected to be positively related to distance and negatively related to the value of imports since there exist economies of scale in transport, but this is perhaps more important for ocean freight. The value of imports may be endogenous in the model since imports also depend on transport costs. Ignoring this endogeneity may lead to biased estimates of the model parameters. When the models were estimated by two-stage least squares using GDP as an instrument, this resulted in implausible estimates with incorrect signs.

In the second specification, the focus is primarily on factors that affect the level of competition on shipping routes. For this, the baseline specification is augmented in turn with several variables that capture either a restrictive regulatory environment or the presence of market power. For these specifications, the baseline model for ocean freight is modified by the addition of the sea index and the model for air freight by the addition of the air index. These indexes capture the degree of restrictions in force on a route. Additional models for ocean freighted imports are estimated, which include various elements from UNCTAD's Liner Services Connectivity Index to capture the competitive features of the route. This second set of market power models therefore includes such things as number of carriers, number of ships or liner services operating on a route, as well as the overall Liner Services Connectivity Index (*LSCI*).

The third focus is on institutional quality in the exporting economy. To capture this feature, we include the Corruption Perceptions Index (*cpi*) for the exporting economy. This index is a general 'catch-all' variable that is expected to be negatively related to freight charges — that is, the higher the index, the better the institutional quality, and the lower the transport charge.

The final focus of this study accounts for the quality of infrastructure and trade facilitation measures. For these specifications, the baseline model is augmented by two measures to capture these features. The first infrastructure variable included is an index of port infrastructure quality (for ocean transport) in the exporting economy and a measure of air infrastructure quality (for air transport), both obtained from Porter and Schwab (2008). For trade facilitation quality, we include the Enabling Trade Index (*eti*) for the exporting economy, also from Porter and Schwab. The *eti* is another 'catch-all' variable composed of four sub-indexes to capture the main enablers of trade: (1) market access, (2) border administration, (3) transport and communications infrastructure, and (4) the business environment. We use the 2009 index, which is the latest available and relates to the year 2008. A higher value of the *eti* index indicates higher quality trade enabling measures in place.

Table 5.6 summarizes the expected direction of the relationships between the various determinants and transport costs.

Table 5.6. Expected Sign of Determinants of Transport Costs

Determinant	*Expected sign*	*Determinant*	*Expected sign*
Value total imports	(–)	Port/air infrastructure	(–)
Value/weight	(+)	Enabling trade index	(–)
Distance	(+)	Corruption perception index	(–)
LSCI and components	(–)		

Source: See text.

Results

The results from estimating transport cost models for ocean and air freight are presented in Tables 5.7 and 5.8. The positive relationship between distance and *ad valorem* transport costs is as expected, with robustly estimated elasticities ranging between 0.26 and 0.4.

The negative relationship expected between import volumes and transport costs is evident in the econometric results: depending on the model specification and other things being equal, the estimated elasticity is between –0.036 and as high as –0.07 for ocean freight (Table 5.7) and between –0.084 and –0.120 for air freight (Table 5.8). The negative

Table 5.7. Transport Cost Regressions for Ocean Shipped Goods

Dependent Variable	*(1)*	*(2)*	*(3)*	*(4)*	*(4a)*	*(4b)*	*(4c)*	*(5)*	*(6)*	*(7)*
Log(dist)	0.268***	0.304***	0.280***	0.322***	0.323***	0.319***	0.328***	0.315***	0.305***	0.273***
	(0.004)	(0.007)	(0.004)	(0.006)	(0.006)	(0.006)	(0.010)	(0.006)	(0.009)	(0.004)
Log(sea imports)	–0.068***	–0.036***	–0.071***						–0.041***	–0.040***
	(0.001)	(0.002)	(0.001)						(0.002)	(0.001)
Log(value/wgt)	–0.390***	–0.403***	–0.386***	–0.423***	–0.429***	–0.430***	–0.418***	–0.431***	–0.410***	–0.396***
	(0.003)	(0.005)	(0.003)	(0.004)	(0.004)	(0.004)	(0.006)	(0.004)	(0.006)	(0.003)
eti		–0.019***								
		(0.004)								
Sea index			–0.487***							
			(0.013)							
Log(ships)				–0.046***						
				(0.003)						
Log(liner services)					–0.024***					
					(0.003)					
Log(liner companies)						–0.033***				
						(0.005)				
Log(max ship size)							–0.027***			
							(0.008)			
LSCI								–0.000***		
								(0.000)		

Table 5.7. Continued.

Port infrastructure									–0.002	
									(0.003)	
cpi										–0.010***
										(0.001)
R-squared	0.271	0.200	0.279	0.214	0.236	0.239	0.210	0.239	0.202	0.244
N	1156239	137035	942441	217018	275996	284779	63115	284779	69601	713108
Years covered	1990–2008	2007–2008	1990–2008	2004–2008	2004–2008	2004–2008	2004–2008	2004–2008	2008	1998–2008

Notes: * p<0.1, ** p<0.05, *** p<0.01. Year dummies included but output suppressed. All models estimated by fixed effects with product fixed effects. Robust standard errors in parentheses. R-squared is the within R-squared. Models 4 and 5 are estimated for containerized shipments only as the LSCI relates to containerized traffic only.

Source: Author's calculations.

relationship reflects economies of scale on routes. However, the coefficient on imports loses all of its explanatory power and changes signs when included in models of ocean freight that also include *LSCI* competition variables (models 4 and 5), and so import volumes have been omitted from these particular models.

Port infrastructure is found to have no significant effect on maritime transport costs. These results are somewhat surprising, since other studies have found this variable significant (for example, Micco and Pérez 2002 and Clark, Dollar and Micco 2004).

Using an alternative measure of port infrastructure (maximum ship size), we find the impact of the size of ships that ports can accommodate has a strong negative impact on shipping costs. The coefficient is not high but is statistically significant. This result has implications for economies of scale and potential cost savings for economies that can take

Table 5.8. Transport Cost Regressions for Air Shipped Goods

Dependent Variable	*(1)*	*(2)*	*(3)*	*(4)*	*(5)*
Log(distance)	0.394***	0.257***	0.239***	0.250***	0.338***
	(0.003)	(0.006)	(0.007)	(0.007)	(0.004)
Log(air imports)	–0.084***	–0.108***	–0.117***	–0.120***	–0.102***
	(0.001)	(0.002)	(0.002)	(0.002)	(0.001)
Log(value/wgt)	–0.362***	–0.304***	–0.278***	–0.271***	–0.333***
	(0.004)	(0.005)	(0.006)	(0.006)	(0.004)
eti		–0.030***			
		(0.005)			
airindex			0.055***		
			(0.004)		
Air infrastructure				–0.099***	
				(0.006)	
cpi					–0.036***
					(0.001)
R-squared	0.274	0.178	0.166	0.170	0.257
N	931667	113728	58054	47516	479416
Years covered	1990–2008	2007–2008	2008	2008	1998–2008

Notes: * $p<0.1$, ** $p<0.05$, *** $p<0.01$. Year dummies included but output suppressed. All models estimated by fixed effects with product fixed effects. Robust standard errors in parentheses. R-squared is the within R-squared.
Source: Author's calculations.

advantage of technological improvements. Ship size and port infrastructure are highly correlated with the total level of imports — if imports are high, then ship size is generally larger.

As expected, the components of the Liner Services Connectivity Index (models 4 and 4b) that capture the competitive environment in which the exporting economy is operating all have a negative and statistically significant impact on shipping costs. Similarly, including the *LSCI* on its own also negatively impacts shipping charges but the effect is very small.

Turning to the restrictiveness index for ocean freight, the coefficient is negative and statistically significant. That is, a higher sea index is associated with a less restrictive environment and we would expect shipping costs to be lower. The estimated coefficient indicates that a one unit increase in the index would see *ad valorem* transport costs fall by approximately 48 per cent, all other things being equal (note that APEC index values are about 0.6 at present, on average). For air freight, the air index is found to have a statistically positive effect on *ad valorem* freight costs: higher values of the index indicate a greater degree of restrictiveness on a route and therefore higher *ad valorem* air transport costs.

Institutional quality, captured by the Corruption Perceptions Index (*cpi*), has more than three times the estimated impact on transport costs for air freight compared to ocean freight. This is plausible if higher value goods, which are generally shipped by air, attract more bribe-taking behaviour. The Enabling Trade Index (*eti*) also has a greater negative impact on air freighted goods compared to ocean freighted goods, suggesting that improvements in trade facilitation measures may be better directed at airport procedures, where the benefits would be greater.

5.5 Conclusion

Transport costs are important and amenable to reduction by technical progress and by policy measures. The richness of the customs data for Australia, Brazil, Chile and the United States allows us to break down transport costs into the various determinants. However, transport costs remain a significant component of the wedge between the prices of domestic and imported goods.

Transport costs depend on more than distance or bulk or scale, and the role of the determinants vary by mode of transport. Transport costs are related to distance and to weight.

Sea freight is cheaper than air per kilogram but imports arriving by air have lower *ad valorem* trade costs because air freight is used for higher value goods. The choice of transport mode is, however, more complex than simply having more valuable lighter goods shipped by air. Air transport will be favoured when timeliness is important, and for such goods, poor exporting-economy institutions may be a particularly significant obstacle.

The econometric results reported in Tables 5.7 and 5.8 indicate that distance and bulk have the expected relationship to transport costs, and that transport costs fall with the volume of trade. The distance and weight variables are statistically significant for both modes, but the coefficients are larger and confidence intervals tighter for sea than for air. Good institutions, as measured by the Corruption Perceptions Index compiled by Transparency International, are associated with lower trade costs, but the impact is larger for air freight.

There are caveats to our conclusions. With just two modes there is an important feedback mechanism because the choice of mode is not simple and it is related to the impact of exporting-economy institutions. There is also an endogeneity concern related to the vicious cycle of high transport costs reducing trade flows and low trade volumes being a cause of high transport costs. Moreover, by focusing only on dollar values of transport costs we do not directly address the role of time, which some authors (Hummels 2001) identify as more important than financial costs, at least for some goods.

Using indicators of restrictiveness in transport services sectors, the econometric results highlight the importance of competitive environments for reducing transport costs for both air and sea transport.

The relevance of research on trade and transport costs is on how transport costs impact on trade flows. Future research should focus on the analysis of the effect of transport costs on exports of the APEC member economies to reporting economies such as the United States,

Australia, Chile and Brazil. Since similar detailed customs level data exist for other economies, notably New Zealand and a selection of Latin American economies through Asociación Latinoamericana de Integración, future research should focus on the analysis of APEC export flows to these economies as well.

Chapter 6

Restructuring and Productivity in Rail Transport[1]

Pedro Cantos, José M. Pastor and Lorenzo Serrano

6.1 Introduction

During the past 50 years the most common market structure in many economies' rail sectors was a single, publicly-owned firm, entrusted with the unified management of both infrastructure and services. Despite some differences in their degree of commercial autonomy, the traditional methods of regulation and control of this sort of company have been relatively homogeneous. In general, it was assumed that the monopoly power of the national company required price and service regulation to protect the general interest. In addition, there was an obligation, often referred to as 'common carrier' status, on the part of the companies to meet any demand at those prices. The closure of existing lines or the opening of new services required government approval. Thus, competition was rare and often discouraged, and the preservation of the national character of the industry was considered the key factor governing the overall regulatory system.

---

[1] This chapter is based on a paper produced with funding from the Asia Pacific Economic Cooperation's Policy Support Unit and material from that paper is reproduced with its permission. Information is taken from The Impacts and Benefits of Structural Reforms in the Transport, Energy and Telecommunications Sectors in APEC Economies APEC#211-SE-01.1. The views expressed in this paper are those of the authors and do not necessarily represent those of the APEC Secretariat or APEC Member Economies.

Under this protective environment, most national rail companies incurred growing financial deficits during the 1970s and 1980s. Furthermore, social obligations to their staff made it nearly impossible to reach any agreement on redundancies or even wage adjustments. In some economies, the companies were forced to finance their deficits by borrowing, so their accounts lost all resemblance to reality. The main problems associated with the traditional policies for railways were: increasing losses, which were usually financed by public subsidies; a high degree of managerial inefficiency; and business activities oriented exclusively toward production targets rather than commercial and market targets.

These distortions did not come from any artificial reduction in the range of services provided or from excessively high fares but, more commonly, from an unjustified increase in the supply of services (and where costs exceeded revenues). Such behaviour implied larger public subsidies. In many cases, the lack of commercially-oriented tariffs and investment policies explained many of the difficulties faced by the companies. Together with the burden imposed by the technical characteristics of the sector, this placed most railways in a very weak position to compete against alternative transport modes. However, fierce intermodal competition alone was not able to improve the competitiveness of the railway system; it was necessary to adopt measures affecting the internal behaviour and structure of the sector itself. Therefore, the sector's overall decline sparked a widespread restructuring movement around the world.

The worldwide restructuring process of the rail industry began with timid reforms. Many economies began by replacing their national railways with autonomous commercial bodies possessing independent, realistic balance sheets, in which only public service obligations could be explicitly subsidized by the government. Other economies opted to substitute their old geographically-based management with a multi-divisional structure, defined by the companies' different lines of business or services.

Some economies have carried out relatively long-term restructuring, whereas others have preferred a quicker implementation. For example, privatization in New Zealand and Japan was phased in over a number of years, while in the non-APEC economies of Argentina and the United Kingdom it took less than two years. All restructuring processes were undertaken to make the companies attractive to private investors, although full privatization has been less preferred than concessioning.

The changes have involved the revision of laws and other regulations affecting railways — reducing staff, dealing with pension issues and deciding how much property should be sold and how much should be retained by the government. In addition, several arrangements for paying for unprofitable (but socially needed) train services have been put into place, together with a precise definition of the concession contracts and their main terms.

With regard to results, in general most of the restructuring experiences detailed below seem to have been positive. The objectives of stopping the industry's drain on public sector resources, along with the stabilization of market share for both passengers and freight, were achieved in most economies. Likewise, the companies succeeded in raising their levels of productivity.

The objective of this chapter is to assess the effectiveness of the main restructuring measures in the world rail sector, with special emphasis on the national rail networks of the Asia Pacific Economic Cooperation (APEC) economies. The study is based on a sample of European and APEC economies with data for the period from 2001 to 2008, and uses non-parametric techniques (Data Envelop Analysis or DEA and the Malmquist productivity index) to calculate indexes of productivity growth, while also disaggregating their various components. This latter aspect is important, as we aim to determine the impact of changes in the sector, not only on efficiency but also on the overall evolution of productivity and its components (technical change and efficiency).

The results of the work show that, on average, the growth of productivity, efficiency and technical change is slightly lower for APEC rail systems than for other national rail systems. In particular, the average rate of productivity growth for APEC rail systems was 3.5 per cent per year, while for non-APEC economies it was 4.8 per cent. We also find that the productivity improvements are mainly explained by technical change, while changes in efficiency are less relevant. In particular, for APEC member economies our results show that no rail system, excepting

Viet Nam's, improved its efficiency. Finally, APEC member economies achieved a rate of technical change of 3.2 per cent a year on average, while non-APEC economies achieved 3.7 per cent.

This chapter describes the restructuring measures for the world rail industry, provides a short literature review on the effects of restructuring, presents the methodology for measuring productivity growth, describes the data used in the study, provides estimations of productivity growth and its components, and finally presents the main conclusions.

6.2 Restructuring Measures for the Rail Industry

Despite all these changes, the most salient characteristic of the restructuring process of the rail industry in the last decades has been the consolidation of different and alternative organizational structures for the industry as a whole. These structures differ in three main features, to be analysed in detail: how access and infrastructure and multimodal competition are considered; what extent of vertical separation is introduced after the change; and what degree of competition (and private participation) is allowed in the industry after the reform.

The degree of vertical separation

The management of rail infrastructure not only includes simple pricing principles, it also encompasses access rights and long-term development provisions. Each economy addresses these matters differently. While most have opted to retain infrastructure in public hands, creating government management agencies to regulate private train operators, others have established nominally independent (actual independence from political control varies) but government-owned enterprises to manage stations and tracks.

One of the most clearly defined patterns emerging from deregulation and restructuring is that they include two critical dimensions — the degree of vertical separation between infrastructure and services and the promotion of competition within the sector. With respect to the first dimension, there are three main options for the vertical organization of the railway industry: vertical integration, competitive access and vertical separation.

The first option of vertical integration corresponds to the traditional, historical model of railway organization described above, where a single (usually public) entity controls all the infrastructure facilities as well as the operating and administrative functions. Less frequently, competitive access is characterized by the existence of an integrated operator, who is required to make rail facilities (tracks, stations *etc.*) available to other operators on a fair and equal basis through the trading of, for example, circulation rights. This has the advantages of integration (economies of scope, coordinated planning and reduction of transaction costs) but its overall effectiveness may be jeopardized if the integrated company has incentives to leave out other operators.

Alternatively, in the complete vertical separation scenario, the management (and possibly the ownership) of facilities is fully separated from other rail functions. This is very attractive, because although infrastructure may remain a natural monopoly, it is separated from rail services, where potential competition among different operators is possible. In general, the main advantage of this vertical unbundling is that rail transport is placed in a similar situation as road transport, especially regarding the tariff system and infrastructure planning. Investment proposals could be studied on the basis of a cost-benefit analysis, while pricing policies could be based on social cost. In addition, separating infrastructure from services greatly facilitates the entry of more than one operator on a single route. For profitable services this would permit notable improvements in efficiency by allowing direct competition among operators. For non-profitable services, infrastructure separation can be accompanied by tendering to stimulate increased efficiency through competition for the market, the introduction of innovations and marketing improvements.

However, the vertical unbundling of the rail industry also implies several disadvantages. The main problem is the potential loss of economies of scope derived from the joint operation of tracks and services. It is often noted that the relationship between the services supplied and the rolling stock used, as well as the quality, quantity and technical characteristics of the infrastructure, is so close that both aspects need to be planned together. Thus, assigning different services to several operators may decrease the utilization of the sector's staff and physical assets. Also, the new system may become less attractive to the user than an integrated system because of higher risk (through the lack of interchangeable ticketing, an integrated national network, and so on). Vertical separation may also require such a complex institutional arrangement that the resulting transaction costs may be prohibitive for many economies. A final consideration with vertical separation is the reduction of investment incentives. For example, an infrastructure owner considering an investment in a facility with only one potential buyer will anticipate bargaining away some of the benefit from the new service once it comes on line. This problem becomes less relevant with more competition in the market, since competition weakens the bargaining position of individual operators by reducing the specificity of the assets.

Promotion of competition (horizontal dimension)

Although it is accepted that infrastructure (characterized by its high levels of sunk costs) may be managed under monopoly conditions, competition can be introduced into operations in two different ways. The first option consists of directly facilitating the free entry of new companies into the railway network. This can be done in either passenger transport or freight transport sectors, but, it has been much more usual in the latter.

The alternative is to foster competition for the market by means of a franchising or concessions system in which the franchised companies compete for the right to use the infrastructure during a certain period of time, which is in all cases notably shorter than the infrastructure concession period. This second option has proved to be very attractive in the European context, in which many railway services are heavily subsidized.

However, this new structure can also have serious drawbacks. As Nash and Rivera-Trujillo (2004) point out, the entry of various companies using the same infrastructure leads to obvious problems in a schedule design that must efficiently assign slots among companies and operations, and at the same time satisfy all of them. These problems significantly affect service quality, since coordination is lost as a result of the separate management of infrastructure and operations.

Table 6.1 summarizes the features of the APEC rail networks. We observe that China, Malaysia, the Philippines, Chinese Taipei and Viet Nam maintain a vertically integrated structure without introducing horizontal reforms. Canada, Japan and the United States maintain a vertically integrated industry but allow the entry of new rail operators, and the rest of the rail systems have fully separated the infrastructure and the rail operations. Finally, some economies such as Chile, Mexico, Peru and Russia have introduced franchising systems and free open systems in their rail networks, while Canada, Japan and the United States have only reformed the sector at a horizontal level by allowing the free entry of new operators.

Table 6.1. Features of APEC Rail Networks

	Vertical dimension			*Horizontal dimension*	
APEC Member	*Integrated monopoly*	*Competitive access*	*Vertical unbundling*	*Franchising system*	*Entry of new operators*
Canada		✓			✓
Chile			✓	✓	✓
China	✓				
Indonesia			✓		
Japan		✓			✓
Repub. of Korea			✓		
Malaysia	✓				
Mexico			✓	✓	✓
Peru			✓	✓	✓
Philippines	✓				
Russia			✓[a]	✓[b]	✓[a]
Chinese Taipei	✓				
Thailand	✓				
United States		✓			✓
Viet Nam	✓				

Notes: [a] Implemented in 2003; [b] Implemented in 2006.

6.3 Literature Review

There are many studies in the literature analysing productivity and efficiency in the railway sector. However, most of the vertical, and particularly horizontal, separation processes have taken place in recent years, and as a result there is very little conclusive empirical evidence on the effects of these processes on productivity and efficiency. Furthermore, most of the studies are focused on analysis in the European rail network — there are few studies devoted to other, and different, experiences.

In general terms, the first studies in this field (see Gathon and Perelman 1992, Oum and Yu 1994, Gathon and Pestieau 1995) indicated that the economies with the most liberalized railway sectors were the most efficient. An excellent survey can be found in Oum *et al.* (1999) covering many of the results obtained in the previous literature.

Likewise, more recent studies have obtained similar results. Cantos *et al.* (1999, 2010) also conclude that rail operators with a higher degree of autonomy and independence are the most efficient, are more technologically advanced and achieve higher gains in productivity. Similarly, Cantos and Maudos (2001) estimate efficiency in costs and revenue, and show that companies need to move towards more commercial policies that also encourage their competitiveness.

Friebel *et al.* (2005) carried out an initial analysis of some of the restructuring measures in the sector for the 1995–2000 period, focusing on measures designed to separate the industry vertically. Their results suggest that, in general, the reforms have furthered more efficient behaviour. However, these reforms must be carried out sequentially if they are to be effective. In addition, Driessen *et al.* (2006) studied the efficiency of a sample of European companies for the period 1990–2001. These authors do not come to a decisive conclusion on the impact of vertical separation of infrastructure and operations. They find that vertical separation does not seem to be necessary to achieve an increase in productive efficiency, although tendering processes do appear to favour an increase in efficiency. In all events, these authors recognize certain data definition problems and particularly acknowledge that many of the predicted effects may still not have been in evidence, since the sample period ended in 2001.

Positions supporting disparate opinions on the efficiency of separating infrastructure and operations are therefore not difficult to find. Evans (2003) stated that the process leads to gains in efficiency, transparency and greater competition. Other authors such as Pfund (2003) believed, however, that the disadvantages clearly outweigh the benefits of separation. In the same vein, as noted above, the initial empirical studies to approach the subject (Friebel *et al.* 2005, Driesden *et al.* 2006) provided no conclusive results.

Very little analysis has been conducted on the changes stemming from the horizontal restructuring of the industry. In particular, Driessen *et al.* (2006) found that processes of competition for the market (through concessions) encourage efficiency more than processes that foster competition in the market (through free entry), and that greater managerial independence does not encourage greater efficiency. These results contradict those from the previous literature (Gathon and Pestieau 1995, Cantos *et al.* 1999, Friebel *et al.* 2005).

Recent works have evaluated some of these reforms, and particularly in those economies that have advanced more in these types of measures. Mulder *et al.* (2005) used an analysis on the basis of cost-benefit techniques in order to evaluate the efficiency of the reforms in the railway industry in the Netherlands. Their results indicate that separating the industry vertically is beneficial when competition is increased in an efficient way in the sector. Furthermore, the authors show that the introduction of competition in the freight sector has increased both efficiency and performance. Passenger transport, however, has had difficulties in realizing historical performance levels. Similarly, in the case of the franchising process in passenger services in Sweden, Alexandersson and Hultén (2005) noted some significant problems associated with very low bids in tenders, and the very low number of firms that compete in each tender. Some of these problems have also been observed in the Australian experience (Kain 2006).

To sum up, results from the majority of studies indicate that most of the reforms have made railway systems more efficient and productive

(Cantos *et al.* 2010). However, a greater effort is still required in order to delineate the relevance and significance of each measure.

6.4 Methodology and Data

The Malmquist productivity index (Malmquist 1953) allows changes in productivity of railway companies to be broken down into changes in efficiency and technical change. The first represents movements towards a given production frontier (a catch-up effect), and the second represents movements of the frontier. Furthermore, Malmquist index methodology allows a different rate of technical change for each railway company. Also, if it is estimated using a non-parametric frontier model (Data Envelop Analysis or DEA), which is the most commonly used approach, it is not necessary to impose any functional form on the data or make distributional assumptions for the inefficiency term, unlike the Stochastic Frontier Approach. The main disadvantage of this approach is that the estimation of inefficiency may show an upward bias, capturing as inefficiency the influence of other factors, such as errors in data measurement and bad luck. The technical details of the Malmquist productivity index methodology used in this study are given in the Appendix to Cantos *et al.* (2011).

The data correspond to a sample of 34 world railway systems from 2001 to 2008 (Table 6.2). The information was taken from reports published by the Union Internationale des Chemins de Fer and completed with data published in the organization's statistical memoranda. Specifically, the different railway systems established in each economy are evaluated. Thus, in the first years of the sample, the systems were run by one single company with vertically integrated infrastructure and operations and horizontally integrated operating services. Over the years, as many of the railway systems began to be separated both vertically and horizontally, different companies took over their management. In this case, the data corresponding to all the companies making up a railway system are aggregated for each variable.

Table 6.2. Average Values for the Variables 2001 to 2008

Economy	*PKT (millions)*	*TKT (millions)*	*LLT (km)*	*LOCOM*	*WAG*	*EMP ('000)*
Austria	8,761	18,176	5,786	1,232	20,457	46
Belgium	9,041	8,309	3,502	776	15,883	39
Bulgaria	2,538	5,041	4,215	602	14,700	35
Czech Repub.	6,749	16,313	9,492	2,180	39,814	69
Denmark	5,478	1,941	2,122	57	5,294	12
Estonia	224	8,838	924	128	3,904	4
Finland	8,017	13,287	5,827	784	14,535	21
France	72,307	45,918	29,456	4,355	57,971	164
Germany	68,707	75,502	34,901	4,976	123,848	201
Greece	1,806	581	2,476	162	4,046	8
Hungary	7,000	8,127	7,951	1,034	18,894	48
Ireland	1,745	305	1,919	94	1,772	6
Italy	47,158	21,589	16,538	3,286	58,449	101
Latvia	855	16,414	2,303	217	5,962	14
Lithuania	446	11,885	1,763	249	9,857	12
Luxembourg	297	461	275	100	3,334	3
Netherlands	14,176	3,848	2,809	275	5,190	26
Norway	2,406	2,723	4,111	156	2,765	9
Poland	17,818	45,115	19,738	3,711	88,993	134
Portugal	3,591	2,474	2,840	182	4,456	9
Romania	7,895	13,656	11,007	1,966	61,314	69
Slovak Repub.	2,352	9,809	3,647	1,041	18,581	38
Slovenia	778	3,239	1,229	165	4,821	8
Spain	19,888	11,820	12,853	732	19,348	23
Sweden	6,042	12,945	10,004	398	8,149	12
Switzerland	14,716	12,216	3,357	1,654	15,854	29
Canada	1,484	334,820	55,893	2,913	94,015	36
China	579,817	1,890,285	61,266	16,157	560,396	1.679
Japan	246,085	22,547	19,884	1,218	34,356	140
Repub. Korea	30,165	10,766	3,260	580	12,225	30
Russia	155,149	1,639,928	86,703	11,945	596,127	1.219
Chinese Taipei	9,285	889	1,096	323	4,692	14
United States	8,985	2,526,146	194,228	22,476	476,044	183
Viet Nam	4,142	2,898	2,804	356	5,588	42
Total	41,202	200,267	18,787	2,610	70,724	130

Notes: PKT = number of passengers/km transported for passenger transport; TKT = tonnes/km transported for freight transport; LLT = number of kilometres of railway infrastructure in each economy; LOCOM = number of locomotives, including light rail motor tractors; WAG = annual fleet wagons (coaches, railcars and railcar trailers); and EMP = number of employees in all of the railways making up the railway system.
Source: Union Internationale des Chemins de Fer.

Two outputs and three inputs are considered. The variables selected as outputs are the number of passengers/km transported for passenger transport and tonnes/km transported for freight transport. In the case of input variables, the following are considered:

- number of employees in all of the railways making up the railway system;
- two measures of the rolling stock:
  - a variable indicating the number of locomotives, including light rail motor tractors; and
  - a variable calculated as the annual fleet wagons and the number of coaches, railcars and railcar trailers; and
- number of kilometres of railway infrastructure in each economy.

6.5 Results

Before presenting the results, we must stress that the railway systems included in the sample vary significantly in terms of technology and quality of service. The comparison of their efficiency levels can therefore lead to misleading or confusing conclusions. For this reason, we will focus our results on the *changes* in productivity, efficiency and technical change and compare these changes mainly between the APEC economies and other economies.

Figure 6.1 shows the accumulated Malmquist productivity index since 2001 for these two groups. The results show that between 2001 and 2005, productivity growth was similar between APEC member economies and other economies. In 2006 the productivity for the non-APEC railway systems increased at a clearly higher rate than the rate for the APEC economies (12.1 per cent against 0.3 per cent). In the following two years productivity increased more for the APEC economies. On average, productivity for APEC economies rose by 3.5 per cent per year, while for non-APEC economies productivity rose by 4.8 per cent.

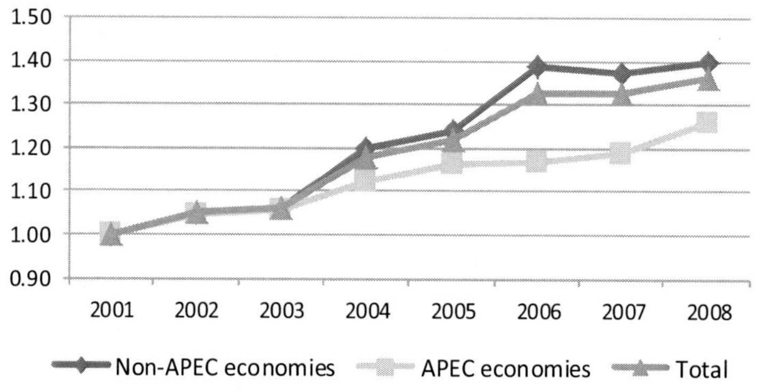

Figure 6.1. Cumulative Productivity Change in Rail Services (2001=1)

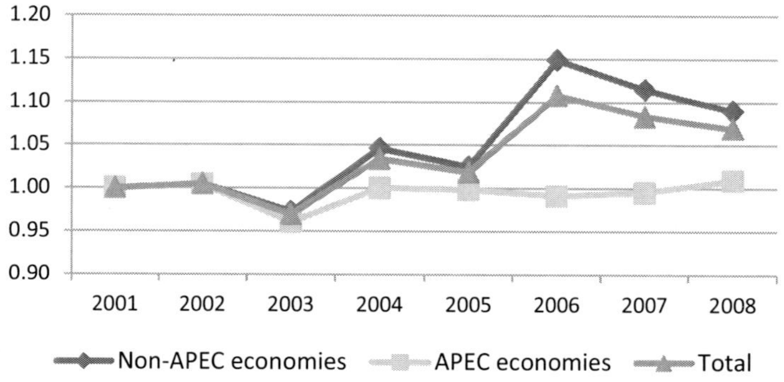

Figure 6.2. Cumulative Efficiency Change in Rail Services (2001=1)

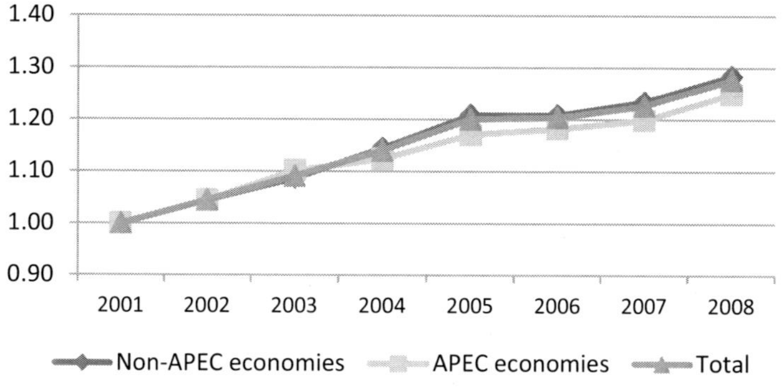

Figure 6.3. Cumulative Technical Change in Rail Services (2001=1)

We then decompose the productivity change between efficiency changes and technical change in order to analyse the causes of the productivity changes. As we see in Figure 6.2, until 2005 the evolution of efficiency is similar, but in 2005 the efficiency notably improved for non-APEC economies, which partially explains the increase in productivity for these economies. But the efficiency of non-APEC economies decreased until 2007. The rates are again similar between the two groups of economies for the last year of the sample. At an aggregate level, there were no significant efficiency improvements for APEC economies, while efficiency improved by 1.4 per cent per year for non-APEC economies.

Regarding technical change, Figure 6.3 shows that the differences are not significant between the two groups of economies. However, from 2005 the technical change improved at a higher rate for non-APEC economies. At aggregate level, technical changes for APEC economies increased by 3.2 per cent per year, while for non-APEC economies productivity increased by 3.7 per cent.

Table 6.3 analyses the annual results per economy for pairs of consecutive years in terms of productivity. The last column expresses the average outcome over the whole sample period per economy.

Regarding productivity change, we can observe that Russia, Viet Nam and China have the highest rates, while Chinese Taipei and the Republic of Korea have the lowest. At the aggregate level, APEC economies obtained an average increase of 3.5 per cent, while non-APEC economies obtained an average increase of 4.8 per cent.

Table 6.4 presents the results for the efficiency change. Firstly, we must indicate that our results show that China, Japan, Russia and the United States were efficient during the whole period and thus cannot obtain efficiency changes. In any case, we observe again that, on average, APEC rail systems improved their efficiency level by only 0.2 per cent, while non-APEC economies improved the efficiency scores by 1.4 per cent.

Finally, rates of technical change are expressed in Table 6.5. At an aggregate level, we can conclude that APEC economies improved their

Table 6.3. Productivity Change in Rail Services (2001=1)

	2001–02	*2002–03*	*2003–04*	*2004–05*	*2005–06*	*2006–07*	*2007–08*	*Average 2001–08*
Austria	1.056	1.055	1.042	0.950	1.088	1.006	1.064	1.037
Belgium	1.067	1.006	1.085	1.042	1.116	0.977	0.999	1.042
Bulgaria	0.919	1.095	1.058	1.025	1.000	1.015	0.910	1.003
Czech Repub.	0.990	1.016	1.002	0.991	1.138	1.048	0.948	1.019
Denmark	0.808	0.914						0.861
Estonia	1.127	1.031	1.064	1.131	1.066	0.791	0.804	1.002
Finland	1.043	1.071	1.320	0.856	2.417	0.465	1.060	1.176
France	1.070	1.030	0.994	0.666	1.640	1.029	1.087	1.074
Germany	0.992	0.854	1.281	0.923	1.019	1.007	1.004	1.012
Greece	1.099	0.889	1.114	1.162	1.040	1.159	1.086	1.078
Hungary	1.009	1.098	1.118	1.006	1.139	0.966	0.964	1.043
Ireland	1.018	1.007	0.989	1.190	1.057	1.143	1.458	1.123
Italy	1.006	0.961	1.029	0.985	1.014	1.010	0.985	0.999
Latvia	1.122	1.203	0.975	1.132	0.877	0.968	1.059	1.048
Lithuania	1.266	1.194	1.019	1.101	1.041	1.016	0.992	1.090
Luxembourg	0.876	0.981	1.026	0.852	1.117	0.848	0.994	0.956
Netherlands	1.152	1.083						1.118
Norway	0.999	1.225						1.112
Poland	1.010	1.085	1.008	0.958	0.970	1.022	0.958	1.002
Portugal	1.137	1.012	1.074	1.043	1.122	1.049	1.049	1.070
Romania	0.915	1.091	1.052	1.102	0.915	1.046	0.821	0.992
Slovak Repub.	0.963	0.971	1.009	0.965	1.065	0.979	1.005	0.994
Slovenia	1.084	1.180	1.056	1.007	0.987	1.047	1.013	1.053
Spain	1.056	1.021	1.010	2.076	1.035	1.010	1.098	1.187
Sweden	1.458	0.291	2.722	0.424	0.896	1.042	1.019	1.122
Switzerland	1.049	0.911	0.948	1.158	1.031	1.131	1.042	1.039
Canada	0.999	1.047	1.088	1.011	1.016	0.979	1.018	1.023
China	1.050	1.022	1.108	1.042	0.931	1.071	1.160	1.055
Japan	1.013	1.055	0.992	1.020	1.023	1.014	1.037	1.022
Repub. Korea	0.981	1.019	0.995	0.998	1.006	1.010	1.014	1.003
Russia	1.210	1.099	1.000	1.079	1.037			1.085
Chinese Taipei	0.963	0.903	1.068	1.023	0.984	0.957	0.978	0.982
United States	1.028	1.035	1.050	1.106	1.028	0.994	1.011	1.036
Viet Nam	1.143	0.891	1.179	1.045	1.000	1.102	1.183	1.078
Total	1.049	1.010	1.112	1.034	1.091	0.997	1.027	1.045
APEC members	1.048	1.009	1.060	1.040	1.003	1.018	1.057	1.035
Non-APEC	1.050	1.011	1.130	1.032	1.121	0.990	1.018	1.048

Note: Blank cells correspond to missing data in the sample.
Source: Authors' calculations.

Table 6.4. Efficiency Change in Rail Services (2001=1)

	2001–02	*2002–03*	*2003–04*	*2004–05*	*2005–06*	*2006–07*	*2007–08*	*Average 2001–08*
Austria	1.024	1.027	0.987	0.896	1.068	0.974	1.014	0.999
Belgium	1.033	0.948	1.026	1.001	1.197	0.940	0.942	1.012
Bulgaria	0.892	1.043	1.002	0.969	0.967	0.991	0.858	0.960
Czech Repub.	0.958	0.969	0.927	0.928	1.189	1.023	0.913	0.987
Denmark	0.753	0.845						0.799
Estonia	1.087	0.984	0.990	1.037	1.054	0.785	0.793	0.961
Finland	1.016	1.006	1.241	0.802	2.345	0.457	1.031	1.128
France	1.032	0.998	0.971	0.628	1.608	1.023	1.058	1.045
Germany	0.981	0.803	1.242	0.874	1.044	0.983	0.966	0.985
Greece	1.081	0.829	1.049	1.135	0.998	1.144	1.050	1.041
Hungary	0.990	1.032	1.083	0.945	1.108	0.964	0.932	1.008
Ireland	1.001	0.939	0.930	1.163	1.026	1.127	1.418	1.086
Italy	0.994	0.895	1.022	0.952	1.000	0.996	0.965	0.975
Latvia	1.098	1.158	0.951	1.044	0.866	0.928	0.991	1.005
Lithuania	1.224	1.129	0.966	1.011	1.023	0.992	0.961	1.044
Luxembourg	0.843	0.934	0.943	0.807	1.223	0.813	0.929	0.928
Netherlands	1.123	1.060						1.092
Norway	0.956	1.317						1.136
Poland	0.980	1.034	0.938	0.894	1.017	0.996	0.921	0.968
Portugal	1.117	0.945	1.011	1.015	1.078	1.036	1.016	1.031
Romania	0.889	1.034	0.999	1.037	0.918	1.034	0.792	0.957
Slovak Repub.	0.920	0.932	0.929	0.917	1.155	0.937	0.940	0.961
Slovenia	1.049	1.128	1.010	0.948	0.973	1.029	0.972	1.016
Spain	1.037	0.954	0.950	2.023	0.994	0.997	1.062	1.145
Sweden	1.024	0.372	2.637	0.394	0.868	1.042	0.984	1.046
Switzerland	1.025	0.854	0.915	1.113	1.075	1.099	0.997	1.011
Canada	1.001	1.025	1.000	1.000	1.000	1.000	1.000	1.004
China	1.000	1.000	1.000	1.000	1.000	1.000	1.000	1.000
Japan	1.000	1.000	1.000	1.000	1.000	1.000	1.000	1.000
Repub. Korea	0.962	0.949	1.010	0.980	0.997	0.990	0.988	0.982
Russia	1.000	1.000	1.000	1.000	1.000			1.000
Chinese Taipei	0.961	0.828	1.153	1.007	0.972	0.943	0.964	0.975
United States	1.000	1.000	1.000	1.000	1.000	1.000	1.000	1.000
Viet Nam	1.105	0.853	1.168	1.000	0.978	1.098	1.147	1.050
Total	1.005	0.965	1.066	0.985	1.088	0.978	0.987	1.011
APEC members	1.004	0.957	1.041	0.998	0.993	1.004	1.014	1.002
Non-APEC	1.005	0.968	1.075	0.980	1.121	0.970	0.978	1.014

Note: Blank cells correspond to missing data in the sample.
Source: Authors' calculations.

Table 6.5. Technical Change in Rail Services (2001=1)

	2001–02	*2002–03*	*2003–04*	*2004–05*	*2005–06*	*2006–07*	*2007–08*	*Average 2001–08*
Austria	1.031	1.027	1.056	1.060	1.019	1.033	1.050	1.039
Belgium	1.033	1.060	1.058	1.042	0.932	1.040	1.061	1.032
Bulgaria	1.030	1.050	1.056	1.059	1.034	1.024	1.061	1.045
Czech Repub.	1.034	1.049	1.081	1.067	0.957	1.024	1.038	1.036
Denmark	1.073	1.082						1.077
Estonia	1.037	1.049	1.075	1.090	1.012	1.007	1.014	1.041
Finland	1.027	1.065	1.064	1.068	1.031	1.018	1.028	1.043
France	1.036	1.032	1.024	1.060	1.020	1.006	1.028	1.029
Germany	1.011	1.064	1.031	1.057	0.976	1.024	1.040	1.029
Greece	1.017	1.072	1.063	1.024	1.042	1.013	1.034	1.038
Hungary	1.019	1.064	1.033	1.064	1.029	1.001	1.034	1.035
Ireland	1.017	1.072	1.063	1.023	1.031	1.014	1.028	1.035
Italy	1.011	1.074	1.007	1.035	1.014	1.015	1.020	1.025
Latvia	1.022	1.038	1.025	1.085	1.012	1.040	1.069	1.042
Lithuania	1.034	1.058	1.055	1.089	1.018	1.025	1.032	1.044
Luxembourg	1.039	1.050	1.088	1.056	0.913	1.044	1.069	1.037
Netherlands	1.026	1.022						1.024
Norway	1.045	0.930						0.988
Poland	1.031	1.050	1.074	1.072	0.954	1.027	1.041	1.035
Portugal	1.019	1.071	1.063	1.027	1.041	1.013	1.033	1.038
Romania	1.029	1.056	1.053	1.063	0.997	1.011	1.037	1.035
Slovak Repub.	1.046	1.041	1.086	1.053	0.923	1.045	1.069	1.037
Slovenia	1.033	1.046	1.045	1.062	1.015	1.018	1.042	1.037
Spain	1.019	1.071	1.063	1.026	1.041	1.013	1.034	1.038
Sweden	1.425	0.783	1.032	1.078	1.032	1.000	1.036	1.055
Switzerland	1.024	1.066	1.036	1.040	0.959	1.029	1.046	1.029
Canada	0.998	1.022	1.088	1.011	1.016	0.979	1.018	1.019
China	1.050	1.022	1.108	1.042	0.931	1.071	1.160	1.055
Japan	1.013	1.055	0.992	1.020	1.023	1.014	1.037	1.022
Repub. Korea	1.020	1.074	0.985	1.018	1.009	1.020	1.027	1.022
Russia	1.210	1.099	1.000	1.079	1.037			1.085
Chinese Taipei	1.002	1.090	0.926	1.016	1.013	1.014	1.014	1.011
United States	1.028	1.035	1.050	1.106	1.028	0.994	1.011	1.036
Viet Nam	1.034	1.045	1.009	1.046	1.022	1.004	1.031	1.027
Total	1.045	1.044	1.045	1.053	1.003	1.019	1.041	1.036
APEC members	1.044	1.055	1.020	1.042	1.010	1.014	1.042	1.032
Non-APEC	1.045	1.040	1.053	1.056	1.000	1.021	1.041	1.037

Note: Blank cells correspond to missing data in the sample.
Source: Authors' calculations.

rate of technical change by an average of 3.2 per cent, while non-APEC economies improved by a rate of 3.7 per cent. Distinguishing between economies, Russia obtained the highest score (8.5 per cent), followed by China (5.5 per cent) and the United States (3.6 per cent). The reasons for this increase may be related in a higher investment in the technology of the railway infrastructure and rolling stock systems.

From these results we conclude that productivity improvements are mainly explained by technical change, while changes in efficiency are less relevant. In particular, for APEC economies our results show that no rail system other than Viet Nam improved its efficiency significantly. Figures 6.4 to 6.6 summarize the results for each APEC member economy.

6.6 Conclusion

We have estimated productivity change indicators for a sample of 34 railway systems during the period from 2001 to 2008. These indexes have been decomposed into efficiency changes and technical change. The methodology used to estimate these indexes has been the DEA approach. We must point out that, as the railway systems are very heterogeneous, it is very difficult to compare them individually.

We first carried out an analysis where APEC rail systems were compared with non-APEC rail systems. The results show that, on average, the productivity, efficiency and technical changes are slightly lower for the APEC rail systems. In particular, the average rate of productivity change for APEC rail systems rose by 3.5 per cent per year, while for non-APEC economies productivity rose by 4.8 per cent. Russia, Viet Nam and China showed the highest rates, while Chinese Taipei and the Republic of Korea had the lowest.

However, China, Japan and the United States were efficient during the whole period. In any case, we observe again that, on average and excepting Viet Nam, APEC rail systems did not improve their efficiency scores, while non-APEC economies did improve their efficiency scores by 1.4 per cent per year.

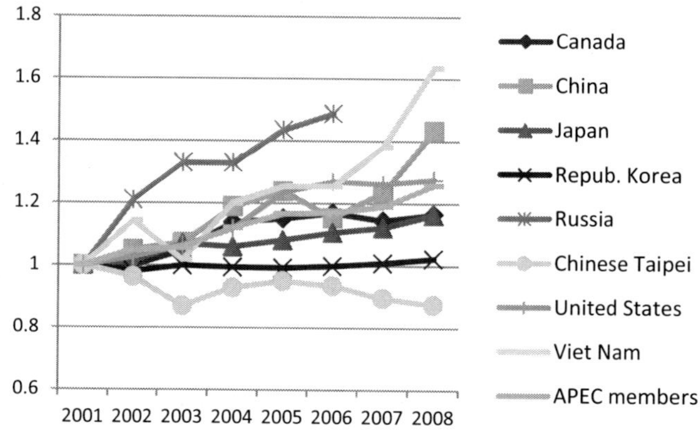

Figure 6.4. Cumulative Productivity Change for Individual APEC Economies (2001=1)

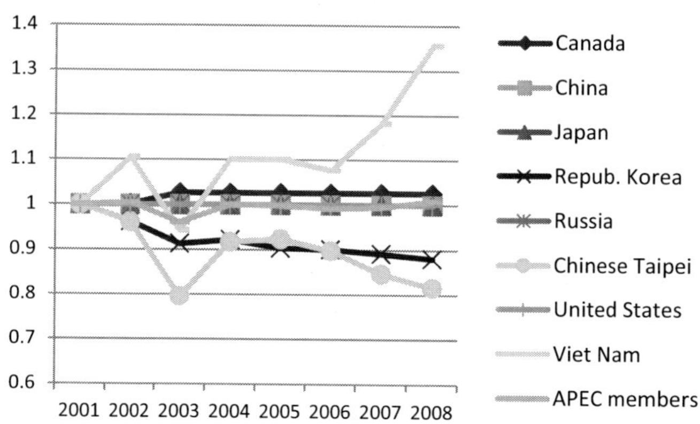

Figure 6.5. Cumulative Efficiency Change for Individual APEC Economies (2001=1)

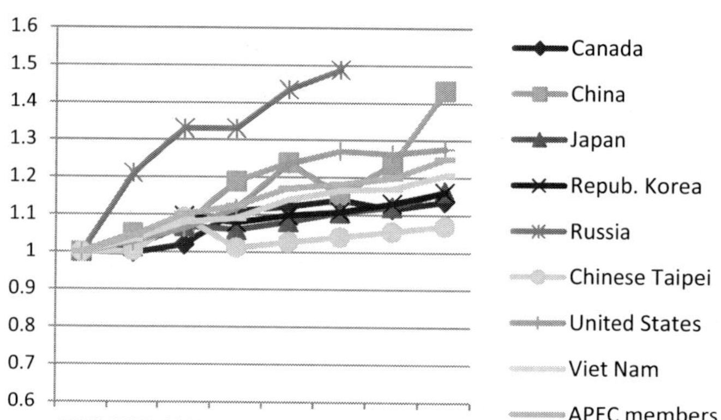

Figure 6.6. Cumulative Technical Change for Individual APEC Economies (2001=1)

Finally, APEC member economies improved, on average, their rate of technical change by 3.2 per cent, while non-APEC economies improved by 3.7 per cent.

Chapter 7

Sectoral Impacts of Reforms in Electricity and Gas Markets[1]

Philippa Dee

7.1 Key Features of Electricity and Gas Markets

The production and distribution of electricity and gas involves networks — networks of electricity transmission and distribution lines, and networks of gas transmission and distribution pipelines. At least some components of the network have the characteristics of a 'natural monopoly', meaning that it is less costly for their operation to be carried out by a single producer using a single set of facilities, rather than having two or more operators with duplicate facilities. In addition, there are strict technical requirements for operating electricity and gas networks, so as to preserve the physical integrity of the distribution systems. For these reasons, electricity and gas have traditionally been supplied by single, vertically integrated monopolies, often in government ownership.

The absence of competition meant that there were few (if any) incentives for electricity and gas providers to keep costs to a minimum and to operate efficiently. Unless prices were regulated, there was also scope for operators to abuse their monopoly power and price above cost.

[1] This chapter is based on a paper produced with funding from the Asia Pacific Economic Cooperation's Policy Support Unit and material from that paper is reproduced with its permission. Information is taken from The Impacts and Benefits of Structural Reforms in the Transport, Energy and Telecommunications Sectors in APEC Economies APEC#211-SE-01.1. The views expressed in this paper are those of the author and do not necessarily represent those of the APEC Secretariat or APEC Member Economies.

Structural reforms in electricity and gas have aimed to overcome these two key problems. The reforms have typically aimed to introduce competition into those parts of the production chain that are not natural monopolies. This requires the competitive suppliers to have access to those parts of the network that are natural monopolies. Successful reform also requires that the restructuring be done in such a way that the benefits of competition in the competitive sectors outweigh the loss of any economies of scope that may have prevailed when the monopoly and competitive activities were operated together under single ownership.

Beyond these common features, there are some differences in the physical characteristics of electricity and gas markets, which have led to differences in the extent of reforms carried out.

Electricity markets

The production of electricity involves: (1) generation, (2) transport over high voltage lines (transmission), (3) transportation over low voltage lines (distribution), (4) marketing to consumers (supply), and (5) buying and selling on wholesale markets (trading). What follows is drawn from European Commission (2007).

Transport operations are considered to be natural monopolies, and typically remain regulated, even after structural reform. But generation is seen as a competitive activity, and is generally the first activity to be opened to competition, followed by wholesale trading and retail supply. However, retail prices may remain regulated in some economies, even after structural reform.

Unlike gas, electricity cannot be stored economically once it is produced. So supply has to be matched to demand on a second-by-second basis, even though demand may vary significantly over different times of the day and over difference seasons. The introduction of new competitive generators needs to be managed in a way that does not jeopardize this supply-demand matching or bring down the grid network. After structural reform, this balancing is typically achieved by having balancing markets run by an independent system operator.

Finally, electricity can be generated using a variety of technologies, each of which has different cost characteristics. Hydro and nuclear plants tend to have low operating (variable) costs, so are typically used for base-load supply (ie operated all the time). However, nuclear plants (and some hydro plants) also have very high capital costs, so the prices to end-users from this source may have to be high if operators are to receive an adequate return on capital. The operating (variable) costs of thermal plants depend largely on the prices of their input fuels. At current prices, coal-fired plants tend to have the next lowest operating costs after hydro and nuclear, and thus be next on the 'merit order'. Combined cycle and gas turbine plants tend to have the highest operating costs, and tend to be used as 'peaking plant' (ie used to meet peak demand). However, combined cycle and gas plants have low capital costs, so end user prices from this source can be relatively low. In general terms, therefore, electricity prices to end users depend not just on the extent of structural reform, but also on the mix of production technologies available.

Finally, like most network industries, electricity transmission and distribution is subject to economies of density — costs are lower, the shorter the distances over which electricity has to be transported. Thus geography also has an impact on electricity prices to end users.

England and Wales took the lead in structural reform of electricity markets in 1990, but many OECD economies and some non-OECD economies have gone at least some of the way down similar paths. In the EU, structural reform has received an additional impetus with the Second Electricity Directive of 2003 (discussed in more detail later). Doove *et al.* (2001) describe the broad outlines of the structural reform agenda as follows:

- structurally separating (*unbundling*) the competitive activities (particularly generation, but sometimes also retailing) from the natural monopoly elements (particularly transmission, but occasionally sometimes also distribution) — this is called *vertical separation*;
- dividing existing generation capacity among a number of different generation companies, who then compete with each other — this is called *horizontal separation*;
- allowing new generators to enter the market — these are sometimes called independent power producers (IPPs);

- guaranteeing open and non-discriminatory access for all generators to the transmission grid (subject to available capacity), so that they can sell directly to downstream suppliers or users, rather than selling to the incumbent — this is called *third party access (TPA)*;
- establishing a *wholesale price pool*, or spot wholesale market for electricity (either mandatory or optional, and broader than, but interconnected with, the balancing market), so that new entrants are not obliged to enter both the generation and retailing sector at the same time, thus lowering entry costs;
- regulating the natural monopoly activities to prevent any abuse of market power;
- introducing a regulator independent of industry players and day-to-day influence, and typically separate from the system operator;
- enabling large customers (retailers and sometimes large industrial users) to buy electricity directly from the generator of their choice;
- introducing competition into metering and billing activities and contract terms, thus allowing retail customers freedom to choose among different electricity suppliers;
- providing a full range of tradable financial instruments (eg futures contracts and options);
- undertaking partial or complete privatization or corporatization of publicly-owned assets;
- introducing cross-ownership restrictions, especially between competitive and natural monopoly activities;
- liberalizing restrictions on foreign investment and ownership;
- mandating service quality standards; and
- allowing retailers to introduce innovative services (eg the ability to switch retailers over the internet, or providing electricity jointly with other services such as telephony and gas).

The possible benefits of these reforms are discussed shortly.

Gas markets

Natural gas is found in underground reserves, often in combination with oil and condensate products. Exploration and production is generally done by oil companies, and there are few synergies between this and other activities in gas markets. In economies without indigenous production, however, the primary supply activity is undertaken by importers, who may also be involved in downstream activities. What follows is also drawn from European Commission (2007).

Natural gas is mostly transported from production to market by high-volume, high-pressure transmission pipelines. Natural gas can also be cooled, condensed, and transported by sea in liquid form (LNG). Both forms of transport are expensive relative to the value of the gas shipped, but pipeline transport is cheaper than LNG shipment for shorter distances, while LNG shipment is viable for longer distances. Both transmission pipelines and LNG terminal facilities involve substantial sunk costs, giving both activities natural monopoly characteristics.

Once natural gas reaches the market, it is distributed to customers over lower-volume, lower-pressure distribution pipelines. These distribution networks also have the characteristics of a natural monopoly.

Unlike electricity, there is essentially only one technology for producing natural gas. Also unlike electricity, natural gas can be stored, so there is no necessity to instantaneously match supply to demand. Nevertheless, flexibility is somewhat limited because the physical characteristics of storage facilities may limit the speed with which gas can be injected or withdrawn. Flexibility is also limited because gas extraction rates from underground reserves may depend on geology rather than demand, and the ability to alter pipeline pressures is also somewhat limited.

In many economies, gas importation, transmission and storage was traditionally undertaken by a single monopolist (or several companies with regional monopolies). Sometimes the monopoly importer also sold to end users, or else these sales were handled by downstream monopolies.

Like electricity, structural reform of gas markets involves allowing new entrants into the potentially competitive segments of the market, without requiring them to be vertically integrated. Possible new business models include the following:

- new companies that produce gas or import it from external sources, in competition with the incumbent(s);
- new shipper/suppliers who buy gas on wholesale markets, arrange for its transportation with the network company, and sign retail contracts with end-users;
- pure traders who buy and sell on wholesale markets to take advantage of arbitrage opportunities.

These new business models rely on the development of functioning wholesale markets, and on third party access to transmission and distribution networks. To reduce the possibility of incumbents using their control over pipeline or terminal facilities to thwart competition, both transmission and distribution should be unbundled into separate transmission system operators (TSOs) and distribution system operators (DSOs). If such operators are sufficiently independent from incumbents, they should have an incentive to maximize, rather than restrict, the amount of gas sold through their networks, thus facilitating competition.

Thus the broad features of structural reform in gas markets are similar to those in electricity markets, though the scope for competition in primary production/importing is somewhat more limited than in electricity generation.

7.2 The State of Play in APEC Economies

The state of play in APEC electricity and gas markets is summarized in Table 7.1, for those APEC economies for which adequate information has been able to be collected via desk research (the exceptions are Brunei and Papua New Guinea). More details on actual policy settings in APEC economies are given in Dee (2011a), which also notes the extent of reforms since 2004.

According to Table 7.1, very few APEC economies have achieved substantial reform of both electricity and gas markets, and those that have are essentially developed economies — Australia, Canada, New Zealand, Singapore and the United States. Japan and Peru have achieved

Table 7.1. Summary of Current Regulation in APEC Electricity and Gas Markets, 2009

	Electricity			*Gas*		
	Unbundling generation	*Third party access*	*Wholesale pool*	*Unbundling transmission*	*Third party access*	*Retail competition*
Australia	Yes	Yes	Yes	Yes	Yes	Yes
Canada		Yes	Yes	Yes	Yes	Yes
Chile	Yes	Yes	Yes	Yes		
China	Yes		Yes			Yes
Hong Kong						
Indonesia				Yes	Yes	
Japan		Yes	Yes		Yes	Yes
Rep. of Korea	Yes	Yes	Yes			
Malaysia						
Mexico					Yes	Yes
New Zealand	Yes	Yes	Yes	Yes	Yes	Yes
Peru	Yes	Yes		Yes	Yes	
Philippines	Yes					
Russia	Yes	Yes	Yes			
Singapore	Yes	Yes	Yes	Yes	Yes	Yes
Chinese Taipei						
Thailand				Yes	Yes	
United States	Yes	Yes		Yes	Yes	Yes
Viet Nam						

Sources: Dee (2011a).

some reform in both markets, though in Japan's case this has been without vertically unbundling its incumbent operators. China has also started to reform both markets, although its electricity reform is only on an experimental basis in a few geographic areas. A few APEC economies have achieved substantial reform in electricity but not in gas — Chile, the Republic of Korea, and Russia — although the extent of electricity reform in the Republic of Korea is rather thin. A few more APEC economies have achieved substantial reform in gas but not electricity — Indonesia, Mexico and Thailand. Some have achieved very little in either market — Hong Kong, Malaysia, the Philippines, Chinese Taipei and Viet Nam.

Dee (2011a) indicates that, to the extent that structural reforms have taken place in electricity and gas markets since 2004, they have tended to be incremental — there have been few big-bang initiatives.

APEC electricity markets

In electricity, this is partly because introducing competition into generation and retail is a highly complex regulatory process. The regulatory requirements for competitive new producers and/or wholesalers to get access to existing transmission and distribution networks need to be compatible with the technical requirements for the safety and physical integrity of the system. Lack of regulatory capacity may explain in part the lack of progress in Viet Nam. It may also explain why China has chosen to undertake reforms on an experimental basis, via two pilot projects in the Northeast and East.

Elsewhere, the California electricity crisis of 2000 and 2001 had a chilling effect on reforms in Malaysia. Reforms have also been stymied by domestic legal or political considerations. For example, in 2004 Indonesia's electricity reform legislation was annulled by the Constitutional Court, and it is only in late 2009 that amended legislation was passed. Similarly, in the Philippines, reform has been handicapped by a legislative requirement that liberalization can proceed only after key players have been privatized. In Mexico, under Article 27 of the Constitution, the State has exclusive responsibility for generating, transporting, transforming, distributing and supplying electricity as a public service. In Chinese Taipei, the incumbent had a legislated monopoly until 2008. In Thailand, after the election of Thaksin, reform plans were converted into a plan to create a 'national champion'.

At the other end of the spectrum, by 2004 some economies in the APEC region had already achieved major structural reforms in electricity generation. This included Australia, Chile, New Zealand, Peru and parts of the United States. In Hong Kong the electricity market is a duopoly, but this appears to be 'natural' as neither has exclusivity.

Thus the post-2004 reform experience in the region has been concentrated in a few economies — Canada and Japan have undergone minor reforms, while the Republic of Korea, Russia and Singapore have undergone more significant ones. In several Canadian provinces and Japan, wholesale price pools have been introduced. The Republic of Korea has gone through a more extensive process of separating transmission from generating capacity and introducing one-way bidding in a wholesale pool. But the Republic of Korea has yet to introduce competition in the retail sector, and the six separate generating companies are still wholly-owned subsidiaries of the majority state-owned incumbent. Singapore had already separated generation from transmission prior to 2004, but has been gradually introducing both wholesale and retail competition since then. Russia has undertaken the most comprehensive reform since 2004, both separating generation capacity into separate companies (though still under partial ownership of the incumbent), and from 2008 introducing both wholesale and retail competition.

APEC gas markets

In general, reforms in natural gas since 2004 have been less extensive than in electricity. In part, this is because the scope for competition in natural gas production depends on the range of sources of supply. Indeed, many of those economies with extensive indigenous reserves had already undertaken significant reform prior to 2004. This includes Australia, Canada, Mexico, New Zealand, Peru and the United States. At the other extreme, the Philippines has little domestic production and no imports, meaning the market is essentially still nascent. In Chile, the scope for competition is limited, given that there is deemed to be little scope for sources of gas other than Argentina. Import-dependent economies such as the Republic of Korea and Chinese Taipei have extended their sources of supply by building terminals to handle LNG, but so far their natural gas industries are still dominated by incumbents.

There have been four main instances of reform since 2004. China has reformed its retail price controls so that these can more closely match production costs. New Zealand has introduced a regulated third party access regime for one of its pipelines. Following earlier reforms in 2002, Singapore introduced a Gas Code in 2005 that details the terms and conditions for gas transportation on an equitable and non-discriminatory basis. Similarly, Thailand has introduced third party access to pipelines to facilitate wholesale competition among its four major producers.

7.3 The Gains from Reform — Evidence to Date

The evidence to date has been both qualitative and quantitative. Most of it has been based on the ongoing reform experiences in the developed economies, particularly in Europe and the United States. Reviews of the reform experience have also had to evaluate several instances of possible reform failure — the first being the California electricity crisis of 2000 and 2001, and the second being the UK retreat from a wholesale price pool back to bilateral contracts in 2001. Empirical evidence on these two issues is presented later.

Qualitative evidence

In several recent papers, Pollitt (2007, 2008) summarizes the gains from reform in electricity markets (and by extension, he claims, in gas markets), based primarily on the UK experience, which in many respects is a best-case scenario.

Competition reduces costs (and prices) significantly, relative to what they might have been without reform, even if it does not reduce them in absolute terms over time. It does this by encouraging efficient operation and least-cost and timely investment. It also exposes pre-existing market power.

Retail competition has been revealed to be an important complement to competition in generation. Retail competition involves more than the choice of buying wholesale power from a non-incumbent generator. It also involves competition in billing, contract terms and bundling of other services, and hence requires competition at the supplier level.

Consumers do respond to price signals, both by switching suppliers and by demand reduction. This contradicts the previous conventional wisdom that demand was very unresponsive to price. Further, Pollitt (2008) claims that household consumers do not need institutionalized protection from fluctuations in wholesale prices — where they prefer fixed tariffs, suppliers have generally offered these voluntarily, providing a form of insurance as part of their bundled package of services. Pollitt (2007) also claims that with sufficient competition in generation, regulation of the *level* of retail prices should also become unnecessary (though incentive regulation of transmission prices, through CPI–X price caps, remains a critical part of the regulatory landscape).

Vertical separation is costly, but the vertical economies of joint operation between networks and competitive segments of the industry are not sufficient to outweigh the increased competitive pressure that comes from clear separation of the monopoly networks from the rest of the supply chain. Pollitt (2008) claims that this has been proved for electricity transmission, gas transmission and may be in the process of being proved for gas distribution in the UK. This finding means that vertical separation should not be pursued for its own sake, but only where it can facilitate greater competition.

However, Pollitt (2007) notes that while the vertical economies between generation and transmission are not sufficient to offset the benefits of competition in wholesale power markets, they do appear to be significant between generation and retail. This is because the integration of generation and retail offers advantages in terms of risk management, and it means that retail-only companies are likely to struggle, as they have in the UK, the Netherlands and New Zealand. One side-effect of generation and retail integration, however, is that it makes wholesale markets much thinner, which can have its own effect on the ease of new entry.

Finally, markets have been good at choosing between technologies on the basis of price, as demonstrated by the move to combined cycle gas turbines in the 1990s, and by the resurgence of interest in nuclear power more recently. It is sometimes claimed that regulated markets are good at ensuring the efficient use of existing capacity, but are not as good at ensuring appropriate investments in new capacity. However, Pollitt (2008) notes that as network capacity limits are reached, the X factor in incentive regulation should become less driven by squeezing monopoly profits, and more driven by the need to finance new investments. Nevertheless, new regulatory mechanisms may be necessary to ensure that the new investments are least-cost, rather than simply undertaken to incumbents' specifications.

Despite these potential gains from structural reforms, they have been taken furthest only in jurisdictions where supranational bodies (the European Commission), national governments (the US Federal

Government) or inspired individuals (in Russia) have pushed hard and consistently. But even parts of the United States do not yet have full retail competition. In many other jurisdictions, reforms have stalled at some early or intermediate stage.

Clearly, local physical, institutional and other factors have a role to play in the ability of reforms to deliver real gains. According to Pollitt (2007), key institutional factors that seem to have been important are significant initial public ownership, and prices that more than cover efficient economic cost (as in Australia, Chile, New Zealand and the UK). Initial private ownership (eg in Japan and the United States) and prices below economic cost (eg in India) have made reform much more difficult. Also critical has been the capacity and flexibility of regulators to tailor reforms to local conditions and to adapt as network conditions change.

Beyond local conditions, Correlje and De Vries (2008) identify four key lessons from the reforms themselves:

- ownership separation (not just accounting or legal separation) of electricity transmission from the rest of the network has been critical to improving access for competitive generation and removing incentives to under-invest in transmission;
- getting the market structure right in electricity generation is crucial for the success of reforms, and allowing new entry alone may not be sufficient — horizontal separation may also be required;
- incentive regulation based on CPI–X price control of monopoly transmission networks can deliver significant incentives to reduce costs and facilitate efficient operation, while proving a stable cash flow for new investment, and economies with tougher incentive regulation of networks have significantly lower network costs as a result;
- regulation can address market failures such as those associated with the quality of supply, but it requires a degree of regulatory sophistication to balance efficiency and quality objectives.

Reviewing the experience of electricity reform in developing economies, Jamasb (2006) notes that the cost savings from wholesale markets or independent power producers will not be passed on to consumers if there is not enough competition in generation. While retail competition may be feasible only in the long term, competition among independent generators is possible even in a single-buyer market, and economies with small markets can also introduce competition *for* the market.

Reform in developing economies can take place even without privatization. Reform requires a well-functioning transmission system, which should probably remain in state ownership in the early stages of reform. Incentive regulation can also drive efficiency improvements in distribution activities and ensure that they are passed on to consumers, even when distribution companies remain in state or local ownership.

Jamasb (2006) also confirms that cost-reflective tariffs and proper subsidy schemes (ie properly funded, and not relying on cross-subsidies) are crucial for the sustainability of reforms. He notes that stable macroeconomic conditions are crucial for attracting the necessary investments from domestic and foreign sources. Finally, he notes that progress in developing economies is likely to be evolutionary, particularly since regulatory experience and the necessary institutional structures take time to develop.

Empirical evidence

The empirical evidence on the gains from reform is mixed. To some extent, the mixed results are themselves a sign that reforms may not have been taken far enough in some economies. Either reforms have not been taken far enough to have any real effects, or there are not enough reforms in the chosen samples for econometric techniques to discern any significant effects.

The mixed results may also reflect the difficulty of the empirical task. Establishing the effects of reform requires a data sample in which there has been a variety of reform experiences. This typically requires a data sample involving a number of different economies, and it can be difficult to correct for all the other country-specific factors (other than reform) that may also account for the performance of the electricity sector. Even if it is possible to establish the effects of reform (correcting for other factors), it is typically very difficult to get robust evidence on which dimensions of the reform experience are responsible for those effects. As noted earlier, reform involves a number of inter-related steps, many of which are often taken together. This makes it very difficult to isolate which particular steps are responsible for the effects.

One of the first empirical assessments of the effects of electricity reform was Steiner's (2000) study of OECD members over the period 1986–96. She found that unbundling of generation, third party access and the introduction of wholesale electricity markets were all associated with lower electricity prices. However, she also confirmed that private ownership was not necessarily associated with increased competition. Nevertheless, both private ownership and unbundling of generation and transmission were found to be associated with a higher rate of utilization of existing generation capacity, and with reserve plant margins that were closer to optimal.

Hattori and Tsutsui (2004) undertook as similar study of OECD members over a slightly later period of 1987–99. Their findings were less definitive than Steiner, although this could in part be because of differences in their measurement of variables (including prices). They found that giving customers access to alternative suppliers (which they argue is highly correlated with third party access) was associated with lower prices. However, unlike Steiner, they did not find a significant effect of unbundling or the introduction of a wholesale spot market on prices.

Nagayama (2007) undertook a broadly similar study of 83 economies over the period 1985–2002. He found that neither unbundling nor the introduction of a wholesale pool market on their own would necessarily reduce electricity prices. In fact, contrary to expectations, there was a tendency for the price to rise. However, coexistent with an independent regulator, unbundling could work to reduce prices. He also found that privatization, the introduction of foreign independent producers and retail competition could lower electricity prices in some regions, but not all.

There have also been in-depth before-and-after studies of reform experiences in individual economies. Two areas of interest are the California electricity crisis, and the UK's apparent reversal of reforms in the early 2000s. Both of these demonstrate the dangers of incomplete or inconsistent reforms.

Joskow's (2001) detailed analysis of the Californian crisis shows that when demand spikes, individual generators may have considerable market power to increase prices and withhold generating capacity, even when there is no collusion among them. This was found to be a factor contributing to a ten-fold rise in wholesale electricity prices in California in 2000. But regulatory problems also contributed significantly. One problem was wholesale market-design rules that prevented a smoothing of wholesale prices. Another problem was the maintenance of retail price caps that prevented signals about market conditions being passed on to consumers. The caps led to the bankruptcy of major suppliers when wholesale prices rose above the capped retail prices.

In the UK, Evans and Green (2003) examined why electricity prices fell after the abandonment of the wholesale price pool and the return to bilateral contracts. One problem with the pool had been collusion or 'gaming' by dominant players (arguably because of insufficient horizontal separation). Evans and Green attempt to distinguish the impact of a subsequent decline in market concentration from the introduction of the new electricity trading arrangements in 2001. They found that it was declining concentration that explained the fall in wholesale prices. This shows that effective regulatory action to reduce incumbent market shares can be more important that market design *per se*.

There are fewer studies of the effects of reform in gas markets. Jamasb, Pollitt and Triebs (2008) studied the effects of US regulatory reform on productivity, and found that encouraging competition has been rather successful in raising productivity. Hawdon (2003) found evidence that the types of reforms introduced in the UK are associated with higher levels of efficiency, good utilization of labour and levels of underutilization of capital sufficient to support the development of competitive markets. Nevertheless, Brakman, van Marrewijk and van Witteloostuijn (2009) warn that lack of competition and capacity constraints in gas production/import can prevent these gains from being passed on to consumers.

7.4 New Evidence on the Gains from Reform in Electricity and Gas Markets

One of the limitations of empirical studies of the effects of regulatory reform is that the studies are somewhat 'captive' to the nature and extent of reforms that are present in the sample. As the recent APEC experience shows, regulatory reform in the developing world has tended to be slow and incremental, so that samples taken from developing economies will not necessarily encompass a wide variety of reform experiences. Samples drawn from the developed world may not match the local conditions of developing economies, so that extrapolation needs to be done with care. But samples from developed economies may capture a wider set of reforms, and therefore give a clearer picture of the *potential* benefits of reform.

A recent round of new EU directives has provided a fresh impetus to regulatory reform of electricity and gas markets in these economies. This provides a rich new source of reform experience with which to test the empirical findings of earlier studies.

The First Electricity Directive (Directive 96/92/EC) of 1996 removed legal monopolies by requiring EU member states to allow large electricity users to choose their suppliers. It also obliged vertically integrated companies to grant third party access to transmission and distribution networks. It also required a minimum level of unbundling of vertically integrated companies. Gradually, this regime was seen to have various limitations. It allowed the terms of third party access to be negotiated rather than regulated. The unbundling obligations were limited, allowing accounting separation as well as legal or ownership separation. And the directive did not require the establishment of a national energy regulator. As a result, there were significant differences across member states in the extent of market opening.

To overcome these limitations, the Second Electricity Directive (2003/54/EC) was introduced in 2003. This obliges EU members to introduce a regulated third party access regime, and removes the possibility of negotiated third party access. It also mandates the appointment of a national regulator that is independent of the industry. It requires legal separation, rather than just accounting or management separation, between network activities (transmission and distribution) and all other activities. Finally, it requires non-household customers to have choice of supplier by mid-2004, and household customers to have choice by mid-2007. These regulations tightened up a range of market opening requirements, and led to significant additional regulatory changes in the lagging member states during the 2000s. In particular, the new regulations also stimulated the development of wholesale electricity markets in lagging member states, so they could meet their obligations regarding consumer choice.

A similar evolution of regulation occurred in EU gas markets. The legislative process began in the 1990s with a series of directives aimed at abolishing import monopolies, gradually opening markets, mandating accounting separation for vertically integrated network companies, and an adoption of regulated third party access. The Second Gas Directive (2003/55/EC) of 2003 requires full market opening, national sector regulators, regulated third party network access, regulated or negotiated access to storage facilities, and further unbundling of integrated companies. Supporting regulation sets obligatory minimum requirements for access to transmission systems, including network tariffs, third party access services, capacity allocation, transparency, balancing and trading of capacity rights.

In analysing the impact of these regulatory frameworks, European Commission (2007) stresses how incomplete unbundling can seriously undermine attempts to introduce competition into electricity and gas markets. If network operators are not sufficiently independent from incumbent service suppliers, they will find a myriad of ways to thwart the activities of new entrants, despite third party access legislation.

The remainder of this section describes econometric analysis of the effects of electricity and gas reforms on prices and non-price measures of efficiency, using data for OEDC members (including a significant number of EU members) over the period 1990 to 2008. Thus the sample captures regulatory changes induced by both the first and second waves of EU reforms. The choice of OECD member economies is dictated largely by the availability of price information. A key source of relatively consistent information on energy prices across economies is the Energy Prices and Taxes publication of the International Energy Agency, the data from which is available for sale online. However, the price information is only available for OECD members. Ideally, the exercise would have included the effects of reform on quality measures such as the reliability of supply. Unfortunately, there is no comprehensive international data on these measures.

Analysis of electricity markets

The analysis closely follows the approach of Steiner (2000). Electricity prices are modelled as being determined by measures of regulatory policy, as well as a number of non-regulatory controls. The regulatory measures are the presence of a regulated or negotiated third party access regime, the existence of a liberalized wholesale market for electricity, the existence of vertical unbundling between transmission and generation, and the prevalence of private ownership. The non-regulatory controls are the level of GDP, the shares of electricity generation accounted for by nuclear sources and hydro sources, and the urban share of the population, as a measure of the density of the network. These explanatory variables are the same as in Steiner, except for the addition of the degree of urbanization, a higher value of which could be associated with lower prices if there are significant economies of density. Missing from the current analysis are Steiner's measures of the time to privatization and the time to liberalization, since these performed perversely in her regressions, suggesting that they were correlated with each other and with other variables, so their own effects would not be established with precision.

Ideally, the model of electricity prices should include the prices of thermal fuel inputs (ie oil, coal and gas) as controls. However, the coverage of input prices from International Energy Agency sources is very patchy, and restricting the estimation to those economies and time periods for which it was available would severely restrict the range and extent of electricity reform in the sample. To some extent, controlling for hydro and nuclear shares helps to control for variations in generating input costs. The estimation also corrects for unobservable differences across economies, as will be explained shortly.

The current analysis also examines the effects of regulatory policy on capacity utilization, and on the extent of deviation of reserve plant margins from optimal. Efficient generators typically plan to meet demands with a capacity buffer that is prudent but not excessive. This analysis follows Steiner in using a 15 per cent margin as a rough indicator of the optimal reserve plant margin. Both measures of efficiency are modelled as being determined in part by the extent of third party access, the extent of unbundling, and the degree of private ownership. The existence of a wholesale price pool is not expected to influence efficiency, though it is expected to influence prices. These measures of efficiency are also affected by non-regulatory controls, including the degree of urbanization. Instead of Steiner's measures of state preferences in favour of coal technology or against nuclear technology (both of which would be expected to reduce measured efficiency), the current formulation uses the actual shares of hydro, nuclear and coal technologies on total generating capacity.

The data sources are similar to those used by Steiner, although the economy coverage is expanded slightly to include two OECD members — the Republic of Korea and Mexico — which are also members of APEC. Electricity prices are taken from Energy Prices and Taxes (third quarter 2009 edition) published online by the International Energy Agency. The necessary data on electricity capacity and generation to compute the efficiency and control measures were taken from Electricity Information (2009 edition), also by the International Energy Agency. GDP and the rate of urbanization are both taken from the World Bank's World Development Indicators. Both electricity prices and GDP are expressed in US dollars converted using purchasing power parities. Electricity prices are the net-of-tax prices to industrial users, since the share of generation costs in end user prices is likely to be highest for industrial users, and reforms are expected to impact most on generation costs. A summary of the data on electricity prices, efficiency measures, and non-regulatory controls is shown in Table 7.2.

The policy variables used in the analysis are defined as follows:

Table 7.2. Economic and Technological Data for Electricity, OECD Economies, 1990 to 2008

Variable	*Variable name*	*Number of observations*	*Mean*	*Standard deviation*	*Minimum*	*Maximum*
Electricity end-user price to industry, net of taxes, US$ PPP/kWh	entpr	349	0.067587	0.028455	0.016	0.187
GDP, PPP (current international $), trillions	gdp_ppp_s	399	1.190218	2.09913	0.046	14.204
Nuclear share in gross production (ratio)	nucshr	399	0.189979	0.2158379	0	0.783681
Hydro share in gross production (ratio)	hydroshr	399	0.2009344	0.2536616	0.0003546	0.9962215
Urban share of population (%)	urban	399	75.3015	10.94613	47.9	97.4
Utilization rate = gross production (GWh)/net capacity (MWe)	eutil	374	4.428908	0.562455	2.715238	5.852232
Deviation of reserve margin from optimal = abs[(capacity – peak)/peak – 0.15]	eres	332	0.304555	0.1984277	0.0004457	0.9926048
Nuclear share in capacity (ratio)	nuccapshr	374	0.1209503	0.1447605	0	0.5509456
Hydro share in capacity (ratio)	hydcapshr	374	0.2659052	0.2393256	0.0006915	0.9907865

Sources: See text.

etpa	Existence of regime for regulated or negotiated third party access to electricity transmission grid 0 = no third party access, 1= third party access
ewpp	Existence of liberalized wholesale market for electricity (wholesale price pool) 0 = no wholesale price pool, 1= wholesale price pool
eunb	Existence of vertical separation between the transmission and generation segments of the electricity market (whether accounting separation or separate companies) 0 = no vertical separation, 1= vertical separation
eown	Ownership structure of the largest companies in the generation, transmission, distribution and supply segments of the electricity market 0 = public, 1 = mostly public, 2 = mixed, 3 = mostly private, 4 = private

Measures of these policy variables for all of the OECD economies in the sample except for the Republic of Korea and Mexico are available up until 2003 from OECD (2005). Measures for the remaining economies and time periods were constructed from information obtained online from the International Energy Regulation Network, the EIA Country Analysis Briefs of the US Energy Information Administration, and the Trade Policy Reviews of the WTO. A full listing of the values of these policy variables for all OECD economies and time periods in the sample is given in Dee (2011a).

As noted earlier, one difficulty in exercises of this sort is distinguishing the separate contributions of different steps in the reform process when the different steps are often taken together. This creates a technical problem of multicollinearity, which manifests itself in econometric estimation on panel data sets as instability or 'flip-flop' in the signs of the coefficients on the policy variables, while the magnitudes of the coefficients are often implausibly large, but apparently highly significant. As an initial reality check, it is therefore useful to look at the *simple* correlations between the policy variables and the resulting measures of performance, prior to correcting for the influence of other variables.

Table 7.3. Simple Correlations between Policy and Performance in Electricity

	Performance measures		
Policy variables	entpr	eutil	eres
etpa	–0.09	0.05	–0.16
ewpp	–0.06	–0.03	–0.04
eunb	–0.04	0.06	–0.17
eown	0.05	0.02	–0.14

Source: Own calculations.

These simple correlations are shown in Table 7.3 (unfortunately, graphical presentation does not show the correlations clearly, because of the zero-one nature of the policy variables). The table shows the same pattern of effects of policy changes on price as in Steiner — third party access, a wholesale market and unbundling all tend to reduce electricity prices, while private ownership can increase them. Third party access, unbundling and private ownership also tend to increase capacity utilization, while a wholesale market can apparently reduce it, although the effect is small, as expected. Third party access, a wholesale market, unbundling and private ownership are all associated with reserve plant margins being closer to optimal (the distance from the optimal margin is reduced), although the effect of the wholesale market again is small, as expected.

The simple correlations do not show whether the strength of these effects are significantly different from zero. They also do not correct for the influence of other, non-regulatory factors. The results of econometric estimation shown in Tables 7.4 and 7.5 overcome these limitations.

The econometric estimation also attempts to control for *unobservable* influences on electricity prices and efficiency that might vary over time or across economies. Unobservable differences over time are controlled using a deterministic time trend. In principle, unobservable differences across economies could also have been controlled using deterministic dummy variables. However, these country dummies are relatively highly correlated with both the policy variables and with the degree of urbanization (which does not vary much over time in many economies). Including deterministic country dummies therefore causes the 'flip-flop' problem noted earlier. Consequently, unobservable economy effects are

Table 7.4. Results of Random Effects Panel Regression for Electricity Prices

Dependent variable	*Industry price*
Constant	0.1571
	[0.000]
Third party access (etpa)	–0.0032
	[0.270]
Wholesale price pool (ewpp)	–0.0049
	[0.072]
Unbundling (eunb)	–0.0075
	[0.008]
Private ownership (eown)	0.0039
	[0.011]
Hydro share in generation (hydroshr)	–0.0276
	[0.047]
Nuclear share in generation (nucshr)	–0.0033
	[0.847]
Urbanization (urban)	–0.0013
	[0.000]
GDP in PPP (gdp_ppp_s)	0.0010
	[0.352]
Time trend	0.0018
	[0.000]
Number of observations	347
Number of time periods	19
Number of OECD economies	21
Wald test that coefficients not significantly different from zero	100.06
	[0.000]
Breusch–Pagan chi-squared test that random effects equal zero	838.65
	[0.000]
Hausman test of no diff. between random and fixed effects estimates	4.34
	[0.888]

Notes: Numbers in parentheses after the coefficient estimates are Prob>|z|. Numbers in parentheses after the Wald, Breusch–Pagan and Hausman tests are Prob>chi^2.

controlled by assuming them to be random and using random effects estimation, even when Hausman tests show that these estimates differ significantly from fixed effects estimates (the fixed effects estimates are not regarded as robust, for the reasons just described).

The effects of the policy variables on electricity prices are qualitatively the same as indicated by simple correlations. Furthermore,

Table 7.5. Results of Random Effects Panel Regression for Electricity Efficiency

Dependent variable	*Utilization rate*	*Reserve margin deviation*
Constant	3.9804	0.5256
	[0.000]	[0.034]
Third party access (etpa)	–0.0638	–0.0023
	[0.289]	[0.919]
Unbundling (eunb)	0.0944	–0.0317
	[0.111]	[0.152]
Private ownership (eown)	0.0077	–0.0019
	[0.780]	[0.871]
Hydro share in capacity (hydcapshr)	0.6381	–0.0126
	[0.152]	[0.939]
Nuclear share in capacity (nuccapshr)	2.3007	–0.2038
	[0.003]	[0.481]
Coal share in capacity (coalcapshr)	0.4208	–0.0126
	[0.284]	[0.939]
Urbanization (urban)	–0.0028	–0.0031
	[0.760]	[0.355]
Time trend	0.0133	0.0036
	[0.014]	[0.078]
Number of observations	330	302
Number of time periods	19	19
Number of OECD economies	21	21
Wald test that coefficients not significantly different from zero	24.30	6.46
	[0.002]	[0.596]
Breusch–Pagan chi-squared test that random effects equal zero	811.45	869.64
	[0.000]	[0.000]
Hausman test of no diff. between random and fixed effects estimates	17.49	6.90
	[0.025]	[0.547]

Notes: Numbers in parentheses after the coefficient estimates are Prob>|z|. Numbers in parentheses after the Wald, Breusch–Pagan and Hausman tests are Prob>chi^2.

the effects are shown to be significantly different from zero. So Steiner's results are again confirmed — third party access, a wholesale market and unbundling all tend to reduce electricity prices, while private ownership can increase them. The apparent insignificance of some of these factors found by other researchers, particularly the presence of wholesale market, has been overcome by using a dataset in which there is more reform 'action'.

The non-regulatory influences on electricity prices are generally also of the expected sign. Prices tend to be higher when GDP is higher, while a higher hydro share in generation tends to reduce prices. A high nuclear share also appears to reduce prices, against expectations, but this effect is not significant. A higher rate of urbanization tends to reduce prices, confirming that there are economies of density in the production and sale of electricity.

The policy variables have less significant effects on efficiency than on prices. The only result that comes close to being significant is that unbundling tends to increase capacity utilization. Note that the European Commission (2007) also identifies adequate unbundling as the key linchpin to promoting effective competition. Utilization also increases significantly when there is a high nuclear share in generating capacity. No policy variable has a significant effect on the deviation of reserve plant margin from optimal. However, this estimation performs poorly on all fronts.

These results should not be taken to mean that structural reform of electricity markets has minimal effect on efficiency. It just means that it has little discernable effect on the particular efficiency measures chosen in this exercise. Reform could still have a large beneficial effect on other measures, such as labour productivity. Indeed, the reforms that are shown to reduce electricity prices could do so in one of two ways — by squeezing the excess profits of incumbent operators, or by encouraging them to reduce their real production costs. Anecdotal evidence from the reform experience in economies such as Australia suggests that reforms can dramatically boost labour productivity, and therefore reduce production costs.

Analysis of gas markets

While there are many models of gas efficiency (eg Lee, Park and Kim 1999, Granderson 2000, Hawdon 2003, Jamasb, Pollitt and Triebs 2008, Farsi and Filippini 2009), there are fewer models of gas prices. Furthermore, many of the price models explain the extent of convergence of gas prices across different geographic markets (eg Walls 1994, Cuddington and Wang 2006) rather than the level of gas prices *per se*.

This may in part reflect the limitations imposed by the way that gas prices are set, especially in Europe. As explained in European Commission (2007), a large majority of gas consumed in the EU is bought by the incumbent wholesale players under long-term contracts from producers, both outside and inside the EU. The prices in European long-term gas contracts are mainly linked to the prices of oil and oil derivatives. Thus the contract prices paid by different producers to different suppliers move in an almost identical manner through time, and do not react smoothly (or at all) to changes in the supply and demand of gas markets. The UK gas market is a little different, with long-term gas prices from UK fields being determined partly by hub gas prices (ie the prices on more-or-less organized wholesale exchanges) and partly by general inflation indexes. But hub trading has been slow to develop. And at the retail end, a majority of EU member states regulate prices to households and small businesses, while at least six member states set a regulated price that is available to all customers (although the proportion of end-users that have stayed with the regulated tariff varies between member states).

Thus if EU structural reform is to be reflected in gas prices at all, is it likely to be reflected in the wholesale-retail margins on gas sold to industrial users. The approach here is therefore to look for any discernable effect of regulatory reform on the net-of-tax price to industrial users. These prices are modelled as being determined by measures of regulatory policy, as well as a number of non-regulatory controls. The regulatory measures are the presence of a regulated or negotiated third party access regime, the percentage of the retail market for gas that is open to competition, the absence of national, state or provincial regulations that restrict the number of competitors, the existence of vertical unbundling between production/import and other segments, the existence of vertical unbundling between gas supply and other segments, and the prevalence of private ownership. The non-regulatory controls are the level of GDP, the total gas pipeline length (to account for economies of scale), and the urban share of the population (to account for economies of density).

Ideally, the model of gas prices to industrial users should include the wholesale price of gas as a control. However, as was the case for electricity, the coverage of input prices from International Energy Agency sources is very patchy, and restricting the estimation to those economies and time periods for which it was available would severely restrict the range and extent of gas reform in the sample. But given the relative unresponsiveness of wholesale gas prices to supply and demand conditions, it was judged adequate to proxy wholesale gas prices by a non-linear time trend.

The current analysis also examines the effects of regulatory policy on gas capacity utilization, as measured by annual gas consumption relative to total pipeline length. This is modelled as being determined in part by the same regulatory variables as for gas prices. It is also affected by non-regulatory controls, including the share of gas in electricity generation (which would be expected to increase the utilization rate), and the degree of urbanization. Urbanization could have an ambiguous effect on the utilization rate. Greater urbanization could increase the utilization rate by allowing economies of density. However, if there were industrial or other users with heavy and reliable gas demands (such as mining operators or electricity generators) located outside of urban areas, this too could increase utilization despite the degree of urbanization.

The coverage of economies and time periods is the same as for the electricity analysis. Net-of-tax gas prices to industrial users are taken from Energy Prices and Taxes (third quarter 2009 edition) published online by the International Energy Agency. The necessary data on gas consumption and the gas share of electricity capacity were taken from Electricity Information (2009 edition) and Natural Gas Information (2009 edition), also by the International Energy Agency. Pipeline lengths are taken from various editions of the CIA World Factbook, available online. GDP and the rate of urbanization are both taken from the World Bank's World Development Indicators. Both gas prices and GDP are expressed in US dollars converted using purchasing power parities. A summary of the data on gas prices, the efficiency measure, and non-regulatory controls is shown in Table 7.6.

The policy variables used in the analysis are defined as follows:

Table 7.6. Economic and Technological Data for Gas, OECD Economies, 1990 to 2008

	Variable name	*Number of observations*	*Mean*	*Standard deviation*	*Minimum*	*Maximum*
Gas end-user price to industry, net of taxes, US$ PPP/10e+7 kcal	gntpr	260	203.2362	118.1389	74.21	644.418
GDP, PPP (current international $), billions	gdp_ppp	399	1190.218	2099.13	46	14204
Pipeline length (thousands of kilometres)	gpipe_s	399	29.32738	87.17871	0	548.665
Urban share of population (%)	urban	399	75.3015	10.94613	47.9	97.4
Utilization rate = gas consumption (million cubic meters)/ pipeline length (kilometres)	gutil	391	6.013908	8.047427	0.023514	47.62
Gas share in electricity generation capacity (ratio)	gascapshr	327	0.1019645	0.1029867	0	0.5691414

Sources: See text.

gtpa Existence of regime for regulated or negotiated third party access to gas transmission grid
0 = no third party access, 1= third party access

gretc Percentage of the retail market for gas that is open to competition
0 = less than 10 per cent, 1= 10 per cent or more

gent Existence of national, state or provincial laws or other regulations that restrict the number of competitors allowed to operate a business in at least some markets in gas production/import
0 = restrictions in all markets, 1= free entry in all markets

gunb_p Existence of vertical separation between gas production/import and other segments of the gas market (whether accounting, legal or ownership separation)
0 = no vertical separation, 1= vertical separation

gunb_t Existence of vertical separation between gas supply and other segments of the gas market (whether accounting, legal or ownership separation)
0 = no vertical separation, 1= vertical separation

gown Percentage of shares in the largest firm in the gas production/import sector owned by government
0 = 100 per cent, 1 = more than 50 per cent, 2 = 50 per cent, 3 = less than 50 per cent, 4 = 0 per cent

Measures of these policy variables for all of the OECD economies in the sample are available up until 2003 from OECD (2005). Measures for the remaining time periods were constructed from information obtained online from the International Energy Regulation Network, the EIA Country Analysis Briefs of the US Energy Information Administration, and the Trade Policy Reviews of the WTO. A full listing of the values of these policy variables for all OECD economies and time periods in the sample is given in Dee (2011a).

As an initial reality check, it is useful to look at the simple correlations between the policy variables and the resulting measures of performance, prior to correcting for the influence of other variables.

Table 7.7. Simple Correlations between Policy and Performance in Gas

Policy variables	*Performance measures*	
	gntpr	gutil
gtpa	0.20	–0.05
gretc	0.20	0.20
gent	–0.40	–0.28
gunb_p	–0.06	–0.29
gunb_t	0.16	–0.18
gown	–0.26	0.22

Source: Own calculations.

These simple correlations are shown in Table 7.7 (once again, graphical presentation does not show the correlations clearly, because of the zero-one nature of the policy variables). The table shows that removing regulatory restrictions on entry can have an apparently large downward effect on gas prices. Unbundling production/import and private ownership are also associated with lower gas prices. Third party access, retail competition and unbundling of gas supply appear to be associated with higher gas prices. But note that there is limited scope for end-user prices to reflect the conditions of supply, demand and competition, especially in Europe.

In simple correlations, the policy variables also appear to have mixed effects on the utilization of gas pipelines. Retail competition and private ownership appear to be associated with higher utilization rates. Third party access, removal of entry restrictions, and any type of unbundling appear to be associated with lower utilization rates. Note, however, that the European Commission (2007) was particularly critical of the adequacy of unbundling and the effectiveness in practice of third party access regimes in European gas markets, even after the reforms, in part because of the prevalence of long-term contracts and the continued close vertical ownership links between incumbent operators. In addition, the methods by which incumbents have been able to reserve storage capacity, whether or not they use it, have had serious deleterious effects on the ability of new entrants to provide adequate services.

The results of econometric estimation shown in Tables 7.8 and 7.9 correct for the influence of other, non-regulatory factors, and also show

Table 7.8. Results of Random Effects Panel Regression for Gas Prices

Dependent variable	*Industry price*
Constant	320.5354
	[0.000]
Third party access (gtpa)	–4.75449
	[0.682]
Retail competition (gretc)	–30.4460
	[0.026]
Absence of entry restrictions (gent)	13.3761
	[0.474]
Unbundling of gas production/import (gunb_p)	–47.5065
	[0.002]
Unbundling of gas supply (gunb_t)	3.8747
	[0.780]
Private ownership (gown)	–2.9226
	[0.595]
Pipeline length (gpipe_s)	–0.3071
	[0.078]
Urbanization (urban)	–1.7877
	[0.124]
GDP in PPP (gdp_ppp)	0.0183
	[0.018]
Time	–11.9693
	[0.000]
Time squared	1.4067
	[0.000]
Number of observations	256
Number of time periods	19
Number of OECD economies	21
Wald test that coefficients not significantly different from zero	531.42
	[0.000]
Breusch–Pagan chi-squared test that random effects equal zero	63.95
	[0.000]
Hausman test of no diff. between random and fixed effects estimates	40.10
	[0.000]

Notes: Numbers in parentheses after the coefficient estimates are Prob>|z|. Numbers in parentheses after the Wald, Breusch–Pagan and Hausman tests are Prob>chi^2.

whether the strength of the policy effects are significantly different from zero.

Table 7.9. Results of Random Effects Panel Regression for Gas Efficiency

Dependent variable	*Pipeline utilization rate*
Constant	15.8143 [0.080]
Third party access (gtpa)	–1.1931 [0.046]
Retail competition (gretc)	1.4587 [0.015]
Absence of entry restrictions (gent)	0.6199 [0.427]
Unbundling of gas production/import (gunb_p)	–0.7744 [0.319]
Unbundling of gas supply (gunb_t)	–0.7000 [0.271]
Private ownership (gown)	1.4720 [0.000]
Gas share in electricity capacity (gascapshr)	2.2703 [0.444]
Urbanization (urban)	–0.1827 [0.132]
Time	0.0089 [0.872]
Number of observations	315
Number of time periods	19
Number of OECD economies	21
Wald test that coefficients not significantly different from zero	49.31 [0.000]
Breusch–Pagan chi-squared test that random effects equal zero	1320.69 [0.000]
Hausman test of no diff. between random and fixed effects estimates	43.26 [0.000]

Notes: Numbers in parentheses after the coefficient estimates are Prob>|z|. Numbers in parentheses after the Wald, Breusch–Pagan and Hausman tests are Prob>chi^2.

As before, the econometric estimation also attempts to control for *unobservable* influences on gas prices and efficiency that might vary over time or across economies. Unobservable differences over time are controlled using a deterministic, quadratic time trend. In particular, this trend is intended to capture the significant and accelerating upward trend in wholesale gas prices over the sample period. Unobservable differences across economies are controlled using random effects estimation, even when Hausman tests show that these estimates differ significantly from fixed effects estimates, for reasons explained earlier.

When non-regulatory factors are controlled for, few of the policy variables have a significant effect on gas prices. The only variable that appears to be significantly associated with lower gas prices is the unbundling of production/import from other market segments. This result accords with the observations of the European Commission (2007) that close ownership links (and long-term contracts) lock new entrants out of being able to secure their own primary gas supplies, creating a serious impediment to competition.

The non-regulatory factors have the expected impact on gas prices. Prices are higher when GDP is higher. Prices are lower when gas pipelines are longer, suggesting economies of scale in gas production. Higher rates of urbanization tend to reduce gas prices, although this effect is not significant.

Few of the policy variables have a significant effect on the utilization of gas pipelines. Third party access appears to reduce pipeline utilization, but third party access in Europe has been effectively thwarted by a variety of other means. Retail competition increases pipeline utilization. The presence of retail competition is the 'acid test' of whether unbundling and third party access regimes create effective competition, and the effect on pipeline utilization is significant. Private ownership also has a significant positive effect on pipeline utilization. Higher rates of urbanization tend to reduce pipeline utilization, although the effect is not quite significant at conventional testing levels, and in any event, the effect is ambiguous *a priori*.

7.5 Implications for APEC Economies

The econometric results of the previous section can be used to project the effects that further structural reforms in APEC electricity and gas markets would have on prices and efficiency.

As noted earlier, such out-of-sample projections need to be interpreted cautiously. The econometric results are conditioned by local factors and details of policy design and implementation that are peculiar to OECD economies in general, and European economies in particular. To the extent that these local factors are adequately captured by the policy and control variables used in the regressions, they can also be taken into account in out-of-sample projections. But many of them will not be adequately captured by these variables. For example, the above policy variables do not distinguish between regulated or negotiated third party access, and this distinction was seen as crucial to the effectiveness of European reform efforts. Nevertheless, while caution is needed in interpreting numerical out-of-sample projections, the general lessons from previous research also provide some guidance about the prerequisites for successful reform.

Dee (2011a) provides a great deal of detail about the current state of play in APEC electricity and gas markets, and this information can be used as the basis for deriving values for the policy variables currently appropriate to each APEC economy. Combined with the coefficient estimates from Tables 7.4, 7.5, 7.8 and 7.9, this information could then be used to project by how much prices or efficiency measures would change if further reforms were undertaken (and hence the values of each of the policy variables were to change). To simplify the process, however, projections can be made for each type of reform, assuming a starting point for prices or efficiency that was the same as the OECD average (as shown in Tables 7.2 and 7.6). Thus a rough guide to the effects of individual reforms can be obtained as follows.

In electricity markets, the introduction of a third party access regime would be associated with about 4.7 per cent lower electricity prices than otherwise, on an indicative basis and holding all other factors constant (where 0.0032/0.067587 = 4.7 per cent). The introduction of a wholesale electricity market would be associated with about 7.2 per cent lower electricity prices, while the unbundling of generation from transmission would be associated with 11.1 per cent lower electricity prices. In reality, the allocation of separate effects to separate reform initiatives is unlikely to be as precise as the combined effect of all initiatives, since the separate initiatives tend to go together. The combined effect of all three initiatives would be electricity prices estimated to be 23.0 per cent lower than otherwise. This is a similar order of magnitude to the effects implicit in Steiner's projections.

Note that the econometric results also suggest that wholly private ownership of electricity operators would be associated with prices that were 23.1 per cent *higher* than if ownership were wholly public (where 4*0.0039/0.067587 = 23.1 per cent). Pollitt (2007) also notes that private ownership can make it difficult to get reforms under way. However, this is an effect of initial conditions that is unlikely to persist over time. Doove *et al.* (2007) also note that ownership is unlikely to be independent of market structure, as the econometrics implies. Any positive relationship between price and private ownership is likely to be strongest when there is a monopoly provider — private sector monopolists might be more likely to pursue higher profits than government monopolists, and hence to raise electricity prices by exploiting their market power. This effect is also unlikely to persist over time as reform efforts continue.

The econometric results also suggest that unbundling of generation from transmission would be associated with 2.1 per cent higher utilization of generating capacity on an indicative basis (where 0.0944/4.428908 = 2.1 per cent). No other reform initiatives were shown to have a significant effect on efficiency.

In gas markets, the introduction of retail competition would be associated with gas prices being about 15.0 per cent lower than otherwise, on an indicative basis and holding all other factors constant (where 30.446/203.2362 = 15.0 per cent). The unbundling of gas production/import from other segments of the market would be associated with about 23.4 per cent lower gas prices. Both these percentages would be lower if initial gas prices were higher than the average in the OECD sample, as they are currently.

The econometric results also suggest that the introduction of retail competition would be associated with 24.3 per cent higher utilization of pipeline capacity than otherwise on an indicative basis (where 1.4587/6.013908 = 24.3 per cent). Third party access was projected to reduce capacity utilization, but this reflects the difficulty of instituting an effective third party access regime in European gas markets. Private ownership is projected to about double capacity utilization, probably reflecting that private gas operations tend to serve dedicated industrial users.

As noted, these results are indicative only, and not fined-tuned to the individual circumstances of each APEC economy. However, they do suggest that the slow, incremental approach to reform of APEC energy markets is worth reviving or continuing, despite the considerable burdens imposed on regulatory capacity. APEC economies can learn by doing, they can learn from the general lessons of reform in other economies, and they can learn from close interaction and cooperation among industry regulators. APEC processes are well-tuned to providing the sort of experience-sharing and capacity-building that can make the regulatory burden easier. The results of this chapter suggest that the gains to industrial users, and by inference to households, would be considerable.

Chapter 8

Impact of Trade Barriers on the Productivity of Higher Education Institutions

Philippa Dee

8.1 Introduction

Higher education is undergoing rapid globalization. Some of this is occurring through the international mobility of students. For example, OECD (2007) notes that the number of foreign students in OECD countries has more than tripled in the last 25 years. But increasingly, higher education is being globalized by the delivery of foreign academic courses, programs and projects to students in their home country. The same OECD report notes that the bulk of cross-border post-secondary education delivered through program and institution mobility is occurring in the Asia Pacific region.

In whatever form it occurs, trade in higher education services is being impeded by a range of regulatory barriers. Some restrict the movement of students, and some restrict the movement of higher education providers. Most affect imports, but some affect exports, as in the case where countries impose restrictions on the inward movement of international students. Examples of the types of barriers to trade in higher education services that are found in various countries are given in Tables 8.1 and 8.2.

In an earlier paper, Dee (2010a) examined the effects of these various trade barriers on the movement of international students between

Table 8.1. Examples of Barriers to Imports of Education Services

Mode	*Limitations on market access*	*Derogations from national treatment*
MODE 1: Cross-border trade, eg downloading course from the internet	Restrictions on downloading educational material from the internet, be it from a domestic or foreign supplier.	Restrictions on downloading educational material from foreign internet sites.
	Requiring foreign suppliers of internet education courses to be in a partnership or joint venture with a local institution.	Restrictions on which courses foreign suppliers of distance education can provide.
	An economic needs test attached to registration, authorization or licensing of all education providers, including those supplying via distance education.	Restrictions on the import and distribution of educational materials or software from foreign institutions providing distance education.
	Restrictions on the recognition of qualifications obtained from any distance education supplier.	Restrictions on the local accreditation of foreign distance education suppliers, or on the recognition of qualifications obtained from a foreign distance education supplier.
		Restrictions on cross-border payment or credit card transactions.
MODE 2: Consumption abroad, eg home students moving overseas to study	Since the home country has no jurisdiction over the foreign service supplier, it can mostly limit foreign supply only indirectly by restricting the local consumer. Such restrictions on consumers are unlikely to also affect local suppliers. Hence it is unlikely that there would be limitations on market access for imports of education services delivered via this mode.	Restrictions on foreign education institutions advertising locally or recruiting local students.
		Quotas on the number of local students going overseas to study.
		Foreign currency restrictions on local students studying abroad.

Table 8.1. Continued.

		Restrictions on the recognition of overseas qualifications for institutional credit. Restrictions on the recognition of overseas qualifications for professional licensing and accreditation.
MODE 3: Commercial presence, eg foreign institutions establishing a local campus	An economic needs test attached to registration, authorization or licensing of all education providers.	An economic needs test attached to registration, authorization or licensing of foreign education providers.
	A requirement that the foreign institution incorporate locally.	A restriction that prevents foreign tertiary institutions from using the term 'university' in the title of their local campus.
	A requirement that the foreign institution operate in a joint venture with a local institution. Restrictions on the number of foreign teachers that local institutions can employ. Limits on foreign equity in local institutions.	Restrictions on the scope of services that the local campus of a foreign institution can provide. Restrictions on the number of students that the local campus of a foreign institution can service. A residency requirement on the management of the local campus of the foreign institution. Discriminatory quality assurance requirements on the local campuses of foreign institutions. Restrictions on the ability of the local campuses of foreign institutions to grant degrees, or restrictions on the recognition of those degrees. Restrictions on the ability of the local campuses of foreign institutions to charge fees. Restrictions on the ability of local campuses of foreign institutions to gain access to producer subsidies. Restrictions on the ability of the students of local campuses of foreign institutions to gain access to consumer subsidies.

Table 8.1. Continued.

MODE 4: Movement of natural persons, eg foreign teachers coming to deliver short courses	An economic needs test attached to registration, authorization or licensing of all education providers, including foreign teachers.	Nationality of citizenship requirements to teach locally.
	Quotas or economic needs tests on the numbers of temporary staff employed by local institutions.	A prior residency requirement to teach locally.
	Labour market testing for the contract employment of foreign teachers.	Restrictions on the recognition of the qualifications of foreign teachers.

Source: WTO (1998a), WTO (2001), IDP Education Australia (2002).

Table 8.2. Examples of Barriers to Exports of Education Services

Mode	*Restriction*
MODE 2: Consumption abroad, eg foreign students entering to take local courses	Numerical limits on the entry of foreign students.
	Limits on what courses foreign students can enrol in.
	Discriminatory enrolment criteria for foreign students.
	Restrictions on local institutions recruiting foreign students.
	Restrictions on foreign students gaining access to local employment while studying.
	Restrictions on foreign students gaining access to tuition or other (eg transport) subsidies while studying.
MODE 4: Movement of natural persons, eg local teachers moving overseas to deliver courses	Exit restrictions on domestic teachers.
	Education or employment bond requiring teachers to serve a minimum term of employment locally before they can go overseas.
	Restrictions on funds transfers overseas by domestic teachers.

Source: WTO (1998a), WTO (2001), IDP Education Australia (2002).

countries. She found that barriers in the source country to importing education services via foreign direct investment (FDI) — the inward movement of foreign campuses — have the effect of boosting the number of students from the source country seeking enrolment in overseas universities. And barriers in the destination country to exporting education services via the inward movement of foreign students have the effect of reducing the numbers of such students. The magnitudes suggest that if a country with sample average barriers to FDI imports were to liberalize completely, it would send about 60 per cent fewer students overseas. If a country with sample average barriers to the inward movement of students were to liberalize completely, it would attract about 250 per cent more students — more than twice as many.

These results are consistent with barriers to education having the effects in the destination country shown in Figure 8.1. In that diagram, it is recognized that tuition levels are typically regulated, so the allocation of tertiary education places is subject to non-price rationing (eg Finnie and Usher 2006). Barriers to imports via FDI in the source country have the effect of moving the demand curve in the destination country to the right. And barriers to exports via the inward movement of students in the destination country have the effect of moving the supply curve to the left. The finding that barriers to imports via FDI in the source country promote imports via the outward movement of students from the source country is evidence of inter-modal substitution.

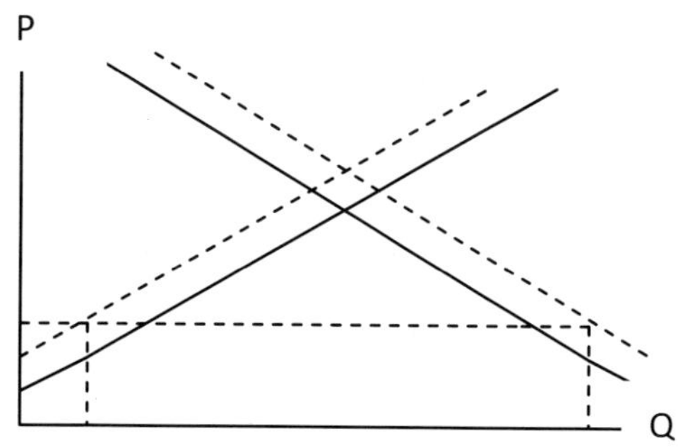

Figure 8.1. The Effect of Services Trade Barriers on Higher Education

The purpose of this chapter is to examine the source of that inter-modal substitution. In the previous paper, it was simply assumed that barriers to the import of education via FDI in the source country would restrict the quantity and/or quality of higher education in that country, thereby making it more attractive for students to seek their higher education overseas. This chapter looks for direct evidence of that effect.

8.2 Possible Effects of Barriers to Trade in Higher Education Services

To establish the welfare effects of barriers to FDI in the source country, it is necessary to do more than just identify by how much they move the supply curve for higher education in the source country. It is also necessary to make a judgement about whether that supply curve shift is 'real' or 'artificial'. If the shift is artificial, then the import barriers may create rents for incumbent higher education providers in the source country, with a relatively small associated loss in producer surplus, shown as the shaded area in Figure 8.2. Alternatively, if the shift is 'real', then the import barriers may raise real resource costs for incumbent higher education providers, with a relatively large loss of producer surplus, shown as the shaded area in Figure 8.3.[1] For the purpose of welfare analysis, it is critical to establish which type of effect occurs.

Theory can provide some guidance. Massy (2004) argues that a useful model of the production side of the higher education market is a model of the non-profit organization. Universities can be seen as optimizing the achievement of some non-profit objective, which could be as diverse as undertaking research, offering a diversity of courses, offering courses to students from a diversity of socioeconomic backgrounds, preserving arcane knowledge, or providing professorial employment. They do so subject to the prevailing production technology, and to the constraint that profits must always be zero. In these circumstances, they produce outputs

[1] These figures are the higher education analogues of the more general taxonomy of effects given in Dee, Findlay and Pomfret (2008).

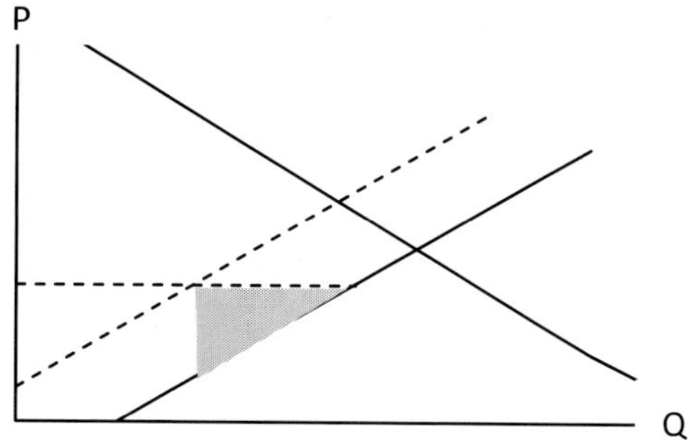

Figure 8.2. Welfare Cost of Rent-Creating Barriers to FDI in Higher Education

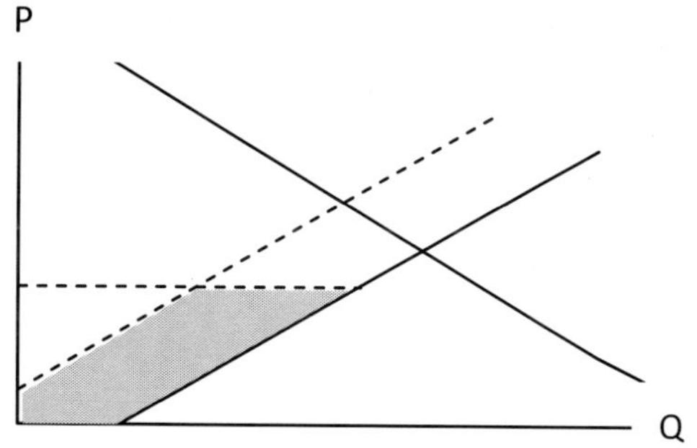

Figure 8.3. Welfare Cost of Cost-Escalating Barriers to FDI in Higher Education

to the point where the marginal revenue from each activity, plus its marginal contribution to the achievement of the non-profit objective, equals its marginal cost. Activities with high marginal revenue but low contribution to the non-profit objective may be exploited so as to cross-subsidize activities with a low marginal revenue but a high marginal contribution to the non-profit objective. Massy (2004) shows that such entities have an incentive to be technically efficient. But by definition, they have an incentive to dissipate any rents on the achievement of their non-profit objective.

In this context, barriers to inward FDI in higher education may have two types of effects. They may artificially restrict the supply of student places, but allow existing institutions to earn revenues above marginal cost from the remaining students. According to the theory of non-profit institutions, they would apply these 'rents' to the production of a non-profit objective, such as more research. The higher education institutions would be seen as teaching fewer students, but producing more research. Their output mix would change, but there would be little evidence of technical inefficiency.

Alternatively, barriers to inward FDI in higher education may mean that institutions with higher cost structures than otherwise are able to survive, or that the quality of higher education activities is lower than otherwise. Thus trade barriers may interfere directly with the production technology, causing genuine technical inefficiency.

Thus barriers to FDI in higher education may either change the output mix of domestic higher education institutions away from teaching towards other activities, or they may cause a reduction in the total output bundle for a given level of inputs. Either phenomenon would explain the observed finding of the previous paper that barriers to the inward movement of FDI in higher education encourage the outward movement of students to seek higher education in other countries. But an outcome of technical inefficiency would be much more costly for the country imposing the barriers. Accordingly, this chapter looks for evidence that barriers to inward FDI in higher education create technical inefficiency in the country imposing the barriers.

8.3 Defining and Explaining Technical Inefficiency in Higher Education

In the production literature, technical inefficiency is measured by the 'distance' of a production unit from the production frontier, where the frontier shows the *maximum* output bundle that can be produced from a given level of inputs. Thus to measure technical inefficiency, it is necessary (i) to specify the relevant inputs and outputs, (ii) to estimate the resulting production frontier, and (iii) to specify the distance measure.

Barriers to the import of higher education via FDI are one possible cause of technical inefficiency, but they are not the only one. In this chapter, it will be necessary to control for other possible causes of technical inefficiency. Many countries are simultaneously importers and exporters of higher education services. For example, Singapore has actively encouraged the establishment of foreign campuses, with a view to improving the quality of its higher education so that it can become a regional education hub. The simultaneous presence of importing and exporting makes it possible to test whether the presence of foreign students themselves is another factor that might contribute to technical inefficiency in higher education.

This possibility is hinted at in some of the literature. For example, in describing the Australian experience, Margison (2006. p. 3) writes

> The rapid growth of foreign student numbers was driven primarily by revenue incentives. The cattle prod has been the sharp decline in public funding per student, now at less than half the level of the 1970s. Growth has now leveled off and some universities appear to be over-exposed.

The author does not explain what is meant by over-exposure — it could mean over-reliance in revenue terms, or it could mean that foreign students have contributed to a perceived decline in standards. Anecdotally, such perceptions do exist.

The theory of the non-profit organization would partly explain such perceptions. The theory predicts that, in the face of a decline in government funding, universities would reduce the proportion of resources devoted to their non-profit objectives. In the limit, they would cease pursuing them altogether, and act like a pure profit-maximizing firm. Thus they would only focus on activities, such as teaching foreign students, that generate marginal revenues at or above marginal cost, and would cease pursuing other objectives, such as preserving arcane knowledge. In the eyes of some, the abandonment of such non-profit objectives would be construed as a decline in standards.

Yet perceptions of a decline in standards go beyond this. In some countries at least, Australia being one of them, foreign students are required to pay high fees to cover the full cost of their education. This is in contrast to the United States, where foreign students pay fees that are subsidized, and to parts of Europe, where foreign students pay no fees. Where foreign students pay particularly high fees, there can be a perception that to ensure them value for money, they cannot be allowed to fail. Thus universities may either spend additional resources to provide foreign students with language training and study skills, or they may allow a decline in academic standards to improve the pass rates of foreign students. To the extent that foreign students are genuinely less able in language skills and/or academic ability than domestic students initially, either of these phenomena could contribute to measured technical inefficiency.[2]

It is of policy interest in its own right to examine whether the presence of foreign students contributes to technical inefficiency. This will be one of the key controls used, when examining the effects of barriers to FDI on technical inefficiency.

Outputs

According to some writers, the core business of higher education institutions is teaching and research. Further, it is both quantity and quality that matter:

> There are other standards that are commonly used to assess the excellence of universities, but the quality of teaching and research are fundamental, capturing what we generally mean when we talk about excellence in a university. (Taylor and Braddock 2007, p. 246)

According to the theory of the non-profit organization, however, universities could also have a range of other non-profit objectives that they pursue. Some of these may be socially productive, for example, ensuring access for indigenous students or students of low-socio-economic backgrounds. Others may not.

> Universities tend to value faculty for their own sake, which inhibits technology-based productivity improvement. They honour the perceived 'property rights' of faculty, which inhibits growth by substitution. They do not resist mission drift,

---

[2] In a separate exercise, Deumert *et al.* (2005) report the results of a survey on the social and economic security of international students while in Australia, focusing on issues such as language, finances, work, loneliness and discrimination. Among other findings, the authors report that 77 per cent of students agree that better or different information should be provided to prospective students, and that 75 per cent agree that better backup systems should be provided to students while studying in Australia.

> which encourages faculty to substitute research for educational tasks to the detriment of students. They under-invest in the provision of information about education quality, which forces the market to rely on surrogates that serve the interests of providers far more than those of consumers. (Massy 2004, p. 31)

Massy argues that one of the policy challenges in higher education, as the institutions become more autonomous, commercial and global in focus, is to keep them 'on mission' — following objectives that are indeed core business. (He also argues that punitive funding cuts are a dangerously blunt instrument for dealing with the problem).

In this chapter, the measures of the output of higher education institutions are restricted to teaching and research. In this way, the analysis will be able to identify whether barriers to inward FDI in higher education have contributed to mission drift, since this will manifest itself as measured inefficiency.

There is a number of ways that the quantity and quality of teaching and research have been measured in the literature. Many of these are surveyed in a recent paper by Carrington, Coelli and Rao (2005). The papers by Taylor and Braddock (2007) and Ab Iorwerth (2005) also address the issue. Various measures used are summarized in Table 8.3.

Since the prime goal of the chapter is to quantify the effects of barriers to FDI, and the prime source of variation in this policy instrument is cross-country variation, the measures of both outputs and inputs used to define technical inefficiency must have a cross-country dimension. This limits the type of measures that can be used for this exercise.

For this exercise, the chosen measure of the quantity of teaching is full-time equivalent enrolments in tertiary institutions, available from the OECD's Online Education Database.[3] This data has been collected for 34 OECD and non-OECD countries for three years — 2000 to 2002. The country coverage of the OECD's data broken down by either level of study (graduate/undergraduate) or field of study (science/other) is incomplete, so only aggregate enrolments have been used.

---

[3] This database is available at
http://www.oecd.org/document/54/0,3343,en_2649_33723_38082166_1_1_1_1,00.html.

Table 8.3. Possible Output Measures for Higher Education Institutions

Output	*Quantity*	*Quality*
Teaching	Student numbers or student completions	Student satisfaction
	Full-time equivalent student numbers	Graduate salary and graduate employment
	Enrolments	Student/teacher ratios
	Full-time equivalent enrolments	
	Numbers of enrolments broken down by level or field of study	
Research	Publication count, either overall, or in selected top journals	Impact = citations per publication
	Citations count	Peer review
	Patents analysis	Numbers of Nobel Prizes and Field Medals
	Peer review	

Source: Carrington, Coelli and Rao (2005), Ab Iorwerth (2005), Taylor and Braddock (2007).

For this exercise, there is no chosen measure of the quality of teaching. There is no comparable cross-country data on student satisfaction, and data on the labour force experience of graduates is hard to come by. The sole remaining measure, student/teacher ratios, *defines* teaching quality as an input/output ratio, and thereby precludes variations in technical inefficiency. Furthermore, using student/teacher ratios or other measures of teaching quality is highly contentious in its own right. This is the reason, for example, that the SCRGSP (2008) report that compares the performance of government vocational education and training providers across State jurisdictions in Australia has found no acceptable measures of teaching quality.

For this exercise, the chosen measure of the quantity of research is data on the numbers of science and engineering articles, taken from National Science Board (2006). This is available for the same countries and years as the enrolment data.

For this exercise, the chosen measure of the quality of research is data on research 'impact', defined as the number of citations per publication in science and engineering for each country. The citations count in the numerator is the number of references made in articles published in 2003 to articles published in 1999–2001. The publication count in the denominator is the number of articles published in 1999–2001. Both are available for science and engineering from National Science Board (2006), for the same countries as the enrolment data. This measure of impact is used for each of the three years in the sample (2000–2002).

Inputs

As in Carrington, Coelli and Rao (2005), a single measure of inputs is used, defined as real current expenditure, which covers the sum of academic salaries and other current expenditure (eg administration costs). As higher education institutions have become more autonomous and commercially oriented, the mix of spending on academic salaries and administration costs has changed over time. The chosen measure covers both activities. Nominal data on current expenditure are taken from the OECD's Online Education Database, for the same countries and years as for the enrolment data. The same OECD source also provides data on capital expenditures, but the time coverage is insufficiently long to be able to use this data to construct a measure of capital stocks using perpetual inventory methods.

The nominal data on current expenditure in national currencies were converted to real data in US dollars as follows. The nominal data were converted to constant price data by deflating the academic salary component by a wage index and the other current expenditure data by a price index, where both the wage and price index data were taken from the International Financial Statistics of the International Monetary Fund (IMF). Where IMF wage data were unavailable, wage data from the International Labour Organization (ILO) were used instead. The 2000 constant price data were then converted to US dollars using the 2000 US dollar exchange rate from the IMF's International Financial Statistics.

Controls

A key interest of this chapter is whether barriers to trade in higher education services contribute to technical inefficiency in the importing country. But there are several other determinants of technical inefficiency that need to be controlled for. One is the proportion of foreign students enrolled in higher education institutions. Data on numbers of foreign students enrolled in tertiary institutions, along with total (full-time plus part-time) enrolments, are available from the OECD's Online Education Database, for the same countries and years as the data on total full-time equivalent student enrolments. These data are used to construct the proportion of foreign students in each country in each year.

Another possible control is the proportion of part-time students in tertiary institutions, since these might imply a less efficient use of university resources. Data on numbers of part-time students enrolled in tertiary institutions is also available from the OECD's Online Education Database, although there is clearly some misreporting. For example, a few European countries, including Denmark, France and Greece, and a relatively high proportion of developing countries in the sample including Brazil, Chile, Indonesia, the Philippines and Uruguay, report having no part-time students. Nevertheless, the data are used to construct a measure of the proportion of part-time students in each country in each year.

The resulting data on outputs, inputs and controls are summarized in Table 8.4 (note that for a few countries, there are missing values for some years). The United States has the largest market for higher education, with the highest levels of full-time equivalent students, publications, and citations per publication, but also the highest real current expenditures. The markets in Europe and Japan are also large in absolute terms. The markets with a relatively high proportion of foreign students are Switzerland, Australia, Austria, Belgium, the United Kingdom and Germany. The markets with a high reported proportion of part-time students are Argentina, Sweden, Poland, Australia, Finland and the United Kingdom.

Table 8.4. Data on Outputs, Inputs and Controls, Averages over 2000 to 2002

Country	*Full-time equivalents*	*Publications*	*Impact*	*Real current expenditure (USD m)*	*Proportion of foreign students (%)*	*Proportion of part-time students (%)*
Australia	656,497	15,103	2.05	5,603	14.7	43.3
Austria	249,878	4,612	2.15	2,175	12.1	3.4
Belgium	331,652	6,174	2.21	3,020	10.8	16.1
Canada	965,626	22,591	2.34	16,583	3.3	27.1
Czech Repub.	248,202	2,783	1.29	444	2.9	7.7
Denmark	192,044	5,006	2.56	2,544	6.9	0.0
Finland	255,352	5,058	2.32	1,982	2.2	40.9
France	2,025,422	31,072	2.14	12,661	7.4	0.0
Germany	2,075,011	43,264	2.34	17,528	9.6	2.3
Greece	476,585	3,491	1.34	806	2.3	0.0
Iceland	9,149	190	2.12	66	4.1	22.1
Ireland	150,082	1,691	1.98	1,156	4.9	24.4
Italy	1,812,176	23,108	2.04	8,992	1.5	0.0
Japan	3,818,501	57,524	1.89	42,596	1.7	7.8
Korea	3,114,513	12,176	1.41	9,577	0.1	0.0
Mexico	2,005,329	3,421	1.16	5,148	0.1	0.0
Netherlands	456,152	12,865	2.63	4,542	3.3	18.5
New Zealand	139,153	2,922	1.73	756	6.8	36.1
Norway	162,672	3,236	1.99	1,997	4.1	28.4
Poland	1,388,486	6,160	1.15	1,736	0.4	44.9
Slovak Repub.	134,366	945	0.98	157	1.1	30.3
Spain	1,722,707	16,088	1.82	5,676	2.3	8.2
Sweden	270,544	10,127	2.36	4,087	6.4	45.0
Switzerland	146,899	8,131	2.98	1,636	16.9	20.2
United Kingdom	1,572,346	47,072	2.41	15,010	10.7	39.2
United States	11,129,326	202,632	3.09	222,208	3.6	35.7
Argentina	629,322	3,059	1.24	2,076	0.4	74.5
Brazil	2,788,011	7,846	1.22	4,200	0.0	0.0
Chile	466,153	1,321	1.38	857	0.7	0.0
India	9,213,204	11,796	0.99	3,283	0.1	15.5
Indonesia	2,932,035	184	1.22	955	0.0	0.0
Malaysia	483,612	490	0.88	845	2.1	10.9
Philippines	2,156,605	172	1.31	340	0.1	0.0
Uruguay	95,158	167	1.77	118	1.6	0.0

Source: See text.

Measures of Trade Barriers

The data on trade restrictions are taken from Nguyen-Hong and Wells (2003). That paper used raw information on regulatory barriers to trade in higher education services, of the type described in Tables 8.1 and 8.2, complied by IDP Education Australia (2002). Because the detailed information was collected to assist Australia in its trade negotiations, it is regarded as 'sensitive' and the IDP report remains unpublished. However, Nguyen-Hong and Wells (2003) have converted the detailed qualitative information into a number of quantitative indices of barriers to trade, by mode of service delivery and also according to whether the restrictions affect higher education imports or exports. Indices of trade restrictions are available for 14 of the countries in the full sample. Most of these are from the Asia Pacific region. The IDP report was completed in 2002 and the barriers that it reports are likely to be those applying in 2000 or 2001, closely matching the time frame of the enrolment data. Thus the cross-sectional data from Nguyen-Hong and Wells (2003) are used for each of the three years in the sample.

The data on trade restrictions are shown in Table 8.5. The top half of the table shows the trade restriction values available for in-sample countries — those that are also in the OECD dataset. The bottom half of the table gives values available for out-of-sample countries. The data show that within the sample, the countries imposing the greatest restrictions on the inward movement of FDI are India, Malaysia and Indonesia. The countries imposing the greatest restrictions on the outward movement of international students (ie restrictions on importing via consumption abroad) are Indonesia and Korea. These countries, along with Brazil, also impose relatively high barriers to cross-border trade in higher education services. Malaysia imposes the highest barriers on the temporary entry of foreign teachers (ie importing via the movement of people), followed by India and Brazil.

Table 8.5. Indexes of Restrictions on Trade in Higher Education Services

Country	*Imports via cross-border supply (0–4)*	*Imports via consumption abroad (0–5)*	*Imports via commercial presence (0–7)*	*Imports via movement of people (0–3)*
In-sample countries				
Argentina	0.50	0.83	0.50	0.00
Australia	0.50	0.25	1.30	0.50
Brazil	1.25	0.83	1.30	1.25
Canada	0.50	0.50	1.45	0.50
Chile	0.50	0.50	1.60	1.00
India	1.00	1.17	4.29	1.50
Indonesia	1.50	1.83	3.76	1.00
Japan	0.50	0.50	1.40	0.50
Korea	1.25	1.83	0.80	0.50
Malaysia	0.75	0.83	4.60	2.00
Mexico	0.25	0.50	0.61	0.25
New Zealand	0.50	0.00	1.45	0.25
United Kingdom	0.00	0.25	0.60	1.00
United States	0.50	0.83	0.60	1.00
Out-of-sample countries				
China	2.50	2.17	4.00	3.00
Hong Kong	0.75	1.33	0.60	0.50
Singapore	1.50	1.50	2.45	1.50
Taiwan	1.00	1.50	1.15	1.00
Thailand	1.00	1.00	2.30	0.50
Viet Nam	1.50	3.67	3.10	2.00

Source: Nguyen-Hong and Wells (2003).

Measures of Distance from the Production Frontier

The standard distance measure in the literature has been adapted to the case of multiple outputs by Coelli and Perelman (1999). To estimate their specification, a functional form must first be chosen for the production frontier. In the current application, there is only one input, so there is no scope for sophistication. Accordingly, a Cobb–Douglas function has been chosen.

The standard distance function $D_O(x,y)$ in outputs y and inputs x is defined as

$$D_O(x,y) = \min\{\theta: (y/\theta) \in P(x)\} \tag{8.1}$$

where P(x) is the feasible output set.

This distance function takes a value less than one if the output vector is strictly within the feasible set, and takes a value one if y is on the production boundary.

In the case of a Cobb–Douglas technology with multiple outputs and one input, the distance of country i from the frontier is measured by

$$\ln D_{Oi} = \alpha_o + \Sigma_m \alpha_m \ln y_{mi} + \beta \ln x_i \tag{8.2}$$

The estimation of this distance measure in the case of multiple outputs uses the fact that the distance function is linearly homogeneous in y, so that

$$D_O(x,\omega y) = \omega D_O(x,y) \text{ for any } \omega > 0 \tag{8.3}$$

If ω is set equal to $1/y_M$, where y_M is arbitrarily chosen as the Mth output, then

$$D_O(x,y/y_M) = D_O(x,y)/y_M \tag{8.4}$$

In the case of the Cobb–Douglas technology above, this means that

$$\ln D_{Oi} - \ln y_{Mi} = \alpha_o + \Sigma_m \alpha_m \ln (y_{mi}/y_{Mi}) + \beta \ln x_i \tag{8.5}$$

or

$$-\ln y_{Mi} = \alpha_o + \Sigma_m \alpha_m \ln (y_{mi}/y_{Mi}) + \beta \ln x_i - \ln D_{Oi} \tag{8.6}$$

This can be estimated in one of two ways. Under corrected ordinary least squares (OLS), the unobservable term $-\ln D_{Oi}$ is interpreted as a random error term. Equation (8.6) is first estimated using OLS. Then the OLS estimate of the intercept parameter α_o is adjusted (by adding the largest negative OLS residual to it) so that the function no longer passes through the centre of the observed points, but bounds them from above. The distance measure for the ith country is then calculated as e^{-u}, where u_i is the (corrected) OLS residual for the ith country.

Using stochastic frontier estimation, the unobservable term $-\ln D_{Oi}$ is interpreted as a one-sided error. A two sided-error is also appended to the formulation in (8.6), and the equation is estimated using maximum likelihood. The distance measure for the *i*th country is then calculated as e^{-u_i}, where u_i is the realization of the one-sided error.

Thus the key difference between corrected OLS and stochastic frontier estimation is that the former attributes all of the random error term to technical inefficiency. In the latter technique, allowance is made for both technical inefficiency (the one-sided error) and an additional random error (the two-sided error). Thus measures of technical inefficiency obtained from stochastic frontier estimation are expected to be smaller than those obtained from corrected OLS estimation.

Another technique that has been used in the literature to estimate technical inefficiency is Data Envelop Analysis (DEA). This is a non-parametric technique, which unlike corrected OLS or stochastic frontier estimation, does not require a functional form to be specified for the error terms. One application in a context similar to this is Johnes and Johnes (1993). However, in DEA, there is no common set of weights applied to inputs or outputs. Each unit of observation is allowed to choose its own weightings of inputs and outputs to maximize its own ratio of weighted output to weighted inputs, subject to the constraint that this ratio not exceed unity. Particularly in a situation of only one input, this would allow weights to be chosen for each country so that most, it not all, were deemed to be totally efficient. This would be neither realistic, nor conducive to testing the effects of trade barriers on technical efficiency. Although techniques have been developed to deal with the problem (as outlined in Murillo-Zamorano 2004), DEA has not been pursued here.

8.4 Estimation Results

Technical inefficiency can be estimated and explained in either a one-stage or a two-stage process. In the two-stage process, equation (8.6) would be estimated as shown, the resulting measures of technical inefficiency would be recovered, and these would then be regressed on the various explanatory variables, such as indicators of trade barriers. As noted by Coelli (1996), however, the two-stage procedure is inconsistent in its assumptions regarding the independence of the efficiency effects in the two estimation stages. Coelli prefers a one-stage process, where the explanators of technical inefficiency are appended to the estimating equation (8.6) directly. The measures of technical inefficiency recovered from a one-stage estimation procedure measure the 'residual' technical inefficiency that cannot be explained by these explanators.

In the current setting, there is more data available on some of the explanators of technical inefficiency — the control variables above — than there is on others — the measures of trade barriers. To maximize use of the data, the control variables were appended to equation (8.6), and this was estimated in a single stage. The resulting 'residual' measures of technical inefficiency were recovered, and regressed on measures of trade barriers in a second stage, for those countries for which the latter were available.

One further variation was made to the above schema. Rather than normalizing the distance function estimation in (8.6) on a single output y_M, it was normalized on the sum of all outputs $\Sigma_m y_m$. This was an attempt to avoid the issue of sensitivity of the results to the particular output chosen. As a sensitivity test, the specification was also normalized on the number of full-time equivalent students. The results were very similar to those reported here.

The results of estimating equation (8.6) with control variables attached using corrected OLS and maximum likelihood are shown in Table 8.6, where the latter estimates were obtained using the estimation program Frontier 4.1 (Coelli 1996). The coefficient estimates are virtually identical in the two approaches, and both specifications fit the data well. Further, the corrected OLS estimates pass the Ramsey reset test for functional form and the Breusch–Pagan test for absence of heteroskedasticity. In each specification, the coefficients on the input and output variables are of the right sign and highly significant.

The coefficients on the control variables measure their contribution to technical *inefficiency*. Thus in both specifications, there is evidence that a higher proportion of part-timers contribute positively to *inefficiency*, although this finding is qualified by the apparent misreporting of part-time numbers. There is no evidence that a high proportion of foreign

Table 8.6. Estimation of Distance Function

Dependent variable = –ln(sum y)

Regressors	*Corrected OLS*		*Maximum likelihood*	
	Coefficient	*t statistic*	*Coefficient*	*t statistic*
ln(FTE/sum y)	9.451***	4.23	9.451***	9.51
ln(pubs/sum y)	0.094***	5.14	0.094***	5.46
ln(impact/sum y)	0.774***	33.41	0.774***	37.90
ln(x)	–0.227***	–11.71	–0.227***	–13.18
Prop. part-time	0.002***	2.99	0.002***	3.16
Prop. Foreign	–0.002	–0.41	–0.002	–0.49
Constant	–1.124***	–6.80	–1.112***	4.64
Number of obs.	90		90	
Adjusted R^2	0.99			

Note: *** significant at the 1 per cent level.
Source: Author's calculations.

students contributes to inefficiency. In fact, the sign of the coefficient suggests the opposite, but in neither specification is the coefficient significant.

Although the two specifications yield virtually identical results for the effects of the inputs, outputs and control variables, they yield different measures of 'residual' technical inefficiency. In the corrected OLS specification, the scores of residual efficiency range from 0.52 to 1.00. The most efficient country is Uruguay in 2000, and the least efficient is Malaysia on 2001. Other countries with high efficiency scores are the United States and Finland, while other countries with low efficiency scores are Mexico and Japan.

In contrast, the maximum likelihood estimates of technical efficiency are all virtually identical to 1.00, suggesting that all countries are efficient. Further, the results suggested that the decomposition of the error into a random component and a one-sided technical efficiency component did not improve the results over those given by the deterministic corrected OLS model. Whiteman (1999) found similar results when estimating the efficiency of electricity, gas and telecommunications industries in a Cobb–Douglas context. Accordingly, the technical efficiency scores from maximum likelihood estimation have been ignored in what follows.

Table 8.7. Estimated Relationship between Technical Efficiency and Trade Barriers

Dependent variable = technical efficiency score from corrected OLS estimation

Regressors	*Model 1*		*Model 2*		*Model 3*		*Model 4*	
	Coeff.	*t stat.*	*Coeff.*	*t stat.*	*Coeff.*	*t stat.*	*Coeff.*	*t stat.*
Barriers to:								
mode 1 imports	–0.055	–0.77						
mode 2 imports	0.025	0.46						
mode 3 imports	–0.031	–1.68	–0.036**	–2.18	–0.015	–1.08		
mode 4 imports	0.088*	2.05	0.086**	2.06			0.029	0.84
Number of obs.	34		34		34		34	
Adjusted R^2	0.06		0.10		0.01		0.00	

Notes: * significant at the 10 per cent level; ** significant at the 5 per cent level;
Source: Author's calculations.

Table 8.7 shows the results from regressing the corrected OLS measures of residual technical efficiency (the distance measure) on the measures of trade barriers, for those countries for which the latter are available. The measures of technical efficiency are time-varying, but the measures of trade barriers are not, so the overall explanatory power cannot be expected to be great. In addition, there is a relatively high degree of multicollinearity between the different types of trade barriers, so the effects of any one kind of barrier on technical efficiency cannot be expected to be identified with any precision.

The first model estimated in Table 8.7 suggests that neither barriers to cross-border trade nor barriers to importing via the outward movement of international students has a significant effect on the technical efficiency of higher education, although this may reflect the particularly high degree of multicollinearity between these two measures. The earlier paper similarly found that neither of these two types of barriers contributed significantly to encouraging an outward movement of international students (Dee 2010a). So both measures are dropped from subsequent models. The subsequent models suggest that barriers to importing via FDI have a negative impact on technical efficiency, as expected, while barriers to importing via the temporary movement of individual teachers have a positive effect on technical efficiency. The first effect has slightly higher significance than the second.

The first effect is consistent with the finding from the previous paper (Dee 2010a) that barriers to inward FDI encourage the outward movement of students. The current finding implies that these barriers also impose a welfare cost, in terms of reducing the efficiency of higher education at home.

The second effect may come about because many of the measured barriers to the inward movement of individual teachers are designed to protect the quality of the teachers that are imported, rather than to restrict their quantity *per se* (see Table 8.1). This may account for the fact that such restrictions appear to improve the technical efficiency of higher education at home. The earlier paper found that such restrictions also tend to reduce the outward movement of international students, although that effect was not significant.

There is a possibility that the above results are driven by a single observation. There is only one year's worth of complete data for Malaysia, and this country had particularly high barriers to inward FDI in higher education, and the lowest technical efficiency score in the full sample. To test whether this observation is dominating the results, both stages of the analysis were repeated without this observation. The results were similar to those reported here in every respect, demonstrating that the phenomena identified here are relatively general.

8.5 Projected Productivity Effects of Liberalizing Inward FDI

The econometric results can be used to project the effects that liberalizing inward FDI might have on the productivity of higher education institutions in the liberalizing countries. Using the results of the preferred model from Table 8.7, the absolute change in the distance measure arising from full liberalization of inward FDI can be calculated as –0.036*(–initial index of barriers to mode 3 imports). The percentage change in the distance measure (equivalent to the percentage change in outputs for a given level of inputs) expresses this absolute change as a percentage of that country's initial distance measure.

The projected productivity gains from liberalization are shown in Table 8.8, for all the countries for which data on barriers to inward FDI are available. The percentage productivity gains for in-sample countries are obtained using their own distance measure averaged across the three years 2000–2002. The percentage productivity gains for out-of-sample countries are obtained using the average of such distance measures across all in-sample countries.[4]

Table 8.8. Projected Productivity Gains from Liberalizing Inward FDI in Higher Education (per cent)

Country	*Productivity gain*
In-sample countries	
Argentina	2.4
Australia	5.8
Brazil	6.3
Canada	7.0
Chile	7.3
India	18.5
Indonesia	18.1
Japan	7.2
Korea	4.0
Malaysia	31.6
Mexico	3.6
New Zealand	6.6
United Kingdom	2.5
United States	2.3
Out-of-sample countries	
China	18.0
Hong Kong	2.7
Singapore	11.0
Taiwan	5.2
Thailand	10.4
Viet Nam	14.0

Source: Author's calculations.

[4] This overall average distance measure is 0.7989. The use of this average for out-of-sample projections is not expected to be problematic. When tested on in-sample countries, the use of this average led to results that were with one percentage point of those shown in Table 8.8 for most countries. The deviation for Malaysia was greater, because its initial distance measure was particularly low.

The results suggest that there can be significant productivity gains from liberalizing barriers to inward FDI in higher education services. The gains can be of the order of 30 per cent for countries such as Malaysia, which had particularly high barriers around 2000, and almost 20 per cent for countries such as China, India and Indonesia. Not only would such liberalization boost domestic productivity, it would also mean that fewer local students were likely to seek their higher education overseas.

8.6 Conclusions

An earlier paper found that barriers to importing education services via FDI has the effect of boosting the number of students seeking enrolment in overseas universities. Thus barriers to importing higher education by one mode appear to increase imports via another. The purpose of this chapter has been to examine more closely the source of that inter-modal substitution.

Conceptually, if higher education were like any other service, then such barriers to inward FDI could either generate rents or raise real resource costs. However, the theory of higher education institutions as non-profit organizations suggests that any rents generated by such barriers are likely to be spent on generating more outputs, such as research. Accordingly, such barriers could change the output mix of higher education institutions. Alternatively, such barriers could raise the real resource costs of higher education institutions, lowering their technical efficiency. If barriers were of this type, they could impose significant welfare costs on the country imposing them.

Accordingly, this chapter has tested whether barriers to FDI in higher education reduce the technical efficiency of higher education institutions. In doing so, it has controlled for two other possible influences on technical efficiency — the proportion of students who are part-time, and the proportion of students who are foreign. The chapter therefore also tests the proposition that exporting education via the inward movement of international students contributes to a decline in technical efficiency in the exporting country.

The results of the chapter suggest that a high proportion of part-timers reduces technical efficiency, although this finding is qualified by the apparent misreporting of part-time numbers. There is no evidence that a high proportion of foreign students contributes to inefficiency, at least at the level of entire countries.

The results also suggest that barriers to importing via FDI have a negative impact on the technical efficiency of higher education institutions. This effect is consistent with the finding from the previous paper that barriers to inward FDI encourage the outward movement of students. The current results imply that liberalizing barriers to inward FDI could lead to productivity improvements of up to 20 to 30 per cent in countries that maintain particularly high barriers. It implies that these barriers impose a significant welfare cost, in terms of reducing the efficiency of higher education at home. There is also weaker evidence that barriers to importing via the temporary movement of individual teachers has a positive effect on technical efficiency. This may come about because many of the measured barriers to the inward movement of individual teachers are designed to protect the quality of the teachers that are imported.

Chapter 9

Barriers to Trade in Healthcare Services in ASEAN Countries[1]

Philippa Dee

9.1 The Benefits of Liberalizing Healthcare Services

The benefits of opening up services markets to foreign competition can potentially be similar to the benefits from opening up goods markets. Foreign suppliers may be able to offer services at lower cost or higher quality. Foreign-invested firms can bring additional resources in the form of capital and skills. And foreign-invested firms may bring better technologies and business processes.

Early estimates of the effects of services trade barriers suggested that the damage they caused could be many multiples of the damage caused by tariff barriers. An early study found that the benefits of services trade liberalization could exceed the benefits of liberalizing agriculture and manufacturing combined (Dee and Hanslow 2001). One of the reasons is that many barriers to services trade do not just inflate price-cost margins, they can also add to real resource costs. This means that they can do much greater economic damage than tariffs.

In markets where foreign firms are providing essentially the same products as domestic firms, then removing all forms of discrimination against foreign suppliers may be sufficient to bring all the benefits of a single market. In services, however, suppliers typically provide highly differentiated services that are customized to each client, and foreign and domestic services providers often focus on different market niches. For

[1] This chapter draws on Dee (2009) and (2011b).

example, foreign-invested hospitals often specialize in particular treatments or focus on providing high quality services to wealthy customers, while domestic hospitals provide a broader range of services.

Where domestic and foreign services providers offer differentiated services, the removal of discrimination against foreign providers may be insufficient to discipline the cost and profit structures of domestic firms. Only by also removing the regulatory restrictions that limit competition by domestic firms, or restrict their performance, can the best economic outcomes be obtained. Recent research has suggested that the economic gains from removing non-discriminatory restrictions, ie those that affect domestic and foreign firms equally, can greatly exceed the gains from only removing discrimination against foreigners (Dee 2007). At best, a policy focus on ensuring national treatment can deliver relatively small gains. At worst, opening up a services market to particular foreign suppliers through preferential arrangements can, in the absence of measures to ensure general contestability, simply hand over monopoly rents to foreigners.

The general theory therefore suggests that a pathway to achieving health services liberalization in ASEAN should pay at least as much attention to removing non-discriminatory restrictions on market access as to ensuring national treatment. It suggests that this would ensure that the gains from liberalization were substantial, and would also maximize the chances that domestic service providers would themselves gain from liberalization, rather than simply being hurt by greater foreign competition.

Nevertheless, special features of health services markets make it difficult to remove all non-discriminatory restrictions on market access. And recent progress in liberalizing the markets for medical professional services in ASEAN has tended to be in the form of removing discrimination against foreigners, although progress has been made in removing non-discriminatory restrictions in a hospital-based environment.

The next section spells out the theoretical reasons why it might be difficult to remove non-discriminatory restrictions on market access in health services. Following sections track recent progress in liberalizing health services markets in ASEAN countries, as well as indicating the additional work that will need to be done if ASEAN is to achieve its liberalization targets. The final section offers some suggested pathways to achieving further liberalization in healthcare in a way that reconciles the potential benefits to ASEAN countries with the special features of healthcare services markets.

9.2 Limitations on Liberalizing Healthcare Services

There are few studies of the conceptual issues associated with barriers to trade in health services. An original contribution was by the World Trade Organization (WTO) Secretariat (WTO 1998b). More recent contributions are by Chanda (2001), Smith (2006), Mikic (2007) and Smith *et al.* (2008). All of these stress the heavy interactions between trade policy and domestic regulation in healthcare. For example, Smith *et al.* (2008, p. 443) list the following as key questions for monitoring the impact of commitments made under the General Agreement on Trade in Services (GATS) on health policy:

- To what extent is the sector already open to foreign service providers, and what have been the regulatory concerns posed by existing foreign competition?
- Do the commitments fit the strategies and directions identified by national health policy?
- What effect would the commitments have on government-provided health-related services?
- What regulatory burdens would the commitments create for the government in health-related sectors?
- Would the commitments eliminate or weaken regulatory approaches necessary for the protection and promotion of health?
- What scientific and public-health evidence and principles can be brought to bear to analyse the possible effect of the commitments?
- Can the commitments be crafted both to protect health policy and to liberalize trade progressively?

Their last question in particular points to the possibility that trade liberalization, if pursued in isolation, might cut across other legitimate regulatory objectives.

In medical and health markets, there are typically at least two such legitimate regulatory objectives. The first is to deal with asymmetric information. Almost by definition, the clients of professional services firms are not sufficiently trained to know whether the services they are receiving are of high quality. In some markets, this problem is dealt with after the event, via mechanisms such as warrantees and product liability legislation. In medical and health markets, this option is typically deemed unsatisfactory, so quality is regulated before the event — via licensing/registration requirements for medical professionals, and by licensing and quality assurance processes for medical and health institutions.

A second regulatory objective in medical and health markets is to ensure equitable and affordable access, either for all, or for particular disadvantaged segments of society.

In some services markets, there is a relatively clear-cut distinction between the policy instruments used to achieve legitimate regulatory objectives, and those that are deemed regulatory impediments to trade. In banking and insurance, for example, the instruments commonly used for prudential purposes are well-defined — minimum capital requirements, capital adequacy ratios, liquidity reserve ratios, disclosure requirements, and possible coverage by an insolvency guarantee or deposit insurance scheme. In most cases, regulatory restrictions on competition in banking and insurance services can be dismantled without jeopardizing prudential objectives, which are achieved using these other means.[2]

In medical and health services, by contrast, the distinction between the instruments used to achieve quality and access objectives and those deemed to be regulatory barriers to trade is less clear-cut. Many of the regulatory restrictions on commercial presence in the healthcare sector have an objective of ensuring quality. And some are justified as ensuring

[2] Nevertheless, there is still a sequencing issue. It would be unwise to open financial markets to competition without adequate prudential regulation and without adequate regulatory capacity to design and enforce it.

that subsidized health care, designed to ensure equitable access, remains affordable to the government. For example, Malaysia, along with Thailand, is one of the few ASEAN countries to have significant government subsidization of public healthcare — according to Arunanondchai and Fink (2007), only 5 per cent of the total cost of public services is covered by fees. Yet foreign providers in Malaysia are not able to access producer subsidies, and their clients are unable to access consumer subsidies. At least in part, this is because the Malaysian government cannot afford to subsidize all healthcare.[3]

Achieving quality objectives in health and medical care will inevitably mean that there are barriers to the entry and operation of at least some providers — not all regulatory restrictions on market access can be removed. But a well-designed quality control framework should ensure that the operators who are locked out are the genuinely low-quality ones. It can afford to be relatively neutral in its treatment of domestic and foreign providers.

Similarly, achieving equity objectives in health and medical care on an affordable basis may mean that not all providers or clients can gain access to government subsidies. Governments could try to ban the rich from attending subsidized hospitals or clinics, but they cannot prevent the rich from misrepresenting themselves as poor. So governments who want to subsidize selectively may need to rely on some degree of self-selection.

The policy challenge here is to design a healthcare system in which those who can afford private healthcare are willing to pay for it, even when subsidized care is also available. This has proven to be a difficult policy challenge throughout the world, particularly when healthcare providers do not know the income status, tastes, or health characteristics of patients in advance. The theoretical literature shows how offering different qualities of health care can encourage the wealthy to self-select to pay for their own care. Sometimes in the policy literature this is seen to be inequitable in itself (eg Chanda 2001). But the theoretical literature

---

[3] Arunanondchai and Fink (2007) point out that if Malaysia were to spend the same per capita amount of money on healthcare as Switzerland, Malaysia's health expenditure would be roughly equal to its GDP, leaving no money for food, housing, clothing or transportation.

shows that in a second-best world, where government budgets are limited, using quality differences to encourage self-selection may be the least-worst outcome.[4]

Gaynor (2006) gives a good review of the recent literature. He concludes that when prices are regulated, competition actually increases quality (because the new entrants compete by offering higher quality rather than lower prices) and improves consumer welfare, although the effect on social welfare is ambiguous (because of the impact on profits of services providers). When firms set both price and quality (as they typically do in ASEAN countries), the effects of competition on both quality and welfare are ambiguous.

However, one model he surveys is revealing. In the model by Mussa and Rosen (1978), a monopolist sells the same product at different qualities to discriminate among consumers who have different valuations. If the monopolist does not know their valuations in advance, she/he will set the quality of the low quality product too low to be socially optimal, in order to get the consumers to self-select. In the ASEAN region, it is not typically the case that a single monopoly provider offers healthcare to both rich and poor. But a private (sometimes foreign-invested) provider often provides healthcare alongside the public system. And while the private provider cannot influence the price or quality of the public system directly, she/he often can indirectly, by offering salaries that will bid the highly trained medical professionals into the private system.

This poaching of talent into the private system has been a key area of policy concern (eg Chanda 2001, Arunanondchai and Fink 2007), and may be the real-world analogue to the policy problem that Mussa and Rosen (1978) outline in theoretical terms. It is a broader problem associated with operating a dual health care system (where high-quality private providers operate alongside a public system) as a way of meeting equity objectives at least budgetary cost. The problem may be exacerbated when trade in healthcare services is liberalized and more

[4] This is particularly the case when quality is differentiated according to the size and amenities of a patient's bedroom, for example, rather than the quality of clinical care.

foreigners join the ranks of private providers. But it is not a trade barrier *per se*.

Nevertheless, achieving equity objectives in health and medical care on an affordable basis may mean that not all providers or clients can gain access to government subsidies. Governments may choose to deny higher-quality private providers access to subsidies, but if the system is to not unduly constrain trade, then this denial of subsidies should be the same for domestically-owned and foreign private providers. However, governments may chose not to be neutral in their treatment of access to subsidies by domestic and foreign patients. For obvious reasons, they may choose to deny the right of foreign patients to subsidized health care.[5]

In health and medical services, it should be recognized that the ASEAN region is already relatively liberal (see also Arunanondchai and Fink 2007). In part, this is because ASEAN has centres of excellence in medical and healthcare, well-placed to export their services, not just to the rest of ASEAN, but also to the rest of the world. In part, it is because at least some ASEAN countries have already bound relatively liberal regimes as part of their WTO accession. But in part, it is also because many ASEAN countries cannot yet afford the expensive universal healthcare subsidies available in the developed world, and so have not instituted the restrictions on access to subsidies that can also restrain trade.

9.3 ASEAN Ambitions for Services Trade Reform

The establishment of an ASEAN Economic Community is intended to deepen economic integration in East Asia as a whole. To achieve that end, the ASEAN Economic Community Blueprint laid out an ambitious reform agenda designed to establish an ASEAN single market.[6] It envisaged the free flow of services, investment, and skilled labour, along with the free flow of goods and the freer flow of capital.

---

[5] Note that the General Agreement on Trade in Services under the World Trade Organization provides disciplines on measures affecting *services* and *service providers*. It does not discipline measures affecting consumers.

[6] The Blueprint is available at http://www.asean.org/21083.pdf.

In services, it was intended that by 2015, there should be substantially no restriction to ASEAN services suppliers in providing services and in establishing companies across national borders within the region, subject to domestic regulations. For four priority sectors — healthcare, air transport, e-ASEAN and tourism — this target was to be achieved earlier, by 2010. It was also intended that ASEAN would work towards recognition of professional qualifications with a view to facilitate their movement within the region.

The blueprint also contained detail about the scheduled sequence of events by which these targets were to be achieved. Liberalization was to occur through consecutive rounds of negotiations, every two years. The number of sectors to be liberalized was to be expanded in each round. For each new group of sectors, the liberalization commitments were to include:

- no restrictions on service delivery via mode 1 (cross-border trade, where neither the producer nor the consumer moves, and trade often occurs via the internet) and mode 2 (consumption abroad, where the consumer moves temporarily to the country of the producer);
- gradual expansion of the foreign (ASEAN) equity participation permitted in each sector, to be no less than 70 per cent by 2010 in the four priority sectors, and eventually to be no less than 70 per cent by 2015 in all sectors; and
- progressive removal of other limitations on market access via mode 3 (commercial presence, where the producer sets up a permanent commercial presence in the country of the consumer) by 2015.

The negotiations were also to set the parameters of liberalization for limitations on national treatment (ie liberalization involving the removal of discrimination against foreign providers), liberalization of service delivery via mode 4 (the movement of natural persons, whereby the individual service provider moves temporarily to the country of the consumer) and the liberalization of horizontal limitations on market access (ie limitations that apply across a range of services sectors, possibly affecting both domestic and foreign providers) by 2009. Commitments were then to be made according to these parameters from

2009. The ASEAN countries were also to complete mutual recognition agreements in architectural services, accountancy, surveying, and medical practitioners by 2008, dental practitioners by 2009, and to identify and develop mutual recognition agreements for other professional services by 2012. These agreements were to be implemented expeditiously, according to the provisions of each respective agreement.

The blueprint allowed for some overall flexibilities in achieving these objectives, including via an ASEAN minus X formula (where countries that were ready to liberalize could proceed first and be joined by others later). In financial services, the process of liberalization was also to take place with due respect for national policy objectives and the level of economic and financial sector development of the individual members.

The next section examines actual policies in healthcare services in ASEAN countries to see whether they meet the ASEAN Blueprint targets. The mapping exercise covers foreign equity limits, as well as some of the more common limitations on national treatment and market access by mode of service delivery. It also covers aspects of the regulatory regimes that may reduce contestability and performance, and may therefore continue to limit trade even when all trade barriers (more narrowly defined) are removed. It is important to monitor these regulatory restrictions as potential additional impediments to achieving the ASEAN Economic Community.

9.4 Scorecards for Assessing Restrictions on Trade in Healthcare Services

Healthcare services can be provided by individual medical professionals, or in a broader institutional setting. Accordingly, the Central Product Classification (CPC), which is used to classify the different services covered by the GATS, recognizes two types of healthcare services:

- the services of *medical professionals*, including medical and dental professionals (CPC 9312) and midwives, nurses, physiotherapists and paramedical personnel (CPC 93191).

- *health services*, including hospital services (including psychiatric hospitals, CPC 9311), and the services of medical laboratories, ambulances, and residential health care other than hospitals (CPC 9319, other than 93191).

One distinguishing characteristic is that medical professional services are provided in clinics or other environments that do not contain residential facilities. This is in contrast to hospital and other residential health care facilities. Another common feature is that the trade barriers affecting medical professional services tend to affect the entry and conduct of the individual professionals as well as the entry and operations of the clinics and other legal entities in which they operate. By contrast, the trade barriers affecting health services are primarily aimed at the institutions rather than the individuals working within them.

The information on actual policies affecting trade in healthcare services in ASEAN member countries was collected using two separate questionnaires — one for medical services and one for health services. The questionnaire instruments and the detailed responses are described in Dee and Dinh (2009). They are a further development of the framework for assessing barriers to trade in the professions that was developed by Nguyen-Hong (2000).

The questionnaires were first administered in each ASEAN economy over the period October 2008 to March 2009 by researchers from think thanks or equivalent institutions in each ASEAN country. These researchers contacted health organizations such as government departments and professional bodies, in order to get up-to-date information about current regulatory policy settings. The same questionnaires were administered in the same fashion two years later, between October 2010 and March 2011.

The questionnaire responses therefore allow an assessment of recent progress toward the ASEAN Economic Community Blueprint targets, as well as defining the remaining liberalization task. Note that except where stated, the questionnaire responses map existing policies on a most-favoured-nation basis, meaning that they map policies without taking into account any real, binding preferences that have been granted to other ASEAN member countries (although often these are noted). The wording of the Blueprint itself suggests preferential liberalization only in the case of foreign equity limits. Whether other types of healthcare services liberalization under the Blueprint should be preferential is examined in more detail in the concluding section.

The remainder of this section describes the questionnaire instruments, while the subsequent section gives the survey results for 2010–11, and an indication of the policy changes over the previous two years that contributed to that result.

A scorecard for medical professionals

Medical professional services can be traded via mode 3 (commercial presence, in the form of medical clinics), and mode 4 (the movement of either individual professionals or the employees of foreign-located professional services firms). Medical, dental and para-medical services are sometimes provided via mode 1 (eg remote diagnostic services) and mode 2 (consumption abroad).

The questionnaire covering barriers to trade in medical services asked about actual policies affecting all these modes of delivery. Under commercial presence, the questionnaire asked whether there were restrictions on the entry of new professional services firms, either domestically-owned, foreign-invested or both, and whether there were restrictions on the legal form of such firms (eg whether they were prohibited from incorporating, whether foreign entrants were required to establish in a joint venture). It also asked about ownership restrictions — whether there were maximum limits on the equity participation of either private (ie non-government) or foreign shareholders in medical service firms, and whether there were restrictions on medical service firms being owned by people who were not licensed medical professionals.

Under mode 4, the questionnaire asked whether there were restrictions on the entry into professional practice of new individual professionals, either domestic, foreign or both, and asked about any nationality, citizenship or residency requirements for individual professionals to practice. The questionnaire also asked about restrictions on the ability of individual professionals to leave their home country, as this can also affect mode 4 trade. Finally, the questionnaire asked about limitations on the movement of intra-corporate transferees (ie the employees of professional service firms), which might take the form of nationality or residency requirements on certain classes of directors, executives, managers or employees, or a requirement for labour market testing to establish that there was no qualified domestic person available for a position before a foreign person could be hired.

Under modes 1 and 2, the questionnaire asked whether foreign medical professionals located abroad could provide services cross-border to patients in the home country (eg via telemedicine), and whether domestic residents could purchase medical services while abroad.

Finally, the questionnaire recognized that certain aspects of the domestic regulatory regime could have a detrimental effect on trade in medical services by unduly restricting the ability of domestic and/or foreign professionals to provide services. A key restriction here is limitations on the recognition of foreign qualifications, which can limit the ability of foreign professionals to obtain a licence to practice. Accordingly, the questionnaire asked about the requirements that foreign professionals needed to undergo to obtain a licence to practice, including whether they needed to retrain or sit a local examination, and whether their foreign qualifications were automatically accepted or were subject to a case-by-case assessment.

The questionnaire also asked about other potentially anti-competitive aspects of the regulatory regime, including whether there were activities reserved by law to the profession, whether there were restrictions on advertising or fee setting, whether there were restrictions on the ability of foreign service providers to access government subsidies (where these were available), either for themselves or for their clients, whether there were limitations on foreign professionals participating in government contracts, and whether there were requirements for foreign-invested firms to train local staff (which could raise their costs).

Finally, the questionnaire revealed information about the transparency of the regulatory regime, by canvassing which stakeholders were consulted in advance of regulatory changes and by asking how regulatory decisions were made public. For information purposes only, it also asked for details about the regulator and about the licensing criteria used.

A scorecard for health services

Health services are primarily facilities-based services that are traded via mode 3, that is, by the entry and operation of foreign-invested operators. Increasingly, however, hospital and medical laboratory services are traded via mode 1 (eg telemedicine or remote diagnostic services). Hospital services are also traded via mode 2 (consumption abroad). Once again, the questionnaire covering barriers to trade in health services asked about actual policies affecting all these modes of delivery. The format was similar to that for medical services, but focusing on restrictions that affected health institutions rather than individual professionals.

Under commercial presence, the questionnaire asked whether there were restrictions on the entry of new health services firms, either domestically-owned, foreign-invested or both, and whether there were restrictions on the legal form of such firms (eg whether they were prohibited from incorporating, whether foreign entrants were required to establish in a joint venture), and whether they were restricted in the scope of services they could provide or the number or type of clients they could service. It also asked about ownership restrictions — whether there were maximum limits on the equity participation of either private (ie non-government) or foreign shareholders in health service firms.

Under mode 4, the questionnaire asked essentially the same types of questions about restrictions on intra-corporate transferees as in the professional services questionnaire.

Under modes 1 and 2, the questionnaire asked whether foreign health services firms located abroad could provide services cross-border to patients in the home country (eg via telemedicine), and whether domestic residents could purchases health services while abroad.

The questionnaire also asked about potentially anti-competitive aspects of the domestic regulatory regime, including whether foreign-invested firms were subject to different licensing or quality assurance requirements from domestic firms, and whether there were restrictions on the ability of foreign health service providers to access government subsidies (where these were available), either for themselves or for their clients.

Finally, the questionnaire revealed information about the transparency of the regulatory regime, by canvassing which stakeholders were consulted in advance of regulatory changes and by asking how regulatory decisions were made public.

Assigning scores

As noted earlier, the questionnaires and the detailed responses are both described in detail elsewhere. For ease of summarizing the survey responses, the qualitative information about trade restrictions and about transparency was coded in a zero-one fashion, where for each question, a score of 1 was assigned if the restriction applied, and 0 if it did not.

Sometimes an intermediate score was assigned for intermediate stages of restrictiveness. In the case of medical professionals, partial scores were assigned as follows. For private, foreign and non-professional equity restrictions, partial scores were allocated in inverse proportion to the equity limitation. For example, if equity participation was limited to 25 per cent, then a score of 0.75 was assigned, while if equity participation was allowed to reach 75 per cent, then a score of 0.25 was assigned. If there were limitations on equity participation, but no numerical limited was stated, this is taken as a sign that bureaucratic discretion was involved, and this was taken to be relatively restrictive — it was assumed to be equivalent to a 25 per cent equity limit, and so received a score of 0.75. When scoring restrictions on cross-border trade, limitations on either the form of services or the groups to which they could be offered were scored at 0.33 each. When scoring restrictions on consumption abroad, limitations in the form of quotas or authorization requirements were scored at 0.5. When scoring the requirements for foreign professionals to obtain a local licence, retraining was scored as the most restrictive (1.0), having to pass an examination is scored as the next most restrictive (0.75), while case-by-case assessment, having to pass an aptitude test or having to have local practice was scored at 0.5. When scoring restrictions on advertising, 'soft' restrictions were scored at 0.5.

Partial scores in health services were assigned in a similar way. For private and foreign equity restrictions, partial scores were allocated in inverse proportion to the equity limitation. If no numerical limit was stated, this was assumed to be equivalent to a 25 per cent equity limit, and so received a score of 0.75. When scoring restrictions on cross-border trade, limitations on either the form of services or the groups to which they could be offered were scored at 0.33 each. When scoring restrictions on consumption abroad, limitations in the form of quotas or authorization requirements were scored at 0.5.

To obtain a restrictiveness score for a broad restriction category, such as a score for all the restrictions affecting a particular mode, the zero-one scores for each of the restrictions affecting that mode were simply added together. This meant that each of the different restrictions affecting that mode was given equal weight — no attempt was made to assess the relative severity of the different restrictions. Accordingly, the overall restrictiveness scores for broad categories of restrictions reflect the frequency, but not necessarily the severity, of individual restrictions. To normalize the scores for a group, they were divided by the maximum possible restrictiveness score for that group. This gave a final restrictiveness score expressed as a percentage, where a score of 75 per cent meant that three-quarters of the restrictions that could potentially apply to that category of trade did in fact apply.

9.5 Scorecard Results for 2010–2011

Medical professions

Most of the survey questions were answered separately for three different types of professionals — medical, dental, and para-medical (nurses, midwives, *etc.*). Summary restrictiveness scores (obtained as described above) are shown in Table 9.1 for each of these medical professions separately, while a summary of the restrictions affecting domestic and

Table 9.1. Restrictions on Trade in Medical Services by Service and Mode of Delivery (per cent)

	BRN	*KHM*	*IDN*	*LAO*	*MYS*	*MMR*	*PHL*	*SGP*	*THA*	*VNM*	*AVE*
Consumption abroad (Mode 2)	0	0	0	0	0	50	0	0	0	0	5
MEDICAL											
Commercial presence (mode 3)	0	0	40	40	20	40	0	0	0	0	14
Inward movt. of persons (mode 4) – individuals	75	25	25	25	50	75	75	0	50	0	40
Outward movt. of persons (mode 4) – individuals	0	50	0	0	50	50	50	0	0	50	25
Inward movt. of persons (mode 4) – intra-corp. transferees	20	80	80	60	100	100	60	0	20	60	58
Cross-border trade (mode 1)	67	0	0	0	33	67	0	0	0	0	17
Ownership	25	0	11	25	10	33	25	0	17	0	15
Regulation – licensing	25	0	100	25	25	75	25	25	88	50	44
Regulation – restrictions on operation	33	33	22	11	72	72	44	11	0	0	30
TOTAL	28	27	34	27	50	64	38	4	17	15	30
Transparency	38	50	63	38	50	25	88	75	38	75	54
DENTAL											
Commercial presence (mode 3)	0	0	40	40	20	40	0	0	0	0	14
Inward movt. of persons (mode 4) – individuals	75	25	25	25	50	75	75	0	50	0	40
Outward movt. of persons (mode 4) – individuals	0	50	0	0	50	50	0	0	0	50	20
Inward movt. of persons (mode 4) – intra-corp. transferees	20	80	80	60	100	100	60	0	20	60	58
Cross-border trade (mode 1)	67	0	0	0	33	67	0	0	0	0	17
Ownership	25	0	11	25	10	33	25	0	17	0	15

Table 9.1. Continued.

Regulation – licensing	25	0	100	25	25	75	25	25	88	50	44
Regulation – restric -tions on operation	33	33	22	11	72	72	22	11	0	0	28
TOTAL	28	27	34	27	50	64	29	4	17	15	29
Transparency	38	50	63	38	50	25	88	75	38	75	54
PARA-MEDICAL											
Commercial presence (mode 3)	0	0	40	40	20	40	0	0	0	0	14
Inward movt. of persons (mode 4) – individuals	75	25	25	25	50	75	75	0	50	0	40
Outward movt. of persons (mode 4) – individuals	0	50	0	0	50	50	0	0	0	50	20
Inward movt. of persons (mode 4) – intra-corp. transferees	20	80	40	60	100	100	60	0	20	60	54
Cross-border trade (mode 1)	67	0	0	0	33	67	0	0	0	0	17
Ownership	25	0	25	25	10	33	25	0	17	0	16
Regulation – licensing	25	0	0	25	25	75	25	0	88	50	31
Regulation – restrictions on operation	33	33	11	11	72	72	22	0	11	0	27
TOTAL	28	27	22	27	50	64	29	0	20	15	28
Transparency	38	50	63	38	50	25	88	100	38	75	56

Source: Dee (2011b).

foreign suppliers (firms or individual professionals) separately is shown, for medical professionals only, in Table 9.2. The detailed scoring for medical professionals is shown in Table 9.3. As will be seen from Table 9.1, the responses for dental and para-medical professions are similar to those for medical professions, so are not shown here.

Table 9.1 shows considerable variation in the prevalence of restrictions across countries. Most restricted is Myanmar. In principle, foreign ownership in medical professional service firms is allowed in accordance with the Union of Myanmar Foreign Investment Law and the

Table 9.2. Restrictions on Trade in Medical Professional Services by Ownership Category and Mode of Delivery (per cent)

	BRN	*KHM*	*IDN*	*LAO*	*MYS*	*MMR*	*PHL*	*SGP*	*THA*	*VNM*	*AVE*
DOMESTIC MEDICAL											
Commercial presence (mode 3)	0	0	0	0	0	0	0	0	0	0	0
Inward movt. of persons (mode 4) – individuals	0	0	0	0	0	0	0	0	0	0	0
Outward movt. of persons (mode 4) – individuals	0	50	0	0	50	50	50	0	0	50	25
Ownership	0	0	0	0	0	0	0	0	0	0	0
Regulation – restrictions on operation	25	50	50	0	63	38	50	25	0	0	30
TOTAL	5	21	11	0	24	18	21	5	0	11	12
FOREIGN MEDICAL											
Commercial presence (mode 3)	0	0	57	57	29	57	0	0	0	0	20
Inward movt. of natural persons (mode 4) – individuals	100	33	33	33	67	100	100	0	67	0	53
Inward movt. of persons (mode 4) – intra-corporate transferees	20	80	80	60	100	100	60	0	20	60	58
Cross-border trade (mode 1)	67	0	0	0	33	67	0	0	0	0	17
Ownership	50	0	23	50	20	67	50	0	34	0	29
Regulation – licensing	25	0	100	25	25	75	25	25	88	50	44
Regulation – restrictions on operation	36	29	14	14	75	82	43	7	0	0	30
TOTAL	37	29	44	37	60	81	45	4	24	16	38

Source: Dee (2011b).

rules of the Ministry of Health. In practice, there are no existing foreign medical professional service firms in Myanmar. At the other extreme, Singapore is the most liberal, followed by Viet Nam and Thailand, and then Cambodia, Laos and Brunei. Singapore and Thailand are well-recognized as centres of medical and health commerce. For example, Singapore's Parkway Group Healthcare has set up joint ventures with hospitals in India, Indonesia, Malaysia, Sri Lanka and the United

Table 9.3. Restrictions on Trade in Medical Professional Services (index 0–1)

	BRN	KHM	IDN	LAO	MYS	MMR	PHL	SGP	THA	VNM	AVE
A. *Market Access – commercial presence (mode 3) – Professional service firms*											
1 Are there restrictions on new entry - by any firm?	0	0	0	0	0	0	0	0	0	0	0
By foreign firms?	0	0	1	1	0	1	0	0	0	0	0.3
3 Are firms prohibited from incorporating?	0	0	0	0	0	0	0	0	0	0	0
4 Are foreign firms prohibited from est. in a joint venture?	0	0	0	0	0	0	0	0	0	0	0
Are they required to establish in a JV?	0	0	1	1	1	1	0	0	0	0	0.4
B. *Market Access – Inward movement of natural persons (mode 4) – Individual professionals*											
5 Are there restrictions on new entry - by any individual?	0	0	0	0	0	0	0	0	0	0	0
Entry by foreign individuals?	1	0	0	0	0	1	1	0	0	0	0.3
7 Is there a nationality or citizenship requirement?	1	0	0	0	1	1	1	0	1	0	0.5
8 Is there a residency or local presence requirement?	1	1	1	1	1	1	1	0	1	0	0.8
C. *Market Access – Outward movement of natural persons (mode 4) – Individual professionals*											
9 Are there restrictions on outward movement?	0	1	0	0	0	1	1	0	0	1	0.4
10 Are there other restrictions on exit?	0	0	0	0	1	0	0	0	0	0	0.1

Table 9.3. Continued.

D. Market Access – Inward movement of natural persons (mode 4)											
– Intra-corporate transferees											
11 Are there requirements to have nationals/residents?	1	1	1	0	1	1	1	0	1	1	0.8
12 Are there restrictions on employing locally trained professionals in foreign firms?	0	0	0	0	1	1	0	0	0	0	0.2
13 Are intra-corporate transferees subject to labour market tests?	0	1	1	1	1	1	1	0	0	0	0.6
14 Are managerial personnel required to be locally licensed as a professional?	0	1	1	1	1	1	1	0	0	1	0.7
15 Are managerial personnel required to be locally domiciled?	0	1	1	1	1	1	0	0	0	1	0.6
E. Cross-border trade (Mode 1)											
16 Are professionals located abroad able to provide services cross-border to patients in your country (eg tele-medicine)?	0.67	0	0	0.00	0.33	0.67	0	0	0	0	0.17
F. Consumption abroad (Mode 2)											
17 Can domestic residents purchase medical services while abroad?	0	0	0	0	0	0.5	0	0	0	0	0.1
G Ownership											
18 Is private ownership allowed - existing operators?	0	0	0	0	0	0	0	0	0	0	0.0
New entrants?	0	0	0	0	0	0	0	0	0	0	0.0
19 Is foreign ownership allowed - existing operators?	0.75	0	0.35	0.75	0.3	1	0.75	0	0.51	0	0.4
New entrants?	0.75	0	0.33	0.75	0.3	1	0.75	0	0.51	0	0.4

Table 9.3. Continued.

20	Are non-professional investors allowed an equity stake in professional service firms - existing operators?	0	0.01	0	0.01	0.01	0	0	0	0	0	0.0
	New entrants?	0	0.01	0	0.01	0.01	0	0	0	0	0	0.0
H.	*Regulation – licensing*											
24	What are the requirements for foreign individual professionals to be licensed to practice locally?	0.5	0	1	0.5	0.5	0.5	0.5	0.5	0.75	0	0.5
25	Are there any other requirements for the licensing and accreditation of foreign individual professionals?	0	0	1	0	0	1	0	0	1	1	0.4
I.	*Regulation – restrictions on operation*											
29	Are there activities reserved by law to the profession?	1	1	1	0	1	1	1	0	0	0	0.6
30	Are there restrictions on the profession having a partnership or association with other professions?	0	0	0	0	0	0	0	0	0	0	0
31	Are there restrictions on the profession advertising, marketing or soliciting?	0	1	1	0	0.5	0.5	1	1	0	0	0.5
32	Are there restrictions on fee setting?	0	0	0	0	1	0	0	0	0	0	0.1
33	Is there a requirement for foreign-invested firms to train local staff?	1	1	0	1	1	1	0	0	0	0	0.5
34	Are there restrictions on the participation of foreign professionals or firms in government contracts?	0	0	0	0	0	1	1	0	0	0	0.2
35	Is there a requirement to have the work of a foreign professional approved by a locally trained/licensed professional?	1	0	0	0	1	1	0	0	0	0	0.3

Table 9.3. Continued.

39	Are foreign providers restricted in their access to producer subsidies?	0	0	0	0	1	1	0	0	0	0	0.2
	Are their clients restricted in their access to consumer subsidies?	0	0	0	0	1	1	1	0	0	0	0.3
36	Which of the following are consulted in advance of regulatory changes (eg licensing requirements)?											
	Service providers	1	1	1	0	1	0	1	1	0	1	0.7
	Professional bodies	1	1	1	1	1	1	1	1	1	1	1
	Users	0	1	0	0	0	0	0	1	0	0	0.2
	Other	0	0	0	0	0	0	1	0	0	0	0.1
37	How are laws and regulatory decisions made public?											
	Government website	0	0	1	0	1	0	1	1	0	1	0.5
	Professional body's website	0	0	1	0	0	0	1	1	1	1	0.5
	Official gazette	1	1	1	1	1	1	1	1	1	1	1
	Other	0	0	0	1	0	0	1	0	0	1	0.3

Source: See Dee (2011b).

Kingdom, while the Bumrungrad Hospital in Thailand has entered into management contracts with hospitals in Bangladesh and Myanmar, and has formed a joint venture with a hospital in the Philippines (Arunanondchai and Fink 2007). According to the survey responses, these commercial endeavours are underpinned by relatively liberal trade and regulatory regimes at home. The Philippines is well-known for exporting nursing services to the rest of the world. Its regime for para-medical services is also relatively liberal, though less so than in Viet Nam and Cambodia, for example, which are liberal as a result of their preparations for WTO accession.

There is a broad tendency for the countries that have a lower prevalence of restrictions on trade in medical services to have a more transparent regulatory regime, in terms of having wider consultation before regulatory decisions are made, and wider dissemination of those decisions after they are made. For example, Singapore has the lowest prevalence of restrictions but the second highest transparency score (behind the Philippines). By contrast, Myanmar has the highest prevalence of restrictions and the lowest transparency score.

It is possible to use the information in these tables to assess the extent to which individual countries have reached the explicit targets of the ASEAN Economic Community Blueprint. Tables 9.1 and 9.2 show that modes 1 and 2 are already relatively liberal. Consumption abroad involves consumption beyond the jurisdiction of domestic quality control processes, so quality control rationales for regulatory restrictions do not apply. Furthermore, most governments recognize that it is impossible in practice to control what their citizens purchase while abroad. It would be a relatively low cost exercise for ASEAN countries to commit formally to keeping this mode of trade free of government restrictions, and on a most-favoured-nation basis (ie for trade with all countries, not just with ASEAN partners).

Mode 1 trade in medical services is less liberal than mode 2 trade. Some countries restrict mode 1 trade to certain procedures, but this runs the risk of locking out trade in new procedures or services that have yet to be developed.

A further liberalization target in the Blueprint is liberalization of limits on foreign equity participation. Four ASEAN countries already meet or exceed the Blueprint's foreign equity target of 70 per cent (where a score lower than 0.3 against question 19 in Table 9.3 indicates that the country allows the foreign ownership share to reach 70 per cent or higher). These are Cambodia, Malaysia, Singapore and Viet Nam. In addition, Indonesia now comes very close to meeting the target. Two additional countries probably meet the target. Brunei has a requirement that at least one of the owners of a medical service firm must be local. Whether this meets a 70 per cent foreign equity target depends on the size of the firm. In the Philippines, professional service firms may be foreign owned as long as the service providers are Filipino citizens. Therefore, there are technically no restrictions on the equity participation of foreigners in corporations. However, for general partnerships and single proprietorships for which the owners are the services providers, foreign ownership is not allowed because of the Constitutional provision restricting the practice of professions to citizens.

Thus it seems that a majority of ASEAN countries already meet, or probably meet, the Blueprint's foreign equity target. This reflects the fact that ASEAN is already relatively liberal in healthcare services, and foreign equity limits have typically been among the first targets of further services trade liberalization initiatives. Furthermore, while some of the ASEAN countries retain restrictions on foreign equity participation, all allow full domestic private equity participation — there are no government-owned monopolies, even though public provision still dominates in practice in at least some countries (Arunanondchai and Fink 2007).

However, the foreign equity targets in healthcare services were to be achieved by 2010. Thus three ASEAN members still need to take definitive action. In Lao PDR there is still a potential disconnect between its relatively liberal investment law and its more opaque sectoral regulation. Thailand still requires government approval for majority foreign ownership. And Myanmar has yet to allow its legislation permitting foreign ownership to be openly reflected in actual practice.

But Tables 9.1 and 9.2 also indicate that the greatest prevalence of restrictions is on Mode 4 trade, with restrictions affecting the inward movement of both individual professionals and intra-corporate transferees. Domestic regulatory regimes (particularly licensing regimes) also impose a relatively high frequency of restrictions. This is particularly significant, as some of these restrictions also affect domestic services suppliers, and may therefore doubly penalize economic performance in the health sector. However, some of these have been justified on the grounds of quality assurance

A visual presentation of the extent of discrimination against foreign providers is shown in Figure 9.1. This plots the prevalence of restrictions against domestic and foreign medical professionals across all modes of delivery — the domestic and foreign totals from Table 9.2. The figure shows that in most ASEAN countries, the *proportion* of restrictions that actually apply is much higher for foreign services providers than for their domestic counterparts. But this only captures one aspect of the discrimination against foreigners. Foreigners also face a higher *total number* of restrictions. So the overall extent of discrimination against foreigners is even greater than indicated in Figure 9.1.

It is likely to be a long and difficult process to ensure that non-discriminatory restrictions only target quality control objectives and are no more burdensome than necessary, although the final section suggests some strategies for doing so. Figure 9.1 demonstrates that a great deal can be done in the meantime. There is considerable scope for ASEAN countries to make additional commitments to remove derogations from national treatment and thereby to remove discrimination against foreign suppliers.

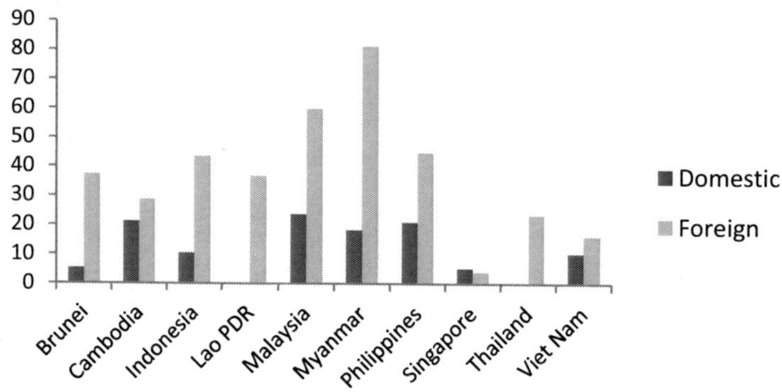

Figure 9.1. Restrictions on Trade in Medical Services by Ownership Category (per cent)

Scorecard results for health services

Tables 9.4, 9.5 and 9.6 give a comparable picture of the prevalence of restrictions affecting the various health services. Table 9.4 indicates that there appears to be little variation in the prevalence of restrictions affecting the different kinds of health services (hospital, medical laboratory, and ambulance), but there is significant variation in the prevalence across countries. Singapore, Thailand and Viet Nam are the most free of restrictions, while Cambodia, Laos and the Philippines are also relatively free. Myanmar is the most restricted. Recognized foreign-invested firms do not yet operate, although there are a few foreign health service organizations such as non-government organizations (NGOs) and volunteer organizations.

The pattern of restrictions across modes of delivery is also similar to that for medical services. Restrictions that are most prevalent are those affecting the movement of intra-corporate transferees and regulatory restrictions.

Table 9.5 and Figure 9.2 indicate that, compared with medical services, the regulatory restrictions in health are entirely aimed at penalizing foreign suppliers, rather than affecting domestic and foreign suppliers more equally. By 2010–11, there were no recorded non-discriminatory restrictions affecting domestic suppliers. As will be seen shortly, the last of these was removed between 2008–09 and 2010–11, when the Philippines removed its last regulatory barrier to entry.

Table 9.4 also indicates that, compared to medical services, health services are slightly more likely to be affected by restrictions on commercial presence that limit the entry, legal form, or scope of operations of foreign-invested firms. The detail supplied by the survey respondents suggests that at least some of the regulatory restrictions and restrictions on commercial presence in health are designed to ensure the quality of foreign health services suppliers. Therefore, the loosening or removal of these restrictions should entail an examination of whether there are better ways to ensure quality in health services. This issue is discussed in more detail in the final section.

Table 9.4. Restrictions on Trade in Health Services by Service and Mode of Delivery (per cent)

	BRN	*KHM*	*IDN*	*LAO*	*MYS*	*MMR*	*PHL*	*SGP*	*THA*	*VNM*	*AVE*
Consumption abroad (Mode 2)	0	0	0	0	0	50	0	0	0	0	5
HOSPITAL											
Commercial presence (mode 3)	43	0	29	0	14	57	29	0	14	0	19
Movt. of persons (mode 4) – intra-corporate transferees	20	80	80	60	100	100	60	0	60	60	62
Cross-border trade	67	0	0	0	33	67	0	0	0	0	17
Ownership	38	0	17	0	15	50	0	0	26	0	15
Regulation	17	17	67	33	67	83	33	17	0	0	33
TOTAL	31	22	46	22	48	72	30	4	22	13	31
Transparency	33	50	83	50	50	50	100	83	67	83	65
MEDICAL LABORATORY											
Commercial presence (mode 3)	43	0	14	0	14	57	29	0	14	0	17
Movt. of persons (mode 4) – intra-corporate transferees	20	80	80	60	100	100	60	20	20	60	60
Cross-border trade	0	0	0	0	33	67	0	0	0	0	10
Ownership	38	0	17	0	15	50	0	0	26	0	15
Regulation	17	17	67	33	67	83	0	0	0	0	28
TOTAL	28	22	42	22	48	72	22	4	13	13	29
Transparency	33	50	83	50	50	50	100	83	67	67	63
AMBULANCE											
Commercial presence (mode 3)	43	0	71	0	14	57	29	0	14	0	23
Movt. of persons (mode 4) – intra-corporate transferees	20	80	100	60	100	100	60	20	20	60	62
Cross-border trade	0	0	0	0	0	0	0	0	0	0	0
Ownership	38	0	50	0	15	50	0	0	26	0	18
Regulation	17	17	83	33	67	83	0	0	0	0	30
TOTAL	28	22	74	22	46	70	22	4	13	13	31
Transparency	33	50	67	50	50	50	0	67	67	67	50

Source: Dee (2011b).

Table 9.5. Restrictions on Trade in Hospital Services by Ownership Category and Mode of Delivery (per cent)

	BRN	*KHM*	*IDN*	*LAO*	*MYS*	*MMR*	*PHL*	*SGP*	*THA*	*VNM*	*AVE*
DOMESTIC HOSPITAL											
Commercial presence (mode 3)	0	0	0	0	0	0	0	0	0	0	0
Ownership	0	0	0	0	0	0	0	0	0	0	0
Regulation	0	0	0	0	0	0	0	0	0	0	0
TOTAL											
FOREIGN HOSPITAL											
Commercial presence (mode 3)	55	0	36	0	18	73	36	0	18	0	24
Movt. of persons (mode 4) – intra-corporate transferees	20	80	80	60	100	100	60	0	60	60	62
Cross-border trade (mode 1)	67	0	0	0	33	67	0	0	0	0	17
Ownership	75	0	34	0	30	100	0	0	51	0	29
Regulation	17	17	67	33	67	83	33	17	0	0	33
TOTAL	37	26	55	26	56	85	36	5	26	15	37

Source: Dee (2011b).

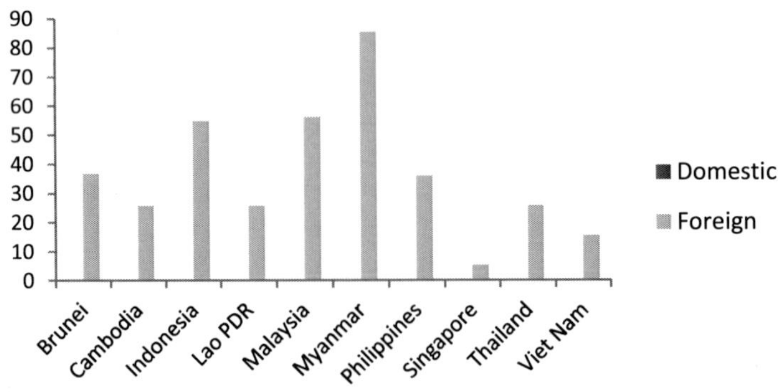

Figure 9.2. Restrictions on Trade in Hospital Services by Ownership Category (per cent)

Table 9.6. Restrictions on Trade in Hospital Services (index 0–1)

	BRN	*KHM*	*IDN*	*LAO*	*MYS*	*MMR*	*PHL*	*SGP*	*THA*	*VNM*	*AVE*
A. *Market Access – commercial presence (mode 3)*											
1 Are there policy restrictions on new entry - by any firm?	0	0	0	0	0	0	0	0	0	0	0
By foreign firms?	1	0	0	0	0	1	0	0	0	0	0.2
3 Are these firms prohibited from incorporating (with limited liability)?	0	0	0	0	0	0	0	0	0	0	0
4 Are foreign health services firms prohibited from establishing in a joint venture with local professionals?	0	0	0	0	0	0	0	0	0	0	0
Are they required to establish in a JV?	1	0	1	0	1	1	0	0	0	0	0.4
5 Are foreign health services firms restricted in the scope of services they can provide?	0	0	1	0	0	1	1	0	0	0	0.3
6 Are foreign health services firms restricted in the number of clients (domestic and/or foreign) they can service?	1	0	0	0	0	1	1	0	1	0	0.4
B. *Market Access – movement of natural persons (mode 4) – intra-corporate transferees*											
7 Are there minimum requirements to have nationals/residents as executives, managers *etc.* in foreign invested health service firms?	1	1	1	1	1	1	1	0	1	1	0.9
8 Are there prohibitions or maximum restrictions on employing locally trained professionals in foreign invested professional service firms?	0	0	0	0	1	1	0	0	0	0	0.2

Table 9.6. Continued.

9 Are there categories of intra-corporate transferees whose entry and stay is subject to labour market tests?	0	1	1	1	1	1	1	0	0	0	0.6
10 Are there categories of managerial personnel who must be locally licensed as a medical professional?	0	1	1	1	1	1	1	0	1	1	0.8
11 Are there categories of managerial personnel who must be locally domiciled?	0	1	1	0	1	1	0	0	1	1	0.6
C. Cross-border trade (Mode 1)											
12 Are foreign health services providers located abroad able to provide services cross-border to patients in your country (eg tele-medicine)?	0.67	0	0	0	0.33	0.67	0	0	0	0	0.2
D. Consumption abroad (Mode 2)											
13 Can domestic residents purchase health services while abroad?	0	0	0	0	0	0.5	0	0	0	0	0.1
E. Ownership											
14 Is private ownership allowed - in existing operators?	0	0	0	0	0	0	0	0	0	0	0
New entrants?	0	0	0	0	0	0	0	0	0	0	0
15 Is foreign ownership allowed - in existing operators?	0.75	0	0.35	0	0.3	1	0	0	0.51	0	0.3
New entrants?	0.75	0	0.33	0	0.3	1	0	0	0.51	0	0.3
F Regulation											
21 Are foreign providers subject to different licensing requirements from domestic firms?	0	0	1	1	0	1	0	0	0	0	0.3

Table 9.6. Continued.

22 Are foreign providers required to train local staff?	1	1	1	1	1	1	0	0	0	0	0.6
23 Do quality assurance obligations on foreign providers differ from those for domestic institutions?	0	0	0	0	0	0	0	0	0	0	0
24 Are foreign providers of these services restricted in their ability to charge fees?	0	0	0	0	1	1	0	0	0	0	0.2
26 Are foreign providers restricted in their access to producer subsidies?	0	0	1	0	1	1	1	0	0	0	0.4
Are their local clients (nationals) restricted in their access to consumer subsidies?	0	0	1	0	1	1	1	1	0	0	0.5
29 Which of the following are consulted in advance of regulatory changes (eg accreditation requirements) affecting service providers?											
Service providers	1	1	1	1	1	1	1	1	1	1	1
Users	0	1	1	1	0	0	1	1	1	0	0.6
Other	0	0	0	0	0	1	1	0	0	1	0.3
30 How are laws and regulatory decisions affecting these service providers (see name of sheet) made public?											
Regulator's website	0	0	1	0	1	0	1	1	1	1	0.6
Official gazette	1	1	1	0	1	1	1	1	1	1	0.9
Other	0	0	1	1	0	0	1	1	0	1	0.5

Source: Dee (2011b).

There is considerable scope for ASEAN countries to make additional commitments to remove derogations from national treatment and thereby to remove discrimination against foreign suppliers. This process is likely to be less difficult and controversial than dealing with the remaining trade barriers in medical professional services. But in places it may need to be preceded by reforms that ensure adequate non-discriminatory quality control procedures.

9.6 Sources of Progress since 2008–2009

A brief summary of the policy changes affecting trade in medical and health services in ASEAN countries since 2008–09 is shown in Table 9.7. It is based on longer country reports in Dee (2011b). The table also shows the extent to which countries in the region have instituted these reforms in response to commitments made under the ASEAN Framework Agreement on Services (AFAS). In medical professional services, Cambodia implemented a mutual recognition agreement with its ASEAN neighbours. In health services, Indonesia relaxed the minimum bed size for foreign-invested hospitals on a preferential basis. In other respects, the reforms recorded in Table 9.7 are unilateral and non-preferential, or if they have a regional dimension, it is because of geographical constraints rather than preferential commitments.

There have been significant reforms in Indonesia and the Philippines, and a slight easing in Myanmar. In Indonesia, new legislation has been introduced to fill the significant gaps in the regulatory framework that were noted in 2008–09 (Dee 2009). In a few cases, the introduction of explicit legislative guidelines has the potential to limit practices (such as the hiring of foreigners into relatively unskilled positions) that might have occurred otherwise. In most cases, however, the legislation will have somewhat reduced the scope for bureaucratic discretion. It also tightens the quality assurance framework in Indonesia by making the hospital accreditation process mandatory every three years. Finally, the Indonesian legislative reforms have also been accompanied by a slight easing of foreign equity limits. In the Philippines, there has been a lifting of the regulatory restrictions on the entry of new hospitals and medical

Table 9.7. ASEAN's Progress in Liberalizing Trade in Healthcare Services during 2008–2010

	Medical Professionals	*Health Services*
Brunei	None.	None.
Cambodia	New mutual recognition agreement signed with ASEAN countries in 2009.	None.
Indonesia	Law no. 44/2009 covers medical professionals for hospitals. Hospitals can employ foreign medical professionals, but the employment must be intended for the purpose of knowledge and technology transfers — this rules out foreigners in unskilled positions. Permenkes no. 028 issued on 4 January 2011 says clinics cannot hire foreign healthcare workers. Foreign equity limits for medical and dental clinics (specialist only) have been raised from 65% to 67%. Those for nursing have been raised from 49% to 51% in Medan and Surabaya, and from zero to 49% in the rest of Indonesia.	Law no. 36/2009 on health requires all foreign healthcare facilities to obtain operating licence. Law no 44/2009 on hospitals regulates their establishment and management and introduces mandatory accreditation every 3 years. Foreign equity limits for hospitals and medical laboratories have been raised from 65% to 67%. The minimum size of foreign hospitals has been lowered from 300 to 200 beds for ASEAN investors, though the hospitals still have to be specialist. Foreign medical professionals can be employed in hospitals and medical laboratories, but this must be intended for the purpose of knowledge and technology transfer — this now rules out foreigners in unskilled positions. Universal services obligations have been spelt out in law.
Lao PDR	None.	None.
Malaysia	PROSPECTIVE: The Malaysian National Healthcare Financing Scheme (similar to Australia's Medicare system) may finally be implemented. The government is keen to push tele-medicine, and has also been promoting medical tourism. It has been promoting the recruitment of foreign doctors and specialists and establishing new medical colleges and twinning programs to raise the ratio of doctors per head of population.	None.
Myanmar	Same as for health services.	Some easing of cross-border trade. Some joint venture hospitals have been established since 2008.

Table 9.7. Continued

Philippines	The process for issuing employment permits to foreign nationals has been extended from 1 to 3 working days. Otherwise, the lack of progress in liberalization stems from the constitutional provision that the practice of all professions in the Philippines shall be limited to Filipino citizens.	A major policy change is the suspension for one year of the need to obtain a Certificate of Need (CON), the only restriction on new entry of private hospitals. The DOH Administrative Order No. 2007-0027 created the improved quality assurance and monitoring program for clinical laboratories in the Philippines and rendered obsolete the DOH-BHFS Circular No. 3 Series of 2003, which suspends issuance of permit to new entry of laboratories. The process for issuing employment permits to foreign nationals has been extended from 1 to 3 working days. In 2009, the Health and Wellness Alliance of the Philippines (HEAL Philippines) was established to organize industry and government stakeholders involved with global healthcare and wellness services, tourism and retirement. PROSPECTIVE: There are emerging demands for the amendment of the Republic Act 4226 or the Hospital Licensure Act to expand the coverage of the law to include health facilities other than hospitals.
Singapore	None.	None.
Thailand	HORIZONTAL: One distinctive change is the replacement of the Working of Alien Act 1978 by the new act, Working of Alien Act 2008. Among other things, it extends the validity period of the work permit from not exceeding one year to not exceeding two years. However, non-immigrants visas are normally granted for one year.	Same as for medical services.
Viet Nam	None.	The Health Insurance Law took effect on 1 July 2009, aiming to ease the load on provincial and central hospitals, and expand policyholder categories to include drug addicts and people with congenital defects who were previously excluded.

Source: Dee (2011b).

laboratories. In Myanmar there has been a growth in cross-border trade in medical and health services and some limited evidence of foreign investment occurring in health, though it is not registered as such.

Thus there is evidence of worthwhile reform efforts since 2008–09. Some of this has been in direct response to AFAS commitments, but most has other proximate causes. A key question is how far these reforms took ASEAN towards reaching its end goal of a single market for services. That question can be addressed by looking at what difference these reforms made to the scorecard results.

For medical professional services, this is indicated in Figures 9.3 and 9.4, for domestic and foreign services providers respectively. These figures compare the overall prevalence of restrictions in 2008–09 and 2010–11. The differences reflect the reforms summarized in Table 9.7. The reforms have made only a slight difference to the overall prevalence of restrictions on foreign suppliers, and no difference to the prevalence of restrictions on domestic suppliers. Thus ASEAN reforms are indeed focused on reducing the extent of discrimination against foreign suppliers. But a great deal more remains to be done.

In health services, Figure 9.5 shows that the last of the non-discriminatory restrictions affecting both domestic and foreign suppliers was removed between 2008–09 and 2010–11, when the Philippines

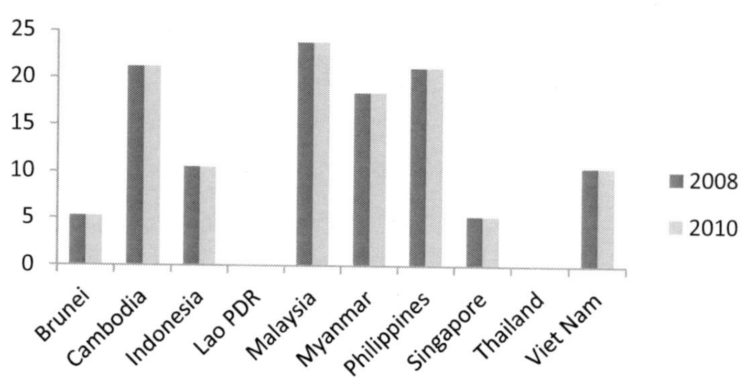

Figure 9.3. Changes in Restrictions on Domestic Medical Services over Time (per cent)

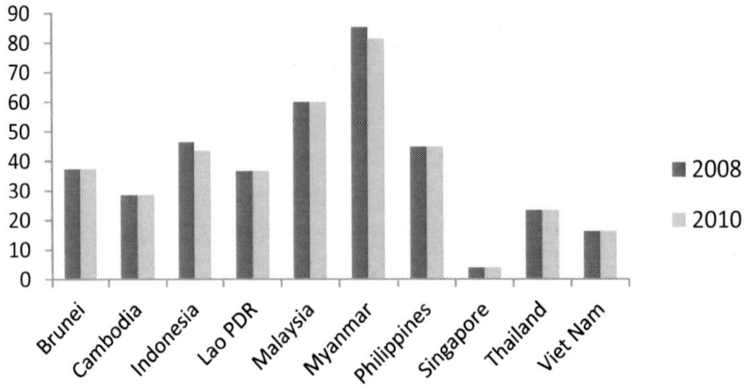

Figure 9.4. Changes in Restrictions on Foreign Medical Services over Time (per cent)

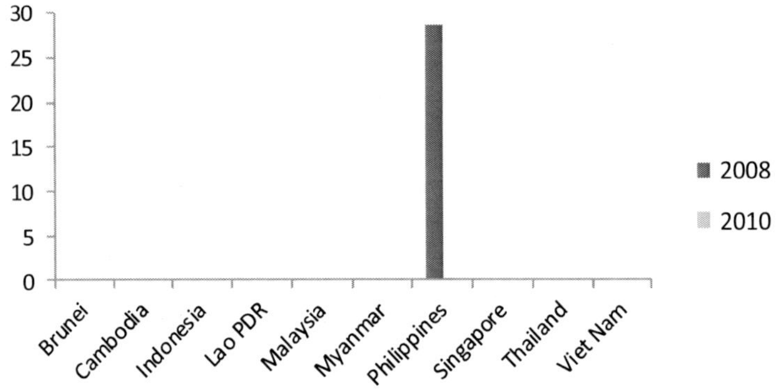

Figure 9.5. Changes in Restrictions on Domestic Hospital Services over Time (per cent)

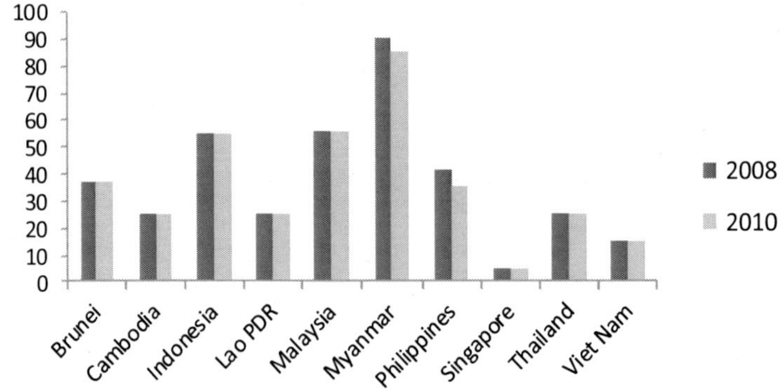

Figure 9.6. Changes in Restrictions on Foreign Hospital Services over Time (per cent)

removed its last regulatory barrier to entry. By contrast, the prevalence of restrictions against foreign health services providers is still quite high, and the recent reforms since 2008–09 have made only slight inroads into those trade barriers (Figure 9.6).

9.7 Pathways to Liberalizing Trade in Healthcare Services

The Government of Singapore developed a Roadmap to advance the region-wide integration of the healthcare sectors. This Roadmap was adopted by ASEAN Trade Ministers in November 2004. Much of the Roadmap is concerned with promoting trade in healthcare goods, including pharmaceuticals and medical equipment. In services, the Roadmap does little more than restate the targets contained in the Blueprint. However, in other areas, it contains recommendations relevant for health services, including:

- accelerating the implementation of mutual recognition agreements;
- setting clear targets and schedules for harmonization of standards, where required;
- facilitating the movement of business persons through an ASEAN Travel Card, and developing an ASEAN Agreement to facilitate free movement of experts, professionals, skilled labour and talents in ASEAN, taking account of domestic laws and regulations;
- more established ASEAN countries to provide training and host attachment programs for medical and health-related workers from less developed ASEAN member states; and
- to strengthen cooperation within ASEAN countries in the area of capacity-building, ie exchange of experts, regulatory infrastructure and human resource development, within available resources.

Some of these recommendations (on mutual recognition, movement of persons) target measures that explicitly discriminate against foreign services providers. The scorecard results suggest that there is much to do in both medical and health services to reduce such discrimination. Others are aimed at harmonization of standards and capacity-building — the latter presumably designed to ensure that the less developed members of ASEAN are (eventually) able to meet the harmonized standards.

However, the experience of harmonization in the EU suggests that this is not a particularly fruitful way to ensure that regulatory regimes are no more burdensome than necessary to meet their legitimate objectives. If anything, it typically has the opposite effect, since those with protectionist motives have an incentive to argue for particularly high 'core' standards with which all suppliers must comply (Messerlin 2009).

Clearly, to facilitate further progress in liberalizing health and medical services, the ASEAN countries will need to work to establish satisfactory regimes for regulating and enforcing acceptable quality standards, both for individual professionals and for healthcare institutions, as Indonesia has recently done. This will be a key prerequisite to dismantling the regulatory and other restrictions that, while having a possible rationale in quality assurance, are either more discriminatory or more burdensome that required.

But this need not involve establishing the same standards in each country. Quality already varies enormously across the region. Thailand has world-class hospitals catering to clients from Japan, but in Cambodia, many private facilities use obsolete equipment and more than half do not have a licence from the Ministry of Health, while in Laos, training is considered to be inadequate, leading to high rates of misdiagnosis and maltreatment (Arunanondchai and Fink 2007). These latter countries do not have the training or regulatory resources to achieve Thai standards immediately. But cooperation among regulatory authorities could help to establish *minimum acceptable standards*, either by country, by discipline, by procedure, or by institution. Countries could choose to adopt standards in their home country that were higher than the minimum acceptable standards. But having a 'ladder' of quality standards across the region would help to do two things:

- it would put a floor under standards, providing a benchmark for standards that were not more burdensome than necessary; and
- it would also provide a viable alternative for the replacement of standards that were discriminatory against foreign providers.

The remainder of this section will demonstrate how such regulatory cooperation would facilitate achieving the Blueprint's targets.

One such target is the completion of mutual recognition agreements. The ASEAN countries have by now completed Mutual Recognition Agreements for medical practitioners, dental practitioners, and nurses. In some respects, these framework agreements are very weak, because in each case, they state that foreign professionals can apply for registration in the host country subject to the following:

- having a relevant qualification — in the case of doctors and dentists, this must be recognized by the professional bodies of both the home and host countries;
- having professional registration in the home country;
- having minimum practical experience (5 years for doctors and dentists, 3 years for nurses);
- being in compliance with continuing professional development;
- being certified at home as not having violated professional or ethical standards; and
- being in compliance with any other requirements as may be imposed by the professional body or other relevant authorities in the host country.

In one sense, this last clause is tantamount to an all-purpose escape clause. In another sense, these agreements mean that recognition cannot be denied so long as all the criteria are spelt out and the foreign professional meets them. Hence, the work still needs to be done to ensure that the requirements imposed by the professional bodies or other relevant authorities are not unduly discriminatory or burdensome. The above regulatory cooperation to establish minimum acceptable professional standards would help to do this. Indeed, at the level of professional qualifications, the regulatory cooperation could involve the same regulatory bodies as were signatories to the Mutual Recognition Agreements.

Another liberalization target in the Blueprint is liberalization of trade via modes 1 and 2. The scorecards show that modes 1 and 2 are already relatively liberal. It would be a relatively low cost exercise for ASEAN countries to commit formally to keeping these modes of trade free of government restrictions, and on a most-favoured-nation basis (ie for trade with all countries, not just with ASEAN partners).

However, an indirect restriction to mode 2 trade is the lack of mobility of health insurance coverage. Often this is because health insurers do not know how to assess the quality of overseas health providers. Mattoo and Rathindran (2005) suggest that hospitals in developing countries could seek accreditation from Joint Commission International, which is the international arm of the Joint Commission for Accreditation of Health Care Organizations, one of the leading organizations certifying hospital quality in the United States. This would provide a strong signal to health insurers around the world that their procedures were worthy of coverage. However, within ASEAN, it may not be necessary or appropriate for all hospitals to meet US standards. But some assurance that a particular hospital met ASEAN-defined minimum acceptable standards, either generally or for a particular procedure, could help to persuade ASEAN insurers to allow intra-ASEAN mobility of health insurance. But this requires ASEAN minimum standards to be defined.

Mode 1 trade in medical and health services is less liberal than mode 2 trade. Some countries restrict mode 1 trade to certain procedures, but as noted, this runs the risk of locking out trade in new procedures or services that have yet to be developed. To the extent that there are quality concerns, the development of ASEAN minimum acceptable standards would facilitate the removal of more burdensome barriers to trade among ASEAN members. But some of the most competitive suppliers of mode 1 diagnostic and medical laboratory services are in places like Hong Kong — outside of the ASEAN region. Hence, to maximize the benefits of mode 1 liberalization, it should also be on a most-favoured-nation basis.

A final concern about mode 1 trade is that the foreign hospitals and medical laboratories should respect the privacy and confidentiality of patient information. Developing rules to ensure the privacy and confidentiality of patient data cross-border is another area requiring regulatory cooperation.

A further liberalization target in the Blueprint is liberalization of limits on foreign equity participation. As noted, a majority of ASEAN members already meet the target in medical services, and on a most-favoured-nation basis. Foreign services providers typically account for small shares of the healthcare market. And while little comprehensive information exists on the origin of foreign investors, in some countries they are from outside the region (Arunanondchai and Fink 2007). For example, in Cambodia most foreign hospitals are of Chinese origin. Further liberalization on a most-favoured-nation basis would maximize the contribution of foreign investment to expanding the resource base in what is an extraordinarily expensive sector. But establishing minimum acceptable ASEAN standards would add to the transparency of the standards that foreign hospitals were required to achieve.

As noted, many of the remaining restrictions on commercial presence and the regulatory restrictions that are measured in the scorecard have been justified on the grounds of quality assurance. While the questionnaire instruments collected information about the general licensing and registration requirements imposed in each country, the scorecard made no judgement about whether they were more burdensome than necessary. It did record whether the requirements on foreign providers were more severe than those on domestic providers. A process of regulatory cooperation that defined minimum acceptable standards in ASEAN would provide a basis for further liberalizing the remaining limitations on market access via mode 3, not just those that discriminated against foreigners, but also those that unduly burdened domestic providers. As noted earlier, this type of liberalization could provide particularly large gains.

A final liberalization target in the Blueprint is liberalization of mode 4 trade. One key to this is the establishment of Mutual Recognition Agreements, which has been discussed above. Another is easing visa and other immigration restrictions on the movement of business people and professionals. The ASEAN Roadmap has useful practical suggestions in this regard.

However, there are residual concerns about brain drain — both from one country to another, and from the public to the private health system within a country. As noted by the ASEAN–ANU Migration Research Team (2005), mechanisms such as bonds and compulsory services are appropriate as an immediate measure. However, in the long term, raising the remuneration in healthcare occupations is also important. This depends partly on raising public allocations to healthcare. It also depends on raising the productivity of healthcare workers. Cooperation in the training of both professionals and regulators, as suggested by the Roadmap, would help in this regard. Furthermore, the social benefits of a medical education accrue very largely to the individual, in terms of higher lifetime earnings. There is therefore a case for ASEAN countries to recover a larger share of the costs of medical training from the students themselves.

Initiatives such as these can help to open up medical and health markets in the ASEAN region so as to increase the quantity and quality of healthcare available, and to improve its 'value for money'. Tools such as the surveys used to map current policy settings in healthcare could be used on a repeated basis to monitor progress towards achieving the Blueprint's liberalization objectives. But because of the inevitable interactions between trade policy and domestic regulation, it should not be anticipated that all of the indicators of regulatory restrictions could be reduced to zero. The aim instead should be to ensure that regulatory structures are no more burdensome than necessary to ensure quality of the service. In most (but not all) cases, however, this means that they should operate on a non-discriminatory basis.

Chapter 10

Assessing Services Reform[1]

Philippa Dee

10.1 Introduction

Structural reform in finance, transport, energy, telecommunications and higher education is a behind-the-border agenda. It is not synonymous with deregulation, but better regulation. Nor is privatization the key. The critical aim of structural reform is to encourage as much competition as is appropriate in these sectors, while configuring the regulation targeted at other legitimate economic and social objectives so that it does least damage to that competition, and therefore to economic efficiency. Competition can come from foreign sources, or it can come from domestic new entrants. It can be a powerful method of squeezing excess profits and driving producers to find lower cost ways of doing business. Ownership matters primarily to the extent that it affects the incentives of producers to respond in these ways to competitive pressures. And government-owned enterprises can respond quite adequately to private sector competition if they operate under the appropriate governance structures. As will be seen, there can be significant gains from structural reforms in some of these sectors, even when they continue to operate with current domestic ownership structures.

---

[1] This chapter is an expanded version of a paper produced with funding from the Asia Pacific Economic Cooperation's Policy Support Unit and material from that paper is reproduced with its permission. Information is taken from The Impacts and Benefits of Structural Reforms in the Transport, Energy and Telecommunications Sectors in APEC Economies APEC#211-SE-01.1. The views expressed in this paper are those of the author and do not necessarily represent those of the APEC Secretariat or APEC Member Economies.

The appropriate level of competition depends on the sector in question. In finance, some regulatory restrictions are designed to ensure systemic stability. Thus prudential controls need to be retained. These may restrict competition by preventing the entry or operation of financial institutions that cannot meet minimum capital or liquidity requirements, for example, but such institutions would be particularly prone to collapse. Other regulatory restrictions that clearly do not have a prudential purpose, but serve to protect privileged positions of incumbent institutions, are the target of structural reform. These include non-prudential restrictions affecting domestic as well as foreign banks or insurance companies.

Problems arise when prudential regulation is under-developed and/or it is not enforced in an effective and impartial manner. When prudential regulation is under-developed, authorities may resort to entry barriers that, while easier to design, are less tightly targeted to checking the financial health and prudent risk management of financial institutions. For example, authorities may resort to screening criteria such as having to be in the top 500 financial institutions. Alternatively, they may place a moratorium on granting new licences, which means they do not have to assess the financial resilience of new entrants. These options have drawbacks — they do not ensure that the best, most competitive and innovative institutions enter the market. And the latter type of screening mechanism can also prevent inefficient, uncompetitive providers from being driven out of the market. While these types of regulations can act as a barrier to competition, reform would probably need to be preceded by the implementation of better designed prudential regulation (Dee 2012).

When capability to enforce prudential regulation is under-developed, similar problems arise. Authorities may resort to screening mechanisms, such as checking the probity of shareholders, that are less tightly tied to the way in which a financial institution is *managed*. Overly restrictive requirements on shareholders may act as a barrier to competition, but reform may depend on building the capability and/or willingness to enforce more traditional methods of prudential regulation (Dee 2012).

Many economic infrastructure industries involve networks — networks of railway lines, of electricity transmission and distribution lines, of gas transmission and distribution pipelines, and of telecommunications transmission and distribution lines. At least some components of these networks have the characteristics of a 'natural monopoly', meaning that it is less costly for their operation to be carried out by a single producer using a single set of facilities, rather than having two or more operators with duplicate facilities.

The structural reforms in these sectors are typically aimed at introducing competition into those parts of the production chain that are not natural monopolies. This requires the competitive suppliers to have access to those parts of the network that are natural monopolies. Successful reform also requires that the restructuring be done in such a way that the benefits of competition in the competitive sectors outweigh the loss of any economies of scope that may have prevailed when the monopoly and competitive activities were operated together under single ownership.

In maritime and air transport, the natural monopoly elements are more likely to be at the ports or airports than in the transport operation *per se*. But maritime and aviation networks operate across national boundaries. In both activities, a degree of regulatory cooperation may be required to ensure safety and coordination along international routes. But such regulation should not unduly impede competition. Nor should competition be unduly stifled in the interests of promoting or protecting 'national champions'.

These network industries are also areas where governments often want to ensure access on an affordable basis to all consumers. A final regulatory challenge is to design ways of imposing universal services obligations on service providers that do not thwart competition.

The details of what constitutes a competition-friendly regulatory environment in economic infrastructure industries vary from industry to industry, and even from country to country.[2] Nevertheless, some key features include (Dee 2012):

---

[2] Natural monopoly essentially occurs when the most efficient scale of operation exceeds market size. Small countries may therefore find it a more extensive problem than large ones, so they may have to pay more attention to the problem of monopoly pricing and less to the problem of access to bottleneck facilities.

- avoiding price controls in competitive segments (which typically include retail);
- finding means other than price controls to ensure universal service (eg explicit budget funding to meet universal service obligations);
- regulating to ensure access to bottleneck facilities on non-discriminatory and reasonable terms, especially when there has not been structural separation of the bottleneck facility;
- having an independent regulator to oversee the above.

Having a competition-friendly regulatory environment is necessary to ensure that foreign providers will in fact be willing to enter the market, once explicitly discriminatory trade barriers are removed. By the same token, it also ensures that structural liberalization does not simply replace a domestic monopoly with a foreign one — it ensures that new domestic providers have the same opportunities as foreign providers in the competitive segments of the market.

A common regulatory objective in social infrastructure industries such as higher education is to ensure quality, given that consumers may not have the information or knowledge to be able to judge quality themselves. Another is ensuring access on an affordable basis for all segments of society.

When quality assurance and accreditation frameworks are under-developed, authorities may resort to entry barriers that are less tightly targeted to checking the quality of the services providers (Dee 2012). For example, they may refuse to grant licences to foreign providers, on the grounds that they cannot check their quality. Alternatively, they may allow foreign providers, but restrict their activities to highly specialized services that are not provided by domestic providers. These types of restrictions can act as a barrier to competition. But reform would probably need to be preceded by the implementation of well-specified quality criteria and better designed quality assurance processes. This can explain why reform of higher education has been slow to occur in some economies.

Authorities may use public funds to subsidize access to higher education for vulnerable groups, but will typically use some type of screening criterion to limit the funds they spend on such subsidies. When screening criteria are under-developed, they may act as barriers to competition. For example, authorities may decide to deny subsidies to the clients of foreign providers, even though some of those clients may perhaps be in vulnerable groups. While there is typically no perfect screening mechanism, some will be less competition-friendly than others. Reform in some economies may not occur until more competition-friendly mechanisms are found (Dee 2012).

This chapter draws on studies in the earlier chapters that identified the types of regulatory structures that unduly impede competition, and quantified their first round impact on economic performance in the sectors in question. The purpose of this chapter is to go one step further — to quantify the effects of reforming those regulatory structures, not just on the sectors in question, but also on sectors that might use these services, on whole APEC member economies, and ultimately on the APEC region as a whole. The chapter also aims to quantify the adjustment costs that these prospective reforms might generate.

Included in the analysis are services trade reforms (narrowly defined), along with pro-competitive domestic regulatory reforms necessary to ensure that the trade reforms deliver on their promise. This includes measures such as the removal of price controls, the establishment of third party access regimes, and the introduction of an independent regulator. However, in finance, the analysis does not explicitly include the better design or enforcement of prudential regulation, while in higher education, it does not explicitly include the design of better quality assurance and accreditation frameworks. In some APEC economies, however, these measures would need to accompany the reforms considered here.

10.2 The Reform Agenda

Insurance

As explained in Chapter 2, insurance services companies are subject to a range of prudential and non-prudential regulation. Insurance companies perform a financial intermediation function by investing their pool of insurance premiums until claims are made. Given that these liabilities typically exceed their paid-up capital by a substantial margin, insurance companies can be susceptible to the same loss of confidence as banks, and thus to the same systemic risks. The prudential regulation is designed to mitigate these risks.

Insurance companies are typically also subject to regulatory restrictions common to other traded services, such as licensing restrictions on entry, legal restrictions on establishment, restrictions on the scale and scope of operations or on the particular types of insurance products that a firm can offer, and restrictions on ownership or pricing. In addition to these general restrictions, there are a few that are peculiar to insurance. One is restrictions on reinsurance — whether it is prohibited, whether reinsurance is restricted to foreign insurance companies, or whether a certain percentage of premiums need to be reinsured with domestically appointed insurers (the so-called ceding percentage). Another is limitations on whether insurance companies can hold assets overseas, or limitations on the form in which they must hold their assets.

Such regulatory restrictions have been found to create artificial barriers to entry that can allow incumbent insurers to charge inflated premiums and earn excess profits. Using a cross-section of regulatory information from around 2002 to 2004, Dihel and Shepherd (2007) estimated that the tax equivalents of barriers to commercial presence ranged from around 20 per cent (in Peru) to around 105 per cent (in Malaysia) and just over 140 per cent (in India). They did not investigate whether these barriers had a significant effect on real resource costs. In Chapter 2, Dee and Dinh used a panel data set from 1997 to 2004 to estimate tax equivalents ranging from 1.6 per cent (for Hong Kong) to 10.5 per cent (for Malaysia) and 10.6 per cent (for India). These estimates are much lower than in Dihel and Shepherd (2007), but are derived from a richer dataset. Dee and Dinh also confirmed that these regulatory restrictions have no significant effect on costs.

The index of regulatory openness compiled by Dee and Dinh (Chapter 2) covers many of the key measures affecting insurance services. Tables 10.1 and 10.2 show the index and its components for

Table 10.1. Index of Policy Restrictions Affecting Foreign Affiliates in Insurance Services

	(1)	*(2)*	*(3)*	*(4)*	*(5)*	*(6)*	*(7)*	*(8)*	*(9)*	*(10)*	*(11)*	*(12)*	*(13)*	*(14)*	*(15)*	*(16)*	*Foreign index*
Australia	0.00	0.33	0.00	0.00	0.66	0.40	0.00	0.00	0.75	0.00	0.75	0.50	0.00	0.25	0.20	0.33	0.21
Canada	0.00	0.00	0.00	0.00	0.66	0.40	0.50	0.00	0.25	0.00	0.75	0.50	0.00	0.25	0.40	0.66	0.21
Chile	0.00	0.33	0.00	0.00	1.00	0.40	0.00	0.00	0.00	0.00	0.00	0.00	0.00	0.25	0.60	0.66	0.15
China	0.50	0.33	0.00	0.50	0.33	0.40	0.00	0.25	0.50	0.05	0.25	1.00	0.00	0.00	0.40	0.00	0.24
Hong Kong	0.00	0.00	0.00	0.00	0.00	0.40	0.00	0.00	0.00	0.00	0.00	0.50	0.00	0.00	0.20	0.33	0.07
Indonesia	0.00	0.33	1.00	0.00	0.00	0.40	0.00	0.00	0.00	0.00	0.00	0.00	0.00	0.50	0.40	0.66	0.19
Japan	0.00	0.00	0.00	0.00	0.33	0.40	0.00	0.50	0.50	0.60	0.25	0.00	0.00	0.25	0.00	0.66	0.18
Rep. of Korea	0.00	0.33	0.33	0.25	0.66	0.40	0.50	0.50	1.00	0.00	0.00	0.50	0.00	0.25	0.40	0.33	0.28
Malaysia	0.70	0.66	1.00	0.75	0.66	0.40	0.00	0.00	0.75	0.15	0.50	0.50	0.66	0.25	0.00	0.33	0.44
Mexico	0.00	0.33	1.00	0.00	0.33	0.00	0.00	0.00	0.00	0.00	0.00	0.00	0.00	0.25	0.80	0.66	0.18
New Zealand	0.00	0.00	0.00	0.00	0.33	0.50	0.00	0.00	0.75	0.00	0.00	0.00	0.00	0.00	0.40	0.00	0.10
Peru	0.00	0.00	0.00	0.33	0.50	0.00	0.00	0.50	0.00	0.00	0.00	0.00	0.00	0.40	0.20	0.00	0.10
Philippines	0.00	0.00	0.00	1.00	0.00	0.00	0.10	0.00	0.00	0.60	0.00	0.60	0.00	0.00	0.00	1.00	0.18
Russia	0.00	0.75	0.33	0.50	0.00	0.00	1.00	0.00	0.25	0.50	0.25	0.00	0.25	0.00	0.00	0.00	0.21
Singapore	0.00	0.33	0.00	0.75	0.00	0.40	0.00	0.00	0.00	0.00	0.00	0.00	0.33	0.25	0.40	0.33	0.16
Chinese Taipei	0.00	0.00	0.00	0.00	0.33	0.40	0.50	0.00	0.50	0.00	0.25	0.10	0.00	0.25	0.40	0.00	0.13
Thailand	0.75	0.33	1.00	0.50	0.66	0.40	0.00	0.00	0.00	0.00	0.50	0.00	1.00	0.25	0.40	0.66	0.38
United States	0.00	0.33	0.00	0.00	0.33	0.40	0.50	0.50	0.50	0.00	0.50	0.00	0.00	0.25	0.40	0.66	0.21
Viet Nam	0.00	0.50	0.00	0.00	0.00	0.00	0.00	0.00	0.00	0.00	0.50	1.00	0.50	0.25	0.40	1.00	0.22

Notes: Index components are as follows: (1) Foreign direct investment, (2) Juridical form, (3) Joint venture arrangements, (4) Licensing, (5) Screening and approval, (6) Scope of services, (7) Restrictions on reinsurance, (8) Broking or agency restrictions, (9) Monopoly provision of insurance services, (10) Ceding percentage, (11) Price control, (12) Placement of assets, (13) Expanding operations — street branches, offices, (14) Movement of people — Temporary, (15) Movement of people — Permanent, (16) Movement of people — Board of Directors.

Source: Chapter 2.

Table 10.2. Index of Policy Restrictions Affecting Domestic Providers in Insurance Services

	Licensing	*Screening and approval*	*Scope of services*	*Restrictions on reinsurance*	*Broking or agency restrictions*	*Monopoly provision of insurance*	*Ceding percentage*	*Price control*	*Placement of assets*	*Expanding operations*	*Domestic index*
Australia	0.00	0.66	0.40	0.00	0.00	0.75	0.00	0.50	0.00	0.00	0.12
Canada	0.00	0.66	0.40	0.50	0.50	0.25	0.00	0.75	0.00	0.00	0.14
Chile	0.00	1.00	0.40	0.00	0.00	0.00	0.00	0.00	0.00	0.00	0.06
China	0.00	0.66	0.40	0.00	0.00	0.75	0.00	0.50	0.00	0.00	0.12
Hong Kong	0.00	0.00	0.40	0.00	0.00	0.00	0.00	0.00	0.50	0.00	0.04
Indonesia	0.00	0.00	0.40	0.00	0.00	0.00	0.00	0.00	0.00	0.00	0.02
Japan	0.00	0.33	0.40	0.00	0.50	0.50	0.60	0.25	0.00	0.00	0.13
Rep. of Korea	0.00	0.66	0.40	0.50	0.50	1.00	0.00	0.00	0.50	0.00	0.18
Malaysia	0.75	0.66	0.40	0.50	0.00	0.25	0.15	0.50	0.50	0.66	0.24
Mexico	0.00	0.33	0.00	0.00	0.00	0.00	0.00	0.00	0.00	0.00	0.01
New Zealand	0.00	0.33	0.50	0.00	0.00	0.75	0.00	0.00	0.00	0.00	0.09
Peru	0.33	0.00	0.00	0.00	0.50	0.00	0.00	0.00	0.00	0.00	0.04
Philippines	0.00	0.00	0.00	0.00	0.00	0.00	0.00	0.00	0.60	0.00	0.03
Russia	0.50	0.00	0.00	0.50	0.00	0.25	0.50	0.00	0.00	0.00	0.09
Singapore	0.75	0.00	0.40	0.00	0.00	0.00	0.00	0.00	0.00	0.33	0.09
Chinese Taipei	0.00	0.33	0.40	0.50	0.00	0.50	0.00	0.25	0.10	0.00	0.10
Thailand	0.50	0.66	0.40	0.00	0.00	0.00	0.00	0.50	0.00	1.00	0.18
United States	0.00	0.33	0.40	0.50	0.50	0.50	0.00	0.50	0.00	0.00	0.13
Viet Nam	0.00	0.00	0.00	0.00	0.00	0.00	0.00	0.50	1.00	0.50	0.11

Source: Chapter 2.

APEC economies, where an index value of 1 indicates full openness, a value of 0 denotes full restrictiveness, and intermediate values denote partial restrictions.[3] The values for most economies were taken directly from Dee and Dinh (Chapter 2) for 2004. The values for the Philippines and Viet Nam were taken from Dee (2011b), using regulatory information that was collected in late 2010. The values for New Zealand, Peru and Russia were derived from regulatory information collected in 2011 using similar sources to those in Chapter 2.

Among APEC economies, Malaysia and Thailand have the highest barriers to trade in insurance services. These economies, along with Indonesia, Mexico and the Philippines, also have a high degree of discrimination against foreign-invested suppliers, as indicated by the difference between the domestic and foreign index values. Peru, Hong Kong and New Zealand have relatively open insurance markets.

Banking

As explained in Chapter 3, banking services providers also face a range of prudential and non-prudential regulation. The non-prudential regulatory restrictions have generally been found to be costly in various ways (Saunders and Schumacher 2000, Kalirajan *et al.* 2000, Barth *et al.* 2004, Dihel and Shepherd 2007, Pasiouras *et al.* 2009). A common finding is that they lead to higher banking net interest margins. For example, using a cross-section of regulatory information from around 2002 to 2004, Dihel and Shepherd (2007) estimated that the tax equivalents of barriers to commercial presence ranged from around 13–14 per cent (in Lithuania and Peru) and to around 25 per cent (in India) and just over 30 per cent (in Malaysia). There is also evidence that at least some restrictions raise costs. For example, Barth *et al.* (2004) found that various restrictions on entry raised overhead costs, while Pasiouras *et al.* (2009) found that restrictions on bank activities reduced cost efficiency.

---

[3] The analysis throughout this chapter is restricted to those APEC members that have been included in the computable general equilibrium model, based on data available from the GTAP model database (Hertel 1997). The analysis therefore excludes Brunei and Papua New Guinea.

In recognition of these adverse effects, there has been a reduction over time in the prevalence of non-prudential regulation in some countries, though the reduction has been larger for foreign banks (Chapter 3). For domestic banks, the reduction has resulted from decreasing government ownership in the banking sector and relaxation of restrictions on licensing. For foreign banks, the reduction has come from relaxations of restrictions on all modes of supply, as well as on their traditional banking activities.

Restrictions on non-traditional banking activities (bank involvement in insurance, securities and real estate business and bank ownership of non-financial firms) have tended to be tightened over time, regardless of bank ownership (Chapter 3). This finding suggests that these restrictions may serve a prudential purpose, and should not be treated purely as barriers to trade in banking services. Recent experience during the global financial crisis showed how bank involvement in non-traditional banking activities could lead to conflicts of interest that were severe enough to outweigh any benefits in terms of risk-spreading. The econometric evidence in Chapter 3 also showed that restrictions on non-traditional activities were not harmful to bank performance.

The index of regulatory openness in Chapter 3 covers some of the key measures affecting banking services. Tables 10.3 and 10.4 show the index and its components for APEC economies, where an index value of 1 indicates full openness, a value of 0 denotes full restrictiveness, and intermediate values denote partial restrictions. The values for most economies were taken directly from Dinh (Chapter 3) for 2006. The value for the Philippines was taken from Dee (2011b), using regulatory information that was collected in late 2010. The values for New Zealand, Peru and Russia were derived from regulatory information collected in 2011 using similar sources to those in Chapter 3.

The index covers many of the same restrictions that were included in the index for insurance services. The restrictions on the scope of operations are specific to banking — whether foreign and/or domestic banks are restricted in their ability to raise funds, to lend, and to undertake settlement or foreign exchange services. Restrictions on banks' ability to undertake non-traditional activities are not included, given that these appear to have a prudential purpose.

Table 10.3. Index of Policy Restrictions Affecting Foreign Affiliates in Banking Services

	(1)	*(2)*	*(3)*	*(4)*	*(5)*	*(6)*	*(7)*	*(8)*	*(9)*	*(10)*	*(11)*	*(12)*	*(13)*	*(14)*	*(15)*	*Foreign index*
Australia	0.123	0	0	0.36	0.66	0	0.25	0	0	0	0	0	0.25	0.2	0.67	0.094
Canada	0.1	0	0	0.19	1	0	0.25	0.1	0	0	0	0	0.25	0.4	0.6	0.103
Chile	0	0.25	1	0.5	1	0.17	0	0	0	0	0	0.2	0.25	0.4	0.58	0.142
China	0.75	0	0	0	0.33	0.69	0.5	0.5	0	0.1	0.1	0.33	0.25	0.4	0	0.156
Hong Kong	0	0	0	0.07	0.33	0	0.25	0.25	0	0	0	0.33	0.25	0.8	0.17	0.099
Indonesia	0.01	0.5	0	0.36	0.33	0.385	0.5	0.5	0	0	0.33	0	0.25	0.4	0.49	0.173
Japan	0	0	0	0.42	0.33	0	0.25	0	0	0	0.33	0.2	0.25	0	0.5	0.087
Repub. of Korea	0	0.25	0	0.28	0.33	0.188	0.5	0.5	0.1	0.33	0	0.33	0.25	0.4	0	0.139
Malaysia	0.51	1	0	1	0.33	0	0.5	0.5	0.5	0	0.33	0	0.25	0	0.33	0.222
Mexico	0	0.5	0	0	0.33	0	0	0	0	0	1	0	0.25	0.8	0.5	0.136
New Zealand	0	0	0	0	0	0.02	0	0	0	0	0	0	0	0.4	0	0.019
Peru	0	0.5	0	0	0.33	0	0	0	0	0	0	0	0.25	0.4	0.2	0.071
Philippines	0.6	0	0	1	0.5	0	0	0.5	0	0	0.5	0	0	0	1	0.158
Russia	0.5	0.5	1	0.33	0.33	0.5	0	0	0	0.33	0.33	0	0.25	0.4	0.15	0.161
Singapore	0.5	1	0	1	0.33	0	0.5	0.7	0.5	0	0.66	0	0.25	0.4	0.083	0.250
Chinese Taipei	0	0	0	0.49	0.33	0.176	0.5	0.5	0	0.5	0.5	0.1	0.25	0.4	0	0.144
Thailand	0.51	0.25	0	0.45	0.33	0.145	0.25	0.5	0	0	0.66	0.2	0.25	0.4	0.75	0.191
United States	0.1	0.5	0	0.15	0.33	0	0.25	0.1	0	0	0.6	0	0.25	0.4	0.51	0.131
Viet Nam	0.51	0	0	0.1	1	0.7	0.5	0.5	0.1	0.33	0.66	0.2	0.25	0.4	0.2	0.199

Notes: Index components are as follows: (1) Foreign equity limit, (2) Juridical form, (3) Reciprocity requirement, (4) Licensing restrictions, (5) Screening and approval, (6) Ownership share of government in the banking system, (7) Fund raising, (8) Lending, (9) Settlement services, (10) Foreign exchange business, (11) Expanding operations — street branches, offices, (12) Price control, (13) Movement of people — Temporary, (14) Movement of people — Permanent, (15) Movement of people — Board of Directors.

Source: Chapter 3.

Table 10.4. Index of Policy Restrictions Affecting Domestic Providers in Banking Services

	Licensing restrictions	*Screening and approval*	*Govt. ownership share*	*Fund raising*	*Lending*	*Settlement services*	*Foreign exchange business*	*Expanding operations*	*Price control*	*Domestic index*
Australia	0.46	0.33	0	0	0	0	0	0	0	0.025
Canada	0.45	1	0	0	0	0	0	0	0	0.037
Chile	0.46	0.33	0.17	0	0	0	0	0	0.2	0.039
China	0	0.33	0.69	0	0.25	0	0	0	0.33	0.059
Hong Kong	0.5	0.33	0	0.25	0	0	0	0	0.33	0.048
Indonesia	0.5	0.33	0.385	0	0.25	0	0	0	0	0.055
Japan	0.46	0.33	0	0.25	0.1	0	0	0	0.2	0.047
Repub. of Korea	0.5	0.33	0.188	0.5	0.25	0.1	0.33	0	0.33	0.093
Malaysia	1	0.33	0	0.5	0.5	0	0.5	0	0	0.106
Mexico	0	0.33	0	0	0	0	0	0	0	0.006
New Zealand	0	0	0.02	0	0	0	0	0	0	0.001
Peru	0	0.33	0	0	0	0	0	0	0	0.006
Philippines	0	0	0	0	0.5	0	0	0.5	0	0.042
Russia	0	0.33	0.5	0	0	0	0.33	0.33	0	0.047
Singapore	1	0.33	0	0.5	0.1	0	0	0.33	0	0.084
Chinese Taipei	1	0.33	0.176	0	0	0	0.5	0.5	0.1	0.088
Thailand	0.638	0.33	0.145	0	0.5	0	0	0	0.2	0.070
United States	0.022	0.33	0	0	0	0	0	0	0	0.007
Viet Nam	0.1	1	0.7	0.1	0.25	0.1	0.33	0.33	0.2	0.100

Source: Chapter 3.

Among APEC economies, Singapore imposes the greatest regulatory burden on foreign affiliates in banking. This finding may seem surprising, given that the Singaporean economy is highly open in many other dimensions, but it is confirmed from an in-country survey of banking regulation reported in Dee (2011b). The other ASEAN members of APEC also have relatively restrictive regulatory regimes, as does China. New Zealand and Peru have relatively open markets for banking services.

Air transport

International air services are governed by a system of bilateral air services agreements. While these agreements cover a wide range of topics that would be deemed legitimate targets of regulation (such as aviation security, incident investigation, immigration and control of travel documents), they also include seven key features that have been identified by the WTO Secretariat (WTO 2006) as restricting scheduled air passenger services.

- **Designation** governs the right to designate one (*single designation*) or more than one (*multiple designation*) airline from the home economy to operate the agreed services between the two economies.
- **Withholding** defines the ownership conditions required for the designated airline(s) of the foreign economy to be allowed to operate the agreed services. The most restrictive conditions require *substantial ownership and effective control* to be vested in the designating economy or its nationals. The most liberal regime (*principal place of business*) removes the substantial ownership requirement, but still requires the designated airline to be incorporated in the designating economy, and to have its principal place of business there. This falls far short of the relatively generous 'rules of origin' typically written into services trade agreements. These would typically require only 'substantial business' in the designated economy, irrespective of ownership.
- **Grant of rights** that define the rights to provide air services between two economies. The dimensions in which air services agreements are

generally being liberalized is in the granting of the fifth, sixth and seventh freedoms and cabotage. The *fifth freedom* is the freedom to carry passengers between two economies by an airline of a third economy on a route with origin or destination in its home economy. The *sixth freedom* is the freedom to carry passengers between two economies by an airline of a third economy on a route that goes via its home economy. (Note that sixth freedoms can also be constructed via a combination of the third and fourth freedoms from different bilateral agreements, and so are rarely specified explicitly.) The *seventh freedom* is the freedom to carry passengers between two economies by an airline of a third economy on a route with no connection to its home economy. *Cabotage* is the freedom to carry passengers within an economy by an airline of another economy on a route with origin or destination in its home economy.

- **Capacity clause** that identifies the regime to determine the capacity of an agreed service, where capacity refers to the volume of traffic, frequency of service and/or aircraft type.
- **Tariff approval** refers to the regime of fare setting. Under the most restrictive regime, the aeronautical authorities of both economies have to approve a fare before it can be applied. Under the most liberal regime, fares are not subject to the approval of either authority.
- **Statistics** provides rules on exchange of statistics between economies or their airlines. If exchange of statistics is (or can be) requested, it is a sign that the parties intend to monitor the performance of each other's airline and is thus viewed as a restrictive feature of an agreement.
- **Cooperative arrangements** define the right for the designated airlines to enter into cooperative marketing arrangements (such as code sharing and alliances). This right is considered as a liberal feature because it provides a means to rationalize networks, in the absence of liberalization of the ownership clause.

These restrictive features of air services agreements have been shown to impose costs, by raising international airfares and restricting international traffic. Gonenc and Nicoletti (2000) and Doove *et al.* (2001) found a positive and significant effect of the restrictiveness of air services agreements on passenger air fares. For example, Doove *et al.* (2001) estimated that the restrictive provisions of the agreements in place at the time had inflated international airfares from Indonesia and the Philippines by over 20 per cent, and from Malaysia, Singapore and Thailand by 16–18 per cent. Piermartini and Rousová (2008) found that an increase in the degree of liberalization from the 25th to the 75th percentile would increase passenger traffic volumes between economies linked by a direct air service by about 30 per cent. In particular, they found that the removal of restrictions on the determination of prices and capacity, cabotage rights, and designation were found to be the most traffic-enhancing provisions.

The restrictive provisions of air services agreements also impose costs on air freight services. Most air freight is carried in the belly of passenger aircraft, and is thus affected by exactly the same provisions as passenger traffic. Freight-only flights are generally also governed by the same provisions as passenger flights, although in some instances they are granted more liberal traffic rights. Grosso (2008) found a positive and statistically significant relationship between relaxing restrictions and the value of merchandise trade. Achard (2009) found a significant correlation between liberal air services agreements and the volume of air cargo.

In recognition of such costs, a growing number of economies are negotiating more liberal air services agreements. The typical 'open skies' agreement grants third, fourth and fifth freedom rights, and removes restrictions on designation, capacity, frequencies, code-sharing and fares. Open skies agreements typically do not grant cabotage rights, nor lift foreign ownership restrictions on domestic airlines. Seventh freedom rights are sometimes included, but often restricted to cargo-only traffic.

Increasingly, economies have also liberalized their domestic aviation services, which they can do on a unilateral basis. Such liberalization has typically included allowing additional domestic and foreign entry on domestic routes, particularly by low cost carriers, and freeing up restrictions on domestic air fares. Sometimes, liberalization has also included the full or partial privatization of government-owned carriers.

The index of policy restrictions compiled by Zhang and Findlay (2011) and reported by Sourdin in Chapter 5 of this volume covers some of the key measures affecting both domestic and international aviation. Table 10.5 shows the index and its components for APEC economies, where an index value of 1 indicates full restrictiveness, a value of 0 denotes no restriction, and intermediate values denote partial restrictions. The index covers privatization of national airlines, foreign equity participation in domestic airlines, the existence of low cost carriers, the number of effective passenger airlines (indicating ease of entry), whether there is multiple designation on international routes, whether there are more than two open skies agreements, and whether seventh freedom cargo rights are granted to at least some foreign carriers.

The table indicates that China, Viet Nam, Russia, the Philippines and Chinese Taipei currently have the most restrictive regulatory regimes

Table 10.5. Index of Policy Restrictions in Air Transport

	Privatized	*Foreign equity*	*Low cost airline*	*Effective competitors*	*Designation*	*Open skies*	*7th freedom*	*Total score*
Australia	0	0	0	0.5	0.5	0	0	1
Canada	0	0.75	0	1	1	0	0	2.75
Chile	0	0	1	1	1	0	0	3
China	0.67	0.5	0.5	0	0.5	1	1	4.17
Hong Kong	0	0	0.5	1	1	0	1	3.5
Indonesia	1	0.5	0.5	0	0.5	0.5	0	3
Japan	0	0.75	0.5	0	0	0.5	1	2.75
Rep. of Korea	0	0.5	0.5	0.5	0	0.5	1	3
Malaysia	0.67	0.5	0	0	0.5	0	0	1.67
Mexico	0	0.5	0.5	0.5	0	0	1	2.5
New Zealand	0.67	0	0.5	0.5	0.5	0	0	2.17
Peru	0	0.5	0.5	0.5	0.5	0	0	2
Philippines	0	0.5	0.5	0	0.5	1	1	3.5
Russia	0.67	0.75	0.5	0	0.5	0	1	3.42
Singapore	0.67	0	0	0.5	0	0	0	1.17
Chinese Taipei	0.67	0.5	1	0.5	0	0.5	0	3.17
Thailand	0.67	0.5	0	0	0.5	0	0	1.67
United States	0	0.75	0	0	0	0	0	0.75
Viet Nam	1	0.5	0.5	0.5	1	0.5	0	4

Source: Chapter 5.

among APEC economies. The United States, Australia, Singapore, Malaysia and Thailand have the least restrictive regimes.

Maritime transport

McGuire, Schuele and Smith (2000) surveyed the maritime policy regimes in a number of APEC, Latin American and European economies. They described the key restrictions affecting shipping services as follows.

- *Right to fly the national flag.* This requires ships to be registered or licensed to provide maritime services on domestic and international routes. The conditions on registration may include legitimate requirements such as meeting seaworthiness and safety requirements, but also include restrictions such as having a commercial presence in the domestic economy, and the ship being built and/or owned domestically.
- *Cabotage restrictions.* These restrict shipping services on domestic and coastal routes to vessels that meet certain conditions. Shipping services between domestic ports may be required to be carried out by domestically owned, operated, built and/or crewed ships.
- *Conferences.* These are private sector arrangements between shippers that are supposed to facilitate the planning and coordination of shipping traffic, but typically also include anti-competitive provisions. Governments that have enacted general competition laws usually permit the existence of conferences through exemptions from the price setting and collusion provisions of their domestic competition legislation.
- *UN Convention on a Code of Conduct for Liner Conferences (UN Liner Code).* This stipulates that conference trade between two economies can allocate cargo according to the 40:40:20 rule, whereby 40 per cent of tonnage is reserved for the national flag lines of each economy and 20 per cent is allocated to liner ships from a third economy.

- *Cargo sharing.* These are other types of arrangements that stipulate the allocation of cargo on particular routes between parties to bilateral and multilateral agreements.
- *Bilateral agreements.* These are agreements between two economies that primarily restrict the supply of shipping services and the allocation of cargo. Some bilateral agreements also restrict the use of port facilities.

Many developing economies do not have general competition law or any legislative framework for regulating the behaviour of shipping conferences. However, in recent times conferences have been subjected to increasing competition. They no longer dominate shipping routes, and are no longer regarded as the impediments to maritime performance that they once were. PDP Australia and Meyrick and Associates (2005) note that within ASEAN, cargo reservation measures have been very significantly reduced and in many cases completely abandoned. Similarly, a growing number of economies have 'open' ship registries, which means that local ship registration is no longer tightly tied to local ownership of the shipping company. This leaves cabotage restrictions, along with inadequate and aging infrastructure, as the main impediments to economic performance in shipping services in many economies.

These regulatory restrictions on shipping services have been shown to be costly, particularly to developing economies. Kang (2000) found that the maritime restrictions imposed by goods exporting economies appear to have a much greater impact on bilateral shipping margins (as measured by cif/fob ratios) than those imposed by importing economies. He also found that in exporting economies, lowering restrictions such as cabotage and port services restrictions had a greater effect on margins than reducing restrictions on the commercial presence of foreign suppliers. In several applications of these findings, the sum total of restrictions on shipping and port services was found to have inflated shipping costs by around 30 per cent in Morocco (Dee 2006) and by around 26 per cent in Indonesia (Dee 2008).

The index of regulatory openness compiled by Bertho (2011) and reported by Sourdin in Chapter 5 of this volume covers some the key measures affecting maritime transportation. Table 10.6 shows the index and its components for APEC economies, where an index value of 1 indicates full openness, a value of 0 denotes full restrictiveness, and intermediate values denote partial restrictions. The index covers cabotage restrictions, cargo handling restrictions, quotas for private or government cargo, the availability of exemptions for carrier agreements from competition law, and the existence of an independent regulatory authority. It also covers measures that fall squarely into the category of barriers to services trade — foreign equity limits, limits on the legal form of establishment (branches, subsidiaries) of foreign greenfield

Table 10.6. Index of Policy Openness in Maritime Transport

	Quotas	*Comp. law exemp-tions*	*Form of owner-ship*	*% of owner-ship*	*Acquis-ition dom-estic entity*	*Nation-ality reqt employ-yees*	*Nation-ality reqt BOD*	*Cabo-tage*	*Cargo handling*	*Indep reg auth.*	*Simple average*
Australia	1	0	0.5	1	1	0	1	1	1	1	0.75
Canada	1	1	0.5	1	1	0	0	0	na	1	0.61
Chile	1	1	1	1	1	na	na	0	na	1	0.86
China	1	1	0.5	0.49	0	1	1	0	1	0	0.60
Hong Kong	1	1	1	1	na	na	na	nr	1	na	1.00
Indonesia	0.5	1	0.5	0.49	1	1	1	0	1	0	0.65
Japan	1	0	0.5	1	1	na	0	0	1	1	0.61
Rep. of Korea	1	0	0.5	1	1	0	1	0	na	1	0.61
Malaysia	1	1	1	0.3	0	na	na	0	na	1	0.61
Mexico	1	1	1	1	1	0	1	0	na	0	0.67
New Zealand	1	0	0.5	1	1	na	na	1	1	1	0.81
Peru	1	1	1	1	1	0	0	0	na	0	0.56
Philippines	0	1	0.5	0.4	na	1	0	0	0	1	0.43
Russia	0	1	0.5	1	1	1	1	0	1	0	0.65
Singapore	1	0	0.5	1	na	na	na	nr	1	na	0.70
Chinese Taipei	1	0	1	na	na	na	na	0.5	0	0	0.42
Thailand	0.5	1	1	0.49	0	1	0	0	0	0	0.40
United States	0	0	0.5	1	1	0	0	0	1	1	0.45
Viet Nam	1	1	0	0	0.5	0	0	0	0	0	0.25

Notes: na = not available, nr = not relevant.
Source: Chapter 5.

operations, whether foreign operators can take a controlling stake in existing private or public entities, and whether there are nationality requirements on the employees or boards of directors of foreign companies.

The table confirms that cabotage restrictions are the predominant restrictions on maritime services among APEC economies. Hong Kong is the most liberal, followed by Chile, New Zealand and Australia. The least liberal APEC member is Viet Nam. It does not have a deep sea port, so most goods are transported to Singapore and Hong Kong before going on to final destinations. Foreign firms usually provide cross-border services via a Vietnamese (wholly domestic) agency, which does everything on behalf of foreign suppliers in Viet Nam and earns a commission from the foreign partners (Dee 2010b).

Rail transport

Rail can be a very efficient means of transporting cargoes, especially bulky ones, once they are loaded onto the trains, but the loading and unloading is costly. By contrast, road freight transport may be less efficient in *moving* large cargos, but can operate door-to-door, often avoiding a cycle of loading and unloading. Similar tradeoffs apply in the economics of rail passenger transport. Furthermore, rail operating costs make it more economic than road for moving freight over longer distances, while over short distances road transport dominates. For these reasons, rail transport often plays a surprisingly minor role in national transport networks. For example, in Indonesia rail transport accounts for only 7 per cent of passenger transport and less than 1 per cent of freight transport (Dee 2008).

In rail services, the natural monopoly elements are the track bed, while rolling stock (ie rail carriages) can be leased or bought by competitors and operated on the incumbent's rail tracks (subject to an adequate access regime, timetabling and safety standards). *Horizontal separation* is the term given to competition *in* the market (eg via the free entry of freight operators) or *for* the market (eg via tendering or franchising arrangements for passenger services). However, to promote effective competition, it may be necessary to require the track operator to become a separate corporate entity, without any interest in passenger or freight operations (*vertical separation*). Without such an interest, the track operator will have an incentive to maximize its revenue by maximizing traffic. With such an interest, it may have an incentive to restrict the access of competitors to promote the profitability of its own passenger or freight operations.

Cantos, Pastor and Serrano (2010) examined the effects of horizontal and vertical separation in European railways. They found that the reforms had been beneficial in terms of efficiency (allowing laggards to catch up to leaders) and productivity (also incorporating the benefits of technical change through innovation). Key drivers of both types of benefits were vertical separation and the free entry of new freight operators. No significant effects on either efficiency or productivity were found for the introduction of tendering systems in passenger traffic.

Table 10.7. Index of Policy Openness in Rail Transport

	Vertical separation of infrastructure and operations	*Free entry in freight operations*	*Franchising in passenger services*
Australia	1	1	1
Canada	0	1	0
Chile	1	1	1
China	0	0	0
Hong Kong	nr	nr	nr
Indonesia	1	0	0
Japan	0	1	0
Rep. of Korea	1	0	0
Malaysia	0	0	0
Mexico	1	1	1
New Zealand	0	1	1
Peru	1	1	1
Philippines	0	0	0
Russia	1	1	1
Singapore	nr	nr	nr
Chinese Taipei	0	0	0
Thailand	0	0	0
United States	0	1	0
Viet Nam	0	0	0

Note: nr = not relevant.
Source: Chapter 6.

The index of policy openness compiled by Cantos, Pastor and Serrano in Chapter 6 of this volume covers some of these elements of rail regimes in APEC economies. Table 10.7 shows their index components, where an index value of 1 indicates openness, and a value of 0 denotes restrictiveness. The index covers vertical separation, free entry in freight operations and franchising in passenger services. The values come from Chapter 6, supplemented by web search for the missing APEC economies.

The table indicates that Australia, Chile, Mexico, Peru and Russia have regimes that are most conducive to competition in rail services. The most restrictive regulatory regimes are in many of the East Asian members of APEC.

Electricity

As noted in Chapter 7, a precursor to allowing new entry and competition in electricity markets is to separate the potentially competitive segments of the industry (typically electricity generation, and sometimes also retailing) from those segments that have natural monopoly characteristics (particularly transmission, but sometimes also distribution). Regulation is also required to ensure that the monopoly provider of transmission services does not use its market dominance in that sector to thwart competition in the competitive segments. Thus the key elements of a competitive regime have included vertical separation and third party access, along with a wholesale price pool to allow distributors and retailers access to energy on commercial terms.

As also discussed in Chapter 7, past empirical assessments of the effects of such reforms have been mixed. This could have been because the reforms under consideration had not been taken far enough to have any real effects, or it could have been because the data samples chosen for econometric analysis did not have enough in-sample variation to discern any real effects. In Chapter 7, Dee found evidence of significant benefits from electricity market opening among OECD members over a period of more active reform, associated with the EU's Second Electricity Directive.

Table 10.8. Index of Policy Openness in Electricity

	Third party access	*Wholesale price pool*	*Unbundling*
Australia	1	1	1
Canada	1	1	0
Chile	1	1	1
China	0	1	1
Hong Kong	0	0	0
Indonesia	0	0	0
Japan	1	1	0
Republic of Korea	1	1	1
Malaysia	0	0	0
Mexico	0	0	0
New Zealand	1	1	1
Peru	1	0	1
Philippines	0	0	1
Russia	1	1	1
Singapore	1	1	1
Chinese Taipei	0	0	0
Thailand	0	0	0
United States	1	0	1
Viet Nam	0	0	0

Source: Chapter 7.

The index of policy openness compiled by Dee in Chapter 7 covers these key dimensions of electricity regimes in APEC economies — unbundling, third party access and the existence of a deregulated wholesale electricity market. Table 10.8 shows the index components, where an index value of 1 indicates openness and a value of 0 denotes restrictiveness.

APEC economies with regimes that are most conducive to competition in electricity generation are Australia, Chile, the Republic of Korea, New Zealand, Russia and Singapore. The most restrictive regulatory regimes are in Indonesia, Hong Kong, Malaysia, Mexico, Chinese Taipei and Viet Nam.

Gas

As also noted in Chapter 7, the broad features of pro-competitive reforms in gas markets are similar to those in electricity markets, though the scope for competition in primary production/importing is somewhat more limited than in electricity generation. There are relatively few empirical studies of the effects of these reforms. Those reported in Chapter 7 were generally positive.

The index of policy openness compiled by Dee in Chapter 7 covers some of these key dimensions of gas regimes in APEC economies. Table 10.9 shows the index components, where an index value of 1 indicates openness and a value of 0 denotes restrictiveness. The index covers unbundling of production/import, unbundling of supply, third party access, the absence of entry restrictions and the presence of retail competition.

APEC economies with regimes that are most conducive to competition in gas markets are Australia, Canada, New Zealand and the United States. The most restrictive regulatory regimes are in Hong Kong, the Republic of Korea, Malaysia, Russia, Chinese Taipei and Viet Nam.

Table 10.9. Index of Policy Openness in Gas

	Third party access	*Retail competition*	*Absence of entry restrictions*	*Unbundling of production/import*	*Unbundling of supply*
Australia	1	1	1	1	0
Canada	1	1	1	1	1
Chile	0	0	1	1	0
China	0	1	1	0	1
Hong Kong	0	0	0	0	0
Indonesia	1	0	1	1	0
Japan	1	1	0	0	0
Rep. of Korea	0	0	0	0	0
Malaysia	0	0	0	0	1
Mexico	1	1	0	0	0
New Zealand	1	1	1	1	0
Peru	1	0	0	1	0
Philippines	0	0	0	0	0
Russia	0	0	0	0	0
Singapore	1	1	0	1	0
Chinese Taipei	0	0	0	0	0
Thailand	1	0	0	1	0
United States	1	1	1	1	1
Viet Nam	0	0	0	0	0

Source: Chapter 7.

Telecommunications

The reforms of the 1990s recognized that efficiency gains could be had by introducing competition into those components of the telecommunications network that were not natural monopolies, but that competitors would need access to the monopoly elements (typically the 'last mile') in order to provide a full retail service. These access principles were incorporated into the WTO Reference Paper on telecommunications, which also stipulated that access charges should be cost-based and non-discriminatory. The appropriate regulation of access charges is a complex issue, although sometimes made more complex than necessary when access charges (as a single policy instrument) are used to pursue multiple objectives (eg Dee and Findlay 2008b).

A related requirement for promoting contestability was to ensure the general interconnectivity of the facilities of various competitors, whether or not they constituted essential facilities. This was required so the subscribers of one provider could make calls to subscribers of all other providers, irrespective of the ownership of the various network components involved. Various regulatory principles were also developed to ensure that interconnection charges were not used by the incumbent to preserve network dominance (eg Economides, Lopomo and Woroch 1996, ITU 2000).

A further component of these reforms was ensuring number portability, so that retail subscribers could take their original phone number with them if they switched providers. This was necessary to reduce the cost of 'shopping around', and thus to increase the competitive pressures on providers.

A key supporting component of these pro-competitive reforms was to revise the ways in which universal service obligations were met. To that point, they had often been met by cross-subsidies built into the retail prices of telecommunications services. These provided competitors with a chance to cherry-pick the lucrative, long-distance parts of the market, and left incumbents with fewer options to cover their fixed costs. Their response was often to inflate the wholesale access prices charged to competitors for access to the essential facility. Of course, this worked to defeat the introduction of competition. A key reform component of the

1990s was therefore to 'rebalance' retail prices to remove the cross-subsidies and ensure that fixed costs were covered, and to find other ways to fund universal service obligations — typically either directly from the government budget, or through an industry levy imposed on all service providers.

Since then, a number of technological advances have in some ways radically transformed the industry. The first key development has been the phenomenal growth of mobile telephony. This technology has few natural monopoly elements, so it has allowed extensive entry by new providers. To the extent that mobile services provide a close substitute to fixed line services, competition from this source can discipline the behaviour of fixed line service providers and reduce the need for regulatory intervention or oversight. The two services are close substitutes for individuals and perhaps even households. But businesses of any size typically also need fixed line connections to meet the sheer volume of their voice and data needs. Most governments have therefore retained the kind of regulatory structures described in the WTO Reference Paper.

A second key development has been the growth of internet, particularly broadband, services. These services, which combine developments in the size and nature of the 'pipe' with developments in switching and signal transmission technology, have made it technologically meaningless to distinguish voice from data traffic. This is the essence of 'convergence'. So now there is an imperative for regulatory structures to acknowledge this convergence. The key way in which this is happening is in the move from 'individual' to 'general' or 'class' licensing, not just for carrier licences, but also for licences to access the spectrum required for mobile and fixed wireless technologies. Typically, individual licences were not only attached to a particular technology, they were also attached to a particular service. General licences are less tied to particular services, and will often allow both voice and data transmission, although most governments are not yet ready to include broadcasting services in the bundle.

The proliferation of delivery technologies for broadband services (eg ADSL, fibre optic, fixed wireless) has also provided an imperative for regulatory structures to be 'technology-neutral'. This is also facilitated by the move from 'individual' to 'general' or 'class' licensing, since general licences are typically no longer tied to a particular technology.

But there are limits on the extent to which regulatory structures can be completely technology-neutral. This is because a key rationale for regulatory intervention remains dealing with 'natural monopoly' components of the network, and the nature and extent of the natural monopoly problem depends on the particular technology in question. Thus given the rapid development and proliferation of technologies, there may be no 'one-size-fits-all' best approach to regulation. A recent ITU survey of trends in reform (ITU 2008) stressed the importance of ensuring interconnectivity across all technologies and all providers, to maximize the use that will be made of any particular facility. The report is subtitled 'Six Degrees of Sharing', and noted (p. 1):

> In a way, many regulatory practices can be viewed as sharing. What is new and innovative is their application to meet the needs of developing economies. What is the same is that they use time-tested, pro-competitive tools, such as the regulation of essential or bottleneck facilities, transparency, and the promotion of colocation and interconnection.

Nevertheless, there is considerable current uncertainty about which technologies may become dominant in the future, and as noted, the scope of such regulation depends on the technology. Economies may not necessarily be sure to 'pick the best winner', but they can at least ensure that their regulatory regimes are internally consistent. For example, economies making a serious commitment to fibre optic technologies could need to put more regulatory effort into access regimes that economies relying more on mobile and fixed wireless technologies.

As well as technological developments, services trade reform has also been an important vehicle for promoting the contestability of markets. The potential benefits have been shown to be significant. Mattoo, Rathindran and Subramanian (2001) estimated that economies with fully open telecommunications and financial sectors grow up to 1.5 percentage points faster than other economies. The analysis of Warren (2000) suggested that in the ASEAN 5, the regulatory restrictions then affecting domestic new entrants would have raised the prices of their services by an average of over 10 per cent, while the additional discrimination (including foreign equity limits) against foreign-invested suppliers would have raised the prices of their services by more than 80 per cent.

The overall coherence of regulatory regimes can ultimately be judged according to whether they have engendered a competitive market structure. An index of policy openness has been compiled for this chapter, using information from Lee *et al.* (2011) and ITU sources. It focuses mainly on market structure, and is based on that used by Warren (2000). Tables 10.10 and 10.11 show the index components, where a higher value denotes more openness and a lower value denotes less. The tables give the number of competitors in fixed and mobile markets

Table 10.10. Index of Policy Openness in Fixed Line Telecommunications

	Number of competitors	*Comp. - local*	*Comp. - long dist.*	*Comp. - internat.*	*Comp. - data*	*Comp. - leased lines*	*Portion incumb. privat-ized*	*Max % FDI in comp. carriers*
Australia	3	1	1	1	1	0.5	0.5	1
Canada	3	1	1	1	1	1	0.5	0.46
Chile	3	1	1	1	1	1	1	1
China	3	1	1	0.5	1	1	0.5	0.49
Hong Kong	3	1	1	1	1	1	1	1
Indonesia	3	0.5	0.5	0.5	1	1	0.5	0.3
Japan	3	1	1	1	1	1	1	1
Rep. of Korea	2	1	1	1	1	1	1	0.49
Malaysia	3	1	1	1	1	1	0.5	0.49
Mexico	3	1	1	1	1	1	1	0.49
New Zealand	3	1	0.5	1	0.5	1	1	1
Peru	3	1	1	1	1	1	1	1
Philippines	3	1	1	1	1	1	1	0.4
Russia	2	0.5	0.5	0.5	1	0	0.5	0
Singapore	2	1	1	1	1	1	0.5	1
Chinese Taipei	3	1	1	1	1	1	0.5	0.6
Thailand	3	1	1	1	1	1	0	0.49
United States	3	1	1	1	1	1	1	1
Viet Nam	3	1	1	1	1	1	0.5	0

Source: Based on Lee *et al.* (2011) and ITU sources.

Table 10.11. Index of Policy Openness in Mobile Telecommunications

	Number of competitors	*Competition*	*Portion incumbent privatized*	*Max % FDI in competitive carriers*
Australia	3	1	0.5	1
Canada	3	1	0.5	0.46
Chile	3	1	1	1
China	3	1	0.5	0.49
Hong Kong	3	1	1	1
Indonesia	3	1	0.5	0.3
Japan	3	1	1	1
Rep. of Korea	3	1	1	0.49
Malaysia	3	1	0.5	0.49
Mexico	3	1	1	0.49
New Zealand	3	1	1	1
Peru	3	1	1	1
Philippines	3	1	1	0.4
Russia	2	1	0.5	0
Singapore	2	1	0.5	1
Chinese Taipei	3	1	0.5	0.6
Thailand	2	1	0	0.49
United States	3	1	1	1
Viet Nam	3	1	0.5	0

Source: Based on Lee *et al.* (2011) and ITU sources.

(where more than three competitors also receive a score of three). It also records the state of competition in the mobile market and various segments of the fixed line market. Finally, it records the portion of the fixed and mobile incumbent operator that is privatized (where any type of partial privatization receives a score of 0.5), and the portion of foreign ownership that is allowed in competitive carriers in fixed and mobile markets.

The results confirm that fixed and mobile markets in most APEC economies are by now fully competitive. Despite this, there are residual restrictions on foreign ownership in a majority of APEC economies. These are hard to rationalize, given the extent of competition that already exists.

Higher education

A key rationale for regulating higher education is to ensure that the education on offer meets certain minimum acceptable standards. Not all countries see the need to regulate higher education in this way. The United States, for example, is happy to leave it to the market-place to assess the relative worth of tertiary degree from Harvard or from a community college, and to allow students to make their choices of tertiary institution, and employers to make their choices of post-graduate remuneration, accordingly.

Other countries take a more pro-active role in regulating the quality of higher education. They establish quality assurance mechanisms to ensure that all the institutions in the sector meet certain minimum standards. They may also institute guidelines for the recognition of qualifications, ensuring that students get recognized credit for the qualifications they receive.

Some of the regulations currently applying to higher education institutions in the APEC region could arguably be seen as measures to ensure quality. But for other regulations, it is questionable whether they can be rationalized on these grounds. A recent survey of measures affecting cross-border exchange and investment in higher education in the APEC region (APEC Human Resources Development Working Group 2009) found that the most restrictive economies did not allow private for-profit or foreign-invested institutions to establish at all. Economies with the most liberal regimes included major exporters of higher education services. The survey also found a negative relationship between the prevalence of restrictions on higher education institutions and the breadth, depth and transparent of quality assurance processes. However, some economies used bans on certain institutions instead of quality assurance processes for them, even when their quality assurance processes for other institutions were relatively extensive, at least in terms of process.

The types of institutions where restrictions were most prevalent were private for-profit and foreign-invested institutions. Nevertheless, government institutions also faced relatively frequent restrictions. Because they were in receipt of significant government funding, they were likely to face relatively high standards of scrutiny and accountability, and some of this was manifest in regulatory restrictions. The institutions facing the lowest prevalence of regulatory restrictions were private non-profit institutions, those in a partnership arrangement with a foreign institution, and institutions delivering online and distance education.

Across all the responding economies, restrictions on the movement of individual students were about as prevalent as restrictions on institutions. Restrictions on the movement of instructors are notably less than on students.

While the survey report provided recent detailed evidence on the prevalence and nature of restrictions on trade in higher education services, survey responses were received from only nine of the 21 APEC economies. The data were not sufficiently rich to support econometric evidence of the effects of services trade barriers on the performance of higher education institutions. Thus the econometric study in Chapter 8 of this volume used an earlier benchmarking study by Nguyen-Hong and Wells (2003), which covered 20 economies from the APEC region and elsewhere. Tables 10.12 and 10.13 give an index of restrictions affecting establishment (ie commercial presence) by both foreign and domestic education institutions, where an index value of 1 indicates full restrictiveness, a value of 0 denotes no restriction, and intermediate values denote partial restrictions. The index components, along with values for most APEC economies, were taken from Nguyen-Hong and Wells (2003). The value for Peru was imputed from the qualitative information in the APEC Human Resources Development Working Group (2009) report.

The index in Tables 10.12 and 10.13 covers restrictions on establishment, including restrictions on the number of providers (registration and authorization requirements as well as explicit quotas), restrictions on foreign direct investment, requirements for joint venture or partnership with a local institution, restrictions on the enrolment of domestic students in international schools, and restrictions on the recognition of qualifications provided by foreign institutions. The index also covers a number of 'other' restrictions on ongoing operation (where

Table 10.12. Index of Policy Restrictions Affecting Foreign Commercial Presence in Higher Education

	(1)	*(2)*	*(3)*	*(4)*	*(5)*	*(6)*	*(7)*	*Foreign index*
Australia	0.5	0	0	0	0.5	0.3	0	1.3
Canada	0.5	0.25	0	0	0.5	0.2	0	1.45
Chile	0.5	0	0	0	0.5	0.1	0.5	1.6
China	0.5	0.5	1	0	0.5	0.5	1	4
Hong Kong	0.5	0	0	0	0	0.1	0	0.6
Indonesia	0.5	0.51	1	1	0	0.25	0.5	3.76
Japan	0.5	0	0	0	0.5	0.4	0	1.4
Rep. of Korea	0.5	0	0	0	0	0.3	0	0.8
Malaysia	1	0.7	1	1	0.5	0.4	0	4.6
Mexico	0	0.51	0	0	0	0.1	0	0.61
New Zealand	0.5	0.5	0	0	0.25	0.2	0	1.45
Peru	1	0	0	0	0	0.3	0	1.3
Philippines	na	na	na	na	na	na	na	na
Russia	na	na	na	na	na	na	na	na
Singapore	1	0	0	0	0.25	0.2	1	2.45
Chinese Taipei	0.5	0	0	0	0	0.15	0.5	1.15
Thailand	0.5	0.5	1	0	0	0.3	0	2.3
United States	0.5	0	0	0	0	0.1	0	0.6
Viet Nam	1	0.5	0.5	0	0	0.1	1	3.1

Notes: Index components are as follows: (1) Number of providers, (2) Foreign direct investment, (3) Joint venture or partnership, (4) Local enrolment in international schools, (5) Recognition of qualifications, (6) Other restrictions — addition categories, (7) Lack of transparency of regulations.
na = not available.
Source: Chapter 8.

each of the following receives a score of 0.1) — restrictions on the legal use of names or university title, quotas for employment of local staff, restrictions on curriculum content, restrictions on fee setting, restrictions on repatriation of earnings, restrictions on advertising, licensing requirements on management, a local language requirement for teaching, limited measures to protect the intellectual property of the education institutions, and limitations on access to public subsidies for foreign

Table 10.13. Index of Policy Restrictions Affecting Domestic Providers in Higher Education

	Number of providers	*Recognition of qualifications*	*Other restrictions – addition categories*	*Lack of transparency of regulations*	*Domestic index*
Australia	0.5	0.5	0.167	0	1.167
Canada	0.5	0.5	0.167	0	1.167
Chile	0.5	0.5	0.167	0.5	1.667
China	0.5	0.5	0.5	1	2.5
Hong Kong	0.5	0	0	0	0.5
Indonesia	0.5	0	0.167	0.5	1.167
Japan	0.5	0	0.333	0	0.833
Republic of Korea	0.5	0	0	0	0.5
Malaysia	0.5	0.5	0.333	0	1.333
Mexico	0	0	0.167	0	0.167
New Zealand	0.5	0.25	0.25	0	1
Peru	1	0	0.3	0	1.3
Philippines	na	na	na	na	na
Russia	na	na	na	na	na
Singapore	0.5	0.25	0.167	1	1.917
Chinese Taipei	0.5	0	0	0.5	1
Thailand	0.5	0	0.167	0	0.667
United States	0.5	0	0	0	0.5
Viet Nam	0.5	0	0	1	1.5

Note: na = not available.
Source: Chapter 8.

providers. According to the report of the APEC Human Resources Development Working Group (2009), the last of these is the most prevalent discriminatory restriction. Finally, the index covers lack of transparency of regulations.

APEC economies that impose the greatest degree of restriction on foreign higher education institutions are Malaysia, China and Indonesia. Malaysia and Indonesia are also the most discriminatory, as indicated by the difference between the domestic and foreign index values. China and Singapore impose the greatest degree of restriction on domestic higher education institutions. Hong Kong, the Republic of Korea, Mexico and the United States have relatively open regulatory regimes.

10.3 Quantifying the First Round Effects of Reform

As noted in Chapter 1, the policy indexes are arbitrary, but are not important by themselves. Instead, they provide inputs into econometric exercises that quantify the first-round effects of policy restrictions on measures of economic performance in the sectors in question, while controlling for all the other factors that affect economic performance in those sectors. The performance measures used in the econometric exercises are often prices or price-cost margins, but sometimes quantities or costs.

The econometric estimates of the effects of policy indexes on these measures of performance can be used to construct the counterfactual — what economic performance would be in the absence of the regulatory restrictions, holding all other factors constant. This counterfactual comparison gives the first-round effects of services reform. It can be seen as a 'tax equivalent', if the restrictions have raised price-cost margins, or a 'productivity equivalent', if the restrictions have raised real resource costs. Ideally, the econometric exercises should include a rich enough menu of performance measures to be able to determine which of these applies.

Insurance and banking

In this chapter, the first-round effects of services reforms in insurance and banking services are derived from the econometric evidence in Chapters 2 and 3. This evidence showed whether non-prudential regulatory barriers affected costs or profits, because both measures of performance were included in the analysis.

In the analysis of insurance services, unit profit and unit cost were modelled using a production structure that recognized two outputs (risk pooling/bearing and real services, and intermediation), one variable input (labour) and two fixed inputs (debt capital and equity capital). The unit profit and unit cost functions were estimated using an unbalanced panel dataset of 369 firms in 29 countries over the period 1997 to 2004, controlling for various fixed effects. Trade barriers were found to have no statistically significant effect on cost. They did have a significant positive effect on profit. The estimated coefficient of unit profit with respect to the services trade restrictiveness index for foreign affiliates was 0.1114958, where unit profit was measured as the pure ratio of total profit to total fixed capital. This coefficient could be used to calculate the tax equivalents of current barriers to trade in insurance services, as shown in Chapter 2.

Similarly, in the analysis of banking services, unit profit and unit cost were modelled using a production structure that recognized one output (loans plus investments), two variable inputs (total deposits and borrowed funds, labour) and one fixed input (fixed capital, measured as the sum of equity capital and fixed assets). The unit profit and unit cost functions were estimated using an unbalanced panel dataset of 7,314 firms in 28 countries over the period 1997 to 2006. In examining the effects of services trade barriers, the estimation controlled for the effects of two measures of prudential regulation, namely the total capital ratio and the liquidity ratio, as well as various fixed effects. Trade barriers were found to have statistically significant effects on both costs and profits. The estimated coefficient of unit profit with respect to the services trade restrictiveness index for traditional banking activities was 0.00826, while the estimated coefficient of unit cost with respect to the same index was 0.0072765, where unit profit and unit cost were measured as the pure ratios of total profit and total cost to total fixed capital. These coefficients could be used to calculate the productivity equivalents of current barriers to trade in banking services, as shown in Chapter 3, as well as the additional tax equivalent effects on profits, over and above the effects on costs.

Given further services reforms in insurance and banking services, it is assumed that the trade restrictiveness indexes for insurance and banking shown above would all reach a value of zero. This implies the removal of non-prudential licensing restrictions on entry, legal restrictions on establishment, and restrictions on the scale and scope of operations, the particular types of insurance or (traditional) banking products that a firm can offer, and on ownership or pricing. In insurance services, it also implies the removal of restrictions on reinsurance and the placement of assets. In banking, it implies the removal of restrictions on fund raising, lending, settlement and foreign exchange services. It does not imply the removal of restrictions on non-traditional banking services (insurance, securities, real estate or non-financial activities), because the evidence cited above suggests that these have a prudential purpose.

The coefficients from the econometric analysis can be used to calculate the resulting percentage reductions in prices in each APEC economy arising from the reductions in costs and/or price-cost margins. The price reductions for foreign-invested insurance firms are shown in Figure 10.1. The price reductions for domestically-owned insurance firms are not shown, but are smaller (because the restrictions they currently face are smaller). The price reductions for foreign-invested

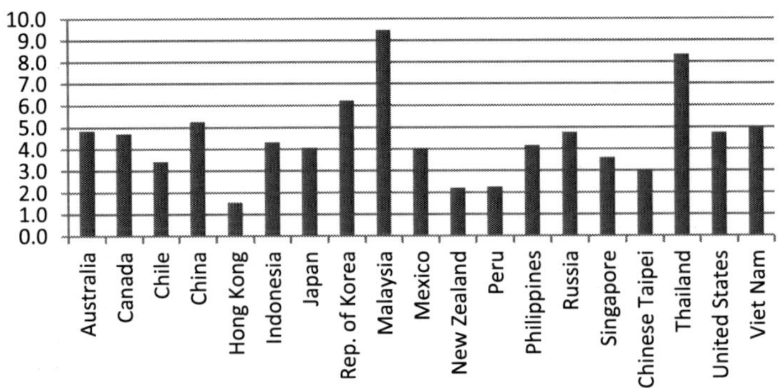

Figure 10.1. Price Reductions from Reforms in Insurance (%)
Source: Table 10.1 and Chapter 2.

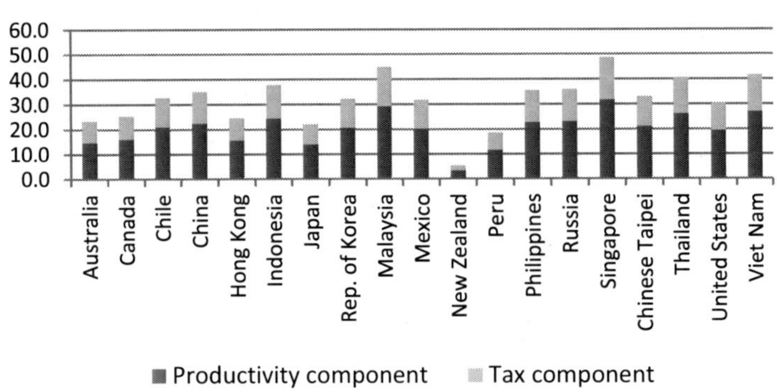

Figure 10.2. Price Reductions from Reforms in Banking (%)
Source: Table 10.3 and Chapter 3.

banks that would come from reductions in both their costs and price-cost margins are shown in Figure 10.2. Comparable estimates for domestically-owned banks are also not shown, but are smaller. Note that the price reductions for banking are sizable in percentage terms — over 40 per cent for some ASEAN members of APEC.

Air and maritime transport

In this chapter, the first-round effects of reforms in air and maritime transport are derived from the econometric evidence in Chapter 5. There Sourdin estimated the effects of policy restrictions using the policy indexes presented in the previous section. Her measure of economic performance was the *ad valorem* transport costs incurred in shipping goods internationally using air or sea transport. She made use of data from four economies — Australia, Brazil, Chile and the United States — that compile detailed (6-digit), consistent data on import values on both a fob (free on board) and cif (cost, insurance, freight) basis. Her measure of *ad valorem* transport costs was the percentage difference between cif and fob valuations, calculated separately (by commodity and source economy) for imports transported by air and by sea. Her controls in the estimation were the value of total imports between the economy pairs, the distance between them, the value-to-weight ratio of the particular import shipment and a product-specific fixed effect. Her estimated semi-elasticity of air transport costs with respect to the air transport restrictiveness index was 0.055. Her estimated semi-elasticity of maritime transport costs with respect to the maritime transport openness index was –0.487.

Given further structural reforms in air and maritime transport in each APEC economy, it is assumed that the air restrictiveness indexes would all reach a value of zero, and the maritime openness indexes would all reach a value of unity. In air transport, this implies a range of reforms to air services agreements, to entry conditions for domestic and foreign carriers, and to ownership. In maritime transport, it implies the dismantling of any remaining entry restrictions, quotas or cargo sharing arrangements, and the granting of national treatment to foreign-owned carriers located domestically. The above semi-elasticities can be used to calculate the resulting percentage changes in air and maritime transport costs for each APEC economy.

One key question for modelling purposes is whether to interpret these prospective cost changes as coming about because the price-cost margins of transport operators would be squeezed, or because the real resource cost of shipping goods by air or sea would fall. Should the first-round effects be interpreted as 'tax equivalents' or 'productivity equivalents'? By itself, the econometrics in Chapter 5 does not resolve the issue.

The issue is decided on *a priori* grounds. Price-cost markups are only likely to be inflated for significant periods of time if regulatory restrictions prevent entry — otherwise the excess profits are likely to be eroded by the entry of new service providers. On the other hand, many kinds of regulatory restrictions are likely to raise real resource costs, particularly regulations that lead to shipping delays or prevent transport operators from configuring their transport routes to achieve network economies. In air transport, restrictive designation provisions can limit the entry of any new carriers on international routes, but other provisions, such as restrictive traffic rights, can prevent the achievement of network economies. In maritime, cabotage restrictions limit foreign but not domestic entry on domestic routes. Quotas and cargo handling restrictions can lead to shipping delays that add significantly to shipping costs.

Overall, it is judged that the regulatory restrictions in air and maritime are likely to have raised transport costs, rather than inflated the price-cost margins of international transport operators. So the first round effects of structural reform are interpreted as productivity improvements. They are shown for each APEC economy in Figures 10.3 and 10.4. Nevertheless, this assumption is subjected to sensitivity testing in the next section, by assessing the economy-wide effects of an alternative treatment, whereby half the first-round impact is assumed to fall on price-cost margins.

A second key question for modelling purposes is whether the first round impacts would fall only on the cost of shipping goods internationally, or whether they would also affect the costs of domestic maritime and air services. In Chapter 5, Sourdin only measured the first

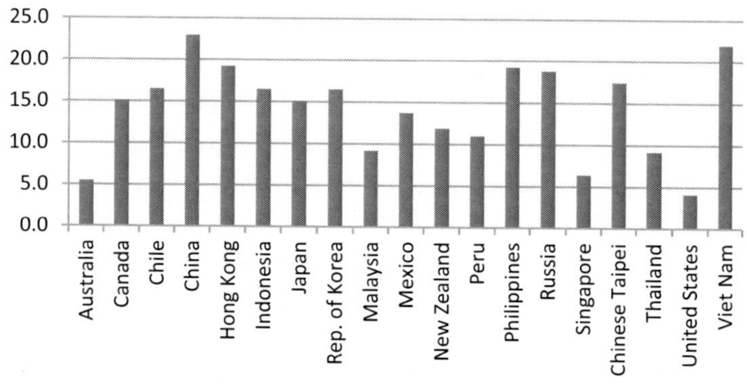

Figure 10.3. Productivity Improvements from Structural Reforms in Air Transport (%)
Source: Table 10.5 and Chapter 5.

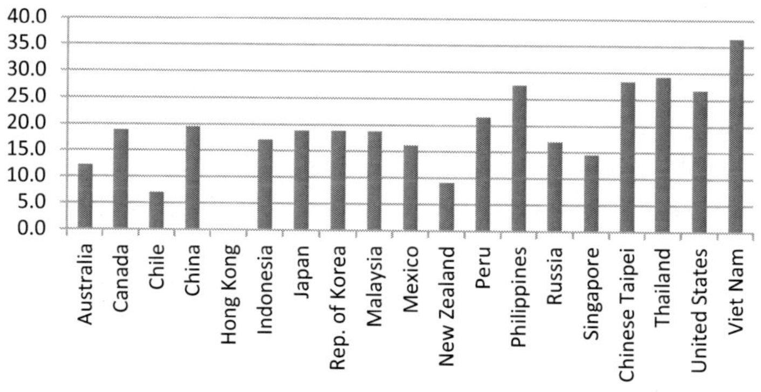

Figure 10.4. Productivity Improvements from Structural Reforms in Maritime Transport (%)
Source: Table 10.6 and Chapter 5.

effect. Nevertheless, the policy indexes for both air and maritime include regulatory restrictions that would also be expected to affect domestic services. Accordingly, in the modelling of the next section, the first-round productivity effects are assumed to fall on international air and sea transport margins, as well as on the domestic production of air and maritime transport services. Further, the effects are assumed to fall equally on domestically-owned and foreign-owned service providers, even though a few components of the indexes would be expected to affect foreign-owned carriers more than domestic ones.

Rail transport

The first-round effects of reforms in rail transport have been derived from the econometric study by Cantos, Pastor and Serrano in (2010). They estimated the effects of horizontal and vertical separation on the efficiency and productivity of rail operations, using data on 16 European railway systems from 1985 to 2005. In measuring efficiency and productivity, they used a production structure that recognized two outputs (passenger and freight transport) and four inputs (employees, passenger train supply, freight train supply, and railway infrastructure). In examining the determinants of efficiency and productivity, they controlled for the share of passengers in the total transport task, measures of the size and density of the network, measures of passenger and freight occupancy, and individual and time fixed effects.

Their measured impacts of reforms on efficiency indicate how reforms can encourage railway operators to move towards the production frontier, from a point inside it (typically by making better use of existing infrastructure facilities). The measured impacts on productivity also show how reforms can encourage technical progress in rail operations, moving the production frontier outwards (typically by encouraging better infrastructure facilities). In the context of rail operations in contiguous European economies, one of the ways in which technical progress could be achieved is via investments that lead to more seamless international rail services. This option is less easily available to APEC economies, which are spread around the Pacific Rim. In recognition of this, the current chapter only makes use of the estimates of the effects of structural reforms on efficiency. Cantos, Pastor and Serrano (2010) estimate the semi-elasticity of efficiency with respect to vertical separation as 0.025, and the semi-elasticity of efficiency with respect to free entry in freight operations as 0.083. Thus free entry has a greater effect on efficiency than vertical separation (the relative impacts on productivity are the reverse).

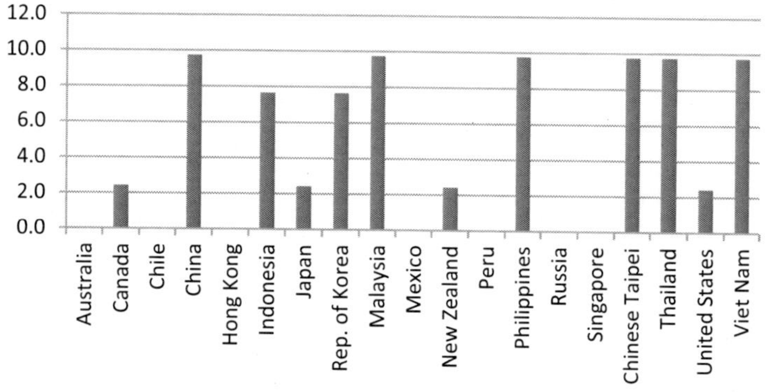

Figure 10.5. Productivity Improvements from Structural Reforms in Rail Transport (%)
Source: Table 10.7 and Cantos *et al.* (2010).

Given further structural reforms in rail transport in each APEC economy, it is assumed that the rail openness indexes would all reach a value of unity. This implies vertical separation and free entry in freight operations in those economies that do not yet have them. It does not necessarily imply any change in ownership.

The above semi-elasticities can be used to calculate the resulting percentage changes in 'productivity' (a term now used more broadly than by Cantos, Pastor and Serrano 2010) in rail operations for each APEC economy. These are shown in Figure 10.5.

Electricity and gas

The first-round effects of reforms in electricity and gas have been derived from the econometric evidence in Chapter 7. This estimated the effects of policy restrictions in these sectors using the policy indexes presented in the previous section. The measures of economic performance were electricity and gas prices to industrial users in OECD economies over the period 1990 to 2008. The controls for electricity prices were per capita GDP, the rate of urbanization, the shares of hydro and nuclear in total generation, and a linear time trend. The controls for gas prices were per capita GDP, the rate of urbanization, pipeline length, and a nonlinear time trend (to capture the upward movement of gas input costs). Looking only at the policy coefficients that were significantly different from zero, the coefficients measuring the impact on electricity prices (measured in US$ PPP/kWh) of third party access, a wholesale price pool, and unbundling were –0.0032, –0.0049 and –0.0075, respectively. The coefficients measuring the impact on gas prices (measured in US$ PPP/10e+7 kcal) of retail competition and the unbundling of production/import were –30.446 and –47.5065, respectively.

Given further structural reforms in electricity and gas in each APEC economy, it is assumed that the electricity and gas openness indexes would all reach a value of unity. This implies third party access, unbundling, wholesale markets and/or retail competition in economies that have not yet implemented these. It does not imply any change in ownership.

The above coefficients can be used to calculate the resulting percentage changes in electricity and gas prices. It remains to decide whether these price changes would come about through changes in price-cost margins or though changes in productivity, because the econometrics does not resolve the issue. Consistent with the presumption of Steiner (2000), and with anecdotal evidence in economies such as

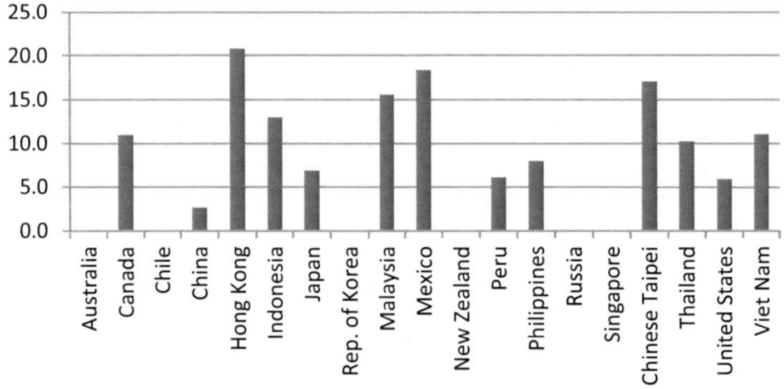

Figure 10.6. Productivity Improvements from Structural Reforms in Electricity (%)
Source: Table 10.8 and Chapter 7.

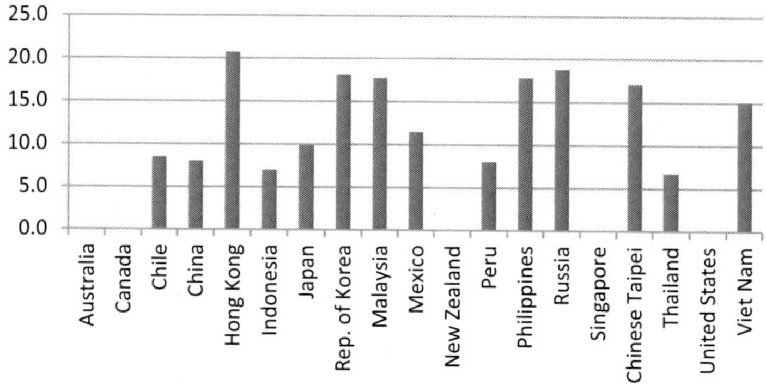

Figure 10.7. Productivity Improvements from Structural Reforms in Gas (%)
Source: Table 10.9 and Chapter 7.

Australia that have undergone significant reform, it is assumed that structural reforms would manifest primarily as productivity improvements. The estimated improvements are shown in Figures 10.6 and 10.7. This assumption is tested later via sensitivity analysis.

Telecommunications

The first-round effects of structural reforms in telecommunications have been derived from an updated version of the econometric study by Warren (2000) (see Dee 2005). The main contribution of the updated study was to use a database with a slightly expanded coverage of economies, and to enter the subcomponents of the policy indexes separately into the econometric estimation. The database covered many more economies than just APEC members. The performance measures were the number of mainlines per 100 inhabitants and the number of cellular phones per 100 inhabitants. The controls in the fixed line estimation were GDP per capita, household density, the percentage of mainlines connected to a digital exchange, and waiting lists as a percentage of mainlines. The controls in the mobile estimation were GDP per capita and population density. In both cases, the relationship with per capita GDP was assumed to be cubic, to allow for 'saturation' levels of penetration. The policy variables were combinations of the indexes shown in Tables 10.10 and 10.11. Separate weighted average indexes of market access and national treatment for fixed and mobile telephony were calculated as in Warren (2000), where these indexes ranged between zero and one. The coefficients of fixed mainline penetration with respect to market access and national treatment were 2.892 and 3.529, respectively. The coefficients of mobile penetration with respect to market access and national treatment were 1.898 and 1.075, respectively.

Given further reforms in telecommunications in each APEC economy, it is assumed that the telecommunications indexes of market access and national treatment would all reach a value of unity. These reforms would predominantly involve the removal of remaining foreign equity limits.

The above coefficients can be used to calculate the resulting small percentage changes in fixed and mobile penetration. With the same price elasticity of –1.2 as assumed by Warren (2000), the quantity effects can be converted to equivalent changes in price. It remains to decide whether these price changes would come about through changes in price-cost margins or though changes in productivity. In previous exercises, when strict licensing requirements limited entry, it was reasonable to assume that reforms would squeeze price-cost margins (as in Dee and Hanslow 2001, for example). By now, most such entry requirements have been relaxed. Accordingly, the remaining small price reductions are assumed to accrue through changes in productivity, though once again this assumption is tested via sensitivity analysis. But as in previous exercises, the impact is assumed to be greater on foreign-invested than on domestic operators, because a greater portion of the limitations on market access and national treatment apply to them. The estimated improvements for foreign-invested operators are shown in Figure 10.8. The values for domestic operators are not shown, but are smaller.

Higher education

In this chapter, the first-round effects of services trade reforms on commercial presence in higher education services are derived from the econometric evidence in Chapter 8. An earlier paper (Dee 2010a) had

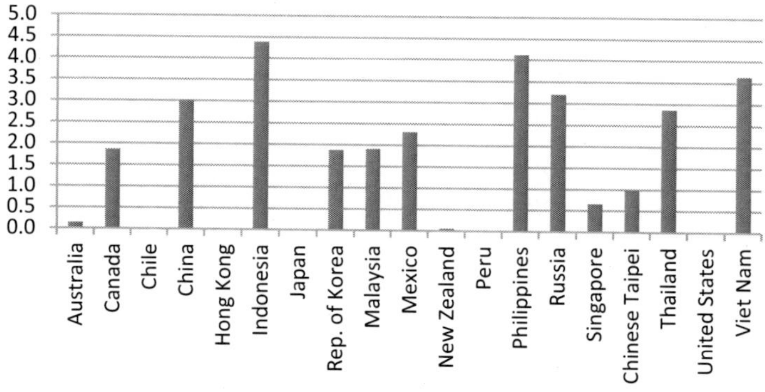

Figure 10.8. Productivity Improvements from Structural Reforms in Telecommunications (%)
Source: Table 10.10 and 10.11 and Dee (2005).

found that barriers to importing higher education services via FDI had the effect of boosting the number of students from that country seeking enrolment in overseas universities. It thus found evidence of inter-modal substitution. The analysis on Chapter 8 was designed to examine the source of that inter-modal substitution, by quantifying the extent to which the barriers to importing education by FDI had been restricting the quality and/or quantity of higher education in the home country.

The analysis looked at the effects of FDI barriers on the technical efficiency of higher education, using a production framework that recognized three outputs (the quantity of teaching, and the quantity and quality of research) and one input (real current expenditure). The analysis controlled for the effects of the proportion of foreign students and the proportion of part-time students. Technical inefficiency was measured by estimated distance to the production frontier, and barriers to importing via FDI were found to have a statistically significant negative effect in technical efficiency — the coefficient of technical efficiency with respect to the index of barriers facing foreign-invested institutions (shown above) was –0.036.

Given further services trade reforms in higher education services, it is assumed that the higher education restrictiveness index would reach a value of zero. This implies the removal of foreign equity limits, as well as a relaxation of restrictions on the number of providers, enrolments and recognition of qualifications. It also implies the relaxation of a number of restrictions on operation, including discriminatory restrictions on access to public subsidies. Finally, it implies greater transparency of regulations.

The above coefficient can be used to calculate the resulting percentage changes in productivity in each APEC economy from services trade reforms in higher education. The resulting productivity improvements for foreign-invested institutions are shown in Figure 10.9. The improvements for domestic institutions are not shown, but are smaller.

The theoretical arguments outlined in Chapter 8 suggested that the main impact of services trade barriers in higher education would be on technical efficiency, rather than on price-cost margins. In most economies, higher education is dominated by non-profit institutions. The theory of non-profit organizations used by Massy (2004) argues that such institutions have an incentive to be technically efficient, but that they have an incentive to dissipate any rents on the achievement of their non-profit objective. Services trade barriers can nevertheless interfere with their ability to achieve technical efficiency.

However, services trade reform in higher education could be expected to have wider effects than just increasing productivity within the higher education sector, as measured by its teaching and research output per unit

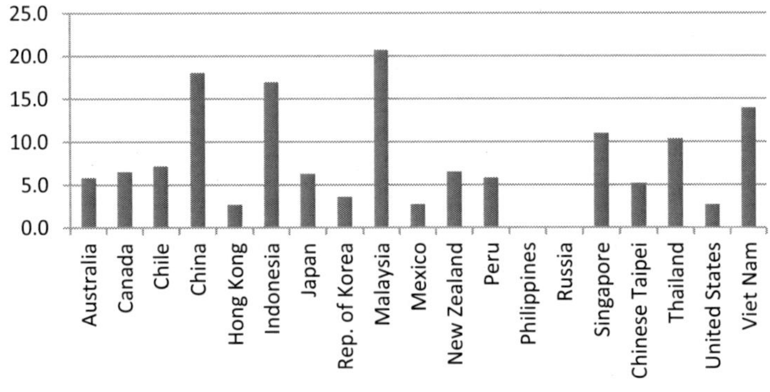

Figure 10.9. Productivity Improvements from Structural Reforms in Higher Education (%)
Source: Table 10.12 and Chapter 8.

of input. As recognized in Chapter 8, one of the missing outputs in the production framework is the quality of teaching, as reflected ultimately in the labour force experience of graduates. If services trade reform were to flow through to the quality of teaching, then it could also improve the workforce productivity of the graduates that the sector produced, thus increasing the productivity of each economy's skilled labour workforce. However, quantifying this effect is difficult, for two reasons. Firstly, data on the quality of teaching is hard to come by, so it is generally excluded from productivity measurement. In addition, not all of an economy's skilled labour will have been educated in higher education institutions at home — some will have been educated in offshore institutions, and some will have other types of qualifications. It is assumed here that there is some positive flow-on effect to the productivity of each economy's skilled labour workforce. It is assumed (hopefully conservatively) that the magnitude of this effect is 25 per cent of the impact on the productivity of domestically-owned higher education institutions.

Summary

In order to get an overall picture of the prospective reform task, Figure 10.10 presents an output-weighted average of the price reductions across all sectors in each APEC economy, arising from productivity improvements and/or reductions in price-cost margins. The weighted average price reductions fall roughly in the range of 4 to 24 per cent. The most extensive reform effort, and largest resulting price reductions (ie above 15 per cent), are projected to occur in Indonesia, Malaysia, Mexico, the Philippines, Singapore, Chinese Taipei, Thailand, the United States and Viet Nam. Singapore and the United States appear on the list primarily because of their barriers to trade in banking services.

To put these projected first-round impacts of services reform in perspective, Figures 10.11 and 10.12 show the simple average tariff rates on agriculture and food, and on manufacturing, in each APEC economy. These would be the targets of further at-the-border trade reforms. (Trade reform in agriculture and food would also target explicit subsidies on output and exports, and implicit subsidies on inputs, though these

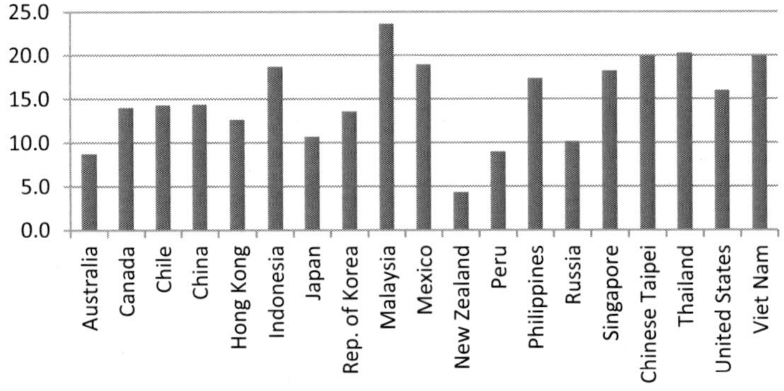

Figure 10.10. Weighted Average Price Reductions from Structural Reforms in Finance, Transport, Energy, Telecommunications and Higher Education (%)
Source: Figures 10.1 to 10.9 and GTAP model database, version 7 (Hertel 1997).

measures are not shown here.) The tariff estimates are derived from version 7 of the GTAP model database (Hertel 1997).[4] The average tariffs on manufacturing are generally slightly lower than the prospective price reductions from structural reforms — up to 13 per cent. The average tariffs on agriculture and food in some economies are higher — up to 35 per cent.

This does not mean that services reforms would generate smaller gains that further trade reforms in agriculture. Tariffs operate in the same way as inflated price-cost margins — inducing large transfers between producers and consumers, but much smaller welfare losses to the economy as a whole. By contrast, the net welfare costs of forgone productivity gains could conceivably be as high as the transfers produced by a tariff, and much larger than its net welfare costs. The relative sizes are examined further in the next section.

---

[4] The model's tariff estimates are import weighted when aggregating from GTAP's 57 sectors to the 25 sectors used in the current model. Simple averages are then taken when aggregating from 25 sectors to the two broad sectors shown in Figures 10.11 and 10.12. Because of preferences, tariffs also depend on the source of imports. Figure 10.11 shows the average values on imports from the United States, while Figure 10.12 shows the average values on imports from the rest of the world.

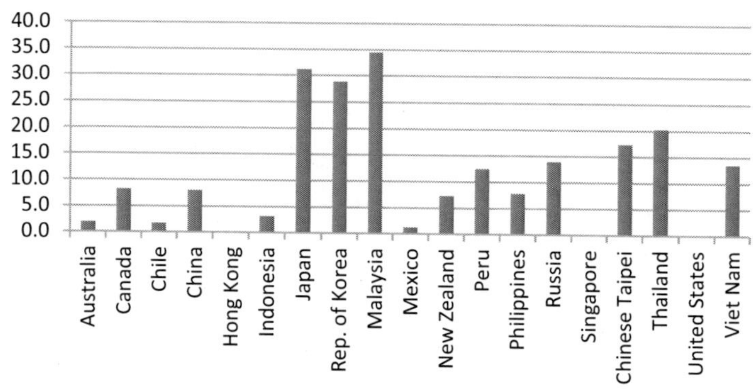

Figure 10.11. Simple Average Tariffs on Agriculture, Forestry, Fishing and Food (%)
Source: GTAP model database, version 7 (Hertel 1997).

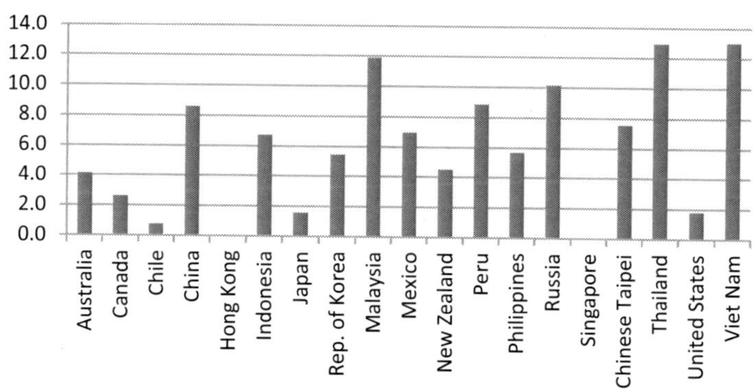

Figure 10.12. Simple Average Tariffs on Manufacturing (%)
Source: GTAP model database, version 7 (Hertel 1997).

10.4 Quantifying the Economy- and Region-wide Effects of Reform

The economy- and region-wide effects of structural reforms in services have been projected using FTAP, a computable general equilibrium model of the world economy that is described in Box 10.1, documented fully in Hanslow, Phamduc and Verikios (1999), and available for download at http://www.crawford.anu.edu.au/staff/pdee.php. This model differs from the GTAP model (from which it is derived) by having a treatment of foreign direct investment, an important mode by which services are delivered.

The measure of welfare in the FTAP model takes into account, not just changes in the level of activity generated in each economy, but changes in the amount of income from that activity that is retained by the residents of each economy. The distinction is important in a long-run context. One of the possible impacts of structural reforms is that they make each economy a more attractive destination for foreign direct investment. Not all the income from that investment will necessarily stay in the economy. However, the model has a fully articulated treatment of savings, investment and capital accumulation (see Box 10.1), so it takes into account how much of the returns on foreign investment are repatriated overseas, and how much are re-invested. Thus the measure of economic well-being is related to the concept of gross national product (the income earned by residents of a region) rather than gross domestic product (the income generated in region).[5]

Box 10.1. FTAP Model

The FTAP model is a computable general equilibrium model incorporating services delivered via FDI. It was developed by Dee and Hanslow (2001). It differs in turn from GTAP (Hertel 1997), the 'plain vanilla' model from which it was derived, in three important respects.

First, because many services are delivered primarily via commercial presence, the modelling framework includes foreign direct investment, and covers separately the production and trading activity of foreign multinationals. In other words, GTAP, the conventional multi-country model, is split out by ownership as well as location. In the current version of FTAP, foreign ownership shares are estimated in the following way. International data on FDI stocks by sector and source economy have been compiled and extrapolated where necessary by the Centre d'Etudes Prospectives et d'Informations Internationales (CEPII). Provisional estimates were kindly made available at the GTAP level of aggregation by Terry Walmsley. These data are scaled up from FDI stocks to the output of foreign affiliates, using FDI to sales ratios obtained from the United States International Trade Commission, and derived from the detailed statistics on the activities of

[5] Hanslow (2000) has a good general treatment of welfare measures and welfare decomposition in computable general equilibrium models.

Box 10.1. Continued

foreign affiliates collected by the US Bureau of Economic Analysis. These estimates of the output of foreign affiliates by sector and source economy are then used to split out their costs and sales structures on a simple *pro rata* basis. Unfortunately, even the best statistics on the activities of foreign affiliates would not support a much more sophisticated derivation of costs and sales structures than this, and few economies collect such statistics.

Second, by virtue of foreign ownership, at least some of the profits of foreign multinationals will be repatriated back to the home economies. Thus the profit streams in the conventional multi-country model have to be reallocated from the host to the home economy, after provision is made for them to be taxed in either the home or host economy. This reallocation leads to a distinction between GDP — the income *generated* in a region — and GNP — the income *received by residents* of a region. The latter forms the basis of (although is not identical to) the welfare measure in FTAP. The information on profit repatriation comes from the Balance of Payments Statistics of the IMF.

Finally, not all profits of foreign multinationals need be repatriated to the home economy. Some may be reinvested in the host economy. To account for this phenomenon, and to allow for the effect that regulatory reform may have on both domestic and foreign direct investment more generally, the model makes provision for savings and capital accumulation. This is particularly important, since some regulatory barriers are aimed directly at limiting domestic or foreign equity participation. It is therefore important to capture how regulatory reform will affect not just foreign ownership *shares*, but also the *total amount* of productivity capacity available to an economy. National savings rates are derived from the macroeconomic data in the International Financial Statistics and Balance of Payments Statistics of the IMF. Government savings rates are derived from the Government Finance Statistics of the IMF. Household savings rates are calculated as a residual.

The FTAP model also differs from GTAP in other respects. In particular, it allows for firm-level product differentiation, economies of scale and large-group monopolistic competition. This is also important, since services tend to be highly specialized, being tailored to the needs of individual customers. In the current version, economies of scale are assumed to be regional for services, and global for all other sectors (Dee 2003).

Source: Based on Dee and Hanslow (2001).

The version of FTAP used here contains 20 regions — 19 APEC regions (excluding Brunei and Papua New Guinea, which are not represented in the underlying GTAP database), and a single rest of the world region. It contains 25 sectors, shown in Table 10.14, 12 of which are services sectors.

The first-round impacts of prospective structural reforms in each economy are modelled via the productivity improvements to banking, air, maritime and rail transport, electricity and gas, telecommunications, and higher education shown in Figures 10.3–10.9 and the productivity component of Figure 10.2. In banking and insurance, where services trade reforms also squeeze price-cost margins, the tax equivalents of the inflated profit margins are first injected into the model's database in as neutral a fashion as possible while maintaining database balance, using an FTAP analogue of GTAP's Altertax procedure (Malcolm 1998). In the FTAP theoretical structure, the rents from such 'tax equivalents' in services accrue to producers rather than to the government. To model the impact of services trade reforms, these tax equivalents are then removed via simulation, generating first-round price reductions of the sort shown in Figure 10.1 and the tax component of Figure 10.2.

In the case of rail transport, the productivity improvement can only be applied to a bigger 'Other Transport' sector, which also includes road transport and storage. In the case of higher education services, the

Table 10.14. FTAP Model Sectors

Agriculture and food	*Other primary products*	*Manufacturing*	*Services*
Agric., for. & fishing	Mining	Textiles and clothing	Electricity
Processed foods		Wood and paper products	Gas
		Chemicals	Construction
		Metals	Trade
		Fabricated metal products	Other transport
		Motor vehicles	Water transport
		Other transport equip.	Air transport
		Electronic equipment	Communication
		Other machinery & equip.	Banking
		Other manufacturing	Insurance
			Government services
			Other services

Source: FTAP model.

productivity improvements can only be applied to a much bigger 'Other Government Services' sector, which also includes public administration and defense, health, community services and sanitation. Detailed input-output data available for Indonesia, the United States and Australia suggested that rail was only about 14 per cent and education only about 30 per cent of the larger sectors of which they were a part. OECD education data suggested in turn that higher education accounting for about 24 per cent of total education spending on average in OECD countries. These proportions provided the basis for scaling down the size of the productivity changes to take account of the fact that they applied to only part of the larger sector.

The productivity improvements and 'tax' reductions are applied to the domestic production of domestically-owned and/or foreign-invested companies, as appropriate. In air and maritime transport, the productivity improvements are also applied to the international air and maritime transport margins used to transport merchandise exports out of each economy. In the model, as in the real world, such transport margins could be provided by transport operators in the source economy, the destination economy, or any third party. As the econometrics in Chapter 5 demonstrates, the regulatory restrictions in these sectors currently penalize all these transport providers. Note that in both cases, some of the services reforms have a bilateral dimension (eg cabotage, air service agreements) and some do not (eg port services). Somewhat arbitrarily, it was decided to apply the productivity improvements in air transport to the margins used to transport goods to other APEC partners. The productivity improvements in maritime were applied to the margins used to transport goods to all regions, including the rest of the world. Because intra-APEC trade is so extensive, the results are not greatly sensitive to this treatment. Finally, to capture the flow-on effects of higher education reforms, productivity improvements were also applied to skilled labour in each APEC economy equivalent to 25 per cent of the improvement to domestically-owned higher education institutions.

For those sectors where the incidence on costs or price-cost margins is uncertain (namely air, maritime, rail, electricity, gas and telecommunications), an alternative treatment of structural reform is examined in which half of the domestic gains are assumed to accrue in the form of productivity gains, and half as reductions in the price-cost margins of domestically located service providers. It is not possible to provide a comparable 'split' treatment of the impact on international air and maritime transport margins, because the FTAP model, like its GTAP source, does not allow for 'taxes' on international transport margins.

The FTAP model provides a long-run snapshot of how different each economy would look about ten years after the reforms, compared to the situation at that same point in time if the reforms had not taken place. During the ten year adjustment period, many other changes would affect each economy, but they are not taken into account in the current analysis. For this reason, the results should not be interpreted as indicating the likely changes that would occur over time — this would require all changes, not just those in regulatory restrictions, to be taken into account.

The distinction is important to keep in mind. Sometimes, to aid fluency, the results are couched as if key indicators 'rise' or 'fall'. This does not mean that the indicators would be higher or lower than they are now. It means that at some future time, they would be higher or lower than they would be otherwise. In both cases, in a growing economy, they could be higher than they are now.

The economy- and region-wide effects of structural reforms

The projected effects of the structural reforms, undertaken jointly, on each APEC economy are shown in Figure 10.13, where to normalize for economic size, the absolute welfare gain in each economy has been expressed relative to its initial GDP. As noted, welfare changes give the effects on the economic well-being of the residents in each economy, while real GDP measures the effects on its level of activity. Figure 10.14 also shows the projected effects on real GDP, measured as the percentage deviations from baseline, ten years after the structural reforms.

In both cases, not surprisingly, there is a reasonably strong correlation between the gains from reform and the size of the reform task. The biggest gain in welfare, at about 6.6 per cent, is projected to occur in Viet

Nam, although the reform task there is not quite as great as in Malaysia.[6] Across all APEC economies, the simple correlation coefficient between the welfare gains in Figure 10.13 and the average price reductions in Figure 10.10 is 0.58. The correlation between the real GDP gains in Figure 10.14 and the average price reductions in Figure 10.10 is 0.54.

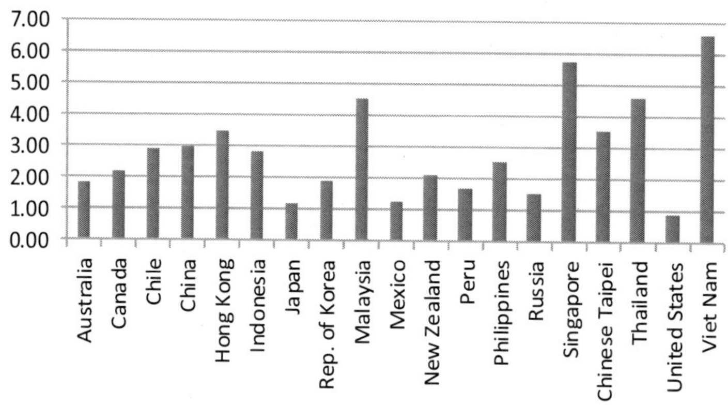

Figure 10.13. Welfare Gains from Structural Reforms, Relative to Initial Economic Size (%)
Source: FTAP model projections.

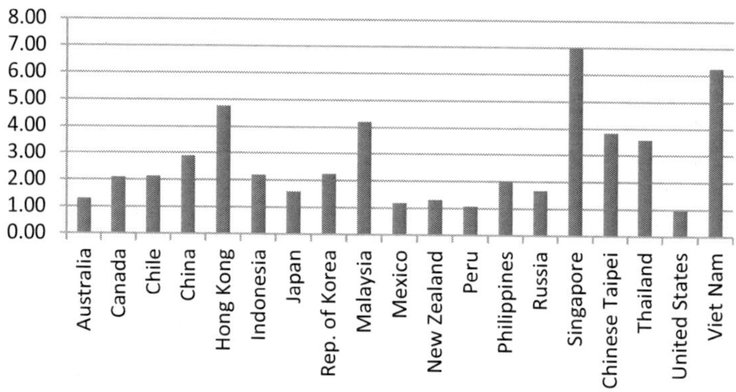

Figure 10.14. Gains in Real GDP (% deviation from baseline)
Source: FTAP model projections.

[6] Both are small open economies, so benefit greatly from services trade reforms in air and maritime services, but Viet Nam's merchandise exports carry larger air and transport margins than Malaysia's in proportional terms.

The latter is slightly smaller than the former because economic activity in each economy is affected, more so than welfare, by reforms in other economies, not just reforms at home.

To get an initial indication of the extent of these 'cross' effects, Figure 10.15 shows the proportion of the welfare gain in each economy that is attributable to reforms at home, relative to reforms in all other APEC economies. The first observation is that in all economies, an overwhelming proportion of the gains comes from reforms at home, rather than reforms in other economies. Thus while the gains from joint reforms are considerable, there is no compelling reason for each APEC economy to wait for others to start.

The second observation is that in most APEC economies, there are small gains to be had from the reforms of others. This is not a foregone conclusion, because many of the gains from services reforms accrue as productivity improvements, and these are typically a two-edged sword — while they increase incomes in other economies and can encourage them to buy more from the home economy, they also improve the price competitiveness of other economies and induce substitution away from the home economy. Typically in these types of simulations, the latter effects dominate. The difference here is that structural reforms in other economies also reduce the cost of transporting merchandise exports from

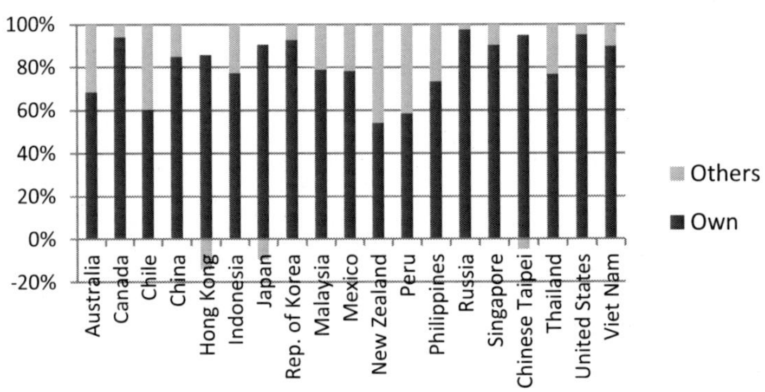

Figure 10.15. Contribution to Welfare from Own and Others' Structural Reforms (% of total)
Source: FTAP model projections.

the home economy, because in most APEC economies, a large portion of that transport task is undertaken by foreign rather than domestic transport operators. So this restores the balance in favour of the home economy.

The three APEC economies that are not projected to gain from reforms elsewhere in the APEC region are Hong Kong, Japan and Chinese Taipei (though all three experience gains from their own reforms). Hong Kong is already an efficient and substantial supplier of maritime transport services to the rest of the region. It is projected to lose its relative position as others become more efficient in maritime services. Japan and Chinese Taipei are projected to lose from reforms in the gas and insurance sectors in other economies. As will be seen later, some of the sectors that are often 'crowded out' in relative terms from services reforms are the motor vehicle, other transport equipment and electronic equipment sectors, and Japan and Chinese Taipei are significant producers of these products, not just at home, but via their foreign direct investments elsewhere in the region.

Figure 10.16 gives the percentage contributions to the overall gains in each economy from the structural reforms in each sector. The biggest gains tend to come from reforms in banking and air and maritime transport, because as Figures 10.1 to 10.9 demonstrate, this is where the biggest reforms tend to occur. As noted, Hong Kong loses in relative terms from maritime reforms because it is already an efficient producer.

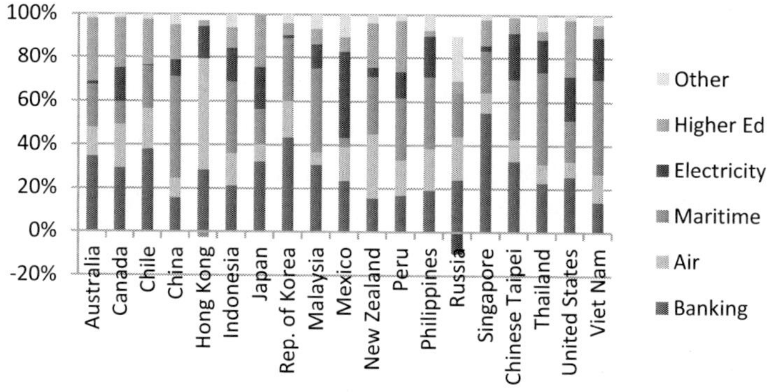

Figure 10.16. Contribution to Welfare from Structural Reforms in Each Sector (% of total)
Source: FTAP model projections.

Similarly, Russia is already relatively efficient in electricity generation, having undertaken a virtual revolution in the organization of its electricity sector in recent years. It is projected to lose from more intensive competition in energy-intensive products as others become more efficient in electricity generation.

Putting the gains in perspective

Across the whole APEC region, services reforms in finance, transport, energy, telecommunications and higher education are projected to generate US$330 billion a year in additional real income (in 2004 dollars), relative to what would have accrued had no reforms occurred. This is a snapshot of the gains after a ten year adjustment period.

These gains can be put in perspective by comparing them with the potential gains from further at-the-border trade reform. Complete liberalization of all remaining trade barriers in agriculture and food, other primary products and manufacturing by all APEC economies is projected to generate real income gains of just under US$100 billion a year, after about ten years. These gains would be generated in sectors that currently produce about US$15,600 billion in output annually. This compares with the annual output of only $5,600 billion annually in the finance, transport, energy, telecommunications and higher education sectors undergoing the structural reforms.

APEC wide, therefore, the projected gains from structural reforms are more than three times as big as the gains from liberalization of merchandise trade. Yet the sectors here where structural reforms occur are about a third the size of those engaged in merchandise trade. When structural reforms lower real production costs as well as squeezing profit margins, they can generate a 'bang for the buck' that is much greater than from merchandise trade reforms.

As noted, however, it is not certain for some sectors that the structural reforms considered here would have their first-round effects on productivity levels rather than price-cost margins, although *a priori* arguments are in favour of this treatment. As a sensitivity test, half of the domestic gains in contested sectors (transport, energy and telecommunications) are modelled as accruing in the form of productivity gains, and half as reductions in the price-cost margins of domestically located service providers. For technical reasons, the impact on international transport margins continues to accrue as a productivity gain, as before. In this alternative treatment, the APEC wide real income gains from structural reforms are smaller, at US$270 billion a year, but still more than double those of merchandise trade reform.

Adjustment costs

Services reforms cannot generate significant gains without also generating significant structural adjustments.

Computable general equilibrium models can help to identify and quantify the extent of structural adjustments, measured by the relative gains and losses to sectoral output and employment in each economy. However, in a model with 20 regions and 25 sectors, the amount of detail that could potentially be presented is considerable. In an attempt to condense the detail, Figures 10.17 and 10.18 show the output-weighted average, across all APEC economies, of the projected deviations from baseline in sectoral output in each economy. Figure 10.17 shows the 'typical' (in this sense) sectoral response to an economy's own reforms. Figure 10.18 shows the 'typical' response in one economy to reforms by all APEC economies. Obviously, the percentage deviations from baseline in at least some individual economies are more severe than the weighted averages. The extremes are examined shortly, in the context of employment changes rather than output changes.

In the typical response to 'own' reforms, the sectors with output higher than otherwise are the services sectors undergoing the reforms.

Their output deviations tend to be in direct proportion to their reform effort. Other sectors to gain in relative terms are those that are heavy users of these services. They tend to be chemicals (an intensive user of gas), metals (an intensive user of electricity), and wood and paper products (an intensive user of domestic transport services). Construction also typically gains slightly from the additional impetus given to industry investment.

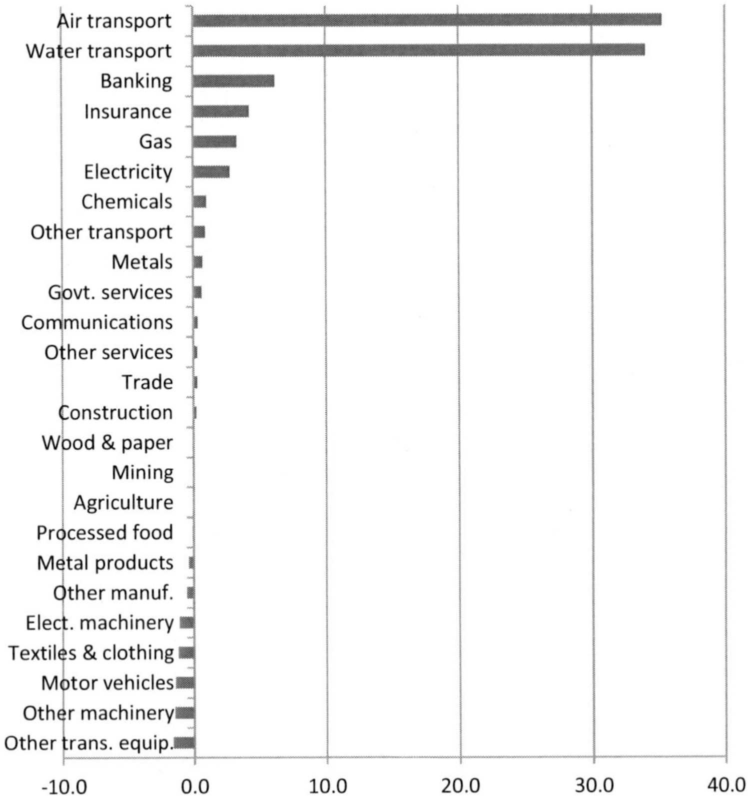

Figure 10.17. Percentage Deviation from Baseline in Sectoral Output from *Own* Structural Reforms — Weighted Average of All APEC Economies (%)
Source: FTAP model projections.

The sectors projected to lose in relative terms from an economy's own structural reforms are typically those that do not fall into the above categories. They suffer indirectly from higher wages and rates of return, effects that are induced primarily by the expansions in overall activity. Industries typically losing in this way include motor vehicles and other transport equipment, electronic equipment and other machinery and equipment, and textiles and clothing. The relative loses in industry output in these sectors are relatively minor, however.

When reforms in other APEC economies are taken into account, the deviations from baseline in sectoral output are typically smaller than for 'own' reforms. Thus structural reforms in other APEC economies can

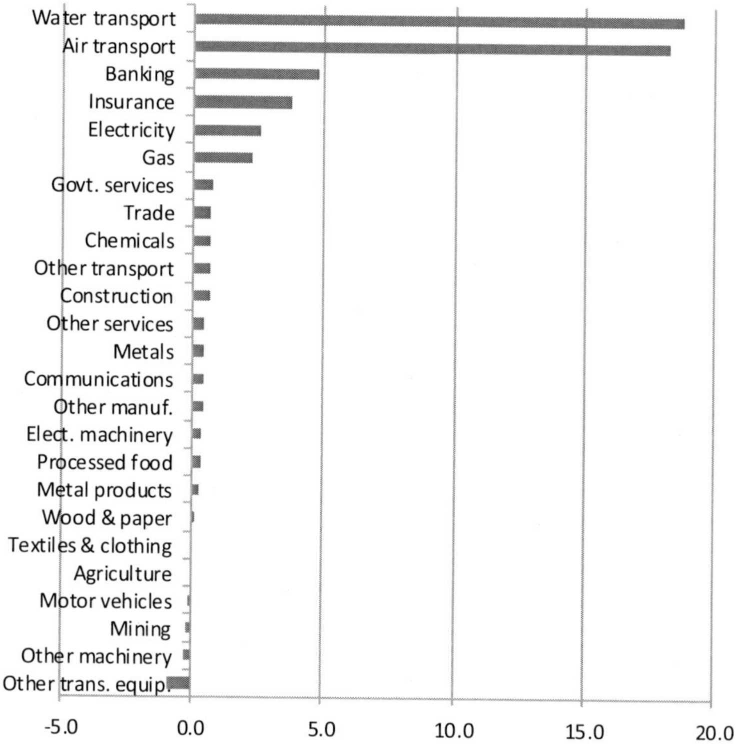

Figure 10.18. Percentage Deviation from Baseline in Sectoral Output from *All* Structural Reforms — Weighted Average of All APEC Economies (%)
Source: FTAP model projections.

play a useful role in helping to cushion the adjustment costs of reforms at home, even if they do not add greatly to the overall gains from reform.

Furthermore, a wider set of industries are projected to gain in relative terms. They now include sectors that are intensive users of international transport margins, and benefit from transport reforms elsewhere. These sectors can include other manufacturing, electronic equipment, processed food and textiles and clothing. The relative output losses are therefore concentrated in a smaller set of industries, but are typically not as severe as with own reforms because of the gains from reforms elsewhere.

A different sort of structural adjustment problem can occur in sectors where reform involves removing a significant margin of discrimination against the commercial presence of foreign services providers. Here the fear is that reform will crowd out domestically-owned businesses in favour of foreign-invested firms, and this fear can carry considerable political weight. To examine this proposition, Figures 10.19 and 10.20 show the effects on domestically-owned firms, relative to the average effects on all firms, in the insurance and banking sectors respectively, as a result of structural reforms in all APEC economies. The insurance and banking sectors have been singled out as those there the margins of discrimination against foreign commercial presence were originally greatest (see Tables 10.1 to 10.4).

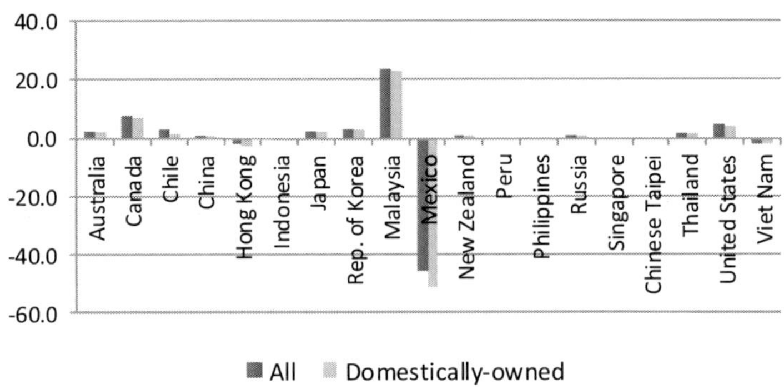

Figure 10.19. Percentage Deviation from Baseline in Sectoral Output in Insurance Industry from All Structural Reforms (%)
Source: FTAP model projections.

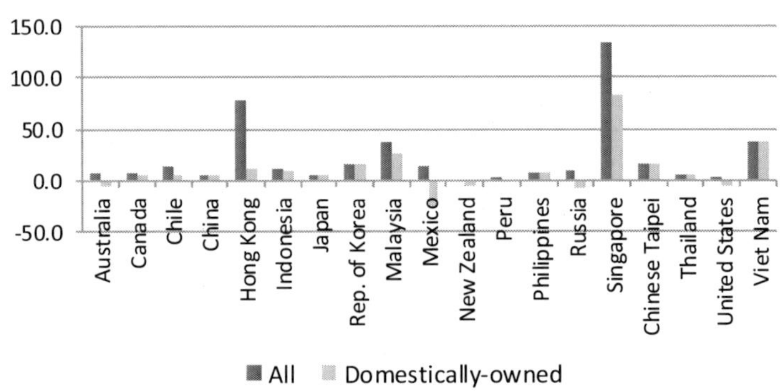

Figure 10.20. Percentage Deviation from Baseline in Sectoral Output in Banking Industry from All Structural Reforms (%)
Source: FTAP model projections.

In the insurance sector, there is very little evidence of crowding out. In the banking sector there is more evidence, although in almost all cases, the banking sector overall is projected to be larger than without the reforms, even though the domestically-owned portion of it may not be. According to the model projections, therefore, crowding out is not of particularly great practical concern.

This apparent lack of crowding out is a function of three things. First, the domestically-owned and foreign-invested portions of each sector are seen as producing differentiated products — these are close, but not perfect, substitutes in demand. This accords with the observation that multinational service firms tend to specialize in market niches, often concentrating on providing services to their multinational counterparts in manufacturing. And in finance, for example, it is often the domestically-owned firms that serve the bulk of the retail market, while foreign-invested banks concentrate on wholesale banking.

Second, the domestically-owned and foreign-invested portions of each sector are not perfect substitutes in capital supply. In the model, investors in each country prefer to hold a mixed portfolio of debt and equity, and a mix of equities across different industries and host countries, albeit with some home country bias to the equity portfolio choice. Because they do not treat equities from different sectors and host countries as perfect substitutes (although they do treat debt as perfectly mobile), they therefore require non-trivial changes in the relative returns to equity from different countries in order to be induced to hold more in their overall portfolio. This is relevant to the current application, because foreign-invested firms can only grow strongly in a particular country if investors are willing to hold those FDI stocks. This aspect of the FTAP model, and the parameter values that govern the extent of substitution in demand and capital supply, are discussed in detail in Dee *et al.* (2011).

Third, services trade reform typically involves more than just removing discrimination against foreign suppliers. In most sectors, there are at least some barriers to market access that also affect domestic new entrants. So services trade reform, if carried out on a wide enough basis, can actually also benefit domestic new entrants. At a political level, this observation can be a counterweight to the crowding out argument.

While Figures 10.17 and 10.18 give an indication of the typical industry output responses to reforms, they do not show the full extent of adjustment costs in employment, for two reasons. Firstly, as noted, they show the average responses rather than the extremes. Secondly, in sectors undergoing productivity improvements, the employment effects can be much more severe than the output effects. The essence of a productivity improvement is that an industry can produce more with less. As a result, input usage can fall, even as output rises.

To capture the full extent of adjustment costs in employment, Figure 10.21 shows, for each industry, the biggest relative gain and the biggest relative loss in sectoral employment of unskilled labour projected in any of the APEC economies. In air transport, for example, Figure 10.21

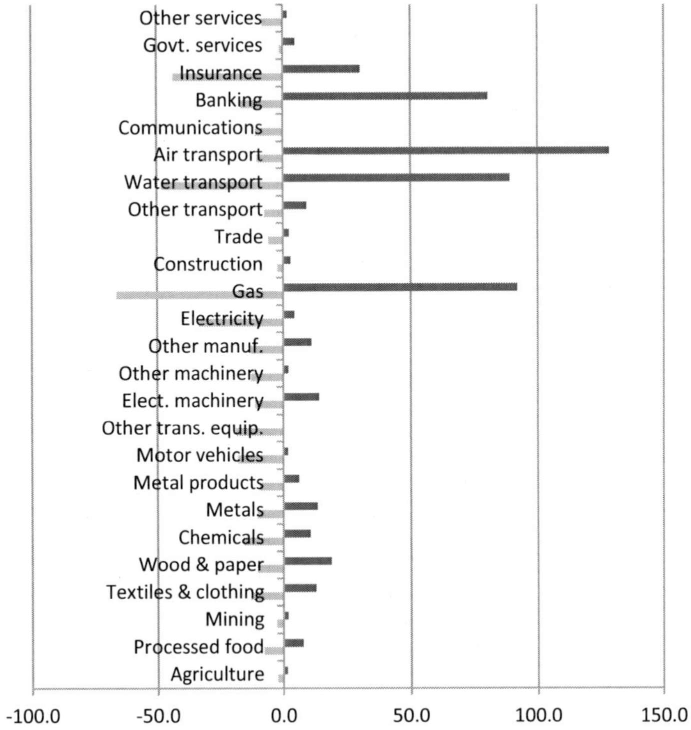

Figure 10.21. Percentage Deviation from Baseline in Unskilled Employment from All Structural Reforms — APEC Minimum and Maximum (%)
Source: FTAP model projections.

shows that the biggest relative gain in unskilled employment is projected to be about 130 per cent (in Hong Kong) while the biggest relative loss in unskilled employment is projected to be about 10 per cent (in Australia).[7] In water transport, the biggest relative gain is shown to be about 90 per cent (in Thailand), while the biggest relative loss is almost 50 per cent (in Hong Kong). In banking, the biggest projected gain is over 80 per cent (in Hong Kong), while the biggest relative loss is around 17 per cent (in Thailand). As the examples show, the particular economies in which the minimums and maximums occur can vary from sector to sector. The corresponding diagram showing the minimum and maximum changes in employment of skilled labour is similar, so it is not shown here.

By far the biggest relative losses in unskilled employment are projected to occur in the gas industry in Singapore (64 per cent), the water transport industry in Hong Kong (48 per cent), and the insurance industry in Mexico (43 per cent). The first two cases are where substantial reform in the home economy has already taken place. These sectors lose employment, not as a result of their own productivity improvements, but because the electricity or gas using industries in these economies lose their position as other economies reform.

These relative employment losses need to be kept in perspective. If unskilled employment in maritime transport in Hong Kong is projected to be 48 per cent lower than otherwise after ten years, then annual economic growth of 6.5 per cent a year over each of those ten years would ensure that the relative loss did not translate into an absolute one. Such a growth rate is not unreasonable for the Hong Kong economy, particularly with the added boost to economic activity arising from reforms in other sectors. Similarly, if unskilled employment in insurance in Mexico is projected to be 43 per cent lower than otherwise after ten years, then annual economic growth of about 5.6 per cent a year would ensure that the relative loss did not translate into an absolute one. Perhaps the only sector that might experience an absolute employment loss as a result of the reforms considered here would be the gas industry

---

7 For clarity of presentation, Figure 10.21 suppresses the very biggest relative employment gains in water and air transport, which are projected to occur in Viet Nam. If these were shown, they would unduly compress the results for other sectors.

in Singapore (where annual growth of about 10 per cent would be required to prevent this outcome).

A further consideration is that while structural reforms may require significant reallocations of unskilled labour between sectors, they also generate higher real wages for unskilled workers. Figure 10.22 shows projected increases in real wages of unskilled labour of up to 8.5 per cent as a result of structural reforms throughout the APEC region, with similar increases in skilled wages (only a small proportion of which come from the assumed flow-on effects of services trade reforms in higher education).[8]

One of the best ways that APEC economies can guard against the adjustment costs associated with structural reforms is to maintain healthy underlying rates of economic growth. To some extent, structural reforms provide their own reward, in terms of stimulating activity and increasing the resilience of the economy, but prudent macroeconomic management is also crucial.

For the particular structural reforms considered here, there is not much prospect that adjustment costs could be cushioned by accompanying the reforms with merchandise trade reforms. The reasons were hinted at earlier — the sectors that tend to lose in output terms from

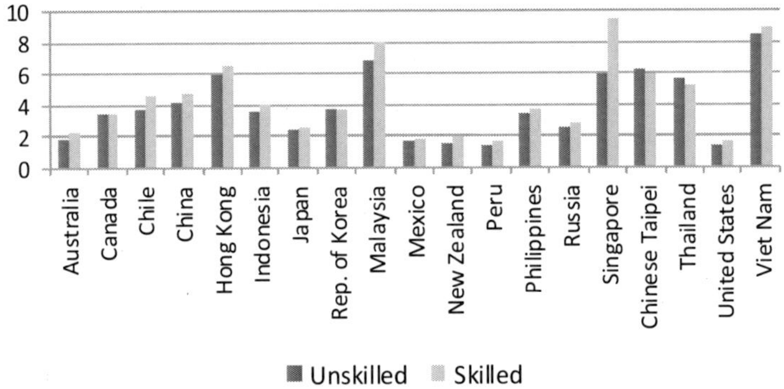

Figure 10.22. Percentage Deviation from Baseline in Real Wages Arising from All Structural Reforms (%)
Source: FTAP model projections.

[8] The economic mechanisms driving the employment effects of services reforms are examined in more detail in Dee *et al.* (2011).

these particular reforms include manufacturing sectors that would also be penalized in at least some economies from merchandise trade reforms. However, there are prospects that a wider set of services reforms could be more complementary with merchandise trade reforms, in terms of cushioning adjustment costs. Such offsets are more likely if reforms targeted at the traded goods sectors are combined with reforms in services sectors that cater more to the needs of households (eg Dee 2008).

10.5 Summary and Conclusions

This chapter has examined the economy- and region-wide effects of prospective reforms in the finance, transport, energy, telecommunications and higher education sectors of APEC economies. Key to these reforms is the introduction of additional competition into each sector — both domestic and foreign.

In insurance and banking services, it implies the removal of non-prudential licensing restrictions on entry, legal restrictions on establishment, and restrictions on the scale and scope of operations, the particular types of insurance or (traditional) banking products that firms can offer, and on ownership and pricing. In air transport, this implies a range of reforms to air services agreements, to entry conditions for domestic and foreign carriers, and to ownership. In maritime transport, it implies the dismantling of any remaining entry restrictions, quotas or cargo sharing arrangements, and the granting of national treatment to foreign-owned carriers located domestically. In rail transport, it implies vertical separation and free entry in freight operations in those economies that do not yet have them. In electricity and gas, it implies third party access, unbundling, wholesale markets and/or retail competition in economies that have not yet implemented them. Note that no privatization of incumbents is assumed in rail, electricity or gas. In telecommunications, the reforms predominantly involve the removal of remaining foreign equity limits. In higher education, it implies the removal of foreign equity limits, the relaxation of restrictions on provider numbers, enrolments, recognition of qualifications, and a range of restrictions on operation (including discriminatory restrictions on access to public subsidies), and greater transparency of regulations.

The estimated first-round impacts of these reforms suggest that they could lead to weighted average price reductions in the range 4 to 24 per cent across the sectors involved, with a substantial proportion of those price reductions coming about through productivity improvements. The most extensive reform effort, but the largest price reductions (ie above 15 per cent), are projected to occur in Indonesia, Malaysia, Mexico, the Philippines, Singapore, Chinese Taipei, Thailand, the United States and Viet Nam. Singapore and the United States appear on the list primarily because of their barriers to trade in banking services.

Once these price reductions flowed throughout each economy and through the region as a whole, it is projected that structural reforms would generate real income gains in each APEC economy of between 1.0 and 6.6 per cent of GDP, relative to what would have happened had no reforms occurred. Across the whole APEC region, these gains would amount to US$330 billion a year in additional real income (in 2004 dollars), relative to the situation without reforms. This is a snapshot of the gains after a ten year adjustment period.

In all APEC economies, an overwhelming proportion of the gains would come from reforms at home, rather than reforms in other economies. Thus while the gains from joint reforms are considerable, there is no compelling reason for each APEC economy to wait for others to reciprocate.

Nevertheless, most APEC economies are also projected to reap small gains from reforms elsewhere. This is not a foregone conclusion, because productivity improvements elsewhere are a two-edged sword. The income and price effects on the home economy work in opposite directions, and very often the adverse price effects dominate. The difference here is that services reforms in other economies also reduce the cost of transporting merchandise to and from the home economy. In most cases, this restores the balance in favour of the home economy.

APEC wide, these projected gains from structural reforms are more than three times as big as the gains from further liberalization of merchandise trade. Yet the sectors here where the structural reforms occur are about a third the size of those engaged in merchandise trade.

When structural reforms lower real production costs, even by half as much as is estimated here, they generate a 'bang for the buck' that is much greater than from merchandise trade reforms. The findings of this chapter therefore vindicate the decision of APEC Leaders to move beyond a 'border' agenda to one that focuses on behind-the-border reforms.

Yet structural reforms cannot generate significant gains without also generating significant structural adjustments. This chapter has also examined the expected size and extent of those adjustments.

At the sectoral level, the projected output gains tend to be in the services sectors undergoing reform, and in the sectors that use their services intensively. These can include chemicals (an intensive user of gas), metals (an intensive user of electricity), wood and paper products (an intensive user of domestic transport services), and a range of industries (other manufacturing, electronic equipment, processed food and textiles and clothing) that are intensive users of international transport services. Construction is typically also projected to gain slightly from the additional impetus given to industry investment.

The sectors projected to lose in relative terms are typically those that do not fall into the above categories. They suffer indirectly from higher wages and rates of return, effects that are induced primarily by the expansions in overall activity. Industries typically losing in this way include motor vehicles and other transport equipment.

The relative losses in industry output are relatively minor, however. And they are even smaller when reforms in other APEC economies are taken into account. Thus structural reforms in other APEC economies can play a useful role in helping to cushion the adjustment costs of reforms at home, even if they do not add greatly to the overall gains from reform.

A different sort of structural adjustment problem can occur in sectors where reform involves removing a significant margin of discrimination against the commercial presence of foreign services providers. Here the fear is that reform will crowd out domestically-owned businesses in favour of foreign-invested firms, and this fear can carry considerable political weight. According to the model projections, however, crowding out is not of particularly great practical concern. Multinational services providers often focus on different market niches than local firms. Investors themselves prefer to retain a diversified portfolio of local and foreign assets. And services trade reform, when carried out on a wide enough basis, can do more than just remove discrimination against foreign providers — it can also benefit domestic new entrants. At a political level, this benefit to domestic players is a counterweight to the fear of crowding out.

The employment effects of structural reforms can be more severe than the output effects. The essence of a productivity improvement is that an industry can produce more with less. As a result, input usage can fall, even when output rises. Nevertheless, two of the three cases where the worst outcomes for unskilled employment are projected to occur are in sectors where substantial reform in the home economy has already taken place. These sectors lose employment, not as a result of their own productivity improvements, but because the home industries that use their services lose their position as other economies undertake structural reform.

In these three worst cases, the relative losses in unskilled employment after ten years are about 40 to 60 per cent. But these losses need to be kept in perspective. Healthy but realistic rates of underlying economic growth in the intervening years would probably ensure that in all but one case, the relative losses did not translate into absolute ones. Furthermore, while structural reforms may require significant relative shifts of labour across sectors over time in some economies, they are also projected to generate higher real wages for all workers in all economies.

Thus one of the best ways that APEC economies can guard against any adverse employment effects of structural reforms is to maintain healthy underlying rates of economic growth. To some extent, structural reforms provide their own reward, in terms of stimulating activity and increasing the resilience of the economy, but prudent macroeconomic management is also crucial.

References

Ab Iorwerth, A. (2005) 'Methods of Evaluating University Research Around the World', Working Paper 2005-04, Ottawa: Department of Finance, Government of Canada.

Achard, P. (2009) 'The Regulation of International Air Cargo Services', Mimeo, Paris: Sciences Po.

Adams, R., Dee, P., Gali, J. and McGuire, G. (2003) 'The Trade and Investment Effects of Preferential Trading Arrangements — Old and New Evidence', Productivity Commission Staff Working Paper, Canberra: Productivity Commission.

Alexandersson, G. and Hultén, S. (2005) 'Strategic Pricing by Oligopolists in Public Tenders of Passenger Railway Services', 9th Thredbo Conference, September 2005, Lisbon.

APEC Human Resources Development Working Group (2009) Measures Affecting Cross Border Exchange and Investment in Higher Education in the APEC Region, Singapore: APEC Secretariat.

Arunanondchai, J. and Fink, C. (2007) 'Trade in Health Services in the ASEAN Region', World Bank Policy Research Working Paper 4147, Washington DC: World Bank.

Arvis, J.F., Mustra, M.A., Panzer, J., Ojala, L. and Naula, T. (2007) *Connecting to Compete: Trade Logistics in the Global Economy*, Washington DC: World Bank.

ASEAN–ANU Migration Research Team (2005) 'Movement of Workers in ASEAN: Health Care and IT Sectors', REPSF Project No. 04/007, Singapore: ASEAN Secretariat.

Asia Pacific Foundation of Canada (2000) *Survey on Customs, Standards, and Business Mobility in the APEC Region*, prepared for the APEC Business Advisory Council, Singapore.

Baltagi, B. and Wu, P. (1999) 'Unequally Spaced Panel Data Regressions with AR(1) Disturbances', *Econometric Theory,* 15(6): 814–23.

Banomyong, R. (no date, c. 2006) 'Logistics Impact on Trade and Economic Development in Lao PDR: the Thai Factor', prepared for the World Bank, Thammasat University.

Barth, J. R., Caprio Jr, G. and Levine, R. (2001) *The Regulation and Supervision of Banks around the World — A New Database*, Washington DC: The World Bank.

Barth, J. R., Caprio Jr, G. and Levine, R. (2004), 'Bank Regulation and Supervision: What Works Best?', *Journal of Financial Intermediation,* 13(2): 205–48.

Barth, J.R., Caprio Jr, G. and Levine, R. (2007) Databases on Banking Regulation and Supervision for 1998–2000, 2003, and 2007, World Bank, http://econ.worldbank.org/WBSITE/EXTERNAL/EXTDEC/EXTRESEARCH/0,,contentMDK:20345037~pagePK:64214825~piPK:64214943~theSitePK:469382,00.html, accessed 15 May 2008.

Berden, K., Francois, J., Tamminen, S., Thelle, M. and Wymenga, P. (2009) *Non-Tariff Measures in EU–US Trade and Investment — An Economic Analysis*, Rotterdam: ECORYS Nederland BV.

Berger, A., Cummins, J.D. and Weiss, M. (1997) 'The Coexistence of Multiple Distribution Systems for Financial Services: The Case of Property Liability Insurance', *The Journal of Business*, 70(4): 515–46.

Bertho, F. (2011) 'Maritime Transport in Australia', in APEC Policy Support Unit, *The Impacts and Benefits of Structural Reforms in Transport, Energy and Telecommunications Sectors*, Singapore: APEC Secretariat: 290–312.

Bikker, J.A. and Bos, J.W.B. (2008) Bank Performance: A Theoretical and Empirical Framework for the Analysis of Profitability Competition and Efficiency, USA and Canada: Routledge International Studies in Money and Banking.

Blundell-Wignall, A., Atkinson, P. and Lee, S.H. (2009) 'The Current Financial Crisis: Causes and Policy Issues', *OECD Journal: Financial Market Trends,* 2(95): 9–28.

Borchert, I., Gootiiz, A. and Mattoo, A. (2012a) 'Guide to the Services Restrictions Database', Policy Research Working Paper 6108, Washington DC: World Bank.

Borchert, I., Gootiiz, A. and Mattoo, A. (2012b) 'Policy Barriers to International Trade in Services', Policy Research Working Paper 6109, Washington DC: World Bank.

Boyd, J.H., Chang, C. and Smith, B.D. (1998) 'Moral Hazard under Universal and Commercial Banking', *Journal of Money, Credit and Banking,* 30(3): 426–68.

Boylaud, O. and Nicoletti, G. (2000) 'Regulation, Market Structure and Performance in Telecommunications', Working Paper No. 237, ECO/WKP(2000)10, Economics Department, Paris: OECD.

Brakman, S., van Marrewijk, C. and van Witteloostuijn, A. (2009) 'Market Liberalization in the European Natural Gas Market: The Importance of Capacity Constraints and Efficiency Differences', CESifo Working Paper No. 2697, Munich: CESifo Group.

Camdessus, M. (1997) 'The Challenge of a Sound Banking System', in C. Enoch and J.H. Green (eds), *Banking Soundness and Monetary Policy*, Washington DC: International Monetary Fund: 535–39.

Cantos, P. and Maudos, J. (2001) 'Regulation and Efficiency: The Case of European Railways', *Transportation Research Part A*, 35(5): 459–72.

Cantos, P., Pastor, J.M. and Serrano, L. (1999) 'Productivity, Efficiency and Technical Change in the European Railways: A Non-Parametric Approach', *Transportation*, 26(4): 337–57.

Cantos, P., Pastor, J.M. and Serrano, L. (2010) 'Vertical and Horizontal Separation in the European Railway Sector and its Effects on Productivity', *Journal of Transport Economics and Policy*, 44(2): 139–60.

Cantos, P., Pastor, J.M. and Serrano, L. (2011) 'Quantifying the Benefits from Structural Reforms in Railway Transport Markets in APEC Economies', in APEC Policy Support Unit, *The Impacts and Benefits of Structural Reforms in the Transport, Energy and Telecommunications Sectors in APEC Economies*, Singapore: APEC Secretariat: 103–23.

Carrington, R., Coelli, T. and Rao, D.S.P. (2005) 'The Performance of Australian Universities: Conceptual Issues and Preliminary Results', *Economic Papers*, 24(2): 145–63.

Chambers, R.G. (1988) *Applied Production Analysis: A Dual Approach,* Cambridge: Cambridge University Press.

Chanda, R. (2001) 'Trade in Health Services', Working Paper No. 70, New Delhi: Indian Council for Research on International Economic Relations.

Christensen, L.R., Jorgenson, D. and Lau, L.J. (1973) 'Transcendental Logarithmic Production Frontiers', *The Review of Economics and Statistics,* 55(1): 28–45.

Claessens, S., Demirgüç-Kunt, A. and Huizinga, H. (2001) 'How Does Foreign Entry Affect Domestic Banking Markets?', *Journal of Banking and Finance*, 25(5): 891–911.

Clark, X., Dollar, D. and Micco, A. (2004) 'Port Efficiency, Maritime Transport Costs, and Bilateral Trade', *Journal of Development Economics* 75(2): 417–50.

Coelli, T. (1996) 'A Guide to FRONTIER Version 4.1: A Computer Program for Stochastic Frontier Production and Cost Function Estimation', CEPA Working Paper No, 7/96, Department of Econometrics, Armidale: University of New England.

Coelli, T. and Perelman, S. (1999) 'A Comparison of Parametric and Non-parametric Distance Functions: With Application to European Railways', *European Journal of Operations Research*, 117(2): 326–39.

Correlje, A.F. and Vries, L.D. (2008) 'Hybrid Electricity Markets: The Problem of Explaining Different Patterns of Restructuring', in F.P. Sioshansi (ed.), *Competitive Electricity Markets: Design, Implementation, Performance*, Oxford: Elsevier: 65–95.

Cuddington, J. and Wang Z. (2006) 'Assessing the Degree of Spot Market Integration for US Natural Gas: Evidence from Daily Price Data', *Journal of Regulatory Economics*, 29(2): 195–210.

Cummins, J.D. and Zi, H. (1998) 'Comparison of Frontier Efficiency Methods: An Application to the US Life Insurance Industry', *Journal of Productivity Analysis*, 10(2): 131–52.

Cummins, J.D., Tennyson, S. and Weiss, M.A. (1998) 'Consolidation and Efficiency in the US Life Insurance Industry', *Journal of Banking and Finance*, 23(2–4): 325–57.

Deardorff, A. and Stern, R. (2005) 'Empirical Analysis of Barriers to International Services Transactions and the Consequences of Liberalization', in P.Dee and M. Ferrantino (eds), *Quantitative Methods for Assessing the Effects of Non-tariff measures and Trade Facilitation*, Singapore: APEC Secretariat and World Scientific Publishing: 549–609.

Dee, P. (2003) 'Modelling the Policy Issues in Services Trade', *Économie Internationale,* (94–95): 283–300.

Dee, P. (2004) 'Services Trade Liberalization in South East European Countries', Mimeo, Paris: OECD.

Dee, P. (2005) 'A Compendium of Barriers to Services Trade', Mimeo prepared for World Bank, Canberra: The Australian National University, available at http://www.crawford.anu.edu.au/pdf/Combined_report.pdf.

Dee, P. (2006) 'The Economy-wide Effects of Moroccan Services Sector Reforms', Mimeo prepared for the World Bank, Canberra: The Australian National University.

Dee, P. (2007) 'East Asian Economic Integration and its Impact on Future Growth', *The World Economy,* 30(3): 405–23.

Dee, P. (2008) 'Benchmarking and Assessing Indonesia's Regulation of Services', Mimeo prepared for the World Bank, Canberra: The Australian National University.

Dee, P. (2009) 'Services Liberalization toward the ASEAN Economic Community', in J. Corbett and S. Umezaki (eds), *Deepening East Asian Economic Integration,* ERIA Research Project Report 2008 No. 1, Jakarta: Economic Research Institute for ASEAN and East Asia.

Dee, P. (2010a) 'International Student Movements and the Effects of Barriers to Trade in Higher Education Services', in C. Findlay and W.G. Tierney (eds), *Globalization and Tertiary Education in the Asia Pacific: The Changing Nature of a Dynamic Market*, Singapore: World Scientific: 39–71.

Dee, P. (2010b) 'Services Liberalization Toward the ASEAN Economic Community', in S. Urata and M. Okabe (eds), *Tracing the Progress Toward the ASEAN Economic Community*, ERIA Research Project Report 2009 No. 3, Jakarta: Economic Research Institute for ASEAN and East Asia: 28–124.

Dee, P. (2011a) 'Quantifying the Impact of Structural Reforms in Electricity and Gas Markets', in APEC Policy Support Unit, *The Impacts and Benefits of Structural Reforms in the Transport, Energy and Telecommunications Sectors in APEC Economies*, Singapore: APEC Policy Support Unit: 124–78.

Dee, P. (2011b) 'Services Liberalization Towards an ASEAN Economic Community', in S. Urata and M. Okabe (eds), *Towards a Competitive ASEAN Single Market: Sectoral Analysis*, ERIA Research Project Report 2010 No. 3, Jakarta: Economic Research Institute for ASEAN and East Asia: 17–136.

Dee, P. (2012) 'Services Liberalization: Impact and Way Forward', paper prepared for ASEAN Economic Community Mid-Term Review, Jakarta: Economic Research Institute for ASEAN and East Asia.

Dee, P. and Dinh, H. (2009) 'Barriers to Trade in Health and Financial Services in ASEAN', ERIA Discussion Paper ERIA-DP-2009-11, Jakarta: Economic Research Institute for ASEAN and East Asia.

Dee, P. and Diop, N. (2010) 'The Economy-wide Effects of Further Trade Reforms in Tunisia's Services Sectors', in J. Gilbert (ed.), *New Developments in General Equilibrium Analysis for Trade Policy*, Frontiers of Economics and Globalization Volume 7, Bingley UK: Emerald: 61–101.

Dee, P. and Findlay, C. (2008a) 'Services: A "Deal-Maker" in the Doha Round?' in B. Blonigen (ed.), *Monitoring International Trade Policy: A New Agenda for Reviving the Doha Round,* London: Centre for Economic Policy Research and Kiel: Kiel Institute for the World Economy: 49–63.

Dee, P. and Findlay, C. (2008b) 'Trade in Infrastructure Services: A Conceptual Framework', in A. Mattoo, R.M. Stern and G. Zanini (eds), *A Handbook of International Trade in Services*, Oxford: Oxford University Press: 338–55.

Dee, P., Findlay, C. and Pomfret, R. (2008) 'Trade facilitation: What, Why, How, Where and When?' in D. Brooks and J. Menon (eds), *Infrastructure and Trade in Asia*, Cheltenham UK: Edward Elgar: 28–53.

Dee, P., Francois, J., Manchin, M., Norberg, H., Nordås, H. and van Tongeren, F. (2011) 'The Impact of Trade Liberalization on Jobs and Growth: Technical Note', OECD Trade Policy Working Paper No. 107, Paris: OECD.

Dee, P. and Hanslow, K. (2001) 'Multilateral Liberalization of Services Trade', in R. Stern (ed.), *Services in the International Economy*, Ann Arbor: University of Michigan Press: 117–39.

Dee, P., Hardin, A. and Holmes, L. (2000) 'Issues in the Application of CGE Models to Services Trade Liberalization', in C. Findlay and T. Warren (eds), *Impediments to Trade in Services, Measurement and Policy Implications*, London and New York: Routledge: 267–86.

Dee, P. and McNaughton, A. (2011) 'Promoting Domestic Reforms through Regionalism', ADBI Working Paper No. 312, Tokyo: Asian Development Bank Institute.

Dee, P. and Sidorenko, A. (2005) 'The Rise of Services Trade: Regional Initiatives and Challenges for the WTO', in C. Findlay and H. Soesastro (eds), *Reshaping the Asia Pacific Economic Order*, London and New York: Routledge: 200–26.

De Souza, R., Goh, M., Gupta, S. and Lei, L. (2007) An Investigation into the Measures Affecting the Integration of ASEAN's Priority Sectors Phase 2: the Case of Logistics, REPSF Project No. 06/001d, Singapore: ASEAN Secretariat.

Deumert, A., Marginson, S., Nyland, C., Ramia, G. And Sawir, E. (2005) 'The Social and Economic Security of International Students in Australia: Study of 202 Student

Cases', Monash Institute for the Study of Global Movements, Melbourne: Monash University.

Diewert, W.E. (1971) 'An Application of the Shephard Duality Theorem: A Generalized Leontief Production Function', *Journal of Political Economy,* 79(3): 481–507.

Diewert, W.E. and Wales, T.J. (1987) 'Flexible Functional Forms and Global Curvature Conditions', *Econometrica,* 55(1): 43–68.

Diewert, W.E. and Wales, T.J. (1995) 'Flexible Functional Forms and Tests of Homogeneous Separability', *Journal of Econometrics,* 67(2): 259–302.

Dihel, N. and Shepherd, B. (2007) 'Modal Estimates of Service Barriers', OECD Trade Policy Working Paper No. 51, TD/TC/WP(2005)36/FINAL, Paris: OECD.

Dinh, H. (2011) 'On Regulatory Barriers to Trade in Banking Services', unpublished PhD thesis, Crawford School of Public Policy, Canberra: Australian National University.

Doove, S., Gabbitas, O., Nguyen-Hong, D. and Owen, J. (2001) 'Price Effects of Regulation: International Air Passenger Transport, Telecommunications and Electricity Supply', Productivity Commission Staff Research Paper, Canberra: Productivity Commission.

Driessen, G., Lijesen, M. and Mulder, M. (2006) 'The Impact of Competition on Productive Efficiency in European Railways', CPB Discussion Paper No. 71, The Hague: CPB Netherlands Bureau for Economic Policy Analysis.

Economides, N., Lopomo, G. and Woroch G. (1996) 'Regulatory Pricing Rules to Neutralize Network Dominance', *Industrial and Corporate Change,* 5(4): 1013–28.

Ethier, W. and Horn, H. (1991) 'Services in International Trade', in E. Helpman and A. Razin (eds), *International Trade and Trade Policy*, Cambridge MA: MIT Press: 223–44.

European Commission (2007) 'DG Competition Report on Energy Sector Inquiry', SEC(2006) 1724, Competition DG, Brussels: European Commission.

Evans, J. (2003) 'The Case for Separation of Infrastructure', *European Transport Forum*, June, available at http://europeantransportforum.eu.

Evans, J. and Green, R. (2003) 'Why Did British Electricity Prices Fall after 1998?', Cambridge Working Papers in Economics CWPE 0326, Cambridge: University of Cambridge.

Farsi, M. and Filippini, M. (2009) 'An Analysis of Cost Efficiency in Swiss Multi-utilities', *Energy Economics*, 31(2): 306–15.

Findlay, C. and Warren, T. (2000) Impediments to Trade in Services: Measurement and Policy Implications, London and New York: Routledge.

Fink, C., Mattoo, A. and Neagu, C. (2002) 'Trade in International Maritime Services: How Much Does Policy Matter?' *The World Bank Economic Review*, 16(1): 81–108.

Fink, C., Mattoo, A. and Rathindran, R. (2002) 'Liberalizing Basic Telecommunications: Evidence from Developing Countries', paper presented at OECD–World Bank Services Experts Meeting, 4–5 March, OECD, Paris.

Finnie, R. and Usher, A. (2006) 'The Canadian Experiment in Cost-sharing and its Effects on Access to Higher Education, 1990–2002', in P. Teixeira, B. Johnstone, M. Rosa and H. Vossensteyn (eds), *Cost-sharing and Accessibility in Higher Education: A Fairer Deal?*, Dordrecht: Springer: 159–87.

Francois, J. and Hoekman, B. (1999) 'Market Access in the Service Sectors', Tinbergen Institute, manuscript, cited in B. Hoekman (2000) 'The Next Round of Services Negotiations: Identifying Priorities and Options', *Federal Reserve Bank of St Louis Review*, 82(4): 31–47.

Freeman, R.B. and Oostendorp, R.H. (2005) 'Occupational Wages around the World (OWW) Database', Cambridge MA: National Bureau of Economic Research, available at http://www.nber.org/oww.

Friebel, G., Ivaldi, M. and Vibes, C. (2005) 'Railway (De)Regulation: A European Efficiency Comparison', March, available at SSRN: http://ssrn.com/abstract=505302.

Gathon, H.J. and Pestieau, P. (1995) 'Decomposing Efficiency into its Managerial and its Regulatory Components: The Case of European Railways', *European Journal of Operational Research*, 80(3): 500–07.

Gathon, H.J. and Perelman, S. (1992) 'Measuring Technical Efficiency in European Railways: A Panel Data Approach', *Journal of Productivity Analysis*, 3(1–2): 135–51.

Gaynor, M. (2006) 'What Do We Know About Competition and Quality in Health Care Markets?', Working Paper 12301, Cambridge MA: National Bureau of Economic Research.

Geehan, R. (1986) 'Economies of Scale in Insurance: Implications for Regulation', in B. Wasow and R.D. Hill (eds), *The Insurance Industry in Economic Development*, New York: New York University Press: 137–59.

Gonenc, R. and Nicoletti, G. (2000) 'Regulation, Market Structure and Performance in Air Passenger Transport', Working Paper No. 254, ECO/WKP(2000)27, Economics Department, Paris: OECD.

Grace, M. and Timme, S. (1992) 'An Examination of Cost Economies in the United States Life Insurance Industry', *The Journal of Risk and Insurance*, 59(1): 72–103.

Granderson, G. (2000) 'Regulation, Open-access Transportation, and Productive Efficiency', *Review of Industrial Organization*, 16(3): 251–66.

Grosso, M.G. (2008) 'Liberalizing Air Cargo Services in APEC', GEM Working Paper, Paris: Sciences Po.

Hanslow, K. (2000) 'A General Welfare Decomposition for CGE Models', GTAP Technical Paper No. 19, Centre for Global Trade Policy Analysis, West Lafayette IN: Purdue University.

Hanslow, K., Phamduc, T. and Verikios, G. (1999) 'The Structure of the FTAP Model', Research Memorandum, Canberra: Productivity Commission, available from http://www.crawford.anu.edu.au/staff/pdee.php.

Hattori, T. and Tsutsui, M. (2004) 'Economic Impact of Regulatory Reforms in the Electricity Supply Industry: A Panel Data Analysis for OECD Countries', *Energy Policy*, 32(6): 823–32.

Hawdon, D. (2003) 'Efficiency, Performance and Regulation of the International Gas Industry — A Bootstrap DEA Approach', *Energy Policy*, 31(11): 1167–78.

Herliana, L. and Parsons, D. (2011) 'Logistics in Indonesia', in APEC Policy Support Unit, *The Impacts and Benefits of Structural Reforms in the Transport, Energy and Telecommunications Sectors in APEC Economies,* Singapore: APEC Policy Support Unit: 446–61.

Hertel, T. (1997) *Global Trade Analysis: Modelling and Applications*, Cambridge: Cambridge University Press.

Hoekman, B. (1995) 'Assessing the General Agreement on Trade in Services', World Bank Discussion Paper No, 307, Washington DC: World Bank.

Hollweg, C. and Wong, M.H. (2009) 'Measuring Regulatory Restrictions in Logistics Services', paper prepared for Economic Research Institute for ASEAN and East Asia (ERIA), Jakarta.

Hummels, D. (2001) 'Time as a Trade Barrier', mimeo, West Lafayette IN: Purdue University, available at http://www.mgmt.purdue.edu/faculty/hummelsd/research/time3b.pdf.

Hummels, D. (2007) 'Transportation Costs and International Trade in the Second Era of Globalization', *Journal of Economic Perspectives*, 21(3): 131–54.

Hummels, D., Lugovsky, V. and Skiba, A. (2009) 'The Trade Reducing Effects of Market Power in International Shipping', *Journal of Development Economics*, 89(1): 84–97.

IDP Education Australia (2002) Identification and Analysis of Barriers to Trade and Investment in Education Services in Selected Countries, Final Report, Sydney: IDP Education Australia.

ITU (International Telecommunications Union) (2000) 'Fixed-Mobile Interconnection Workshop', Document WFMI/04, ITU New Initiatives Program 20–22 September 2000, Geneva: International Telecommunications Union.

ITU (2008) *Trends on Telecommunication Reform 2008,* Geneva: International Telecommunications Union.

Jamasb, T. (2006) 'Between the State and Market: Electricity Sector Reform in Developing Countries', *Utilities Policy*, 14(1): 14–30.

Jamasb, T., Pollitt, M. and Triebs, T. (2008) 'Productivity and Efficiency of US Gas Transmission Companies: A European Regulatory Perspective', Cambridge Working Papers in Economics CWPE 0812, Cambridge: University of Cambridge.

John, K., John, T.A. and Saunders, A. (1994) 'Universal Banking and Firm Risk Taking', *Journal of Banking and Finance,* 18(2): 307–23.

Johnes, G. and Johnes, J. (1993) 'Measuring the Research Performance of UK Economics Departments: An Application of Data Envelopment Analysis', *Oxford Economic Papers*, 45(2): 332–47.

Jolliffe, I.T. (2002) *Principal Component Analysis,* 2nd edition, New York: Springer.

Joskow, P. (2001) 'California's Electricity Crisis', *Oxford Review of Economic Policy*, 17(3): 365–88.

Kain, P. (2006) 'Pitfalls in Competitive Tendering: Addressing the Risks Revealed by Experience in Australia and Britain', paper presented to European Conference of Ministers of Transport 'Workshop on Competitive Tendering for Rail Services', 12 January 2006, Paris, published as Staff Paper, Canberra: Bureau of Transport and Regional Economics.

Kalirajan, K. (2000) 'Restrictions on Trade in Distribution Services', Productivity Commission Staff Research Paper, Canberra: Productivity Commission.

Kalirajan, K., McGuire, G., Nguyen-Hong, D. and Schuele, M. (2000) 'The Price Impact of Restrictions on Banking Services', in C. Findlay and T. Warren (eds), *Impediments to Trade in Services, Measurement and Policy Implication*, London and New York: Routledge: 215–30.

Kang, J. (2000) 'Price Impact of Restrictions on Maritime Transport Services', in C. Findlay and T. Warren (eds), *Impediments to Trade in Services, Measurement and Policy Implications*, London and New York: Routledge: 189–200.

La Porta, R., López-de-Silanes, F. and Shleifer, A. (1999) Government Ownership of Banks,
http://mba.tuck.dartmouth.edu/pages/faculty/rafael.laporta/publications.html, accessed 15 May 2008.

Lawrence, D. (1988) 'Recent Developments in Applying Duality Theory', *Review of Marketing and Agricultural Economics,* 56(3): 375–82.

Lee, J.D., Park, S.B. and Kim, T.Y. (1999) 'Profit, Productivity, and Price Differential: An International Performance Comparison of the Natural Gas Transportation Industry', *Energy Policy*, 27(11): 679–89.

Lee, R., Ure, J. and Lee, H.C. (2011) 'Quantifying the Impact of Structural Reforms in Telecommunications Markets in APEC Economies', in APEC Policy Support Unit, *The Impacts and Benefits of Structural Reforms in Transport, Energy and Telecommunications Sectors*, Singapore: APEC Secretariat: 179–208.

Llewellyn, D.T. (1986) The Regulation and Supervision of Financial Institutions, London: Institute of Bankers.

Löthgren, M. (1997) 'Generalized Stochastic Frontier Production Models', *Economics Letters*, 57(3): 255–59.

Malcolm. G. (1998) 'Adjusting Tax Rates in the GTAP Database', GTAP Technical Paper No. 12, Centre for Global Trade Policy Analysis, West Lafayette IN: Purdue University.

Malmquist, S. (1953) 'Index Numbers and Indifference Surfaces', *Trabajos de Estadística*, 4(2): 209–42.

Marginson, S. (2006) 'Australian Universities in a Global Context', paper presented to Business Higher Education Round Table conference Tomorrow's Universities, 7 June, Melbourne.

Massy, W. (2004) 'Markets in Higher Education: Do They Promote Internal Efficiency?', in P. Teixeira, B. Jongbloed, D. Dill and A. Amaral (eds), *Markets in Higher Education: Rhetoric or Reality?*, Dordrecht: Kluwer: 13–35.

Mattoo, A. and Rathindran, R. (2005) 'Does Health Insurance Impede Trade in Health Care Services?', World Bank Policy Research Working Paper 3667, Washington DC: World Bank.

Mattoo, A., Rathindran, R. and Subramanian, A. (2001) 'Measuring Services Trade Liberalization and its Impact on Economic Growth: An Illustration', World Bank Working Paper No. 2655, Washington DC: World Bank.

Mattoo, A. and Wunsch, S. (2004) 'Pre-empting Protectionism in Services: The WTO and Outsourcing', World Bank Policy Research Working Paper No. 3237, Washington DC: World Bank.

McGuire, G. and Schuele, M. (2000) 'Restrictiveness of International Trade in Banking Services', in C. Findlay and T. Warren (eds), *Impediments to Trade in Services, Measurement and Policy Implications*, London and New York: Routledge: 201–14.

McGuire, G., Schuele, M. and Smith, T. (2000), 'Restrictiveness of International Trade in Maritime Services', in C. Findlay and T. Warren (eds) *Impediments to Trade in Services, Measurement and Policy Implications*, London and New York: Routledge: 172–88.

McKinnish, T. (2005) 'Lagged Dependent Variables and Specification Bias', *Economics Letters*, 88(1): 55–9.

Messerlin, P. (2009) 'The EC Approaches to Services: Tensions between Domestic and Foreign Goals', Mimeo, Paris: Sciences Po.

Micco, A. and Pérez, N. (2002) 'Determinants of Maritime Transport Costs', IADB Working Paper 441, Washington DC: Inter-American Development Bank.

Micco, A. and Serebrisky, T. (2006) 'Competition Regimes and Air Transport Costs: The Effects of Open Skies Agreements', *Journal of International Economics*, 70(1): 25–51.

Mikic, M. (2007) 'Health-related Services in Multilateral and Preferential Trade Arrangements in Asia and the Pacific', Asia-Pacific Research and Training Network on Trade Working Paper Series No. 30, Bangkok: United Nations Economic and Social Commission for Asia and the Pacific.

Mirza, D. and Zitouna, H. (2009) 'Oil Prices, Geography and Endogenous Regionalism', Working Paper 2009-26, Paris: CEPII Research Centre.

Moreira, M.M., Volpe, C. and Blyde, J.S. (2008) *Unclogging the Arteries: The Impact of Transport Costs on Latin American and Caribbean Trade,* Washington DC: Inter-American Development Bank.

Mulder, M., Lijesen, M., Driessen, G. and van de Velde, D. (2005) 'Vertical Separation and Competition in the Dutch Rail Industry: A Cost-Benefit Analysis', paper submitted to Third Conference on Railroad Industry Structure, Competition and Investments, 21–22 October 2005, Stockholm.

Murillo-Zamorano, L.R. (2004) 'Economic Efficiency and Frontier Techniques', *Journal of Economic Surveys*, 18(1): 33–77.

Mussa, M. and Rosen, S. (1978) 'Monopoly and Product Quality', *Journal of Economic Theory*, 18(2): 301–17.

Nagayama, H. (2007) 'Effects of Regulatory Reforms in the Electricity Supply Industry on Electricity Prices in Developing Countries', *Energy Policy*, 35(6): 3440–62.

Nash, C.A. and Rivera-Trujillo, C. (2004) 'Railway Regulatory Reform in Europe: Principles and Practice', Mimeo, Institute for Transport Studies, Leeds: University of Leeds.

National Science Board (2006) *Science and Engineering Indicators 2006, Volume 2*, Arlington VA: National Science Foundation, available at www.eric.ed.gov.

Nguyen-Hong, D. (2000) 'Restrictions on Trade in Professional Services', Productivity Commission Staff Research Paper, Canberra: Productivity Commission.

Nguyen-Hong, D. and Wells, R. (2003) 'Restrictions on Trade in Education Services: Some Basic Indexes', Productivity Commission Staff Working Paper, Canberra: Productivity Commission.

Ochiai, R., Dee, P. and Findlay, C. (2010) 'Services in Free Trade Agreements', in C. Findlay and S. Urata (eds), *Free Trade Agreements in the Asia Pacific*, Singapore, Hackensack NJ and London: World Scientific: 29–80.

OECD (Organization for Economic Cooperation and Development) (2005) 'Indicators of Regulatory Conditions in Seven Non-manufacturing Sectors', Paris: OECD, available at http://www.oecd.org/document/32/0,2340,en_2649_37421_35791136_1_1_1_37421,00.html, accessed 2 December 2005.

OECD (2007) Cross-border Tertiary Education: A Way Towards Capacity Development, Paris: OECD and IBRD/The World Bank.

Oum, T.H. and Yu, C. (1994) 'Economic Efficiency of Railways and Implications for Public Policy', *Journal of Transport Economics and Policy*, 28(2): 121–38.

Oum, T.H., Waters II, W.G. and Yu, C. (1999) 'A Survey of Productivity and Efficiency Measurement in Rail Transport', *Journal of Transport Economics and Policy*, 33(1): 9–42.

Pasiouras, F., Tanna, S. and Zopounidis, C. (2009) 'The Impact of Banking Regulations on Banks' Cost and Profit Efficiency: Cross-Country Evidence', *International Review of Financial Analysis*, 18(5): 294–302.

PDP Australia Pty Ltd and Meyrick and Associates (2005) 'Promoting Efficient and Competitive Intra-ASEAN Shipping Services', REPSF Project No. 04/001, Final Report, Singapore: ASEAN Secretariat.

Pfund, C. (2003) 'The Separation of Infrastructure and Operations Constitutes a Fundamental Mistake', *Public Transport International*, 3/2003: 32–33.

Piermartini, R. and Rousová, L. (2008) 'Liberalization of Air Transport Services and Passenger Traffic', Staff Working Paper ERSD-2008-06, Economic Research and Statistics Division, Geneva: World Trade Organization.

Pollitt, M. (2007) 'Liberalization and Regulation in Electricity Systems: How Can We Get the Balance Right?' Cambridge Working Papers in Economics No. 0724, Faculty of Economics, Cambridge: University of Cambridge.

Pollitt, M. (2008) 'The Future of Electricity (and Gas) Regulation', Cambridge Working Papers in Economics No. 0819, Faculty of Economics, Cambridge: University of Cambridge.

Pomlaktong, N., Jongwilaiwan, R., Theerawattanakul, P. and Pholpanich, R. (2011) 'Road Transport in Thailand', in APEC Policy Support Unit, *The Impacts and Benefits of Structural Reforms in the Transport, Energy and Telecommunications Sectors in APEC Economies,* Singapore: APEC Policy Support Unit: 267–89.

Porter, M.E. and Schwab, K. (eds) (2008) 'Global Competitiveness Report', Davos: World Economic Forum (and earlier years).

Sampson, G. and Snape, R. (1985) 'Identifying Issues in Trade in Services', *The World Economy*, 8(2): 171–82.

Saunders, A. and Schumacher, L. (2000) 'The Determinants of Bank Interest Rate Margins: An International Study', *Journal of International Money and Finance,* 19(6): 813–32.

SCRGSP (Steering Committee for the Review of Government Service Provision) (2008) *Report on Government Services 2008*, Canberra: Productivity Commission.

Sealey Jr, C.W. and Lindley, J.T. (1977) 'Inputs, Outputs, and a Theory of Production and Cost at Depository Financial Institutions', *The Journal of Finance,* 32(4): 1251–66.

Sequeira, S. and Djankov, S. (2008) 'On the Waterfront: An Empirical Study of Corruption in Ports', Mimeo, Cambridge MA: Harvard University, available at http://www.doingbusiness.org/documents/Corruption_in_Ports.pdf.

Sidorenko, A. and Findlay, C. (2003) *Regulation and Market Access*, Canberra: Asia Pacific Press.

Smith, R. (2006) 'Measuring the Globalization of Health Services: A Possible Index of Openness of Country Health Sectors to Trade', *Health Economics, Policy and Law* 1(4): 323–42.

Smith, R., Blouin, C., Drager, N. and Fidler, D.P. (2008) 'Trade in Health Services and the GATS', in A. Mattoo, R.M. Stern and G. Zanini (eds), *A Handbook of International Trade in Services*, Oxford: Oxford University Press: 437–58.

Snape, R. (1998) 'Reaching Effective Agreements Covering Services', in A. Krueger (ed.), *The WTO as an International Organization*, Chicago and London: University of Chicago Press: 279–92.

Sourdin, P. 2011, 'Quantifying the Impact of Structural Reforms on International Transport Margins', in APEC Policy Support Unit, *The Impacts and Benefits of*

Structural Reforms in the Transport, Energy and Telecommunications Sectors in APEC Economies, Singapore: APEC Secretariat: 69–87.

Steiner, F. (2000) 'Regulation, Industry Structure and Performance in the Electricity Supply Industry', Working Paper No. 238, ECO/WKP(2000)11, Economics Department, Paris: OECD.

Stephenson, S., Findlay, C. and Yi, S. (2002) *Services Trade Liberalization and Facilitation*, Canberra: Asia Pacific Press.

Stiglitz, J. (2010) Freefall: Free Markets and the Sinking of the Global Economy, London: Penguin.

Taylor, P. and Braddock, R. (2007) 'International University Ranking Systems and the Idea of University Excellence', *Journal of Higher Education Policy and Management*, 29(3): 245–260.

Trewin, R. (2000) 'A Price-impact Measure of Impediments to Trade in Telecommunications Services', in C. Findlay and T. Warren (eds), *Impediments to Trade in Services, Measurement and Policy Implications*, London and New York: Routledge: 101–18.

United States International Trade Commission (2005) *Logistic Services: An Overview of the Global Market and Potential Effects of Removing Trade Impediments*, USITC Publication 3770, Washington DC: United States International Trade Commission.

USTR (United States Trade Representative) (2000) *National Trade Estimate Report on Foreign Trade Barriers*, Washington DC: United States Trade Representative.

USTR (2002) *National Trade Estimate Report on Foreign Trade Barriers*, Washington DC: United States Trade Representative.

Varian, H.R. (1992) *Microeconomic Analysis,* USA: W.W. Norton and Company Inc.

Walls, W.D. (1994) 'A Cointegration Rank Test of Market Linkages with an Application to the US Natural Gas Industry', *Review of Industrial Organization*, 9(2): 181–91.

Warren, T. (2000) 'The Impact on Output of Impediments to Trade and Investment in Telecommunications Services', in C. Findlay and T. Warren (eds), *Impediments to Trade in Services, Measurement and Policy Implications*, London and New York: Routledge: 85–100.

Warren, T. and Findlay, C. (2000) 'Measuring Impediments to Trade in Services', in P. Sauvé and R.M. Stern (eds), *GATS 2000: New Directions in Services Trade Liberalization*, Centre for Business and Government, Harvard University, Washington DC: Brookings Institution Press: 57–84.

Whalley, J. (2004) 'Assessing the Benefits to Developing Countries of Liberalization in Services Trade', *The World Economy*, 27(8): 1123–53.

Whiteman, J.L. (1999) 'The Measurement of Efficiency Where There Are Multiple Outputs', General Paper No. G-134, Centre of Policy Studies, Melbourne: Monash University.

Wilmsmeier, G. and Hoffmann, J. (2008) 'Liner Shipping Connectivity and Port Infrastructure as Determinants of Freight Rates in the Caribbean', *Maritime Economics and Logistics*, 10(1): 130–51.

Wilmsmeier, G., Hoffmann, J. and Sanchez, R. (2006) 'The Impact of Port Characteristics on International Maritime Transport Costs', in K. Cullinane and W. Talley (eds), *Port Economics: Research in Transportation Economics 16*, Amsterdam: Elsevier: 119–42.

Winter, R. (1994) 'The Dynamics of Competitive Insurance Markets', *Journal of Financial Intermediation*, 3(4): 379–415.

World Bank (undated) 'Questionnaires to Assess Services Trade Policy and Performance: Long Version', World Bank Research Program on Trade in Services, Washington DC: World Bank, available at http://siteresources.worldbank.org/INTRANETTRADE/Resources/QuestionnaireV20-long.pdf.

World Bank (2010) 'Connecting to Compete in Indonesia', paper associated with the release of the World Bank LPI Rankings 2010, available at http://siteresources.worldbank.org/INTINDONESIA/Resources/Publication/280016-1264668827141/LPI.indo.en.pdf.

WTO (World Trade Organization) (1998a) 'Education Services: Background Note by the Secretariat', S/C/W/49, WTO, Geneva: World Trade Organization.

WTO (1998b) 'Health and Social Services: Background Note by the Secretariat', S/C/W/50, Geneva: World Trade Organization.

WTO (1998c) 'Trade Policy Review — India', WT/TPR/S/33, Geneva: World Trade Organization.

WTO (2000) 'Trade Policy Review — Brazil', WT/TPR/S/75, Geneva: World Trade Organization.

WTO (2001) 'Guidelines for the Scheduling of Specific Commitments under the General Agreement on Trade in Services', Adopted by the Council for Trade in Services on 23 March 2001, Geneva: World Trade Organization, available at http://tsdb.wto.org/wto/guidelines.html.

WTO (2006) 'Second Review of the Air Transport Annex: Developments in the Air Transport Sector (Part Two), Quantitative Air Services Agreements Review (QUASAR)', Volumes I and II, Note by the Secretariat, S/C/W/270/Add.1, Geneva: World Trade Organization.

WTO (2009) *Trade Policy Review — Malaysia*, WT/TPR/S/225, Geneva: World Trade Organization.

Yuengert, A.M. (1993) 'The Measurement of Efficiency in Life Insurance: Estimates of a Mixed Normal-gamma Error Model', *Journal of Banking and Finance,* 17(2–3): 483–96.

Zhang, S. and Findlay, C. (2011) 'Quantifying the Impact of Structural Reforms on Air Traffic Flows in APEC', in APEC Policy Support Unit, *The Impacts and Benefits of Structural Reforms in the Transport, Energy and Telecommunications Sectors in APEC Economies*, Singapore: APEC Secretariat: 290–312.